AI WEIWEI

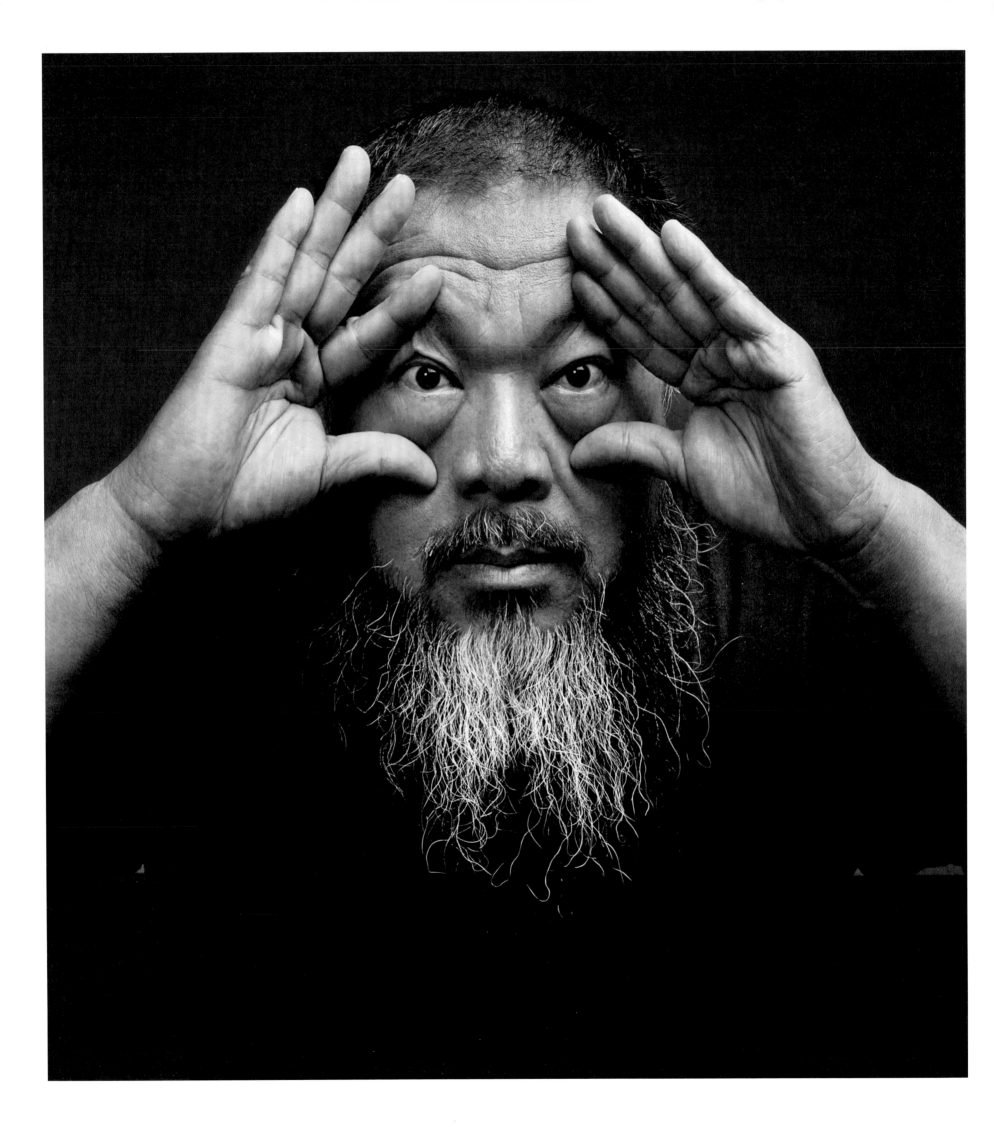

AI WEIWEI

Royal Academy of Arts

First published on the occasion of the exhibition
'Ai Weiwei'

Royal Academy of Arts, London
19 September – 13 December 2015

Supported by

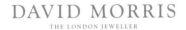
DAVID MORRIS
THE LONDON JEWELLER

LISSON GALLERY

Iwan and Manuela Wirth

The Royal Academy International Patrons

The Henry Moore
Foundation

This exhibition has been made possible by the
provision of insurance through the Government
Indemnity Scheme. The Royal Academy of Arts
would like to thank HM Government for providing
Government Indemnity and the Department for
Culture, Media and Sport and Arts Council England
for arranging the indemnity.

Department
for Culture
Media & Sport

EXHIBITION CURATORS
Tim Marlow, Artistic Director
Adrian Locke

EXHIBITION MANAGEMENT
Idoya Beitia
Jasmine Fenn
Katharine Oakes
Elana Woodgate

EXHIBITION CATALOGUE
Royal Academy Publications
Beatrice Gullström
Alison Hissey
Carola Krueger
Simon Murphy
Peter Sawbridge
Nick Tite

Picture research: Sara Ayad
Design: Lizzie Ballantyne
Colour origination: DawkinsColour, London

Printed in Italy by Graphicom

Texts by Ai Weiwei (interview), Cui Cancan, Jacques
Herzog, Anish Kapoor, Daniel Rosbottom, Sean
Scully and John Tancock © 2015 The authors

Copyright © 2015 Royal Academy of Arts, London

British Library Cataloguing-in-Publication Data

A catalogue record for this book is available from
the British Library

ISBN 978-1-910350-42-3
(boxed limited-edition hardback)
ISBN 978-1-910350-16-4 (hardback)
ISBN 978-1-910350-23-2 (paperback)

Distributed outside the United States and Canada
by Thames & Hudson Ltd, London

Distributed in the United States and Canada
by Harry N. Abrams, Inc., New York

EDITORIAL NOTE
Dimensions of all works of art are given in
centimetres, height before width (before depth).

ILLUSTRATIONS
Page 2: Portrait of Ai Weiwei. Photograph by
Gao Yuan
Page 7: detail of cat. 1
Page 8: detail of cat. 25
Pages 10–11: Ai Weiwei with *Souvenir from Shanghai*
(cat. 19) at the Royal Academy of Arts, 2015
Pages 12–13: Ai Weiwei arranging *Coloured Vases*
(cat. 22) at the Royal Academy of Arts, 2015
Pages 14–15: detail of cat. 45
Page 100: detail of cat. 1
Page 106: detail of cat. 3
Page 112: detail of cat. 8
Page 128: detail of cat. 13
Page 142: detail of cat. 19
Page 154: detail of cat. 22
Page 168: detail of cat. 24
Page 174: detail of cat. 30
Page 186: detail of cat. 32
Pages 188–89: installation view of Gallery 8
Page 196: detail of cat. 39
Page 210: detail of cat. 43
Page 218: detail of cat. 45

CONTENTS

PRESIDENT'S FOREWORD

On 3 April 2011 Ai Weiwei was detained at Beijing International Airport as he waited to check in on a flight to Taiwan, where he was planning his first solo exhibition in the Chinese-speaking world. His illegal and secret detention sent shockwaves throughout the international art world. As a gesture of support and in recognition of his work as both an artist and an architect, the General Assembly of the Royal Academy of Arts elected Ai an Honorary Royal Academician on 26 May of that year. He was released on 22 June, having been held in solitary confinement for 81 days. The suitably titled exhibition 'Ai Weiwei: Absent' opened that October at the Taipei Fine Arts Museum.

Ai Weiwei was born in Beijing in 1957. Shortly after his birth his father, the celebrated poet Ai Qing, became a victim of a government-led crackdown on free-thinking intellectuals, and was sent with his family to a remote labour camp in northwest China. The family returned to Beijing only after the death of Chairman Mao in 1976 had heralded a brief relaxation of state restrictions. In 1978 Ai entered the Beijing Film Academy, and became part of the avant-garde 'Stars' group of artists the following year. State censorship of artists was soon reintroduced, however, and Ai, like many artists of his generation, decided to leave China to seek freedom of expression abroad. He moved to America and in 1982 settled in New York. Eleven years later he returned to Beijing and started creating a body of work that has established him as an artist of international standing, whose output represents a powerful and coherent exploration of Chinese tradition, history and materials as well as a fearless confrontation of issues surrounding free speech and expression. 'Ai Weiwei' at the Royal Academy is the first major survey of his art in the UK, and represents a comprehensive view of his work of the last twenty years.

As I write we have just learned that Ai has received his passport. We look forward with great anticipation in the hope that we will be able to welcome him here at the Academy in person, and we are delighted that he will have the opportunity to see his work exhibited in the Annenberg Courtyard and the Main Galleries. Because he was unable to leave China this exhibition has been curated through a number of different initiatives, and we are very grateful to the dedicated staff of his studio for making this complex operation work so smoothly in a short space of time. The exhibition has been curated by Adrian Locke and Tim Marlow, who have worked very closely with Ai on the selection and display of his work at the Royal Academy. Special thanks are due to Darryl Leung, Gui Nuo and Siri Smith of Ai Weiwei's studio in Beijing, and to all Ai's studio staff in Berlin, Beijing and Hong Kong, as well as to our Senior Exhibitions Manager Idoya Beitia and Exhibitions Assistant Elana Woodgate: all have made the process seem effortless.

We are grateful to the Royal Academy's Publications Department for producing this handsome catalogue, and to the authors of the essays and reflections included within it.

We would also like to thank our lenders Lisson Gallery, M+, Tate, Honus Tandijono and Larry Warsh, as well as those who prefer to remain anonymous. Nicholas Logsdail, Greg Hilty and Rute Ventura of the Lisson Gallery have generously supported the exhibition financially and logistically. We are also hugely grateful to all those who have given us valuable support for the exhibition, including David Morris – the London Jeweller, Jake and Hélène Marie Shafran, Iwan and Manuela Wirth, Stephen and Julie Fitzgerald, Paul and Susie Kempe, Christian Levett, the Royal Academy International Patrons and those who wish to remain anonymous.

Christopher Le Brun PRA
President, Royal Academy of Arts

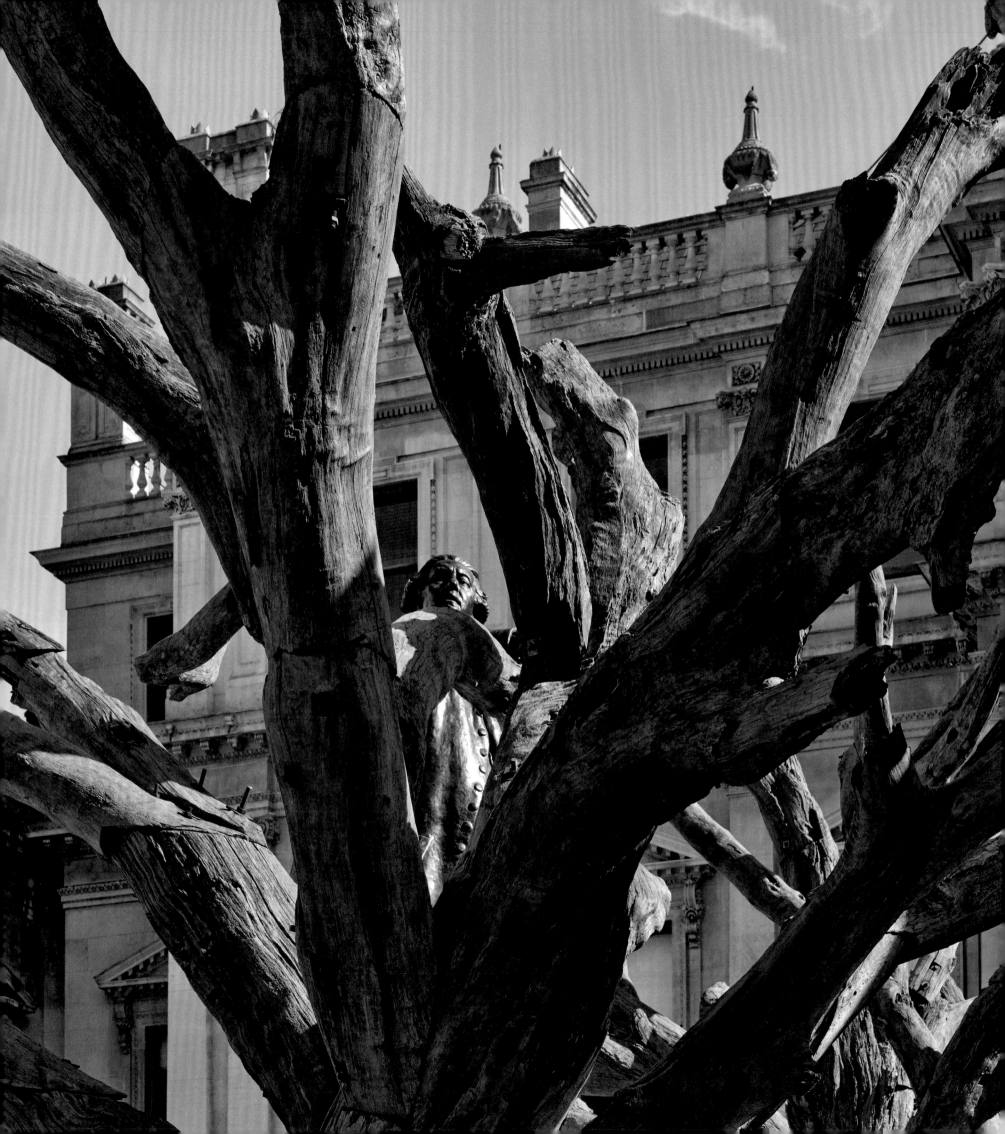

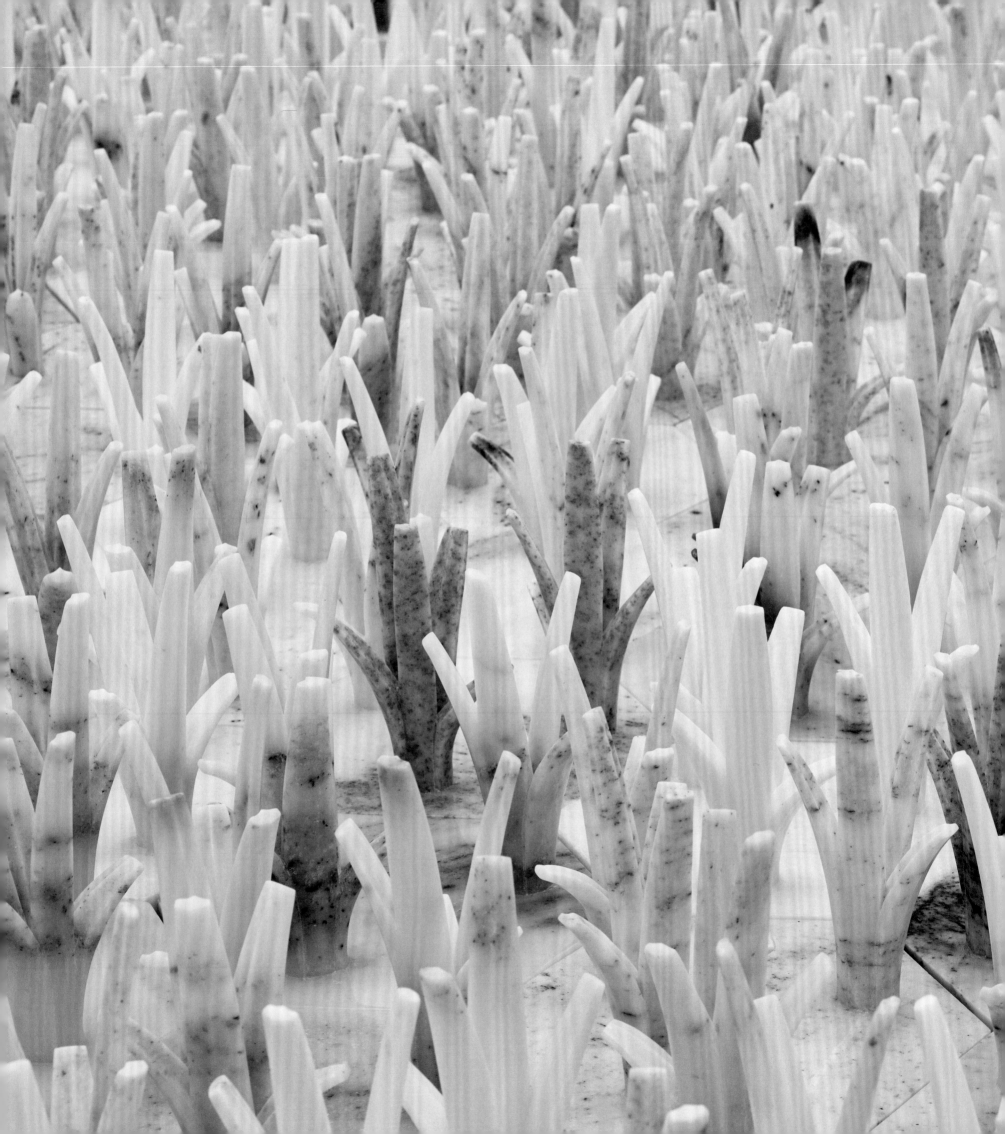

ACKNOWLEDGEMENTS

The Royal Academy of Arts would like to thank the following individuals for their invaluable assistance during the making of this exhibition and its catalogue:

Lisa Baxter, Sebastian Bustamente-Brauning, Eva Carbo Estrada, Julia Carver, Verónica Castillo, Patricia García Sáez, Purificación García Soler, Heli Harni, Christopher Higgins, Pascaline Monier, Ana Jiménez Muñoz, Harry Pearce, Rosa Pera, Erja Pusa, Dorothy Rowe, Gereon Sievernich, John Tancock, Julie Traitsis, Marc Tutt, Ossian Ward, Wang Zhongxia

Ai Weiwei Studio

Eleonora Brizi, Chan Kin Sing, Chen Chao, Cui Xing, Dong Tai Qi, Ga Rang, Gui Nuo, Josh Harks, Hui Xiao Xuan, Luis Játiva, Jiang Li, Kam King Yip, Kang Sunkoo, Tom Lau, Darryl Leung, Leung Pui Hei, Li Chang Ting, Li Dong Xu, Edmond Li, Li Jie Pu, Ma Yan, Jennifer Ng, Eric Gregory Powell, Siri Smith, Song Xiao Jing, Nadine Stenke, Sun Mo, Kimberly Sung, Wibke Tiarks, Jennifer Tran, Xu Ye, Zeng Yi Lan

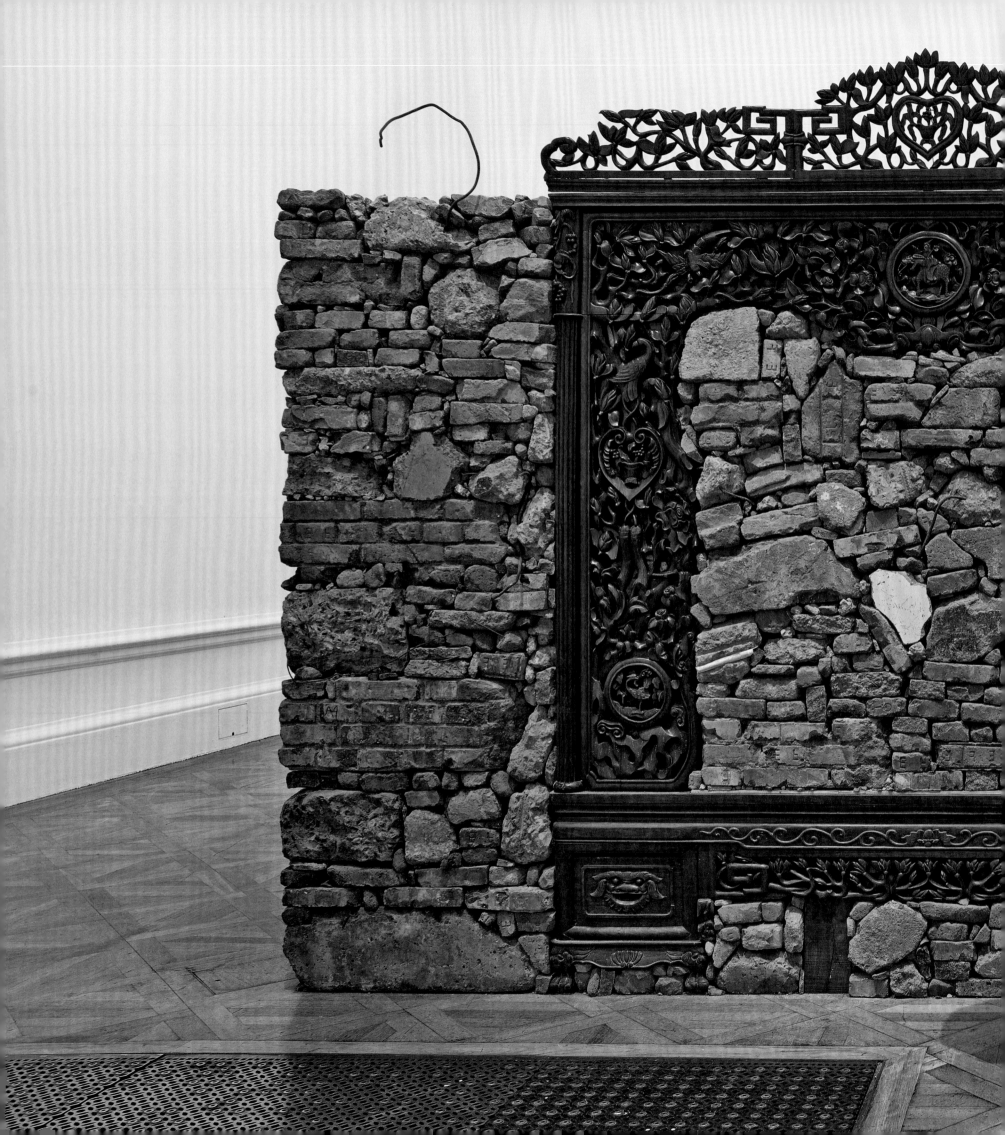

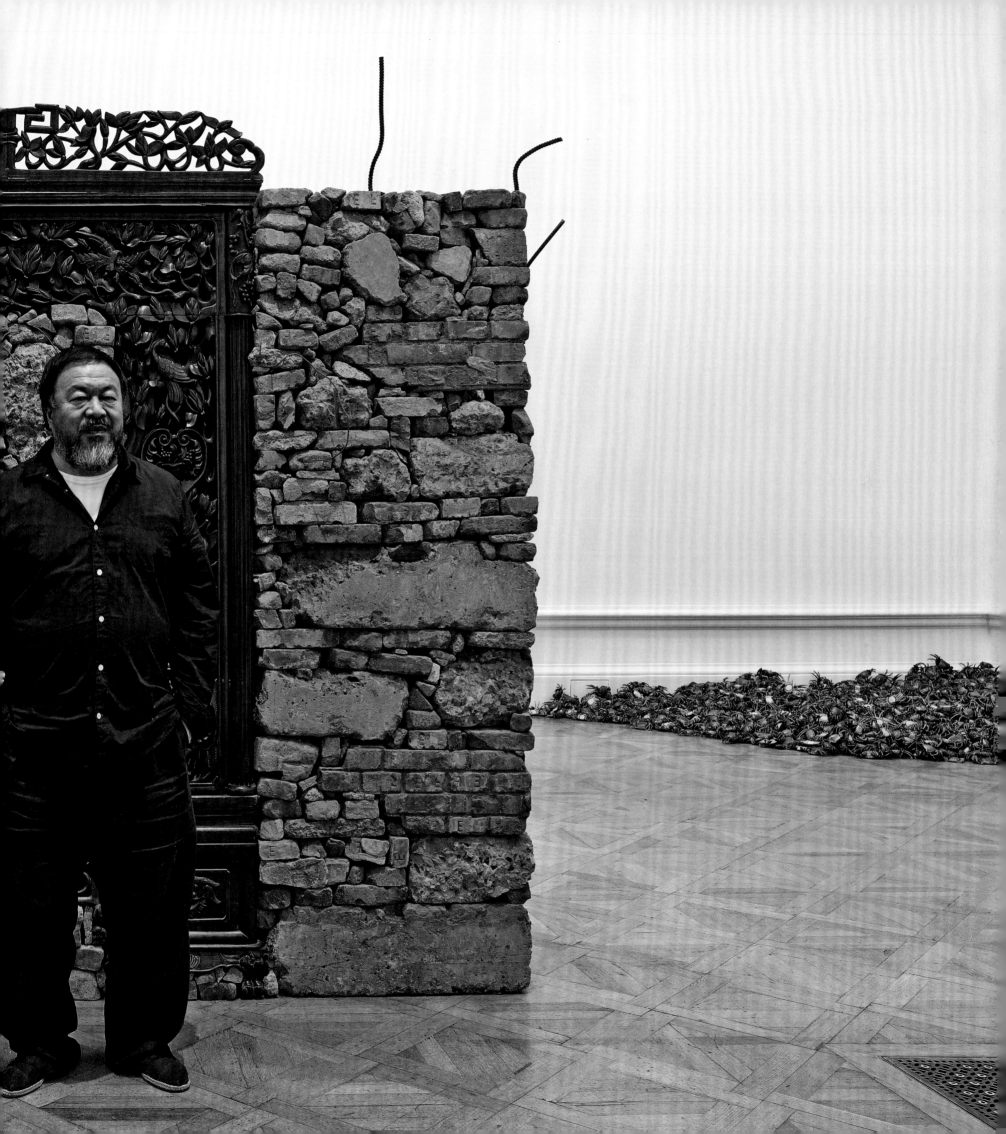

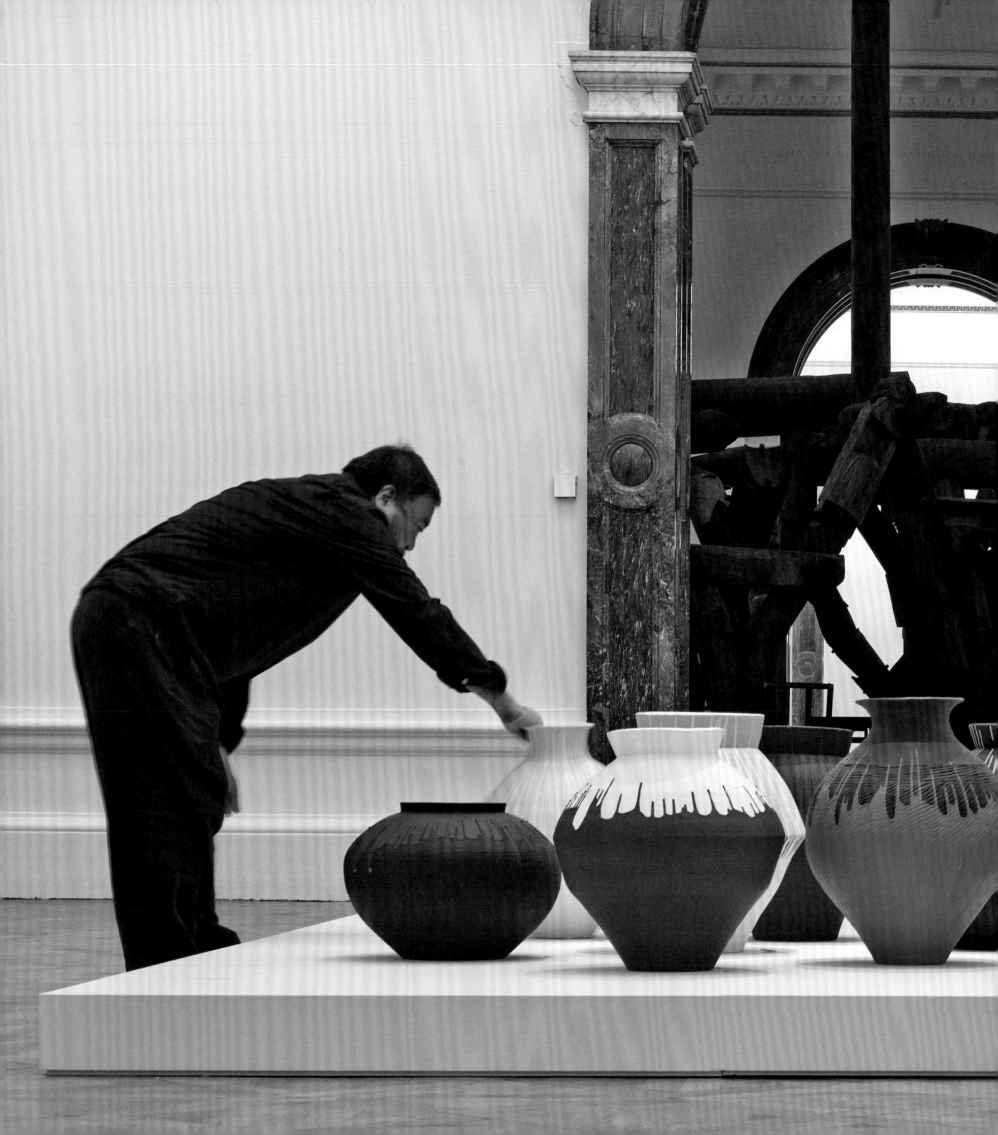

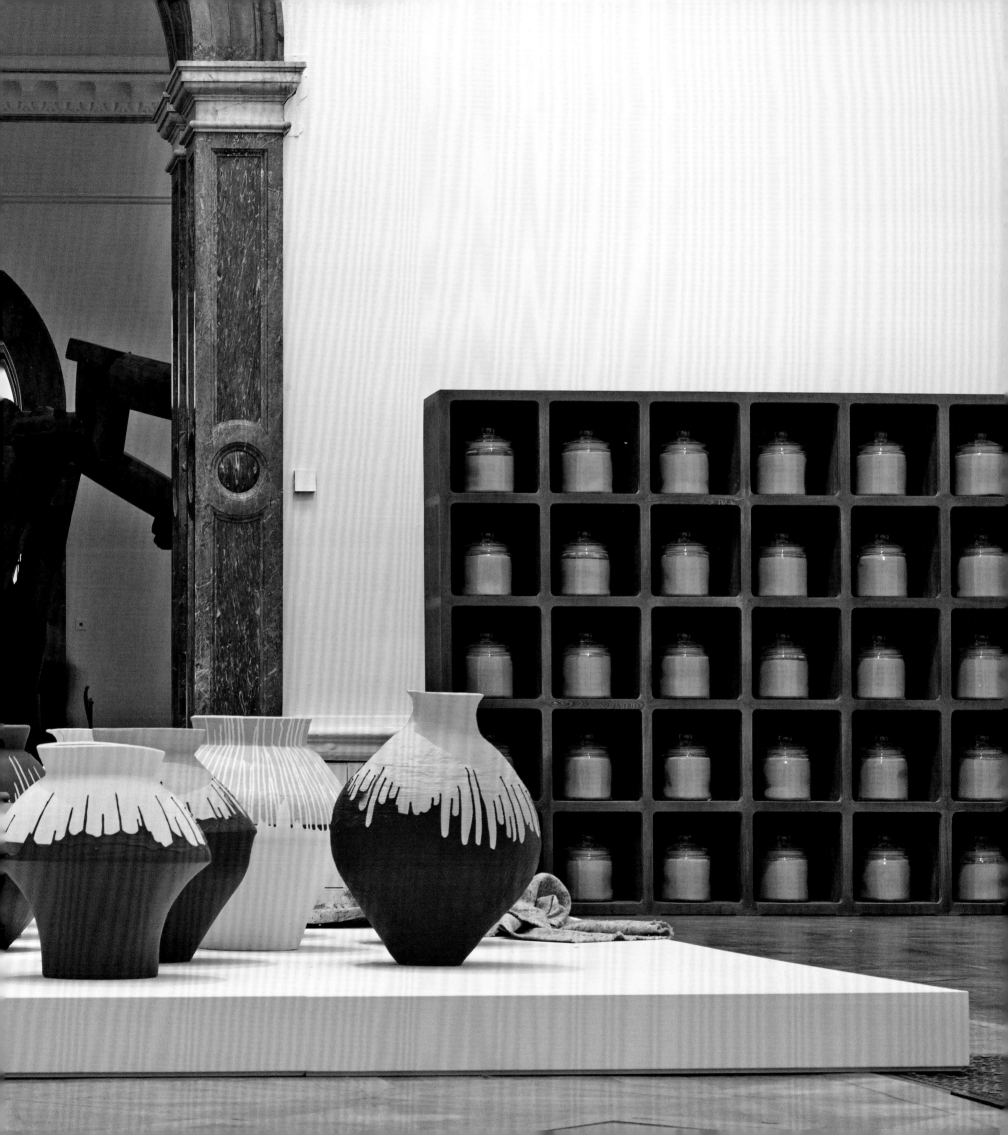

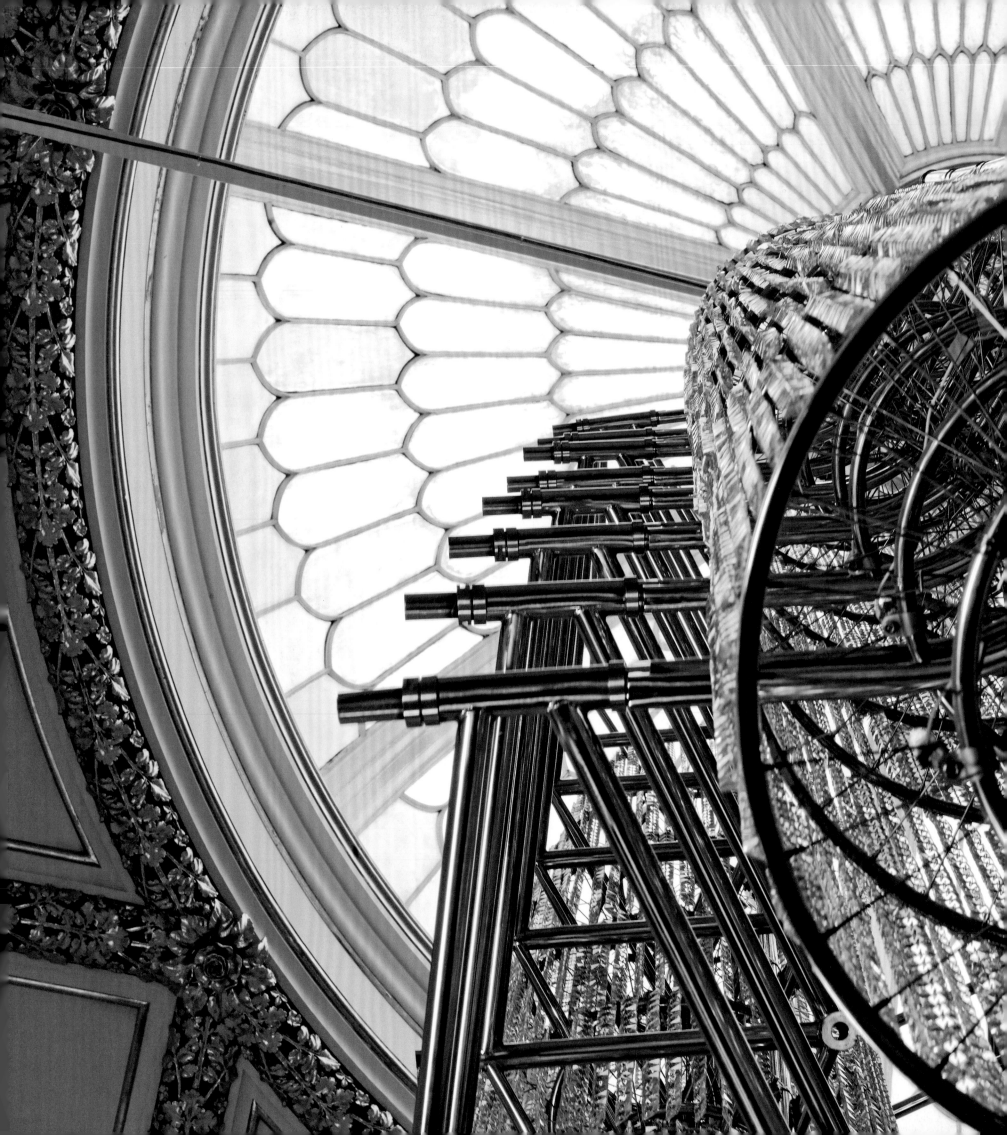

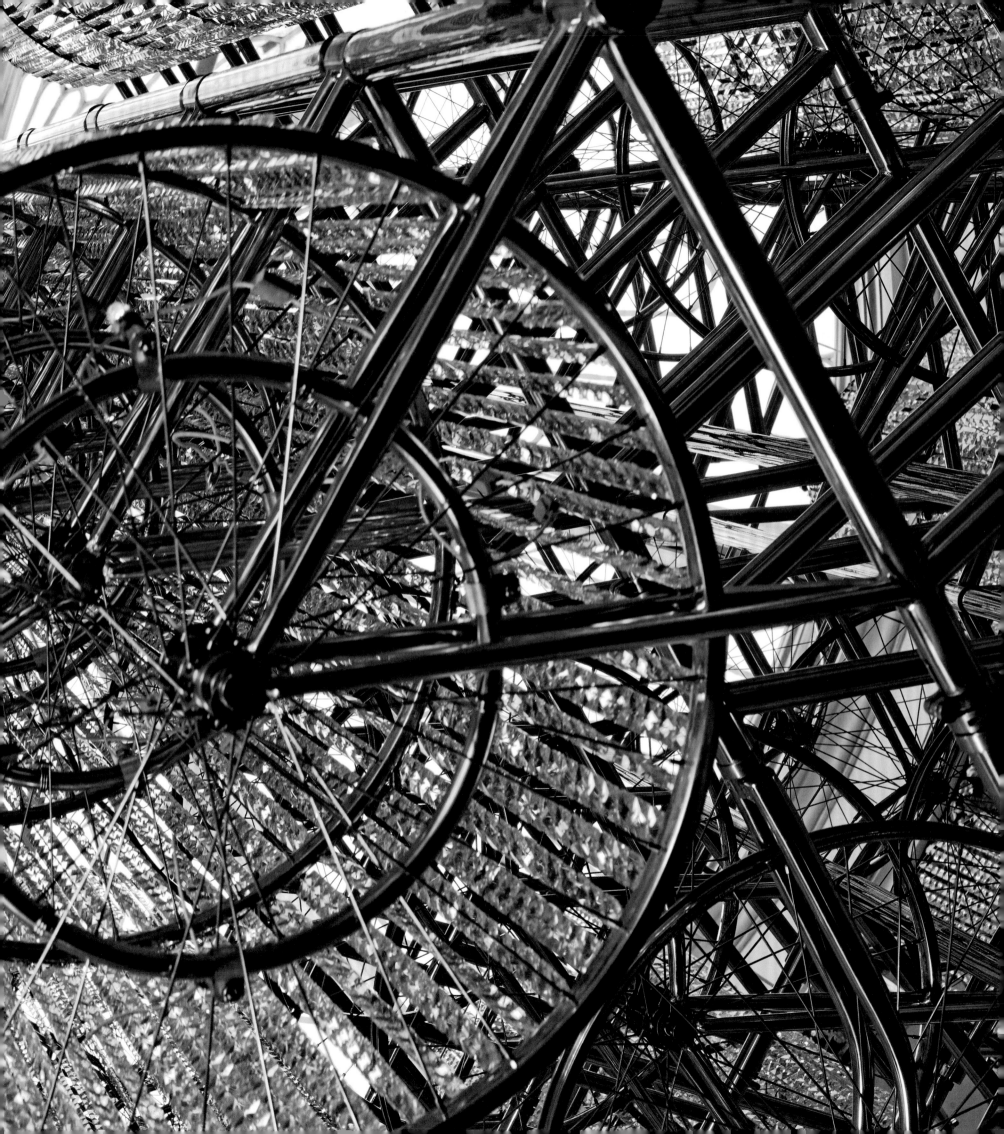

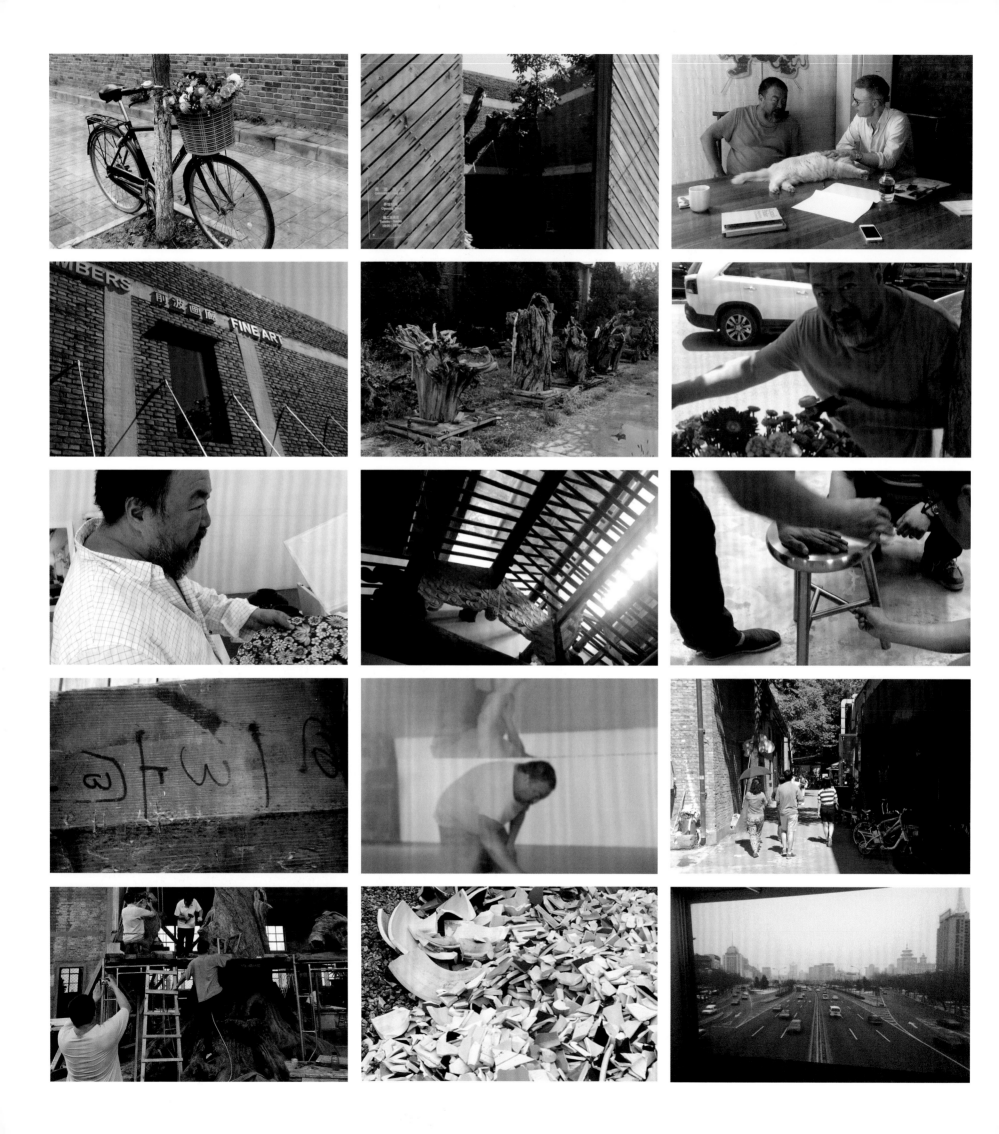

AI WEIWEI

IN CONVERSATION

TIM MARLOW

TIM MARLOW: I'd like to start by asking why you have only included work in the Royal Academy show made after your return from New York to Beijing in 1993, and nothing from during or before the Stars period?

AI WEIWEI: Actually before 2000 I didn't make much artwork. I spent about 12 years in New York and in that whole period I made artworks for less than six months. The rest of the time I just wandered around. There was no need to call myself an artist: I had no gallery and I didn't think I would ever have a show. I moved about ten times in the city, and every time I moved the first things I threw away were artworks.

TM: But you still saw yourself as an artist when you were in New York?

AW: Yes. Two things: first, I didn't have a steady job and I didn't have a clear sense of what I was going to do. And second, if you tell people

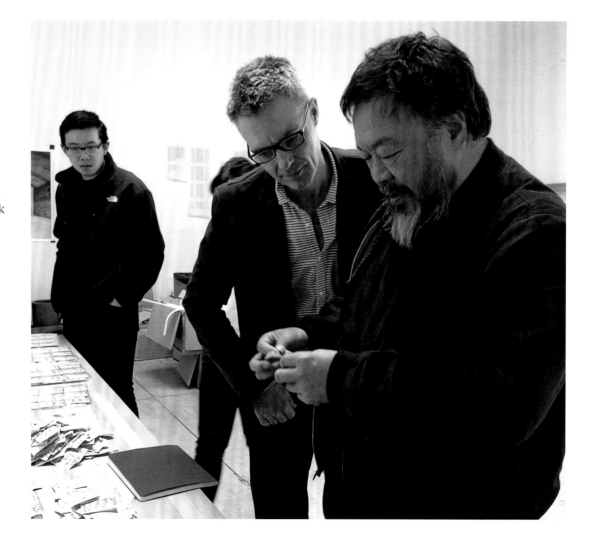

Fig. 1 Photographs from Tim Marlow's visits to Ai Weiwei in Beijing while organising the exhibition, 2015. Photographs by Tim Marlow

Fig. 2 Tim Marlow with Ai at the artist's studio-house, Caochangdi, Beijing, 2015

you're an artist nobody asks any more questions: they all seem to know what an artist does, so I didn't need to give explanations. If you tell people you're a banker they talk about stocks or whatever. Artist? OK, you're an artist.

TM: When did you first realise you wanted to be, or indeed were, an artist?

AW: Well, that's a good question. Maybe I'm still not in that mode yet! I'm still questioning that. I think art is an attitude or lifestyle, one type of activity, but to think about it as a profession is kind of questionable: you know, this guy does nothing but art. It's kind of strange.

TM: Strange? A privilege?

AW: A privilege, I don't know about that. If you're successful maybe you can call it a privilege, but for most people... Yes, if you can make art without worrying about anything else, maybe that is a privilege.

TM: Your parents were both artists in the broadest sense of the word, they were both poets, so this was the culture in which you grew up, although, obviously, during the Cultural Revolution you grew up in fairly brutal circumstances.

AW: Being a poet is very different. I think writing is a very natural act, you write down what's in your mind and maybe you publish it, or maybe you don't. A poet cannot make money from poetry. But today, if you say you're an artist, that's really a problem because you produce things that are not just for yourself. You know, you make a large canvas: who's going to look at it except museums or big collectors? And of course installations are even more of a luxury, it takes so much space to show them.

TM: So poetry is a much more intimate medium as well?

AW: Yes, it's like using Twitter, 140 characters, you just put up one line and somebody will look at it and smile because they get it. OK, they understand: stop the poetry!

TM: It's interesting that for you Twitter, the blog and so on are a form of contemporary poetry, so in a way your activity online does connect you back to your parents.

AW: I see it this way. Online communication to me is like poetry, or it can be like a manifesto: it clearly states your mind and you can communicate very precisely, of course, although you cannot trust that people will understand. But at least it is one form of expression.

TM: I know it's more of a tendency for art historians and curators to see careers in terms of particular works as staging posts or manifesto pieces, but when you're thinking about an exhibition like the one at the Royal Academy, do certain works of yours seem more important to you than others?

AW: If I look at this group of works and just think 'it's my work', I still have trouble really to make sense of it fully because it covers a very large variety of topics or very different depths or levels of interpretation, through materials, through skills, and very different concerns in terms of aesthetics or on a political level. The only way I can describe it is that it's like opening up a garbage can: you see things and you think oh, that's related to yesterday, or somebody else threw that in there. It's very mixed.

TM: One man's postmodern pluralism is another man's garbage can. But you've long seemed to be someone who's interested in different ways of working and different ideas. Has that always been so or were you more focused when you were younger?

AW: I never had a chance to focus, actually. I grew up in the Gobi Desert when my father was forced to do hard labour there or be exiled. I remember my family always moving around, not by choice but because they were made to live in very difficult conditions. My father later became rehabilitated, a very respectable poet again, but even then it was not by his own choice but to serve some political purpose for the Party. So then in New York I had the chance to study outside my situation, as a new immigrant, and had to worry about how to survive and at the same time how not to lose my original interest, which was in art and literature. So my childhood and youth were quite fragmented, and later, when I came back from America, facing China as an opened-up society, totally capitalist and materialist, so I just tried to catch up and I made architecture and later became an artist. Today I have been practising art since the late 1970s, but I started again in 2005, so now is a ten-year anniversary of my new life. So it's quite disparate, so many different experiences.

TM: It's very interesting that you categorise your career like this, and that you see your second phase as an artist beginning in 2005. In the 1990s – from 1993 when you returned to China – you published three books, starting with the *Black Cover Book* (fig. 12), which is very interesting in itself, but you were also making those furniture pieces at the same time.

AW: I started making several books to explore and to try and build up a platform for underground art, because at that time contemporary art had still not been accepted by Chinese society; there was absolutely no chance even to discuss it, so I thought I would make underground prints and printed matter to record that piece of history. Before 2000 I had already started to make some furniture pieces because at that time I was collecting Chinese antiques, furniture, jade and other old artefacts. It's fascinating why we collect. I started to make fun of those things, by painting 'Coca-Cola' on an old Han Dynasty vase (cat. 23) or to drop some pots to test my camera's ability to catch those images (cat. 20). And at the same time I gave my carpenter some work, saying why don't you fix this up, and make this table a different shape (cats 5, 6), to keep him busy. And later the pieces became artworks. But I never thought I would have the chance to show these things.

TM: So they weren't made specifically as sculptures to show?

AW: No. One day a collector said, 'Oh that vase is interesting' and I said 'Take it.' The first Coca-Cola vase basically I just gave to friends, because it stayed in my home for a long time and nobody paid any attention to it.

TM: Let's just think about the furniture then. I've always thought that very smartly you were playing with fragments of history and subtly reconfiguring it. These are very formally engaging objects but also amusing. They're absurd as well: you were playing with the whole construct of furniture. You admit all that's the case, but that they weren't intended as sculptures in the way we might conventionally see a work of sculpture?

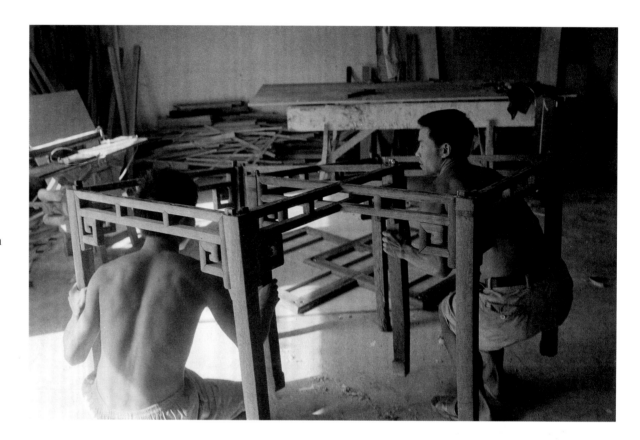

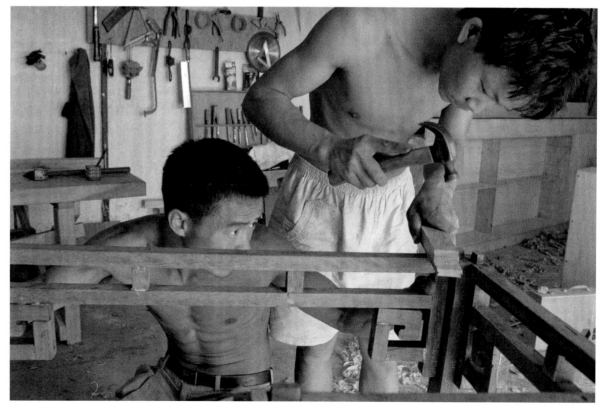

Fig. 3 Making **Tables with Crossed Corners**, 1998

AW: At that time I was very convinced that art has attitude, and it's about the way we treat things. It's not necessarily the way we show people how we treat things, it's just for myself. And also at that time Chinese artists had no opportunities to show their work, until foreigners started to buy works in China, and to collect. Then all my exhibitions started showing outside China. And of course they said this old nation has such history and there must be some interesting artists or art activities, so they started to select Chinese artists for their art shows.

TM: People think there's an ambivalence in the way you use historical fragments: on one level it can be argued that you're reconstructing the past, you're using historical detritus to remake something for the present and the future. In other works, like *Dropping a Han Dynasty Urn*, or *Dust to Dust* (cat. 21), you're being wilfully destructive. Are those critical works or are they provocations, or a mixture of the two?

AW: You could say it's neither, it's just this guy being bored. To me it's not so subversive, it's just a silly act. Boys will be boys.

TM: So you admit there's a silly, childish, playful, but also destructive streak in all this?

AW: Not really destructive, it's just an attitude.

TM: And yet as a collector you seem to have a very respectful – you might even say reverential – attitude to the past in certain ways, if you collect these exquisite objects. Therefore, to paint over or temporarily or permanently to destroy historical fragments, that is a contradiction isn't it?

AW: You call it being destroyed. I'm not like the Taliban, their hatred destroys things. I think I change the form; it's just a different way to interpret the form. One summer a very good collector, an expert in Chinese furniture, said when he saw my furniture: 'Oh, that's the moment you make me really understand Chinese furniture.' So I think in my interpretations I still pose a very philosophical question about how and why those forms have been respected and for what reason. I'm still questioning those very essential aesthetic judgements, where those judgements come from, and in that sense it has followed the tradition of making that pot. I wouldn't call it being destroyed, it just has another life, you know, it's a different way of looking at it.

TM: I would accept that, although you could argue that physically breaking something or grinding it to dust is destructive. But I certainly take the philosophical argument.

AW: I think if there is only one left in the world, if you end that tradition, that's destruction, but if there are 100 then you try to say what happens to one is a break – I think that is discovery, not really destruction.

TM: Your architectural company is called FAKE, as the label outside the studio we're sitting in now states. It's a very interesting area, the authentic and the fake, and I think it operates universally as well as in specific cultures. Is Marcel Duchamp an important antecedent for you in all this? Can we trace your interest in the authentic and the fake back to your encounter with Duchamp's work in New York, or does it pre-date that?

AW: I think Duchamp is the most, if not the only, influential figure in my so-called art practice. We all benefit from what he has done: as a person and a mind, he's very influential on all artists. There's no doubt about it.

TM: The coat hanger, *Hanging Man* (1985; cat. 10), in the exhibition: it's part drawing, part homage, but it's playing with Duchamp, being a readymade in a way.

AW: Yes, I think it was around 1983, when I got to New York, that I was introduced to Duchamp by reading Jasper Johns. I felt he was such a fascinating character, very witty, almost like an oriental thinker or a chess player, and so admirable. So I paid my homage to him, using a coat hanger to make a profile of his face.

TM: I'm interested in the way you would locate yourself art historically. You're part of a long Chinese tradition but part of contemporary Chinese art, and also in the Western tradition Duchamp is one of your influences. How would you describe yourself?

AW: I had very little knowledge about Chinese art before I came back, and now I think I have learnt much more, but basically I was a contemporary artist because my father was a contemporary poet, so I was very influenced by him to read contemporary poetry. And then, I liked Duchamp, Surrealism, Dada, you know, and later in the tradition, conceptual art, all those characters, and of course I loved Warhol's attitude, his communication and all his anxiety as a modern man, so maybe all these have been a strong influence on me.

TM: Duchamp, Warhol, Jasper Johns and others don't engage explicitly with the politics of the world in which they live, but of course all great art does engage socially and politically in different kinds of ways. How much was your artistic engagement with politics personally driven? How much did it stem from your childhood or from what happened when you came back to China, and how much do you think is just what you are as an artist, intrinsically?

AW: If I were very serious about being an artist I would stay away from so-called politics. You know, talking about art in political terms does not suit most artists. But I have to face my reality: I did grow up in this society, my father and a whole generation were victimised by the political struggle, and today I am also being hurt or at least restricted by the situation. I am just the one who does not avoid or try to escape from that. I think if I am an artist I will find my way in my language to deal with my problem. It may be solely my problem, but I do think it's a problem of a nation, and if I truly feel the same way I have a responsibility to let other people know about it. So it's not my choice, it's my life, and if I have to make sacrifices I have no regrets about that. So if we have to examine my art or my politics I think the two are inseparable. Artistically I profoundly relate to philosophy and I cannot avoid all political opinion. No respectable artists, thinkers or poets try to separate them. To me that would be incomprehensible, so I just do my job. I couldn't care less what other people think that is.

TM: It becomes quite clear talking to you that you're very thoughtful but quite restrained. I wonder how often anger fuels your art?

AW: I couldn't say there's immediate anger. Even when I put my imprisonment into those cases in *S.A.C.R.E.D.* (cat. 43). I reduced it to half the scale, to make people feel that it's more like a play than a reality. I think in art you have to transform your primitive feelings into something that has clear language so that the story can be clearly told to another person. Of course you cannot force anybody to think or feel the same way, but you have a responsibility to make sure your language is clear.

TM: Let's talk about *Straight* (cat. 13), which was part of your eventual response to the Sichuan earthquake. When you went down to Sichuan in the immediate aftermath you didn't do so specifically as an artist, is that right? You were invited to go down there, friends needed your support and you went and then realised that social and political work and messaging had to be done about this.

AW: Before I went to Sichuan in 2008 I'd been involved with the internet for three years.

I would write my opinions daily because I wanted to exercise the skill of writing, to practise that – there's so much to say – and that was still a golden time for the internet in China. It was the very beginning, because the government didn't know how effective or how important it was to become. They still hadn't found the right skills to shut it down. So we really had some good times, each day I just anchored myself sitting in front of the screen and I would talk to anybody. I really enjoyed it, I could do it 24 hours a day. And suddenly the earthquake came and, confronted with that disaster, for six or seven days I didn't write anything. Everybody felt really strange, and people said, 'Weiwei, what's happened to you?' Giving opinions about such a disaster seemed futile, I just felt speechless. It was too overwhelming for me, I couldn't find the right language to describe that incident. I was not prepared for it. So I told myself I must go, to be there; only when I'm there will whatever I say be relevant. Otherwise I should stay away because this is beyond my comprehension.

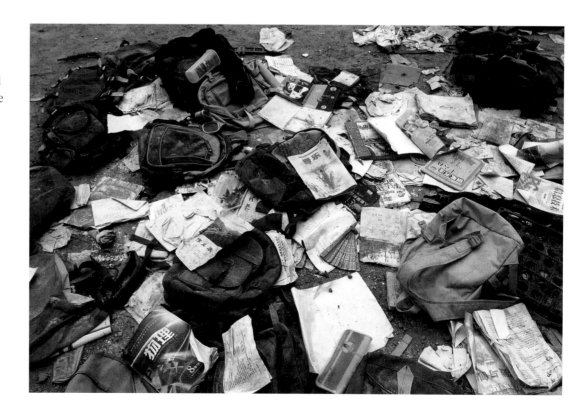

Fig. 4 Ai Weiwei, **Sichuan Earthquake**, 2008.
Part of a series of photographs taken by Ai Weiwei at the earthquake disaster zone, May 2008

So I went to the disaster area, to those ruins. Standing in the earthquake zone, I felt the wind, the air, it was really horrifying: you have bodies underneath the rubble and you feel the wind, you feel that death is there. I never before had such a feeling. I came back and didn't know what to do, so I thought the least I could do would be to find out who was killed in the earthquake, and I wanted to focus on the children because I had seen many students' backpacks strewn everywhere, textbooks, pencils, all their school things. I said let's just ask who those people were and how old they were, and nobody would give us an answer. So I said OK, maybe I can do the research myself, so we did a so-called citizens' investigation, asking people on the internet.

You send out one message and there are thousands or hundreds of thousands of people watching and they say, 'We want to join you.' They had both the emotion and the will to participate but they didn't know how to do it. So I said let's just start from here. So we sent out a message to about 40 groups and of course they were all arrested by the local police, who deleted their research, their photo-images and also the names they found. So we started making a documentary film, of those who needed to be recorded, and we interviewed hundreds of parents of those students, and in the end we found about 5,000 students, and I daily put those names on my blog – some days there were a few, some days a few dozen. So that act really became

so powerful, it became a symbol or some kind of testimony to show this whole nation how an individual can act against the whole system.

TM: By naming individuals whose lives had been lost?

AW: Yes, who they were, when their birthdays were, how old they were, which class they were in and their parents' names. And it's so shocking, we were totally mobbed. I don't think it's art or not art, it was an expression that had a lot of people listening and a lot of people cared and they related to life. But we needed a symbol. So every day I would light a candle, and put its image on the internet, so that people were

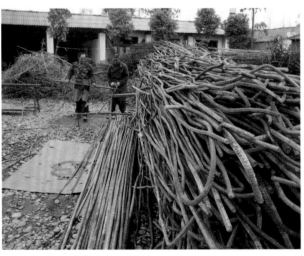
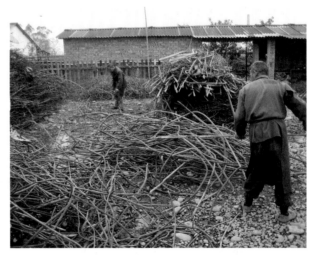
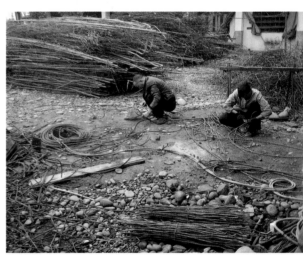
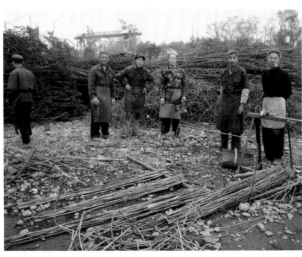
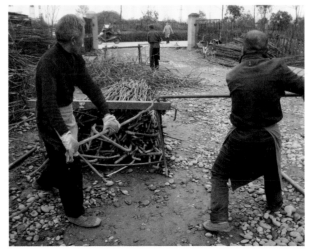
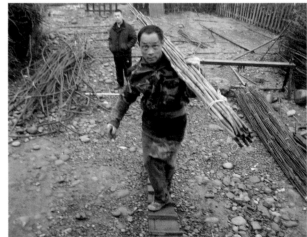

just waiting for our names, until my blog was totally shut down by the government. Then later I got into all kinds of trouble, but that was the beginning. I didn't know how to take all those emotions to the public, you know, how to make it remembered, be recognised.

TM: How to make a memorial I suppose.

AW: The first showing was at the Haus der Kunst in Munich, where I did the façade with one line of words: 'She had been living in this world happily for seven years.' That came from the mother of a victim, a dancer who had just lost her life. So her mum said, 'I don't want state money, I just want her to be remembered,' so I used 9,000 students' backpacks to construct one line, *Remembering* (2009; fig. 61). Years later I realised I could still get the steel rebar they took out of the rubble because they were reselling it for melting down. We managed to buy all that rebar, which was all twisted and I didn't know what to do with it, so I came up with the minimal way to straighten it so that it would look as though it had just come out of the factory. So we had a lot of people start to bend and knock it straight. Then I was arrested, and after 81 days I was released and I went to my studio and before I arrived I heard 'ding ding ding', and people were still working on it. That gave me such joy. I shall always remember those sounds.

TM: So *Straight* is also testament to the resilience of the artistic process, in that it was going on while you were in prison; the piece was still being made.

AW: Yes, we continued to make it until the last Venice Biennale (2013), and we presented it there. But that was only half of it, because it's 150 tons; the volume was too large.

TM: I think people are fascinated by your ideas and processes. So you had the opportunity to acquire that rebar that was being sold off to be recycled. You had the idea of restoring it to its original form, which I suppose is a way of looking back historically, trying to bring things back to their original state. What then led you to decide to show it as a kind of minimalist floor piece in the configuration that you did? How is the work resolved, how does that process come about?

AW: I think the meaning or the message should be carried through knowledge rather than just visual presentation, and besides, no visual presentation could adjust itself to that kind of disaster. So if I could have a machine to rewind time from the ruins to the buildings, the students would have their classes there, and before the building was built, the rebar came from the factory like that: that's how you rewind this time machine. And I think it should stay quiet because there is so much to talk about.

TM: So the simplest configuration in some ways is the most powerful, because it lets the material and the history of that material speak?

AW: Yes, it will speak and it carries a lot, and I don't think it needs to be disturbed by any other form.

TM: You mention your 81-day incarceration and the fact that *Straight* was being made at that time and its making was one of the first sounds you heard when you came back to the studio. It's a lovely idea, a moving story. I'm curious as to how the idea of *S.A.C.R.E.D.* came to you. When you were thinking of ways of surviving in prison, and asking yourself whether you were going to get out, was one of your thoughts 'I will make works of art about this'?

AW: First, when I was in prison I never thought I would be released. The situation was so severe you never have that kind of thought, that you could get out without a heavy sentence, and they had clearly told me I would be there for over ten years. So at that time being an artist or not being an artist didn't seem very important. But what did make me satisfied was that I had spoken my mind clearly before I got into this situation. I had no regrets about having to stay there a long time for that reason.

TM: When I first saw *S.A.C.R.E.D.* in Venice in 2013, in a church, it reminded me of the Stations of the Cross, those images of fourteen moments in Christ's journey to the Crucifixion. I'm not suggesting that you were depicting a moment of martyrdom, but did that Christian tradition have some kind of resonance for you?

AW: Once I was released, people were not really curious about why I had been in prison but, rather, about how they had treated me. It's really too hard to describe that, how they treat you. They never beat me and they fed me well and they had doctors measure my physical condition every day, sometimes seven times a day. It's as though you have been checked into a scientific centre: you're being heavily monitored, and you can see how much care they take of you. But of course it's extremely tough psychological warfare. I thought the best way to describe my situation in prison would be to make a piece to simulate the condition, and of course the reference comes from religious ritual, which can be Christian or even Buddhist. Early temples I have visited always have drawings, how Buddha lets the tiger eat his own meat [he pitied a starving mother tiger and allowed her to eat his own flesh],

Fig. 5 Fabrication of **Straight**, 2008–12

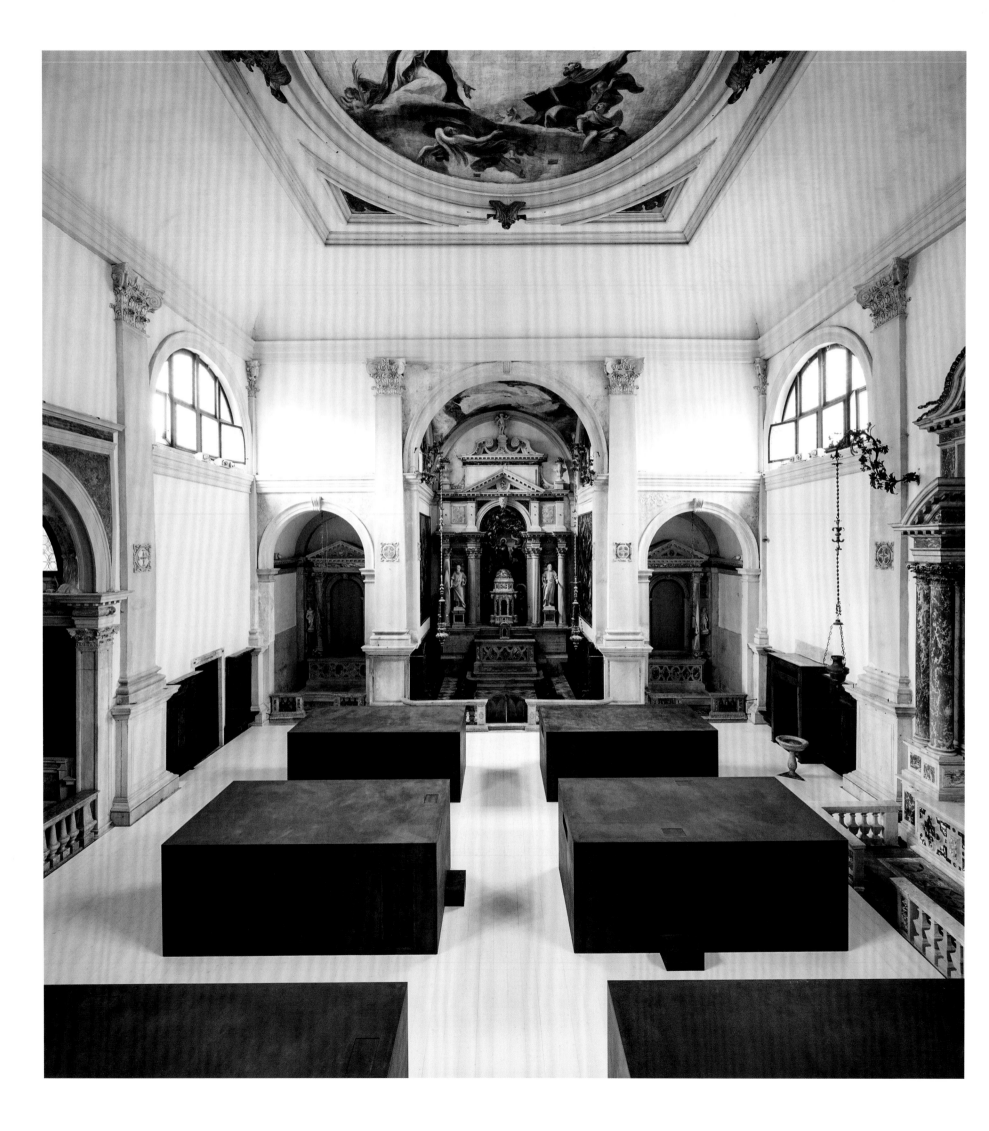

and also in the Natural History Museum you see those dinosaurs. I think those are very effective settings, so that children and people who do not necessarily understand exactly what they're looking at can still clearly see some details. So that was the idea.

TM: But your means of display are reduced, minimal, and the six block-enclosed dioramas themselves suggest incarceration but also a post-minimalist installation – when you first encounter the work you're not aware of the internal detail, but it still works as an installation. It's architectural and sculptural to me.

AW: Yes, all my works play with art history. As a contemporary artist I can never leave the context of what contemporary philosophy and aesthetics are about, so I think I am fully aware of that. It's like a Communist member is always aware of the flag: I'm contemporary, by definition, but I definitely speak art-historical languages too. But in the end everything has to carry my message.

TM: I'm also interested in the relationship between art and architecture in your work. Does architecture feel something apart from what you do artistically, or are the two absolutely linked?

AW: I have worked as an artist, a critic, an architect or planner or designer, so I think those roles can be distinct although they have very strong similarities. They are all trying to set up a condition, to give definition about who we are and how we want people to look at us and what we want to show other people; it's about our minds. Some aspects are more practical, some are less practical or abstract, and I think it's interesting to play with those different kinds of qualities. There are always some very indistinct

boundaries between the practical and the non-practical worlds.

TM: Is it important to you that your studio and the space you live in are designed by you? Was that a matter of convenience or is it culturally important to you to live in a space that you've created rather than one loaded with previous history?

AW: I'm not very self-indulgent, I think any space can work, and recently I have started to like being in hotels, I think they can work very well for artists. Warhol said he liked airport waiting areas or stations. If we think about life, we're just passengers. Sometimes we can feel very familiar or comfortable, but after all we're just passing through, there's no question about it. So it's hard to say what kind of condition would lead to a better mood for work, that depends on the kind of work and who you are working with.

TM: So you want to create a straight-forward, practical, stripped-back place in which to work, and that's the design that surrounds us now: it's very elegant, modernist to a certain extent.

AW: What I've created here is a kind of emptiness, you don't see much art here and if people come and they don't know me it's very hard for them to identify with the space. And even the builders, when I said 'OK, we'll stop here,' they said, 'Oh, we haven't finished,' and so I said, 'Well, I don't have any more money,' so then they can believe, OK, and they're satisfied. Otherwise they would think this house is half finished.

TM: What about your relationship with China now: you can't travel because you don't have a passport. I remember reading that when you

were in America in the late 1980s and early 1990s, it was said that you never intended to come back. And then because of your father's illness you did. If you were given your passport back – let's hope that you are – do you still envisage living and working the majority of your life here in China? Are your art and life so inextricably linked to this place? Or could you conceive of living and working in different places again?

AW: The question reminds me of the story of a German poet [Heinrich Heine, 1797–1856] who was trying to cross the border and saw the police search all his books to try to find out if any were illegal or dangerous. He wrote, 'You know, what is most dangerous is in my mind, you cannot stop that.' So I have the same attitude. I don't think anybody can stop me, our thinking is so free and we can be much braver than anybody thinks we can, so this is our life, we defend it, we defend the dignity of life. Of course I should be allowed a passport, come on, this is beyond question. And this is my nation, this is where I grew up, it's where my father and my ancestors grew up, and I try to defend that. I love comfort but I'm not just seeking my private safety and comfort. If I were to do so, I would have made the biggest mistake in my life. I would not even start with this. So I think they just underestimate me, and they don't understand those values.

TM: I presume becoming a father has changed certain attitudes for you.

AW: It does make me much more vulnerable because you bear some kind of responsibility. You do feel that you're not just speaking for yourself but for the people you care about, and you think twice. So that's my condition. So this interview has only half my mind!

Fig. 6 Ai Weiwei, **S.A.C.R.E.D.**, 2011–13 (cat. 43).
Installation view in Chiesa di Sant'Antonin,
Venice, 2013

TM: I'm glad to hear that, it's as it should be! Do you think you will continue to communicate in the broadest possible way with the broadest number of people? Is that now part of what you're compelled to do as an artist?

AW: I still don't have the chance to do so. I was prepared for a much worse situation, for never having a show, never having an interview or writing, so I think I will be OK. You always have to prepare for the worst. In history this happened, it's not fantasy, it happened to my family, it still happens to many people in the world or in this nation.

TM: How different do you think the exhibition that you're making for the Royal Academy would be if you could come to London? I'm very curious because the architectural side of your thinking has been very detailed in the way you've considered the spaces and where the works are going to go.

AW: I wouldn't think it would have been very different. Of course if I had had more time or could have adjusted myself to different conditions I may have included different works or even had different intentions, but basically it's about me, it's about what I have done and it's about my feeling for the Royal Academy as an artists' institution and London as a city. I don't know, it's very hard to say.

TM: Do you think art can make a difference? Does it have the potential to do this? And are there examples in your own life where you feel making art does make a significant difference?

AW: I prefer to think of art as offering a possibility to help or accommodate me with my situation and it gives me so much. And also I can share my situation with others, and it certainly changes things, and if I'm part of that world I hope I can change at least the spirit of the times with art. I think we'd have a better society if imagination, fantasy or passion – the qualities realised through art – were more valued.

TM: If you want to change the world, try and change the way people see it?

AW: First, I think artists are the ones who use their own lives to feel the world, to understand the world, so by doing that maybe at least they add to other people's understanding. I think people have to live some of this life through art and through doing things, so art practice cannot be separated from life.

TM: I want to talk to you now about a series of works made in marble, some of which have been made specifically for the exhibition at the Royal Academy. These include various objects, a pushchair, a video camera and a series of grass leaves that in effect make a marble lawn on the gallery floor. Where did the idea come from?

AW: When I talk about one piece, normally it doesn't come from a particularly rational development, it comes from an amalgamation of vague aspects. You know the place we live here we call Caochangdi, which in Chinese means a grass field, and the grass always relates to grass roots, and poetically we Chinese always have an apposite proverb: 'Wildfire cannot destroy the grass because when the spring comes it becomes green again.'

TM: The grass will always grow again.

AW: Yeah, it's always like that. It's not so poetic if you have to talk about it but it's interesting for me to see if I can transform grass into marble. It's not easy because both materials are very fragile in different ways, grass is beautiful because it's not stiff, it can really move. But I have done iron casting and I have worked in marble and each has its own form; there's a sense of discovering what is possible through the process of transformation.

The baby's pushchair came from an incident after I was released from prison. Daily I would take my boy to the park – I wanted to spend as much time with him as possible because I was afraid I would lose him – so one day my driver said, 'Oh, someone is following us and taking photos.' I was angry and I ran after this guy and said, 'You're taking photos of us: why?' and he said 'No, I don't know you, I'm just a tourist and don't try to bother me.' I was very frustrated because my boy was there; if it had been just myself I wouldn't have bothered. So I grabbed his camera, took out the memory card. Before I gave it back I said, 'If you promise me you will never follow me again I will give back your camera.' He said, 'I will never follow you again,' so I gave him back his camera and he said, 'This is my job,' and I said OK, but I took his memory card and I still feel a little bit bad as maybe I made a mistake. I put the memory card in my computer and was shocked. An image of my boy's pushchair jumped out at me from the screen, and there's a series of terrible photos not just of my boy's pushchair, but also of the restaurant I was at last night, every room, the counter, the hallway. I was speechless to see how the State functions, how they invade people's privacy and how powerful they are. They are so powerful but only because they violate essential values – all the values we care about, they don't. That's what makes them so powerful.

TM: And you have also made a surveillance camera out of marble too. When I arrived at your studio here, there were red Chinese lanterns hung on all the lampposts where actual surveillance cameras are sited, so in a way you're playing a kind of game with the voyeuristic State, the State that is obsessed with surveillance.

AW: My condition sometimes becomes so dry, so meaningless and almost dreadful that I try to use humour to force myself to make a move. It's a difficult game, but I still have to play. I always say: You make a move, I'll make a move. It's the same, still, a fair game. But it's very difficult.

TM: Marble is of course a very important and rich material in art history. It tends to be the conventional material of monuments. I suppose you could say that the grass, the pushchair, the surveillance cameras are all part of a tradition of anti-monuments as well: they're both monuments and anti-monuments at the same time.

AW: Yeah, it's a send-up of this kind of monumentalism. My work always has some kind of contradiction within it.

TM: I'm curious about your interest in different materials, marble but also wood and glass. I'm thinking of the Cube pieces (cats 31–34), and particularly the boxes that you made that seem to be both architectural and sculptural again, but very material-led as well, almost a celebration of materials and craftsmanship. Is that a fair comment?

AW: I think you're right, I think you've noticed that I use essential physical or even mathematical elements, the better to carry our questions about our modern history, about minimalism and conceptual art. They are also part of our state

of mind as artists, and relate to questioning the world around us. For me, the Cube pieces remain a question rather than being a perfect product. They're not the answer but the question.

TM: And traditional craftsmanship? Again, that seems to be something that you celebrate in your work.

AW: Yes, those traditions are alive because they've been developed through a classic understanding of materials and of how best to use them, and to show how humans are capable of interacting with materials. I think this is also part of the balance between humans and nature, and this is something that is being broadly ignored at present and the consequences are not always so happy. But there is also the question of whether there is a need for such a perfect manual skill, which could be seen by some as a utopian type of practice.

TM: Are you saying, among other things, that traditional skills are exploited by capitalism, for example? Is that one of the points you're making, that we lose sight of skill in that sense because everything is mass-produced?

AW: I think so, I think in many ways high-volume production serves a very different purpose, and sometimes it can be devastating.

TM: It's interesting seeing the metre-cube of glass, because we're so used to industrial manufacturing processes, these thick glass structures that make buildings now. But your glass cube is the result of an intricate handmade process, and it seems miraculous but also it seems rough as well. I love its perfection and its imperfection too.

AW: By chance I visited this state-owned company, probably the largest crystal company in China, but what they produce there is very pitiful: beer mugs and candlesticks and in such

Fig. 7 Ai Weiwei, **Sunflower Seeds**, 2010.
Ai's son Ai Lao during installation at the Tate
Modern, London, 2010

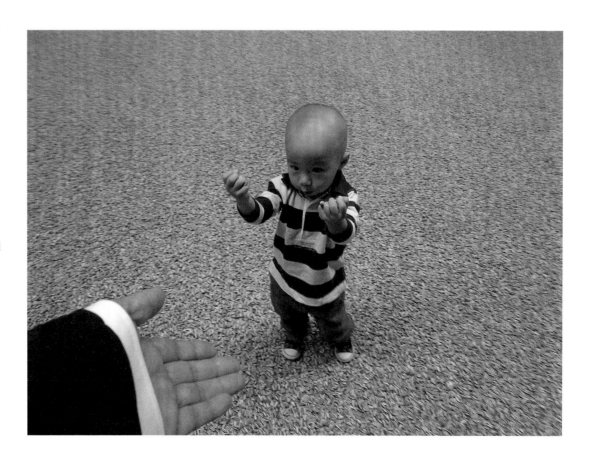

bad taste. I don't know who uses the things they make. So then you look at those products made from a material that has its own power and roughness. I like those qualities, I want to see what the glass looks like, but they could never make such a large piece because the heat is over 1,000 degrees, they take half a year to cool down, and many times they fail because once you open them, they crack. So in the end I had to work with my own team with a material that has a very interesting nature, you know, its own temperament.

TM: So it's truth to materials but it's also the complexity of process, and there's an element of thinking this will never work.

AW: It's hard to handle because we don't understand it.

TM: You've included a sex toy in the exhibition, not made from glass but from jade (cats 35, 36). Where did that come from?

AW: I thought you brought it to me?

TM: Busted! No, I can safely say I didn't.

AW: Our friends brought it to me from New York, but I think works in jade were appreciated by the Emperor, the material is of such fine quality and craftsmanship. And those modern sex toys, even though they're so common, they're never really displayed, they're private objects. I thought it would be nice to produce one for public display in this fine material.

TM: It reminded me that when Brancusi's celebrated erotic sculpture *Princess X* went to New York it was censored on the grounds of obscenity, and this was in the second decade of the twentieth century.

AW: Why was it censored?

TM: Because it looked very phallic, it is phallic – this was around the same time that Duchamp at the Armory was making *Fountain* – and I think people commented then that the Brancusi looks like a sex toy, so I wondered if there was any distant connection?

AW: So this would be a homage to that piece? This is a sex toy. It doesn't look like a sex toy, every inch of it is a sex toy.

TM: So I'll take that as an emphatic no then! It does however connect in my mind to the fact that your first show in New York was called 'Old Shoes – Safe Sex'. That seems obviously connected to an awareness of AIDS?

AW: Yes, by 1983 there was already a lot of speculation about AIDS and many artists lost their lives because there was still no way to cure it. Everybody was so scared. Actually AIDS is not so scary, but without the knowledge we now have, it was.

TM: So that was part of that culture of protest and also of enlightening people or trying to bring to their attention something that was being buried, effectively. So it relates a little to the situation you're dealing with now, in a funny kind of way, of censorship and people putting their heads in the sand and not acknowledging what's going on.

AW: Yes, sex is always an area through which you can see different moments in history with a certain clarity.

TM: I just want to talk to you finally about bicycles: in the Wohl Central Hall at the Royal Academy you're going to make a new piece featuring a chandelier made of Forever bicycles (cat. 45). I think I'm right in saying that the bicycle pieces began because of the loss of the life of an activist with whom you had become friendly. Could you just explain how they have evolved? They're political as well as social and universal I suppose?

AW: The bicycle is very symbolic in China because it's just like grass really, it belongs to ordinary life and the way we grow up, and yet a bicycle is also a luxury and practical. The first chandelier I did used scaffolding, which reflects some architectural aspects and China's understanding of luxury life and power, and I never thought to combine the two ideas. I don't even know how the Royal Academy chandelier is going to look, we're still testing it.

TM: When you say luxury, you mean because it's the scaffolding of new, high-rise buildings?

AW: Well, scaffolding belongs to high-rise buildings, but it doesn't matter what kind of building, the chandelier is always the finishing touch of a new building, and normally the scaffolding and the chandeliers don't meet. So I think it's a structure of two sets of different kinds of usage together. Wittgenstein once said, 'The meaning of a word is its use.' So, I think it's interesting.

TM: Absolutely. He also said, 'Whereof one cannot speak, thereof one must be silent,' on which note we should probably end this interview.

AW: Yes, maybe for my next show I shouldn't give interviews.

This text is based on a conversation that took place between the author and Ai Weiwei at Caochangdi, Beijing, on 16 March 2015.

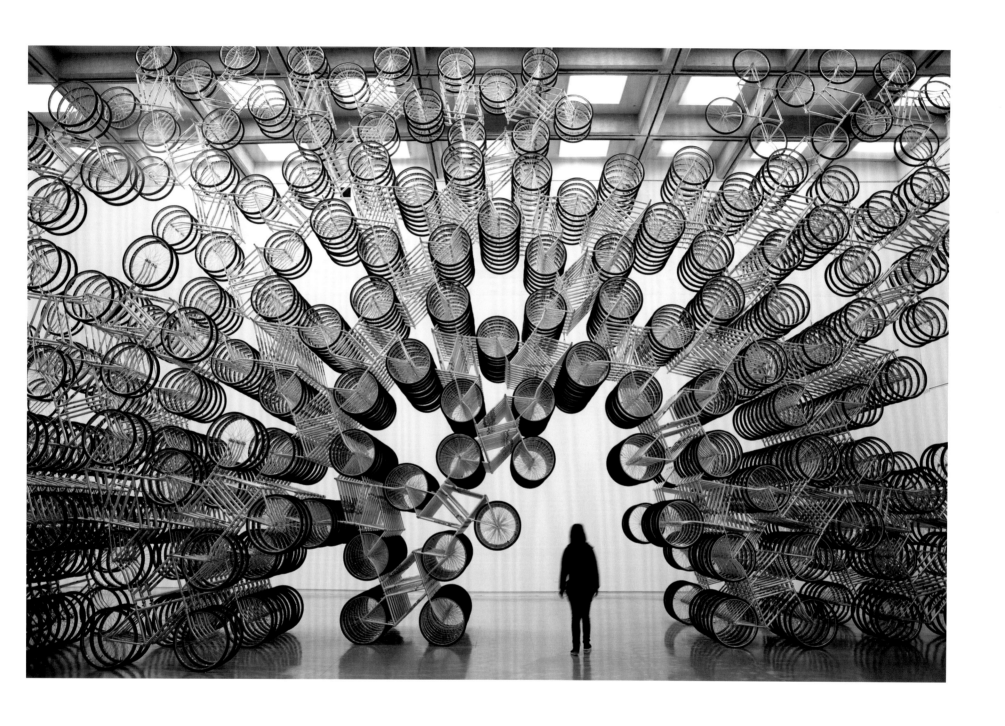

Fig. 8 Ai Weiwei, **Forever Bicycles**, 2011.
1,200 Forever bicycles, installation view,
Taipei Fine Arts Museum
Courtesy of Taipei Fine Arts Museum

BORN RADICAL

JOHN TANCOCK

No contemporary Chinese artist has greater name recognition worldwide than Ai Weiwei, and yet within China, until the exhibitions of his work in Beijing in June and the announcement on 22 July that his passport had been returned, his name could not be mentioned.[1] Following his career over three decades, it seems almost inevitable that this would have been the case, since on several major issues – the importance of human rights, freedom of speech and what he refers to as 'modernism' – Ai has not wavered. There were times when this was less apparent than it is today. During the decade he spent in New York (1983–93) his photographs reveal a keen awareness of what was happening in American politics, although he was powerless to effect any change. For the first few years after he returned to Beijing in 1993 he diverted this conviction into artistic channels but it was always present.

When Ai returned to Beijing in 1976 after growing up in remote Xinjiang province, where his father, the poet Ai Qing (1910–1996), had been sent into exile during the Cultural Revolution (1966–76), he immediately gravitated to the circle of young creative people in all fields – poets, filmmakers, painters and sculptors – who were trying to establish themselves in a cultural and political environment in which all the certainties of the previous three decades had vanished. Art academies that had been closed during the Cultural Revolution reopened in 1978 but the official art world held little attraction for the minority of like-minded individuals who valued self-expression above everything else.

Ai entered the Beijing Film Academy in 1978, in the same year as Chen Kaige and Zhang Yimou, who were later to gain celebrity as two of China's outstanding film directors, and he also participated in the Democracy Wall where on 5 December 1978 Wei Jingsheng posted an essay stating that the 'Four Modernisations'[2] advocated by Deng Xiaoping should be expanded to include a fifth, namely democracy. Ai's interest in the visual arts began at about the same time. Artist-friends of his father had given him basic tuition and, as a member of a distinguished intellectual family that had been reinstated, he had access to books on such modern masters as Picasso and Matisse, which were exceedingly rare in China at the time. In his lack of experience and knowledge, however, he was no different from any of his contemporaries.

For the underground painting club 'Wuming' ('No Name'),[3] it had been an act of courage during the Cultural Revolution to paint landscapes and still-lifes small enough to be hidden in a pocket if an unfriendly security guard

Fig. 9 Ai Weiwei, **Sunflower Seeds**, 2010. Installation of 100 million painted porcelain seeds in the Turbine Hall at the Tate Modern, London

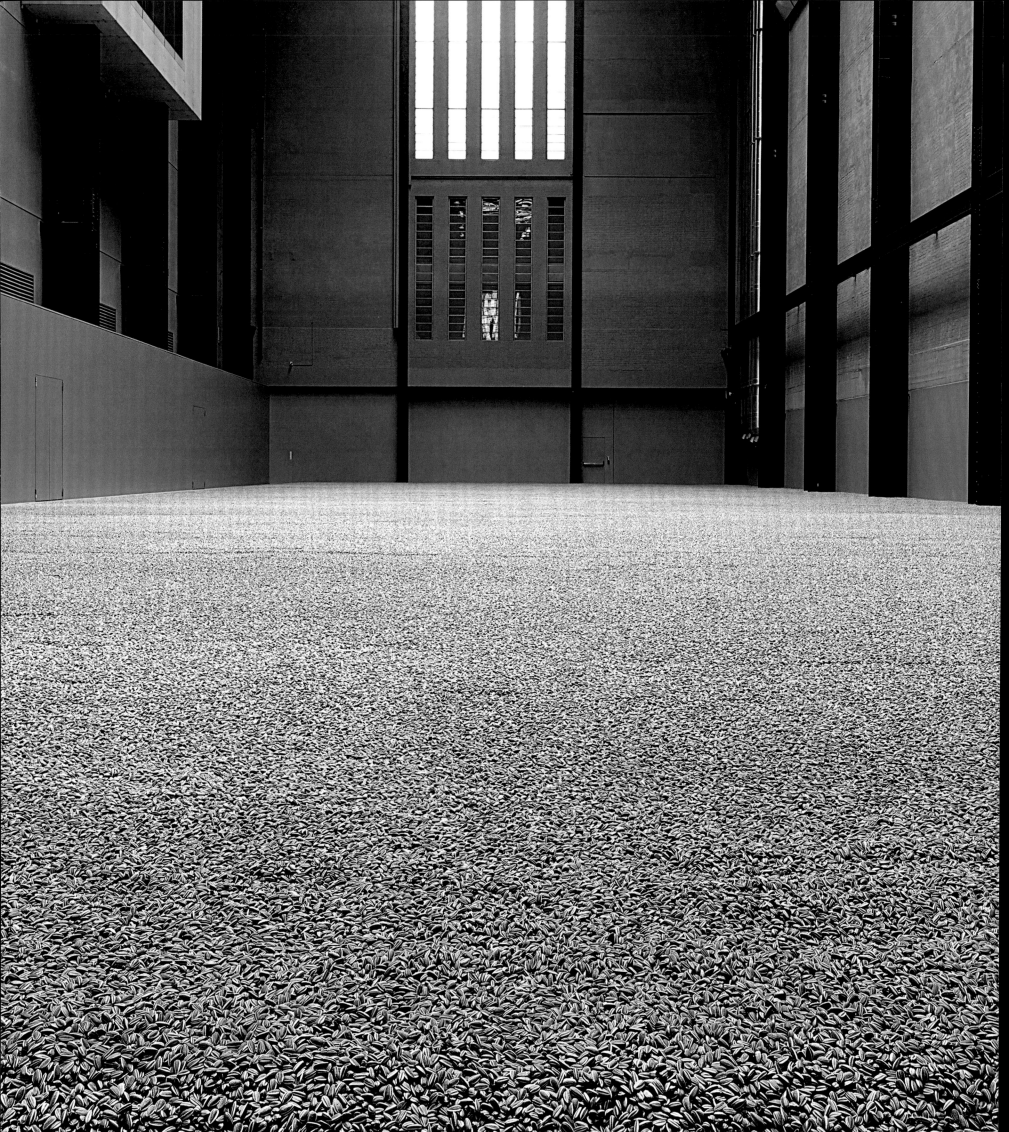

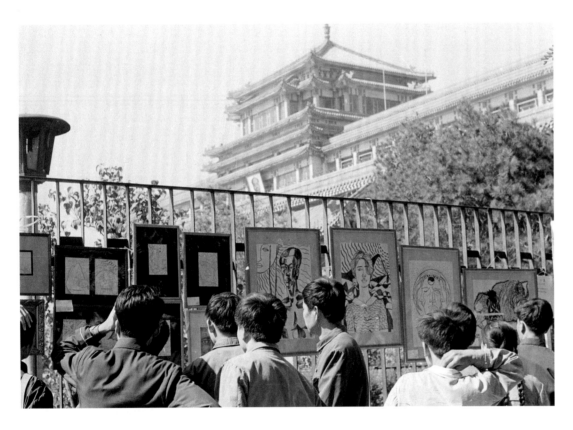

Kollwitz had been a revered figure since the time of the influential left-wing writer Lu Xun.[5]

This period of youthful idealism was not to last very long. The temporary lull in censorship that had permitted the brief existence of the Stars group was followed by a cultural crackdown, and Wei Jingsheng was given a thirteen-year prison sentence. Ai was disillusioned: 'I left because the activists from our same group were put in jail. The accusation was that they were spies for the West which was total nonsense. The leaders of the Democratic Movement were put in jail for thirteen years, and we all knew these people, and we all got absolutely mad and even scared – you know, "this country has no hope".'[6]

New York, 1983–93

Ai Weiwei arrived in the United States in 1981 and lived in New York from 1983 to 1993.[7] He arrived with little money and few possessions, for the greater part of the next decade supporting himself through a number of unlikely temporary jobs ranging from babysitting to pavement art. Absorbing much of what was happening around him by osmosis rather than by direct contact with American artists, and establishing an attitude towards the creative process that was fully formed when he returned to Beijing, he took no part in such key events such as the 1985 Art New Wave movement and the 1989 'China/Avant-Garde' exhibition at the National Art Museum of China in Beijing. Although Chinese knowledge of developments in contemporary art in the West was severely limited, there was a proliferation of artist groups throughout China during this period, including the conceptually oriented Xiamen Dada and the Pond Society in Zhejiang, which offered radical alternatives to official and academic art. Certain works such as

happened to be nearby. In 1979 the painter Huang Rui felt that the time had come for a more public approach. With Ma Desheng, Wang Keping and Qu Leilei, he selected the group of 23 artists including Ai Weiwei who participated in the first exhibition of the 'Stars' group, which is generally considered to be the first major event in the short history of contemporary Chinese art. Since this was an unofficial exhibition, the works were hung on the fence surrounding the China Art Gallery (now the National Art Museum of China) in Beijing on 27 September 1979 and attracted a large, enthusiastic audience (fig. 10). Closed down after two days, the exhibition reopened on 23 November in a different location. A second Stars exhibition in which Ai also participated took place the following year inside the China Art Gallery from 24 August to 7 September.[4]

Believing in self-expression following years during which this had been suppressed as a bourgeois indulgence, the artists painted in a variety of styles, Ai's watercolours revealing a preference for a colourful, expressive manner. When asked to name the artists who meant most to members of the Stars group at the time, the sculptor Wang Keping mentioned Käthe Kollwitz and Picasso, an odd pairing for a Western audience but not for a Chinese one, for whom

Fig. 10 The first Stars exhibition displayed on the railings outside the China Art Gallery, Beijing, 27 September 1979. Collection Li Xiaobin

Huang Yong Ping's *'The History of Chinese Art'*
and 'A Concise History of Modern Painting' after
Two Minutes in the Washing Machine (1987) and
Xu Bing's *Book from the Sky* (1987–91) are now
recognised as milestones in the early history of
contemporary Chinese art. Developments in
oil painting outside the official academies also
occurred, a tendency that the critic Li Xianting
was to nurture and eventually to identify as
Cynical Realism and Political Pop, both of which
had gained international recognition by the time
Ai returned to Beijing.

During this period Ai's small apartment
became a crucial stop for the numerous Chinese
artists, writers and composers who were visiting
New York. The film director Chen Kaige, the
composer Tan Dun, Wang Keping (fellow
exhibitor with Ai in the Stars exhibitions), Xu
Bing and Liu Xiaodong all make an appearance
in Ai's extensive photographic documentation.
He also made new acquaintances, such as the
rigorous Taiwanese performance artist Hsieh
Tehching, who was to become a close friend, and
the poet Allen Ginsberg, a neighbour who had
been welcomed by Ai's father when he visited
China in 1984.

Unlike his contemporaries in China, who
were finding out about recent developments
in the West from hard-to-come-by periodicals
and Xeroxed documents, Ai was able to see
everything the New York galleries had to offer at
first hand. As can be seen from his paintings, the
currently popular neo-expressionism of artists
such as Julian Schnabel and David Salle left him
cold. By contrast, the cerebral approach of Marcel
Duchamp, and the two artists who benefited
in totally different ways from their mentor,
Andy Warhol and Jasper Johns, found in Ai an
enthusiastic admirer. Duchamp's readymades

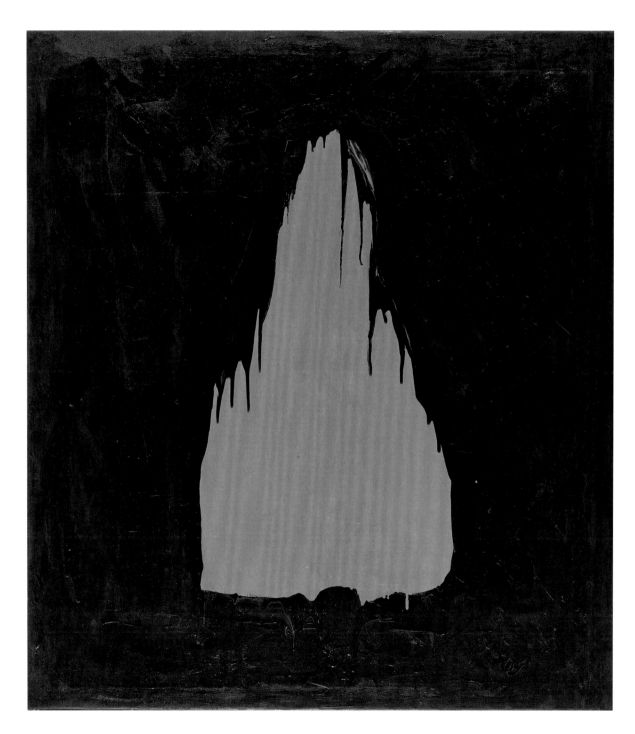

Fig. 11 Ai Weiwei, **Untitled**, 1986. Oil on canvas,
172 x 142 cm

inspired him to make a small number of three-dimensional works during this period and were to lead ultimately to a practice based to a large degree on pre-existing materials and the belief that anything at all could be 'readymade' material for his art. Even more far-reaching was Ai's recognition that 'after Duchamp … being an artist is more about a lifestyle and attitude than producing some product'.[8] As a result Ai had abandoned painting by the early 1990s, never to return to it.

Concurrent with this gradual evolution in his definition of what it meant to be an artist was the realisation that there were alternatives to the fatalism with which he had reacted to the political realities of China before he decided to leave for the United States in 1981. In the confrontations between demonstrators and the police around Washington Square Park and Tompkins Square Park in 1988, and in the ACT UP AIDS demonstrations of 1989, he saw democracy in action, although he had had to watch from afar the terrible outcome of the confrontation between unarmed students and the People's Liberation Army on Tiananmen Square in Beijing on 4 June 1989. Ai stayed in New York for another four years after this and despite the fact that he felt isolated there, had no intention of returning to China. The declining health of his father led him to change his mind early in 1993.

Dongshi Shisantiao Courtyard, Beijing, 1993–99

At the age of 36 Ai returned to Beijing and for the next six years lived with his mother and his brother Ai Dan in the family home, a traditional courtyard house of the kind that was rapidly disappearing as urban development completely transformed the character of the city, which

had remained largely unchanged until then. He had missed not only the early stages in the development of contemporary Chinese art that had occurred in the 1980s but also the accelerated pace at which it had coalesced into several highly visible movements that found ready international acceptance. The exhibition 'China's New Art, Post 1989', curated by Chang Tsong-zung (a.k.a. Johnson Chang) in Hong Kong and Li Xianting in Beijing, opened in Hong Kong in 1993. In the same year thirteen artists including Wang Guangyi, Fang Lijun, Yu Youhan and Xu Bing were included in the Venice Biennale. Although he was of the same generation, Ai Weiwei was not mentioned in any of the early studies of contemporary Chinese art or included in any of the major travelling exhibitions or biennales until 1999, when he participated in the Venice Biennale with more than twenty other artists.[9]

Circumstances are partly to account for this, but a much stronger reason is surely that Ai was temperamentally ill-suited to be part of any group, official or avant-garde in character. Ironically the aura he had acquired after his decade in New York was a major attraction for a generation of younger artists who were associated with a short-lived informal grouping based in an area of Beijing that they named East Village after the part of Manhattan where Ai had lived for nearly a decade. Although it only existed from 1992 to 1994, the Beijing East Village has gained almost mythical status for the extreme nature of the performances that took place there, notably Zhang Huan's *12 Square Meters* (3 June 1994) and *65 Kilograms* (11 June 1994), memorably photographed not only by Ai himself but also by RongRong, founder of the Three Shadows Photography Art Centre in Beijing.[10] As Ai later observed, 'The art events that took

place in Beijing's East Village marked the first time that contemporary Chinese art voluntarily took up the theme of existence itself in a sober attitude, focused on the connection between art and existential realities, as well as the spiritual and physical experience of the artists themselves.'[11]

Simultaneously Ai was also considering ways in which he might reach a much broader audience than the small circle of artists with whom he had direct contact. Since contemporary art was actively discouraged by the Chinese authorities and there were no museums or galleries in which it could be displayed, he decided to assemble documentation on recent artistic developments in the West and in China and circulate it as a book. *Black Cover Book* (fig. 12), published in 1994, contained an extensive interview with Hsieh Tehching by Ai and Xu Bing, information on Andy Warhol and Jeff Koons, as well as three important texts by Marcel Duchamp: 'The Richard Mutt Case', 'The Creative Act' and 'Apropos of Readymades'. There was also a section devoted to young Chinese artists, including Song Dong, Wang Jianwei, Zhang Pei-Li, Huang Yong Ping and Geng Jianyi, who were accorded the same degree of seriousness as the more established Western artists who were being introduced to a Chinese audience.

Commenting on the lack of contemporary activity after 1989, Ai later explained that 'We tried to establish a base to encourage more experimental and performance-based work through the *Black Cover Book*. I think that, through it, we succeeded in creating a kind of platform through which artists saw really experimental work, and it gave them great encouragement in the face of the dominant

Fig 12 Double-page spread from **Black Cover Book**, 1994, showing Duchamp's readymade *Urinal*. Museum of Modern Art, New York. Inv. 962.2011

practices: "political pop", "social realism", export art made for foreign travellers, depictions of the Cultural Revolution.'[12] Taking to his new role as impresario and advocate for contemporary art in a society that was still reluctant to recognise it, Ai acted as joint editor on two further volumes, the *White Cover Book* (1995) and the *Grey Cover Book* (1997). In 1997 he also co-founded, with the Dutch art historian Hans van Dijk, the China Art Archives and Warehouse (CAAW), a pioneering gallery and source of information on recent activities.

Although Ai shipped many of the works he had created in New York back to Beijing and decorated the walls of his mother's house with them, he recognised that he could not continue in that vein. He was a committed conceptualist but the way forward was to be refashioned through close observation of the current political and social situation in China and immersion in its classical material culture. Contradictory as this may seem, the distinctive character of the large body of three-dimensional works in many media that Ai continues to make to this day owes

as much to his knowledge and appreciation of classical Chinese art as it does to contemporary theory and practice. While he was in New York he had focused exclusively on contemporary art, but once he was back in Beijing the range of his interests expanded to include many aspects of Chinese art, from the Neolithic period to the Qing Dynasty (1644–1911).

As a result of the massive urban development that took place in China in the wake of Deng Xiaoping's capitalist reforms of the 1980s, a vast amount of archaeological material

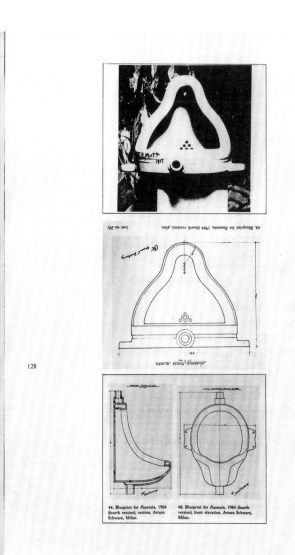

128

43. Blueprint for *Fountain*, 1964 (fourth version), plan. [cat. no. 24]

馬塞爾・杜香
《噴泉》設計圖
1964(第4版)

馬塞爾・杜香
《噴泉》
1917
美國紐約

44. Blueprint for *Fountain*, 1964 (fourth version), section. Arturo Schwarz, Milan.

45. Blueprint for *Fountain*, 1964 (fourth version), front elevation. Arturo Schwarz, Milan.

創作的行爲

馬塞爾・杜香

我們來考慮一下兩個重要的因素，即藝術創造的兩個角色：一方面是藝術家，另一方面就是以後要爲成後人的觀衆。

很顯然，藝術家的行爲猶如巫士，他從超越時空的迷宮中尋找通往光明的途徑。

如果我們將媒介的屬性賦予藝術家，那麼我們就會在美學層面上否認他對自己在做什麼和爲什麼這樣做等問題擁有清醒的狀態。他在作品的藝術創造中所作出的一切決定都出於純粹的本能，並且不可能被譯解爲自我分析，無論是口頭的、文字的甚或是思考中的。

T.S.愛略特在《傳統與個人天賦》一文中寫道："藝術家越是完美，那麼在他身上肉體的人與創造的大腦之間就越是徹底分離；大腦也就越是完全地吸收和改變作爲其素材的情感。"

億萬個藝術家都在創造，只有數萬個藝術家被觀衆討論和接受，而受後人所敬仰的就更少。

在上述分析中，藝術家也許會大聲疾呼自己是天才；他會耐心等待觀衆的裁決以使自己的名聲產生社會價值，並最終使後人將他收入藝術史的入門書籍中。

我知道我的這段話不會得到很多藝術家的同意，他們不願承認巫士的角色，而是一味堅持認爲他們的創造活動中確實很清醒——然而藝術史決定一件藝術作品的價值所依據的想法與藝術家本人理性化的解釋全然無關。

如果藝術家作爲一個對自己和整個世界充滿了最美好的意圖，但對

129

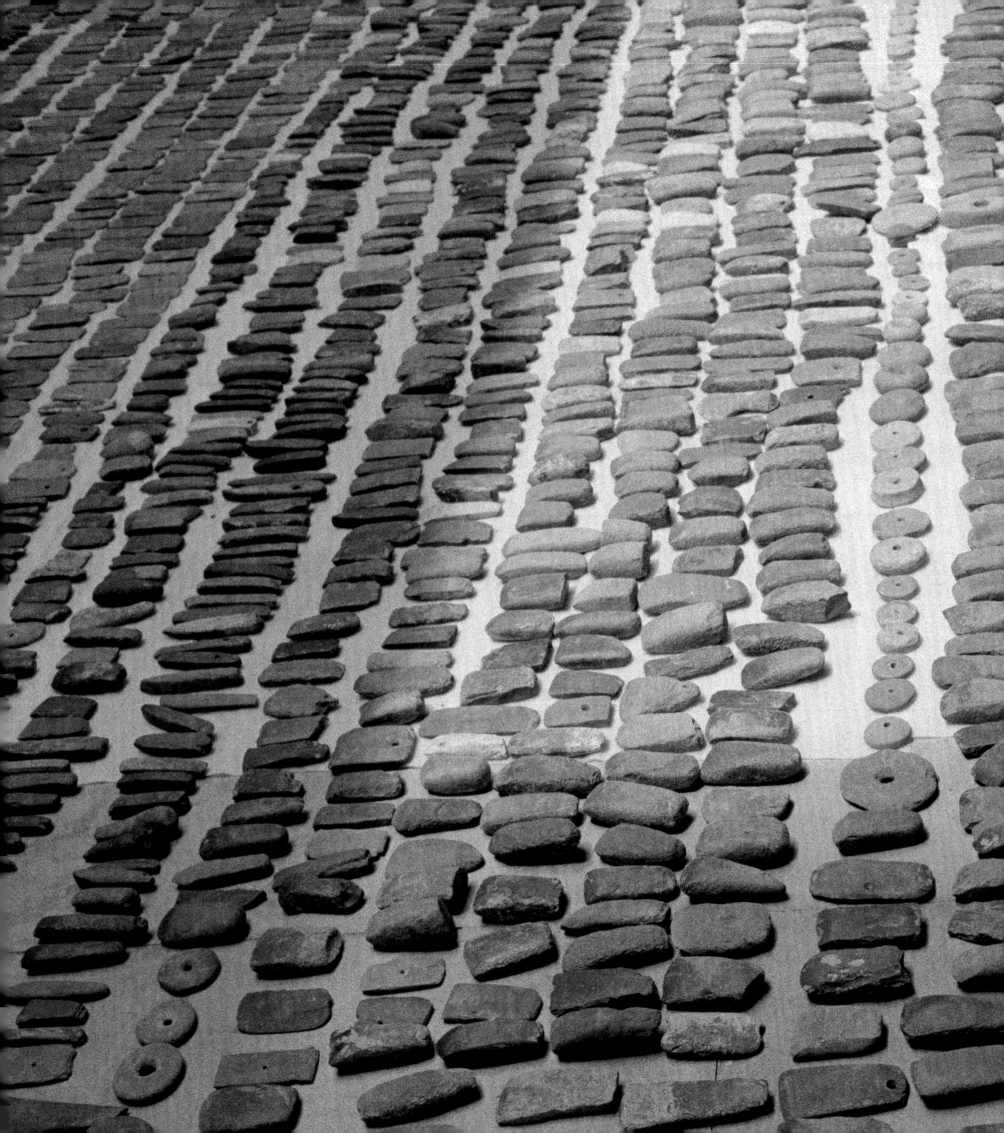

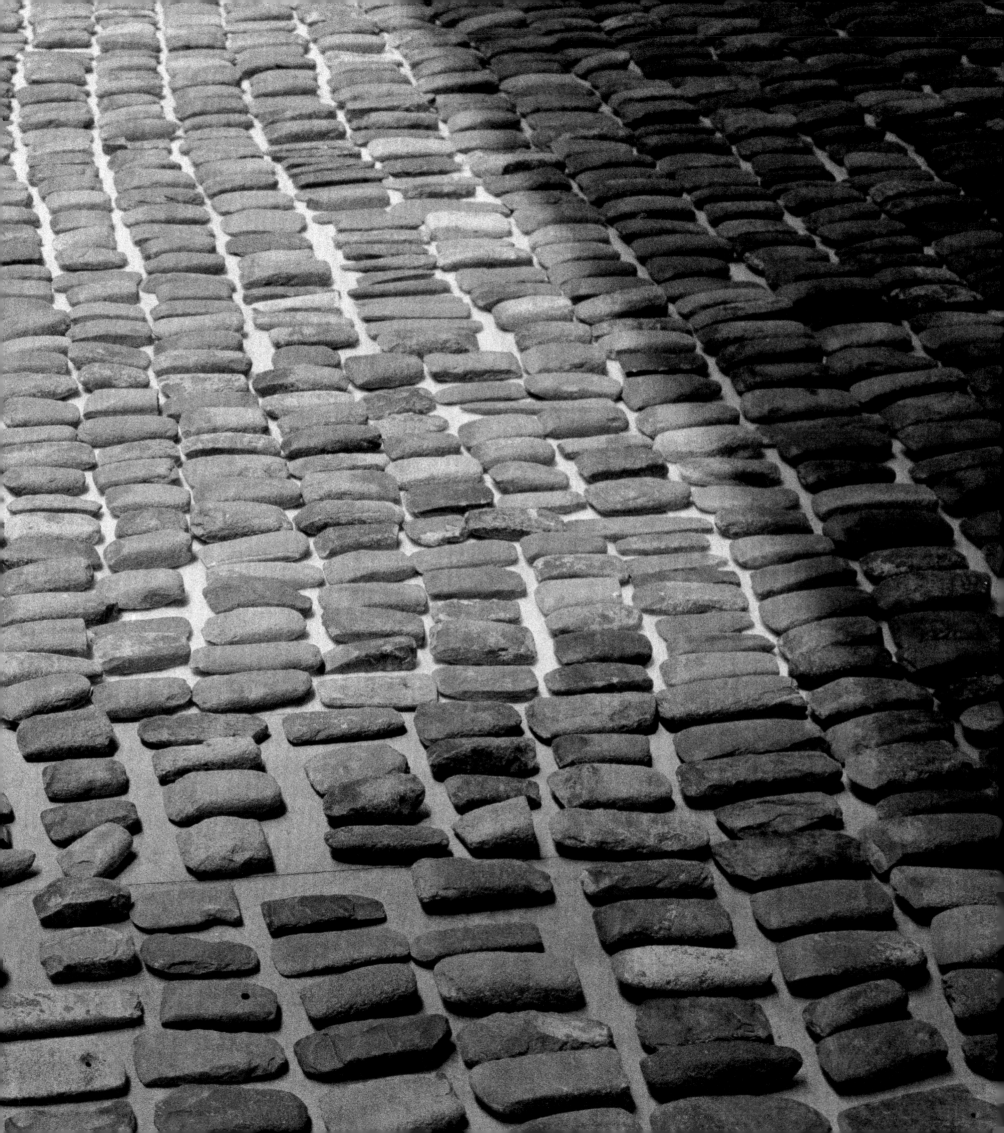

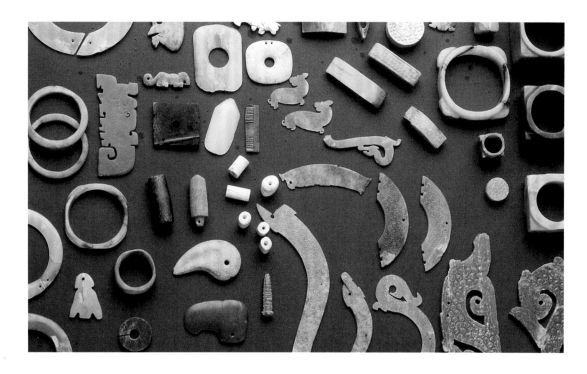

was unearthed and offered for sale in markets such as Panjiayuan[13] near the Temple of Heaven in Beijing and Hollywood Road in Hong Kong. Frequently accompanied by his brother Ai Dan, who is well recognised for his expertise in many different aspects of Chinese art, Ai began frequenting the markets in Beijing and elsewhere in China. Among their first purchases were stone tools dating from the Stone Age to the Shang Dynasty (c. 1766–1122 BC), at that time available for very little money, which became the basis of Ai's *Still Life* (1993–2000; fig. 13), a collection of 3,600 stone tools laid out in an orderly fashion on the floor and later housed in specially crafted boxes. This mounting interest in antiques can be gauged from study of the photographs that Ai continued to take after he returned from New

York. Interspersed with personal photographs and documentation of events in the art world are many images of Buddhist sculpture, jades and beads (fig. 14) that he either owned or that had attracted his interest.

At this early stage in his exploration of archaeological material, Ai was buying and selling reluctantly, collecting, although he did not as yet regard himself as a collector, and using objects in his own work to consider questions of authenticity and value through methods that still have the power to shock. *Dropping a Han Dynasty Urn* (1995; cat. 20) and *Breaking of Two Blue and White Dragon Bowls* (1995) document two events that took place in his mother's house and were both reproduced in the *White Cover Book*. When questioned about these, Ai is not

forthcoming about his motivation, leaving plenty of room for later commentators to speculate on his reasons for treating cultural relics in a way that inevitably recalls the worst excesses of the Cultural Revolution. In conversation he has remarked that when he does something, he is not always aware initially of his reasons for doing so, hence putting in jeopardy any attempts to seek explanations that are too narrowly defined.[14] That said, the Socratic question that Ai poses in these works continues to underpin every aspect of his practice to the present day.

In the unregulated atmosphere of the markets, Ai enjoyed the challenge of distinguishing the real from the fake, aided by Ai Dan, but also by some of the more knowledgeable dealers, notably Liu Weiwei,[15] whom he met when he first began buying classical Chinese furniture. He was also acquainted with some of the major dealers in the field, notably James J. Lally in New York. Ai has commented that he grew up in a privileged, educated family in which there was an innate feeling for the great achievements of the past, although the Cultural Revolution intervened, removing all opportunities to develop these interests.[16] Through his sudden immersion in the world of antiques, however, he began to develop considerable expertise and to realise the importance of connoisseurship, an approach to the appreciation of art that is diametrically opposed to his conceptual bias although it was soon greatly to enrich it. By handling and comparing a vast quantity of antiques, identifying their distinguishing characteristics and looking for minute differences between apparently identical objects, Ai developed a sense of quality that is crucial to his activities in every field.

In addition to his admiration for the works

Fig. 13 (previous pages) Ai Weiwei, **Still Life**, 1993–2000. 3,600 stone tools dating from the Stone Age to the Shang Dynasty (10,000–1100 BC), dimensions variable

Fig. 14 Ai Weiwei, **Jades**, 1994. Photograph

of art and artefacts themselves, Ai also has the highest regard for the craftsmen who continue working in the same traditions. In 1996, a year in which the death of his father Ai Qing occupied much of his time, Ai concentrated on the production of works in porcelain, further complicating the theoretical debate by selecting and later exhibiting as his own work a series of entirely convincing replicas of blue-and-white porcelain vases from the Qing Dynasty Kangxi (1662–1722) and Qianlong (1736–96) eras made at Jingdezhen, site of the former Imperial porcelain workshops and still a major centre for the production of porcelain on an industrial scale.[17] Another important encounter was with Lao San, a carpenter, whose first work for Ai was the memorable *Table with Two Legs on the Wall* (1997; cat. 5). Ai has noted:

In 1997, I started making furniture. By then I already had a profound knowledge of Chinese artefacts, jade, silk, bronze, wood. I was deeply impressed with the objects that had been made in the past five thousand years, and how these reflected the thinking of the people who ordered them, designed them and who created them: what it was they wanted to express through these objects, as well as the technical difficulties they had to overcome. I came back from New York and jumped into another world. I wanted to see how to work with it, to overcome it. The furniture began there; combining the New York experience with the Chinese conditions, its history and my understanding of it all.[18]

Although it is common practice to consider Ai's series of furniture works as examples of 'deconstruction', aligning them with his career-defining 'destructive' acts of 1995, the attention he gives to the process of reconfiguring a pre-existing functional object, his understanding and respect for traditional joinery techniques, and the care he gives to maintaining the patina all point in a different direction. The manner in which he redefines the space-occupying characteristics of these tables also looks forward to the beginning of his architectural practice two years later.

Since his return, Ai had been active in many different fields but had produced only a small body of work. Whereas many of his contemporaries were gaining international recognition, Ai had only participated in several group exhibitions outside China. That situation began to change in 1999 when the former Swiss Ambassador to China, Uli Sigg, a major collector of contemporary Chinese art and one of Ai's earliest supporters, introduced him to the legendary curator Harald Szeemann, who recognised the quality of his work and invited him to participate in 'dAPPERTutto' at the 48th Venice Biennale.

Studio-house, Caochangdi, Beijing, 1999–

In 1999 Ai designed and built a house for himself and his wife Lu Qing (b. 1964) at Caochangdi, a village on the outskirts of Beijing. Based on sketches made on his mother's dining-room table, it was constructed by local builders and announced the beginning of Ai's major career in the field of architecture (discussed further on pp. 46–65). Ai is able to multi-task, a gift that enables him to become a forceful presence in whatever medium he decides to investigate. In 2000, for example, in addition to working on a building for the China Art Archives and Warehouse (CAAW) at Caochangdi, and two monumental sculptures, *Concrete* and *In Between*, for SOHO New Town, Beijing, Ai and Feng Boyi co-curated the exhibition 'Fuck Off' at the Eastlink Gallery, Shanghai, which offered a radical alternative to the officially sponsored Third Shanghai Biennale at the Shanghai Art Museum.

In an interview in 1995,[20] Ai had given a striking definition of the role that artists should play in society. 'In a rational social society,' he remarked, 'the artist should play the role of a virus, like a computer virus. A very small design is capable of effecting change throughout the entire rational world, and this change brings about chaos, so it is actually a process of eliciting the vigilance of the rational world. This is a very important function of art today. Otherwise, if art is just a public service, its effects will never be as great as those of various scientific activities. Art is one of mankind's inordinate ambitions.'

Five years later in his role as curator, Ai was able to show exactly what he meant. Believing that there is an inherent conflict between the agenda of organisations recognised by the State and truly independent art, Ai and his co-curator Feng Boyi assembled a group of mostly younger artists whom they believed reflected the current state of Chinese society. Although the minimalist abstractions of Lu Qing and Ding Yi were notably restrained, there was a strong emphasis on violence and works that tested all ethical and legal limits, as in the contributions by Peng Yu and Zhu Yu that utilised human corpses. 'Fuck Off', they maintained in the introduction to the catalogue, 'emphasises the independent and critical stance that is basic to the existence of art. Within a state of countless contradictions and conflicts, it maintains its status of independence, freedom and plurality. It tries to provoke an artist's responsibility and self-discipline, and searches for a way in which art lives as "wildlife", and raises issues about some issues of contemporary Chinese art.'[21]

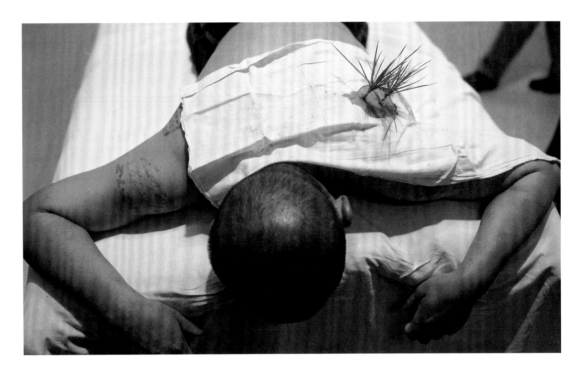

stark contrast to the prevailing mediocrity and stylistic polymorphism of contemporary Chinese architecture – also had a major impact on his artistic practice. Although he had seen and admired works by Donald Judd and Carl Andre while he was in New York, minimalism had not been a major focus of interest, but as the scale of his works increased dramatically, it entered his formal vocabulary as a way of giving order to multiple layers of cultural references. It also affected the way in which he insists that his works should be presented, their relationship to the space in which they are exhibited being of fundamental importance.

Presented as an ensemble, for example, the four Cubes, made from tea (2008; cat. 31), ebony (rosewood) (2009; cat. 32), marble (2011) and crystal (2014; cat. 34), belong to a tradition that began with Tony Smith's *Die* (1962), a six-foot steel cube based on the proportions of Leonardo da Vinci's *Vitruvian Man*; but for Ai the nature of the material is as important as the form. The unmodulated surfaces of the marble and crystal cubes contrast with the intricately carved surface of the ebony cube, while the slowly fermenting cube of pu-erh tea (a type that is preserved in blocks and improves as it ages) offers an organic riposte to all three. In contrast to the customary impersonality of minimalism, the ebony cube introduces an autobiographical element: it was inspired by a small Qing Dynasty box that once belonged to Ai's father (fig. 16).

In addition to theoretical questions arising from his immersion in the world of antiques, Ai was also deeply disturbed by the ongoing destruction of traditional architecture and associated ways of living being caused by thoughtless urban renewal in China. In this he was not alone: in the mid-1990s a number

Ai is noteworthy for the clarity with which he sees important issues for the development of contemporary art within China. Although his statements and activities have not always been received with enthusiasm domestically, in Europe his independent voice has been increasingly appreciated. Approaching his fiftieth birthday in 2007, he had reached the stage in his development when he had gained enough confidence to work on a larger scale, producing sculptures, installations and buildings that for the first time gained the kind of international recognition that had so far been lacking. Despite the fact that his architectural career had only begun four years earlier, in 2003 he was invited to act as consultant to Jacques Herzog and Pierre de Meuron on the design of the stadium for the

2008 Olympics in Beijing (see fig. 28) and in 2004 he had his first solo museum exhibitions at the Kunsthalle Bern in Switzerland and in Ghent. In Bern for the first time he was able to see how his works could be displayed in an institutional setting, the elegant simplicity that characterised the installation echoing his own recently completed studio-house in Beijing.

By now whatever influences there might have been from Duchamp, Warhol and Johns in his work of the 1980s and 1990s had been deeply interiorised and transformed, in large part through the dialogue with Chinese tradition that had been a major preoccupation since he returned to Beijing. Without question his architectural practice – the creation of unadorned, minimal spaces that offered a

Fig. 15 Yang Zhichao's performance, **Planting Grass**, during the 'Fuck Off' exhibition at Eastlink Gallery, Shanghai, 2000

of artists including Yin Xiuzhen incorporated fragments and debris from demolished buildings in their installations and free-standing works,[22] but the matter continues to be a major preoccupation for Ai until the present day. While documenting the destruction in the photographic series *Provisional Landscapes* (2002–08; fig. 27), he began to accumulate quantities of massive beams, doors and windows from Qing Dynasty temples and domestic architecture for use in his sculptural projects. *Bed* (2004; cat. 3) and *Fragments* (2005; cat. 24) are two outstanding examples, demonstrating the diversity of his approach in the use of 'readymade' materials. *Bed* hugs the floor and commands the space within which it is situated with as much authority as a floor sculpture by Carl Andre, although its rippling surface and fine patina endow it with a physical allure that is alien to minimalism. In contrast, *Fragments* is rough-hewn and archaic in feeling, assembled from reclaimed pillars, beams, tables and chairs

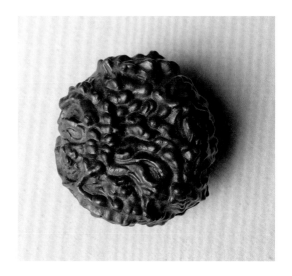

by carpenters who had been working for Ai for eight years and to whom he gave only the most cursory instructions.[23]

The recognition that Ai was finally beginning to receive around 2002 increased dramatically after 2005 when the Chinese website sina.com invited him to open a blog. Surprisingly, he did not even know how to use a computer at this time, although once he had mastered the basics, he spent many hours on it each day, realising that through modern technology he could reach many more people than he ever could through his art. Posting thousands of photographs along with thoughts on current issues, which became increasingly political and aimed at specific targets as his own disenchantment mounted, Ai was able to reach 100,000 people each day as they visited his blog. In a discussion with Uli Sigg,[24] the architect Yung Ho Chang remarked that 'If you really want to have an impact on today's China, you have to be a public intellectual, which is what Weiwei is. It means that you have to be willing to spend a lot of energy and time doing just that, dealing with the media, for instance, instead of producing your own work.' Ai responded: 'But that is my own work.'

Although Ai continued to be productive as an artist, and the range of works coming out of his studio was more varied than ever, it was clear to those who followed his career in detail that his art was only one aspect, albeit a significant one, of a far-reaching agenda that largely ignored the demands of an increasingly voracious art market. Even as early as the mid-1990s, when he had commented on the proliferation of 'export art made for foreign travellers', he had recognised the danger signals. Nothing had happened to lessen their impact. In fact, the situation had

considerably worsened as growing interest in contemporary Chinese art had resulted in a bull market and steadily rising prices for a handful of artists, without exception painters in oils. These veterans of the late 1980s and early 1990s – Yue Minjun, Fang Lijun, Zhang Xiaogang and Wang Guangyi – achieved record prices at auction but were not accorded any serious critical attention.[25] Lacking the versatility of Ai, many of these artists have found it difficult to move beyond the artistic formulae with which they first gained success.

Ai continued to be supportive of artists of many different persuasions, posting articles on Liu Xiaodong, Yan Lei, Li Songsong, Wang Xingwei and Zhao Zhao on his blog between 2005 and 2008,[26] but, in keeping with his definition of art as a 'virus', he believes that by agreeing to co-operate with the agenda of the Chinese State the artist inevitably sacrifices his independence. After a decade of actively seeking to declaw contemporary art in the 1990s, the authorities clearly recognised that the best way to control it would be instead to co-opt it. For many artists of Ai's generation the offers proved irresistible, Cai Guo-Qiang agreeing to design the firework displays for the AsiaPacific Economic Cooperation (APEC) Summit in 2001 and for the opening of the 2008 Beijing Olympics, and Xu Bing, at one time a good friend of Ai's, becoming vice-president of the Central Academy of Fine Arts, Beijing (CAFA), the most prominent art academy in China, in 2008. And in 2009, the year that Ai established a citizens' committee to investigate the deaths of thousands of schoolchildren in Wenchuan County, Sichuan province, the Ministry of Culture established the China Contemporary Art Academy and 21 of China's most prominent contemporary

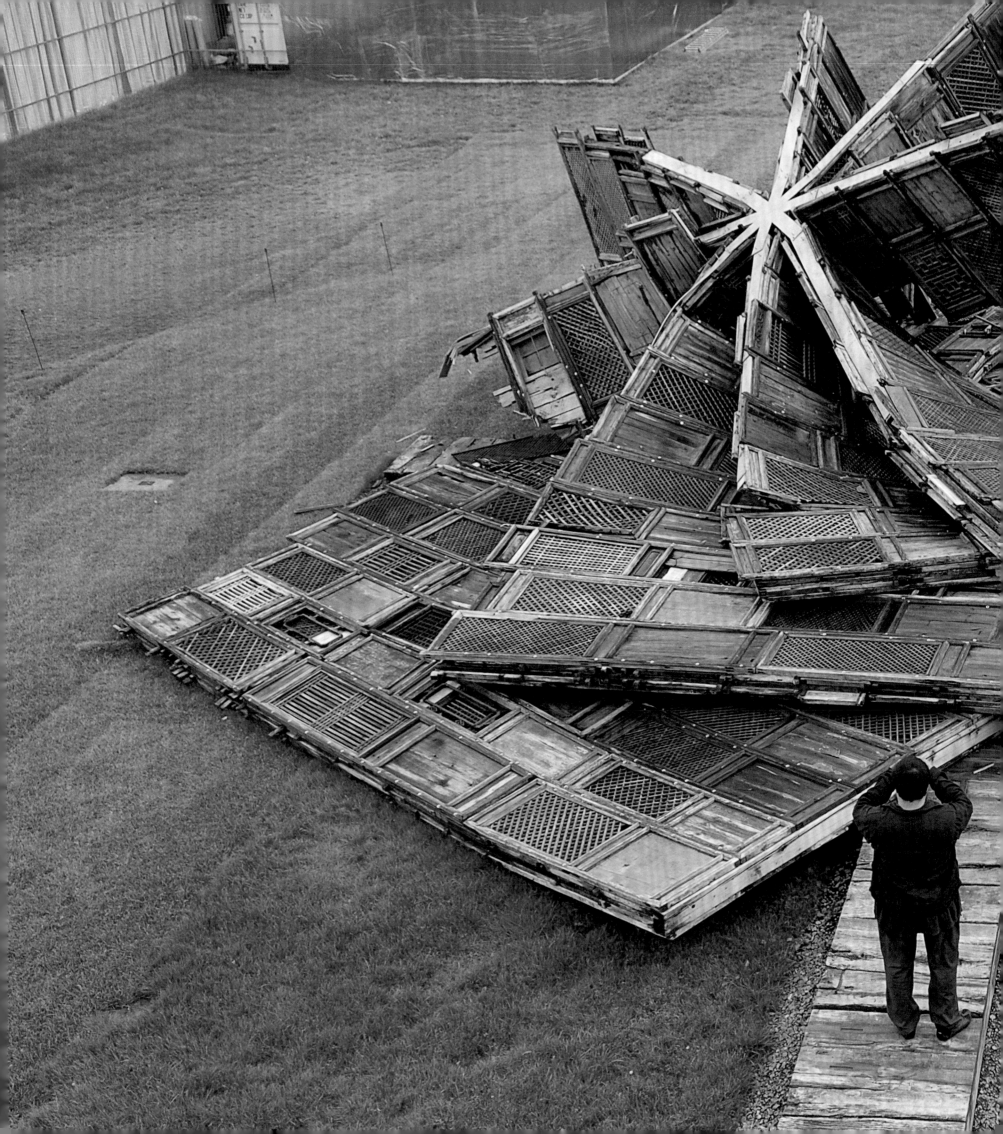

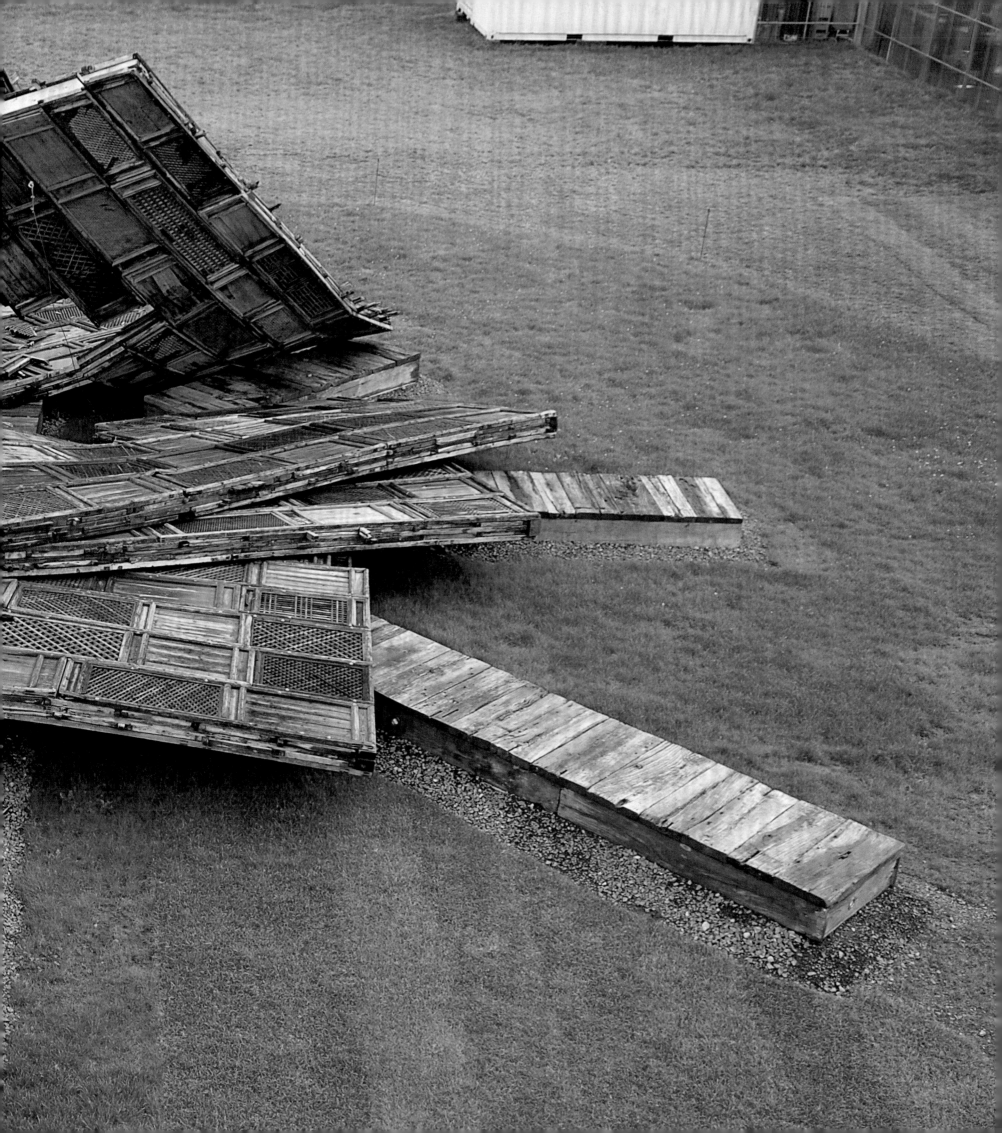

artists became members.[27] Within China, Ai had become an isolated figure, increasingly at risk for his outspokenness.

As the range of possibilities open to him in China narrowed, Ai began to attract increasing international recognition as China's most intellectually challenging artist, whose heterodox position blended conceptualism, deep respect for traditional skills and a significant architectural practice. This unique fusion of diametrically opposed approaches was further complicated by his growing political activism, and a move towards the orchestration of large-scale works that have much in common with the concept of 'social sculpture' associated with Joseph Beuys. One of Ai's most complex works, *Fairytale* (2007), conceived for Documenta 12, involved making arrangements for 1,001 individuals from all over China to travel to Kassel, Germany, for the duration of the exhibition. Once there, accommodation was provided and they were free to do whatever they wished. 'People have become the medium,' Ai has commented, 'and are also the inheritors, beneficiaries, or victims, and this adds to its complexity. But it is still consistent in asking fundamental questions about culture, values, and judgement.'[28] In addition to the human components and 1,001 Qing Dynasty chairs that were placed throughout the exhibition spaces Ai also conceived for Documenta 12 a free-standing sculptural ensemble, *Template* (fig. 17), which he constructed from multiple doors and window frames from destroyed Ming and Qing Dynasty buildings, leaving a hollow space in the shape of a temple in the centre of the towering structure. When on 20 June a violent storm caused the work to collapse, Ai remarked that he liked it better that way, recalling Marcel Duchamp's

preference for the *Large Glass* (1915–23) after it had been shattered while being shipped from an exhibition in 1926.

Ai's installation *Sunflower Seeds* in the Turbine Hall at Tate Modern in 2010 has as a distant antecedent Walter De Maria's *Earth Room* (1977), now permanently installed at 141 Wooster Street in Soho, New York, which consists of 250 cubic yards of earth in 3,600 square feet of floor space. By locating the earth within an enclosed interior, relatively small in scale, De Maria stressed its space-filling qualities, rather than seeking to draw attention to any metaphorical associations. In contrast, by choosing to fill the massive interior of the Turbine Hall with 100 million hand-painted ceramic sunflower seeds, Ai was operating on many levels, not least the huge collaborative effort required to orchestrate the labours of 1,600 workers in the ceramic capital Jingdezhen. In addition to being a popular snack in China, sunflower seeds were at one time also likened to the Chinese people following the light emitted by Mao Zedong at the height of his power (fig. 9).

Since Ai's 81-day detention in 2011, his works have gained an added dimension as he can no longer be regarded as a detached observer on social and political events but rather as an active participant whose principled position makes him exceptional among visual artists. Exhibited together, *He Xie* (2011; cat. 18) belongs to the group of porcelain works in which Ai challenges the craftsmen at Jingdezhen to produce ever more complicated forms, while *Souvenir from Shanghai* (2012; cat. 19), a large stack of bricks and rubble in a wooden frame, appears to be a continuation of his concern over the continuing destruction of the urban environment. In this case, however,

Ai was the victim. *Souvenir from Shanghai* is all that remains from the studio he was invited to build by the local authorities on the outskirts of Shanghai in 2008, while the 3,600 porcelain crabs commemorate the banquet he organised on 7 November 2010 to publicise the announcement that it would have to be torn down because of a purported lack of planning permission. One year to plan, one year to construct and a day to demolish, Ai's Shanghai studio was never used by the artist but survives in fragmentary form as vivid testimony to the imbalance in power between the individual and a totalitarian state. An admirer of Franz Kafka, Ai reveals the nature of the society in which he lives both through exact reconstruction of horrific circumstances, as in *S.A.C.R.E.D.* (2012; cat. 43), and metaphorically in the heap of porcelain crabs and his jade handcuffs (2011; cat. 37).

Without question, Ai Weiwei is a deeply controversial and divisive artist. As recently as 2009–10 he was co-curator with Luc Tuymans and Fan Di'an of an exhibition of contemporary art from Belgium and China held in Brussels and at the National Art Museum of China in Beijing.[29] For the four years between 2011 and 2015 during which Ai Weiwei's political situation was unresolved, that kind of direct involvement with the Chinese art world was out of the question. Until June 2015 he was essentially a non-person within China, his name too dangerous to post on the walls of exhibitions in public institutions and even removed from the Chinese edition of *The Art Book* (cat. 40), celebrating 'the greatest painters, photographers and sculptors from medieval times to the present day'.[30] Agostino di Duccio was not perhaps an obvious choice as his substitute. In June, however, four exhibitions of Ai's work opened in Beijing, three in commercial

Fig. 17 (previous pages) Ai Weiwei, **Template**, 2007, after collapsing at Documenta 12, Kassel, 2007. Wooden doors and windows from destroyed Ming and Qing Dynasty houses (1368–1911)

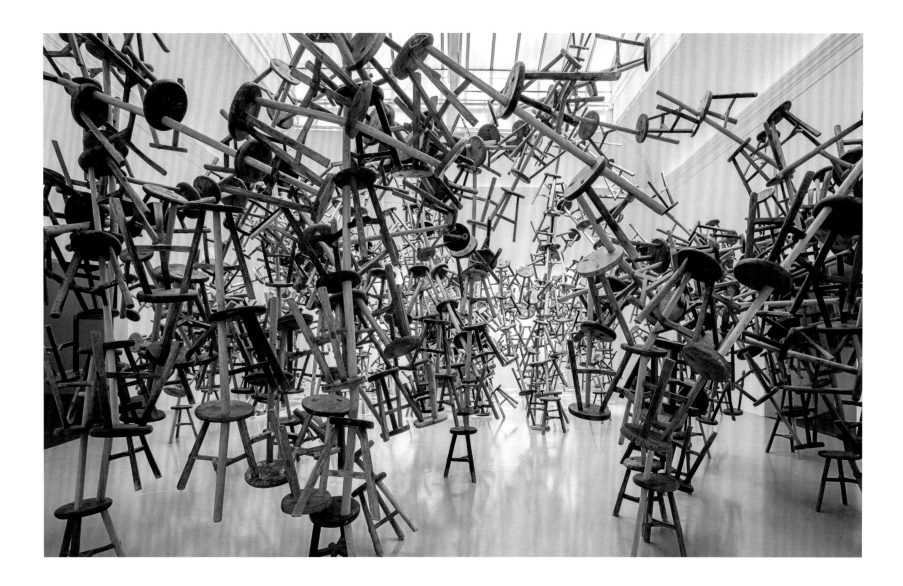

galleries and a one-day exhibition in an artist's studio, the first time this had been permitted since 2009.[31]

Inspired by the example of his father, Ai does not flinch from the hardships caused by his unwillingness to compromise, among them the head injury he suffered at the hands of the police in Chengdu, his 81-day imprisonment in 2011 and the subsequent frustration caused by the refusal of the Chinese government to return his passport. Although his situation gave rise to a tremendous outpouring of international support, the huge disparity within China between the attitude of the many thousands of his online supporters, mostly unknown to him, and the artistic community, was a source of major personal disappointment. None of this has prevented him from producing an impressive body of work and from being the subject of solo exhibitions in Asia, Europe, the United States and now at the Royal Academy of Arts in London. Notable also was the inclusion of his large installation *Bang* in the French Pavilion at the 55th Venice Biennale in 2013. Unsurprisingly, the enthusiasm with which the international art world has embraced an artist who has always professed his independence and his spirit of 'non-co-operation' has hardened the attitude of the Chinese authorities who have created a situation for which there is no easy solution. Interviewed with Luc Tuymans, Ai explained why this is so: 'Being an artist, no matter how one looks at it, is to take action and be a visionary. It is to think about making an event, and the event for me is ultimately historical, intended to make a mark [on] history.'[32]

Fig. 18 (above) Ai Weiwei, **Bang**, 2013. Installation view of the German contribution to the French Pavilion, 55th Biennale, Venice

ARCHITECTURE CAN ALSO BE SILENT

DANIEL ROSBOTTOM

Perhaps unusually, it was architecture rather than art that provided my first physical encounter with the work of Ai Weiwei. In early 2008, a few months before his inaugural London exhibition offered me the possibility to experience his art directly for the first time,[1] my practice was fortunate to be among one hundred young architecture offices from around the world who were invited by him and the Swiss architects Herzog & de Meuron to take part in a project called 'Ordos 100'.

Looking back seven years, it seems remarkable how little we knew then about his work. Indeed it was only a rather scant knowledge of his outspoken politics that overcame our misgivings,[2] ethical and otherwise, with regard to his ambitious plan to 'curate' part of a new city within the desert landscape of China's Inner Mongolia.

That project remains unrealised, yet our participation in it offered an opportunity to meet and talk with Ai and to visit buildings, including his own home and studio, that he had designed for the urban village of Caochangdi, on Beijing's periphery (fig. 22). Despite the eloquence and energy that emanated from the many young architects with whom we met and conversed during those intense few days in China, it was the quiet yet emphatic material presence of Ai's sculpted yet elemental volumes and spaces, simply constructed using brickwork and concrete frame, that informed our own contribution and which continues to resonate in my imagination.

As Ai writes, 'Architecture can also be silent. It can stay aloof from the popular words of this world, like a stone statue buried in a river bed.'[3] This early encounter with his powerfully experiential buildings made explicit for me the extent to which their concerns and qualities,

Fig. 19 Courtyard 104, Caochangdi, Beijing, 2005

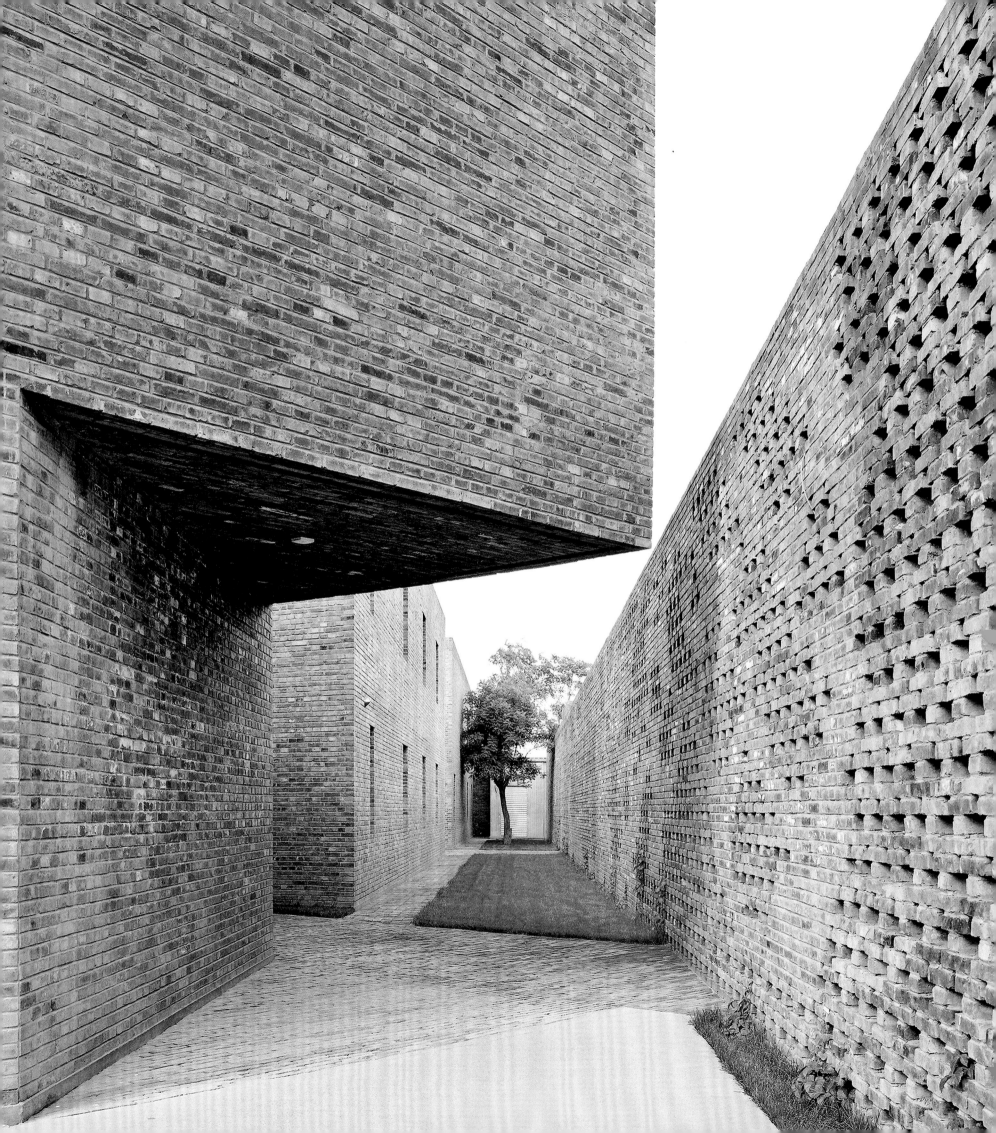

ones that could be considered fundamental to architecture, are also embodied within his artworks and installations. One continually senses architecture's possibilities within them and they often go further in appropriating its forms and conventions or in literally re-appropriating its materials. Architecture's structures of space, material and movement are not only imbued within the pieces themselves, but are also described through the relationships that they form with one another and in the dialogues they create with the rooms and spaces in which they are placed. Although Ai's built works are not explicitly represented in the Royal Academy exhibition, architecture could be said to be, silently, everywhere.

Ai makes, he claims, 'ordinary architecture',[4] rooted in the idea of home and our individual and collective need to dwell in the world. He seeks to work with fundamental concerns, forming spaces that may be both practically and poetically inhabited and which, through their material qualities, embody something of the essential structure of human life. Yet he equally recognises the complexities of this apparently 'basic activity'.[5] His musings on the subject reflect upon contemporary architecture's increasing fragility and troubling disengagement from human needs, as it struggles and often fails to address a continually evolving condition of

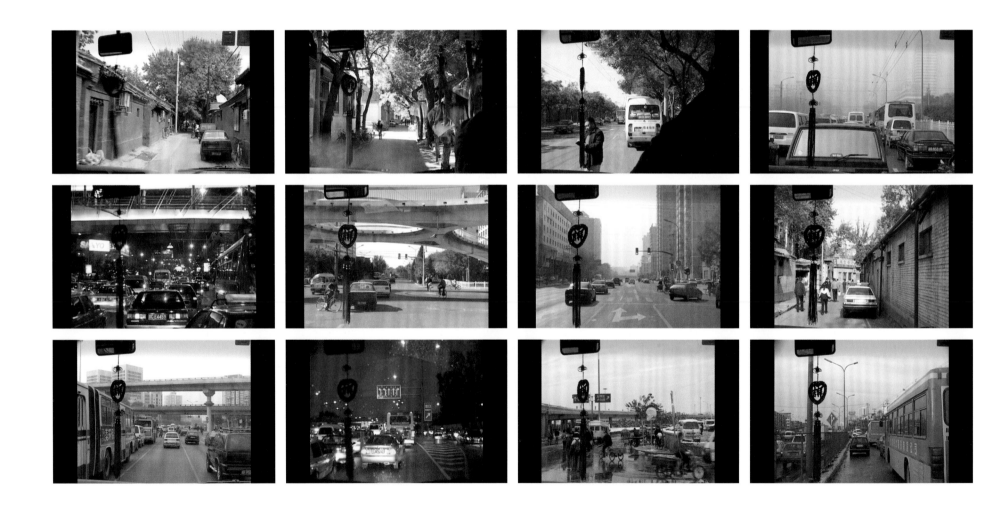

Fig. 20 Ai Weiwei, **Beijing 2003**, 2003
Video, 1 hour 50 minutes (video stills)

radical and often brutal social and physical transformation. For Ai the context is China, a country whose extreme pace of change led to it using more cement between 2011 and 2013 than the United States did during the entire twentieth century.[6] Yet to a greater or lesser extent the critique could be applied universally.

Although he is harsh in his criticism of modern China, going so far as to call contemporary Beijing 'unfit for human habitation',[7] Ai embraces what he calls 'authentic modernism'[8] as both an attitude and a critical method. There is no substitute, he says, for the 'here and now'.[9] Ai's ordinariness is not therefore nostalgic, nor is it a simple reiteration of what has been. Rather, it might be understood as a resituating and restructuring of the architecture of everyday life, in response to contemporary conditions and future possibilities, in ways that can encompass many traits.[10] It embodies an open attitude that seeks to address both individual desires and collective need through a sense of 'leeway and possibility',[11] which Ai in turn translates as freedom.

His concerns seem unsurprising when one considers his background. His father, the renowned poet Ai Qing, was expelled from Beijing to Xinjiang, in China's barren northwest, during Mao's anti-intellectual campaign of 1957 and lived there in hardship with his family for the next twenty years, until his reinstatement in the late 1970s. Ai recalls the first time he applied himself to an architectural problem as the moment when he dug out and deepened the underground chamber in which they were required to live, so his father could stand upright in it.[12] One can only speculate how such juxtapositions – between a necessarily private but intensely artistic and intellectual family life and the reduced realities of an everyday existence that involved his father cleaning the public lavatories – shaped his understandings, reinforcing the importance of architecture's role in providing shelter and comfort and through them, in nurturing and enriching the continuum between mind, body and world.

For Ai 'the many efforts that people make when creating architecture represent an understanding of their own place within the natural world, of order and of potential … No matter what type of architecture from what time or place one considers, they all reveal who the builder was.'[13] It is tempting then, to ask who the builder *is* and whether it is through the architecture, which he made for himself and for those around him, that Ai has explored and revealed some of his most fundamental concerns. Through its materialisation of the issues and themes that underpin his own life and those of his neighbours and fellow citizens, the act of building must surely have been instrumental in coalescing the emerging critical dialogues that Ai has subsequently explored across a diverse range of artistic forms and media.

Situated in the village of Caochangdi, a once-autonomous community now subsumed into the outer folds of Beijing's ever-lengthening skirts, it was the modest and unadorned brick volume of his own house and studio that in 1999 instigated Ai's brief but extremely productive career as an 'accidental architect'.[14] He apparently sketched the design one evening at his mother's kitchen table, before taking advantage of the village's legal informality and the strange slippages of bureaucratic oversight that can occur at the overlooked margins of the vast, centralised structures of the Chinese State, to build it over the next one hundred days.

Set within a walled courtyard to the rear of its plot and announced to the passer-by only by the vibrancy of its turquoise gates, the building is deliberately unassuming. Inside its walled forecourt only two openings punctuate its long, closed façade of local black-grey brick: a large window centred within a projecting gable, and a canopied entrance door, discretely set into the resulting corner. Both open into a double-height living space of red brick, which relates two intersecting bars of accommodation creating a T-shaped plan. The first contains the domestic functions of the house, arranged over two storeys, the other a large roof-lit studio, which also serves as a temporary gallery.

With strong echoes of the traditional Chinese courtyard houses and *hutongs* that once defined the urban grain and social structure of Beijing, what might seem an introverted typology can instead be interpreted as a deep and intricate space of threshold, capable of enfolding the intimacies of private life within the mediating territories of a public one. Its interior and exterior spaces are arranged as a connected sequence of rooms of varying scales and degrees of enclosure. Collectively these establish a common ground, accommodating friends, family and an itinerant feline community alongside the array of visitors and collaborators who have together supported Ai's complex and overlapping creative activities as an artist, architect, gallerist, curator, collector, writer and political activist.

Within these logical arrangements the potential for slippage or juxtaposition between one and another, a central concern in Ai's work, becomes embodied through the experience of inhabitation. The generous scale of the table occupying the main living space anticipates its

shifting usage and the transition from greeting to meeting to eating together over the course of a day. Yet the table's proximity to the large, centrally positioned master bathroom, which overlooks it from the top of an open stair on the floor above, simultaneously questions that sense of public-ness (fig. 21). With the bathroom's most intimate functions screened only by a projecting brick wall at one end of an otherwise open gallery, the humorous yet disconcerting immediacy of this relationship, between an innately social space and what is usually considered an intensely private one, exemplifies the attitudes of an artist whose own identity and unclothed form are regularly used to personify often uncomfortable questions about society, culture and the human condition.

Since its construction, his studio-house has offered Ai the freedom to develop the many aspects of his work alongside the structures and relationships that support it. Yet his wider experience equally demonstrates the limits of architecture's ability to embody freedom of a more fundamental kind. *Surveillance Camera* (2010; cat. 29), a CCTV camera carved in marble, is an ironic monument to the overbearing power of a state security apparatus, which has employed its functioning counterparts to maintain a constant surveillance over the house's walled enclosure, finally transforming it into a space of confinement when Ai was placed under house arrest in 2010. His subsequent 81-day detention during 2011 is viscerally described in *S.A.C.R.E.D.* (2012; cat. 43), whose six chilling dioramas set within his detention cell depict the drab, institutionalised banality of an architecture whose purpose has been subverted to that of subjugation and oppression.

The philosopher Michel Foucault once proposed, 'It can never be inherent in the structure of things to guarantee the exercise of freedom. The guarantee of freedom is freedom.' To those for whom ideas exist in things, this is a salutary thought, although one that is encouragingly qualified by his preceding statement that 'Liberty is a *practice*.'[15] The notion that freedom might exist in the doing, rather than in what is done, is a possibility that Ai appears to pursue continually, through both thought and action. From behind the limited sanctuary of his overlooked gates, his response to surveillance has been to expose himself to the collective gaze; broadcasting his life and thoughts through digital photography, Twitter and a blog, with an intensity that renders external monitoring practically superfluous. His riposte to detention is to turn the gaze of the world upon the actions of his oppressors. Through *S.A.C.R.E.D.* the watchers become the watched.

It is clear however that, for him, the material of architecture has come to offer more than mere enclosure for human activity, no matter how charged. His realisation that when 'compared to other man-made objects, architecture is probably closer to politics'[16] increasingly leads him to employ it or its material directly, its physicality becoming a tangible agency through which he is able to offer critical resistance to the prevalent conditions of contemporary Chinese society and culture.

Prior to the construction of his house, Ai professes to have had no formal knowledge of architecture. The only book he owned on the subject was apparently a monograph on the house that another rarified 'amateur', Ludwig Wittgenstein, built for his sister in Vienna in 1926.[17] Both Wittgenstein's ideas and his

architecture appear to have had a considerable influence on Ai, whose observation that the philosopher's 'effort, the repeated effort, made all his practice become one – just one act'[18] seems to reflect equally upon his own trajectory. Intriguingly, the plan arrangement of the *Haus Wittgenstein* bears a marked similarity to that of Ai's studio-house, albeit with the Viennese house's formal sequence of hallway, grand staircase and salon replaced by the single space of the studio.[19] The sensibilities inherent in Wittgenstein's precise yet elemental forms and spaces, which seem capable of simultaneously addressing and condensing both history and modernity into a singular expression, also have much in common with his own.

In his seminal work *Tractatus Logico-Philosophicus* (1921) Wittgenstein posits the idea that 'ethics and aesthetics are one and the same'.[20] This tenet seems central to Ai's developing architectural discourse and is echoed in his demands that architecture should have an intellectual component and an ethical-moral relevance. Even before his active involvement, Ai forcefully expressed a disdain for architecture's role in embodying power and authority through his ongoing photographic series *Study of Perspective* (1995–). These works depict his middle finger raised in ironic salute to landmarks from around the world, among them the White House in Washington (fig. 46) and Tiananmen Square in Beijing. Yet the moral and ethical issues that principally concern him have less to do with the representational qualities of individual structures. Instead they increasingly focus on the physical and social consequences of the massive programmes of urbanisation and urban transformation, instigated by the Chinese State as a means to facilitate the policies of growth and

Fig. 21 Studio-house (interior), Caochangdi, Beijing, 1999

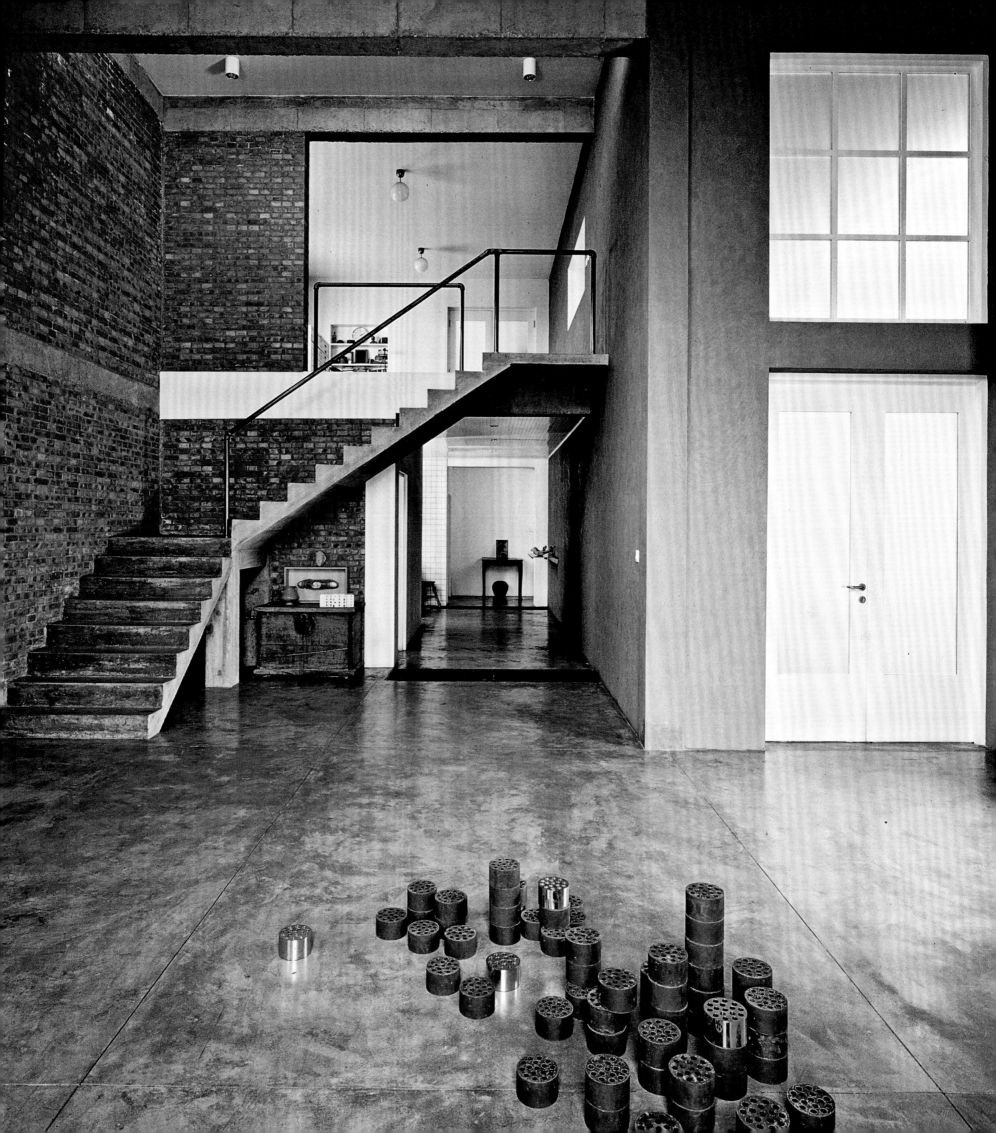

liberalisation introduced by Deng Xiaoping in the period following Mao's death in 1976.

The controversial triptych of photographs that depict Ai *Dropping a Han Dynasty Urn* (1995; cat. 20) was the catalyst for a series of works, including *Coloured Vases* (2015; cat. 22) and *Dust to Dust* (2008; cat. 21), that question the value placed on historical and cultural artefacts of many kinds in the making of the new China. They are pieces that might arguably be considered counterpoints to *Fountain* (1917), the seminal piece by Marcel Duchamp, whose artistic influence on Ai is captured in *Hanging Man* (1985; cat. 10), where the Frenchman's profile is fashioned from a coat hanger. However, whereas the urinal that Duchamp appropriated to create his work lacked any cultural status until it was placed into an art context, Ai's 'readymades' are archaeological artefacts of great antiquity and cultural gravitas. By destroying them or dipping them in industrial paint to all but obliterate their past, the artist questions where value resides. In the dark humour of these startlingly wanton yet deliberate actions, he draws attention to the loss of countless other pieces of China's heritage over the period since the Cultural Revolution; during which time the ideological zeal that sought to replace the past has been supplanted by a *laissez-faire* acquisitiveness.

Many of those lost artefacts are buildings, whether individual houses or the ancient temples that once drew their inhabitants together into neighbourhoods and communities. Ai describes how 'China's cities are striving to dress themselves up, as if they are rushing to attend a lavish masquerade ball',[21] a transformation propelled by the rapid expansion of an affluent middle class and the accompanying influx of poor workers who service their needs.

Across China, vast areas of historic urban fabric have been cleared to make way for this explosion in development, while what little remains has been clumsily re-dressed for the tourist. He recalls experiencing this directly when, in preparation for the 2008 Olympic Games, the brick façade of his mother's house was refaced in concrete by the Beijing authorities, as part of a large-scale gentrification programme. 'All the fake walls,' he remonstrated, 'it's crazy, the old town disappeared in one night.'[22] Defiantly he removed the majority of the replacement wall but left a fragment of it in place, exposing just one of the many 'scars left by authoritarianism'.[23] Creating in effect a work in situ, this critique echoes the concerns of a number of significant gallery pieces and installations that emerged from Ai's creative focus on architecture in the years after the millennium. When seen in parallel with his developing architectural practice, these works continue to reflect on China's struggle to find an appropriate balance between preservation and transformation.

Pieces such as *Kippe* (2006; cat. 8) become measures of the scale of destruction, with each of the 6,000 wooden blocks from which it is assembled being fashioned from a fragment of a temple of the Qing Dynasty (1644–1911) that was demolished to make way for new construction. The monumental installation *Fragments* (2005; cat. 24) goes further in spatialising this loss. Ai muses that 'you know an old temple was beautiful and beautifully built. We could once all believe and hope in it. But once it has been destroyed, it's nothing. It becomes another artist's material to build something completely contradictory to what it was before.'[24] Utilising pillars and beams of iron wood collected from dismantled temples in Guangdong province,

he worked with a team of carpenters skilled in traditional techniques to create a complex, visually ungainly yet extremely precise structure. Its individual pieces of timber are held in delicate balance by elaborate jointing and wooden pegs, establishing a sense of equilibrium between the destructive and the creative act that appears at once solid and yet transient and uncertain. The piece's constellation of elements maps out China's borders, but it is in the re-appropriation and re-engagement of the material, understood through the presence and physicality of both viewer and maker, that the work attains its significance.

At a more intimate scale, works such as *Table with Three Legs* (2011; cat. 6) and *Table with Two Legs on the Wall* (1997; cat. 5) continue this process of re-articulation. A similar process of artful brutality, employing traditional craftsmanship of the highest standard, transforms the domesticity and familiarity of these antique furniture pieces, mutating them into 'foreign objects' of 'unknown purpose'. They reflect Ai's interest in the contradiction of putting 'a tremendous effort ... into something useless or even nameless'.[25] Recalling the *Prop* pieces of American minimalist sculptor Richard Serra, they create structures of dependency that draw the space and fabric of the gallery itself into the composition, thus making it an active participant in the dialogue between subject and object. In *Table and Pillar* (2002; cat. 9) the leitmotifs of column and table become fused together as two lost figures locked in a precarious embrace. The seamlessness of their carefully crafted junction belies the inherent violence of this enforced union and offers them both an uncertain future, rejecting their individual identities and obliging them to occupy space collectively, without purpose.

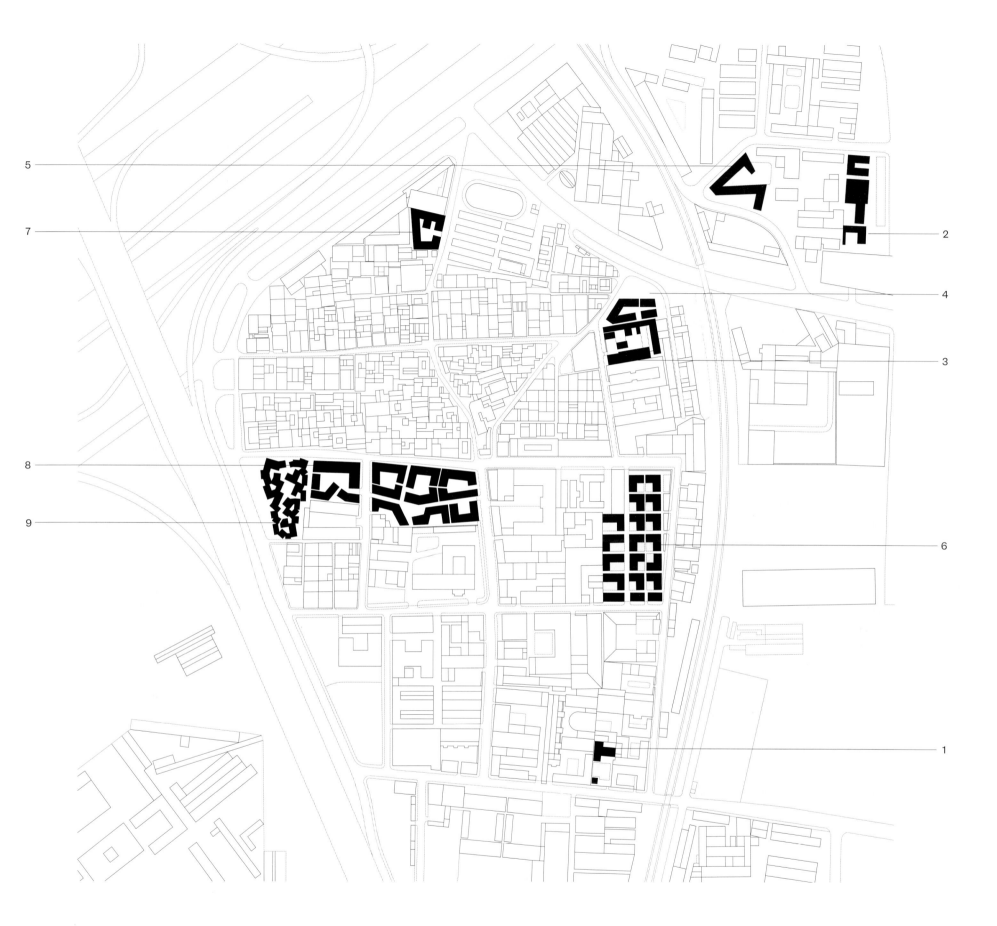

Fig. 22 **Ai Weiwei / FAKE works in Caochangdi**

Drawn by Liam J. Andrews

1. Ai Weiwei house and studio 1999
2. China Art Archives and Warehouse 2000
3. Courtyard 105 2004–05
4. Courtyard 104 2005

5. Three Shadows Photography Art Centre 2005
6. 241 Caochangdi 2007
7. Curved Wall Studios 2007
8. Red Brick Complex 2008
9. Courtyard 211 2009

If these and other works can be understood, in part, as a critique of what has been lost to the choking banality of the contemporary Chinese city, then the architecture that Ai made in parallel takes a further step in offering both a resistance and an alternative to it. The critical success of the studio-house, which received considerable exposure across China and internationally, brought with it a steady stream of building commissions that, in turn, led to the establishment of Ai's studio, FAKE Design. At its most active in the period up to 2008, when Ai announced his withdrawal from architecture, FAKE completed a substantial and wide-ranging body of work, amounting to more than eighty commissions.

Yet it is in the sequence of buildings made within the immediate environs of his residence that his architecture is most compelling. These low, brick volumes, which reiterate and develop the simple forms and construction techniques of his own project, might appear formally neutral. Yet in the context of the wider city their form, scale and materialisation place them in opposition to both the alienating, systemised monotony of Beijing's new residential towers and the gaudy objectification of its often imported trophy architecture. Equally emphatically they reject the historicist, faux-vernacular tendencies often employed to signify domesticity. Despite its highly controlled nature, Ai's architecture declines to close itself off into self-contained, aestheticised systems. Instead it adopts, adapts and refines readily available local materials and the expedient construction techniques of local tradesmen, establishing a modest, robust language that has grown out of the village context and within which it continues to propagate.

In common with much of Ai's creative output, the power of this collection of buildings is reinforced through their seriality and proximity. The balance of repetition and variation within their various arrangements allows them to be understood as an adaptive type, malleable enough to be responsive to a particular situation while retaining a strong familial character when considered as an ensemble. Each grouping of buildings organises a suite of rationally ordered interior volumes, for use as living, working or gallery space, within the constraints of a given site. 'I search for maximum flexibility because I don't know who will end up using the space,' Ai explains. 'Since I know nothing about the interior's final function, I try to control the proportion, the material and the openings.'[26] Exterior courts and passages form charged voids between the resulting volumes, negotiating their relationship with the irregular grain and form of the unplanned village context.

In its loose grid of nineteen rectangular and L-shaped studio-houses, each a variant of Ai's original, one project, 241 Caochangdi (2007;

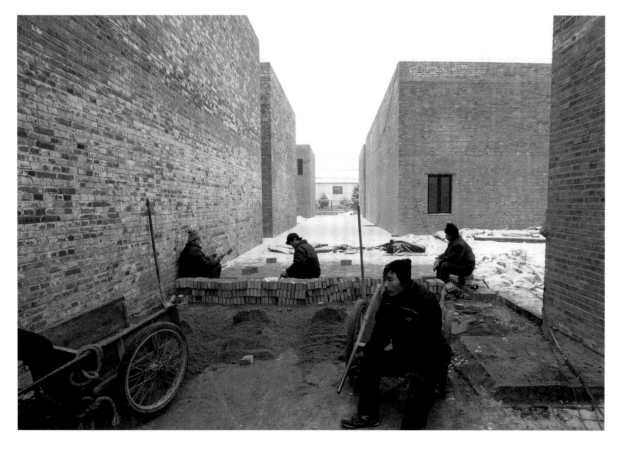

Fig. 23 Construction of 241 Caochangdi, Beijing, 2007

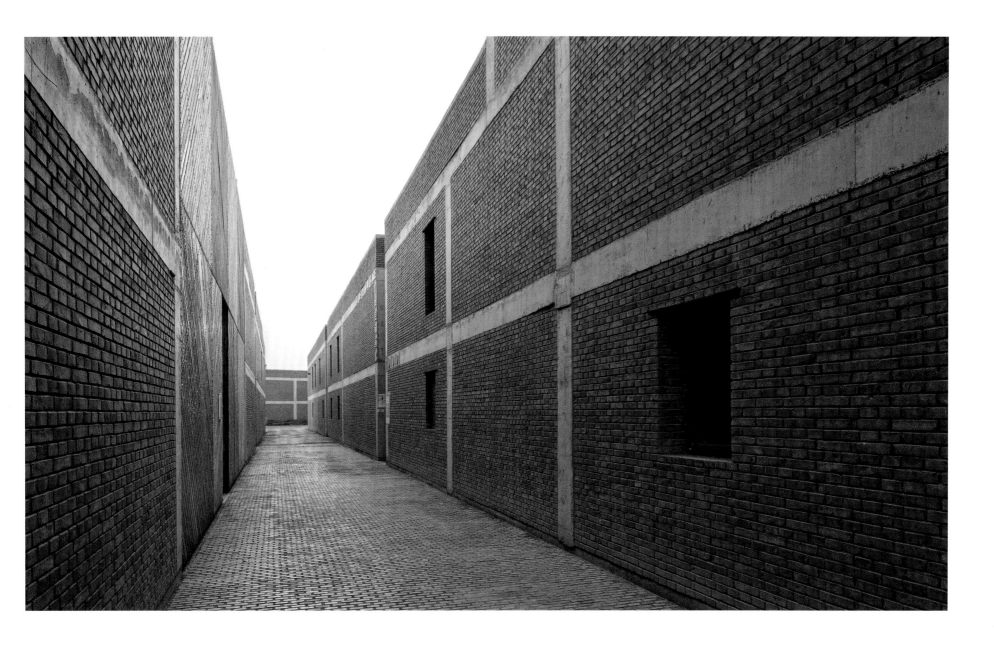

fig. 23), subsumes the series within itself. Echoing his cubic metres of material, including *Ton of Tea* (2008; cat. 31) and *Cube in Ebony* (2009; cat. 32), this adjusting repetition of simple forms makes manifest a relationship between his architecture and minimalist art, proposing, in the buildings' incidental evocation of work by Donald Judd or Sol LeWitt, that meaning is established through the experience of them as simultaneously object, space and idea.

Beyond similarities in their scale and layout, it is the use of brick as a unifying material that draws the Caochangdi projects into coherence (fig. 26). Ai is not the first artist to become fascinated with brick and its possibilities. Per Kirkeby's brick sculptures might be one reference point, while the persistent geometries of the twelve sculptural grey-brick pavilions that the German artist Erwin Heerich constructed for the Museum Insel Hombroich near Düsseldorf offer immediate counterparts, albeit in very different circumstances. Reflecting upon the laconic walls of Caochangdi, one also recalls the *Equivalents* of Carl Andre, stacks of brick whose titles draw attention to the fact that each work is not only composed of repeated elements but is also conceived as part of a larger whole.

While brick might be regarded as the most ordinary of building components, it has an elemental nature; a material made of earth, water, fire and air, it transcends cultures and eras. The size of a brick is such that it can be picked up with one hand, laid in place and through that simple, repeated action a wall is made. It is the smallest unit through which architecture can be manifested and no matter what scale the

Fig. 24 Red Brick Complex, Caochangdi, Beijing, 2008

resulting wall might be, one can still recognise each individual component within it and the artisanship inherent in the act of stacking them, one upon another.

Souvenir from Beijing (2002) places a single grey Beijing brick into a box of salvaged timber, highlighting the increasing scarcity of this once-prevalent material within the city, while simultaneously celebrating its physical characteristics. Courtyard 105 elevates the crafted, textural qualities of the same brick as a component within a larger surface. Relieved of its structural

responsibilities, it is utilised purely as a lining, masking a series of existing concrete structures in order to form a unified courtyard interior. In doing so it constitutes a small reversal in a context where concrete increasingly dominates.

Conversely, the external expression of the Red Brick Complex uses brick within a constructional language of frame and infill, revealed elsewhere only through the interior. Here the vestiges of façade, present in other works, are stripped away to expose what the architectural historian Kenneth Frampton

describes as 'a potentially poetic manifestation of structure in the original Greek sense of *poiesis*, as an act of making and revealing ... the *tectonics* of the frame, in which members of varying lengths are conjoined to encompass a spatial field and the *stereotomics* of compressive mass, that whilst it may embody space, is constructed through the piling up of identical units.'[27]

Many of Ai's works demonstrate his concern with juxtaposing the qualities and character of an individually worked element against its placement within the multitude. Brick translates this idea into the realm of architecture. Humble yet sensuous, it remains inseparable from both the place and time of its making and the temperament of the bricklayer who places it, allowing their practice to be drawn into collaboration with the artist's own. The architecture that results both acknowledges his appreciation of the skills of his workforce and reveals the extent to which Ai conceptualises the act of making itself. 'Most of the buildings are located within five minutes' walk of my place,' he says, 'although I never paid a visit to the building site during construction. The craftsmen understood the design and I know that they are doing things right' (see fig. 25).[28]

As with many of his large-scale collaborative art projects the rough precision of the resulting buildings demonstrates 'his use of architectural process as a critical medium',[29] made by many hands. The outcome is not a reversion to the vernacular but, instead, its inversion. By reframing the expedient possibilities of local skills and resources Ai encourages both construction workers and fellow villagers to profit from the cultural and economic impetus that his burgeoning international profile has brought to Caochangdi. The spare aesthetic of

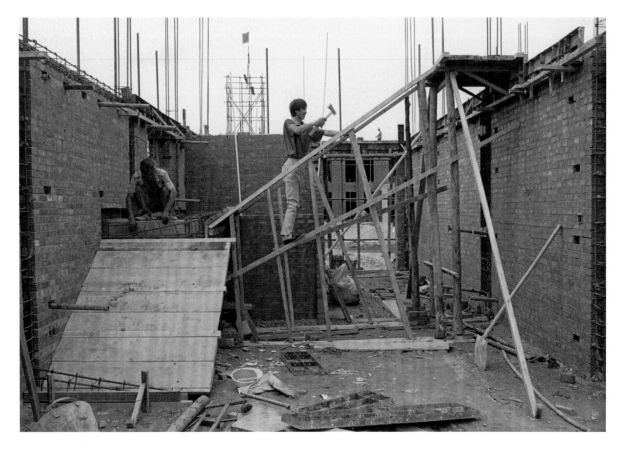

Fig. 25 Construction of Ai Weiwei's studio, Caochangdi, Beijing, 1999

Fig. 26 (opposite) Three Shadows Photography Art Centre, (detail), Caochangdi, Beijing, 2006–7

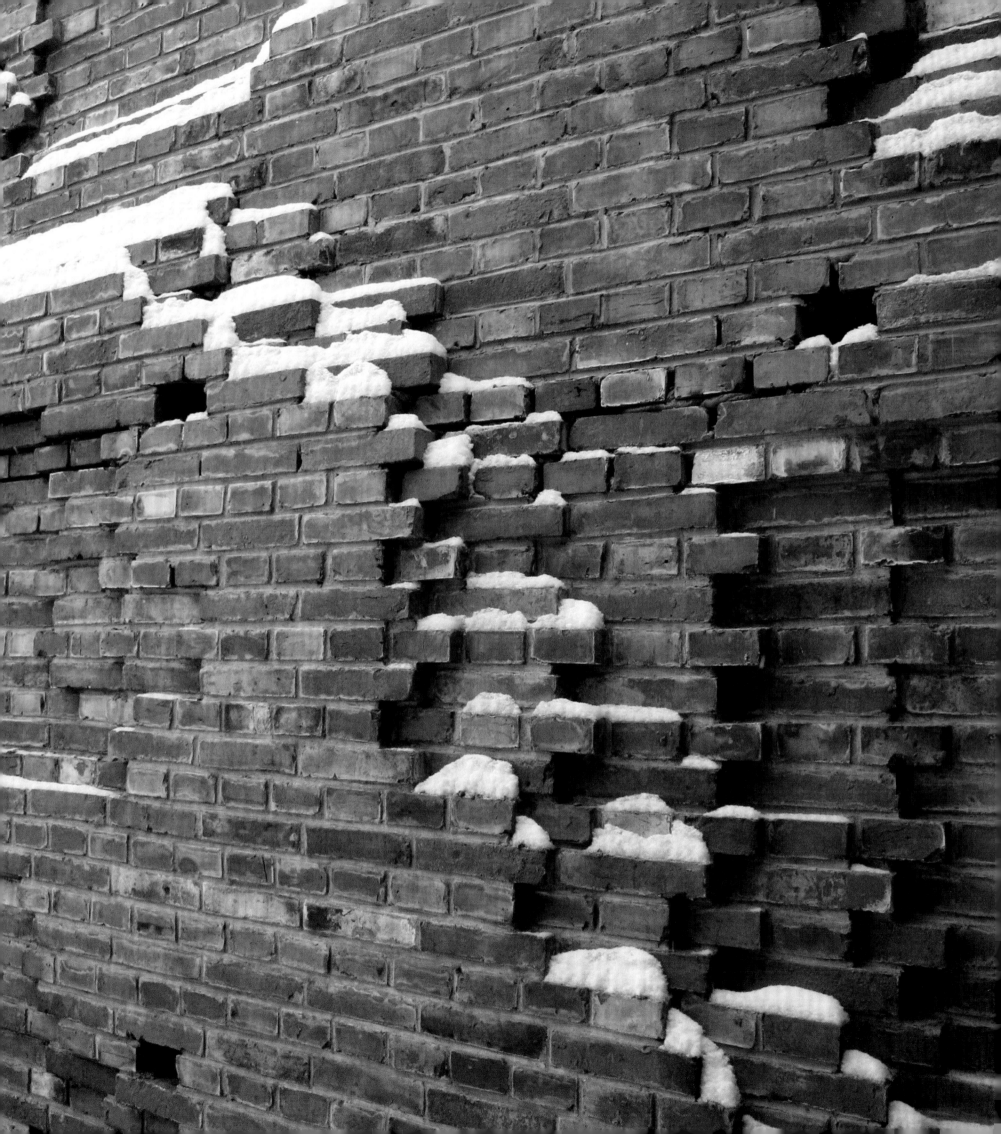

Fig. 27 Ai Weiwei, **Provisional Landscapes**, 2002–08. C-prints, various dimensions

his architecture has thus become a commodity, appropriated through any number of fake FAKES, which borrow its identity without ever quite achieving its eloquence.

The result has been to propagate Ai's ongoing influence as an architect far beyond his actual output and involvement in practice. It has led to the emergence of a *type*, which has been instrumental in setting the village apart from the other 300 or so urban villages to be found within the expanding city edge. Not unlike Marfa, the isolated town in New Mexico that Donald Judd relocated to in the early 1970s, Caochangdi now plays host to a heterogeneous and heady mix of artists, high-end galleries and cultural tourists,

alongside a shifting population of mostly migrant workers. It is not without irony that this agglomeration of mostly illegal construction has undermined the very anonymity that allowed the phenomenon to occur in the first instance. Noting its cultural and economic success, the authorities re-designated Caochangdi a model 'Socialist New Village'. Yet as with all such places in China, the encroachment of officialdom only exacerbates uncertainty over its future.[30]

Through a number of photographic and video projects Ai has critically observed the cycles of destruction and construction that accompany such processes of change across the city. While a student in New York, between 1983

and 1993, he photographed life around his home in Manhattan's Lower East Side, recording its often troubled evolution from a space of urban dereliction and counterculture into a valuable piece of real estate.[31] It is tempting to imagine that his personal experience as part of that threatened community established the ground for his subsequent interest in the plight of the buildings, spaces, people and communities caught up in the turmoil and aftermath of Beijing's rampant redevelopment. Leaving the act of judgement or interpretation to the viewer, each piece is didactic and objective in its methods. Yet their intention is not to document the city but rather, Ai suggests, 'to materialise our physical life,

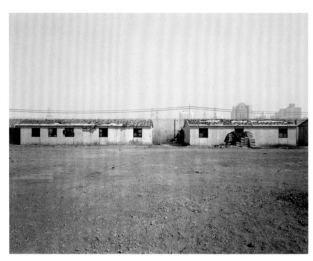
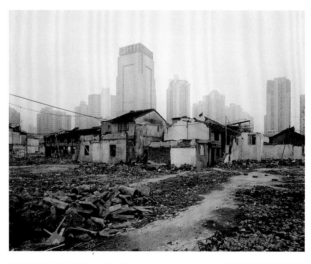
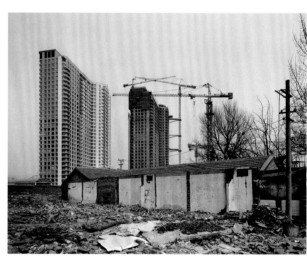
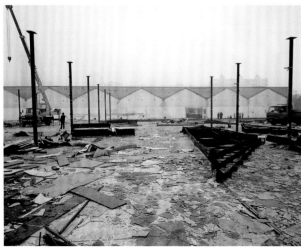
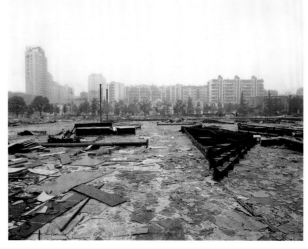
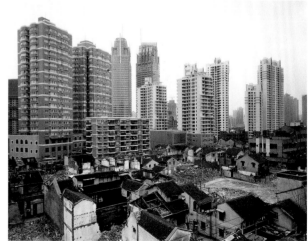

its condition in the moment.'[32] The films *Beijing 2003* (2003; fig. 20), *Chang'an Boulevard* (2004), *Beijing: Second Ring Road* and *Beijing: Third Ring Road* (both 2005) recall the serial photography of Bernd and Hilla Becher or films like Ed Ruscha's *Every Building on Sunset Boulevard* (1966) in their collation of the spatial taxonomy of a changing city. Made in parallel, Ai's photographic series *Provisional Landscapes* (2002–08; fig. 27) captures the many voids and transitional spaces left in limbo by the same entropic processes of change.

Ai has commented that the area of Beijing being redeveloped each year is larger than the entire area of the city in 1949, when land was sequestered and placed into collective ownership.[33] Speaking of *Beijing 2003*, he says: 'I think what happens around us is often more massive than what we can interpret ... This is my sense of the massive change that has happened in this city, which we are all part of. I wanted to find an almost mathematical and unemotional way to show this: to show the powerlessness of the people, and the blind nature of the redevelopment.'[34] The rules and order he imposes on each piece only serve to reinforce the shifting, transient nature of their subject-matter. While they might be made with reference to official maps and particular places, those reference points are themselves unstable and impermanent 'non-sites', comparable to Robert Smithson's notion of 'ruins in reverse'.[35] Far from seeking to offer an authoritative documentation of the urban condition, this systematic body of work instead records its provisionality and, in doing so, questions why it is happening, who is in control and who profits?

In 1976, quoting their artist namesake, British architects Alison and Peter Smithson wrote: 'A building under assembly is a ruin in reverse; at certain times of a building's construction, the anticipatory pleasure of ruins is made manifest.'[36] In the short history of its construction and subsequent demolition, the fate of Ai's final building in China, his own

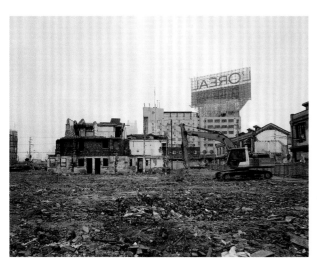
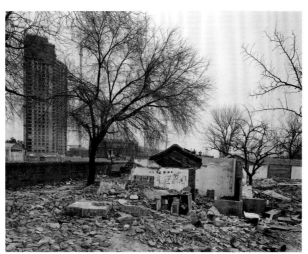
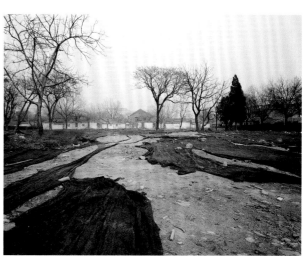
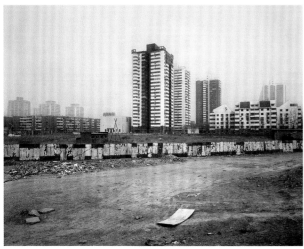
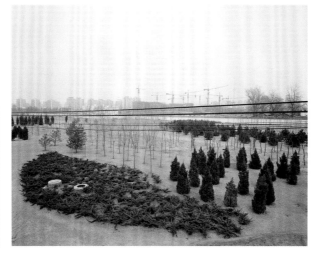
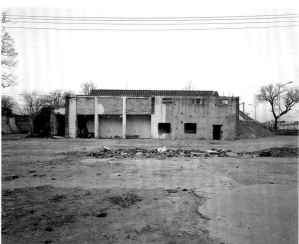

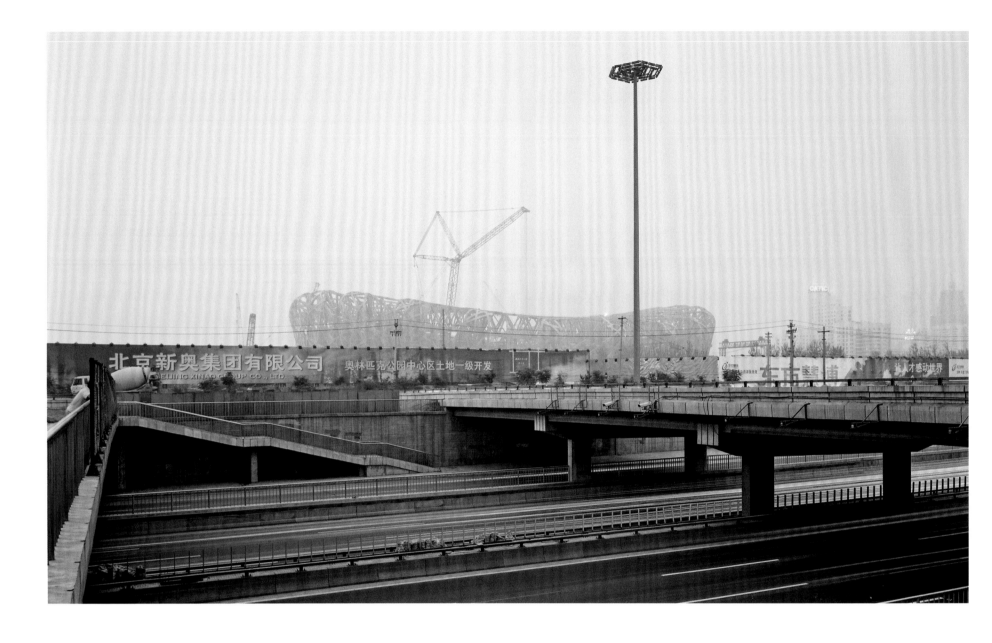

studio complex in Shanghai (fig. 29), draws the threads of his work into a curious confluence.

By 2008, when the commission arrived, Ai had already announced his intention to withdraw from architecture. When he began to engage in it, he must have envisioned the possibility of initiating social change by means of building. However, his urban observations led to the realisation that no matter how productive he might be, his buildings ultimately counted for little, while within his own village they had unwittingly contributed to the area's uncertainty.

Meanwhile his celebrated collaboration with Herzog & de Meuron on the design of the 'Bird's Nest' stadium (fig. 28) for the 2008 Beijing Olympics also ended in disappointment, not as a consequence of its bold entwining of form, structure and space, but because its co-opting by the authorities negated its designers' intention that it should act as a 'Trojan horse',[37] which 'could really have a chance to become a place representing civil society, a place in which citizens can celebrate'.[38] Ai therefore initially refused when the city of Shanghai approached

him to construct a new studio and gallery complex, apparently as a cultural catalyst, only to be eventually persuaded by the enthusiasm and perseverance of the young official involved.

With its brick and concrete frame construction and asymmetric pitched roof enclosing a courtyard, the resulting building briefly represented the dénouement of the series Ai had developed in Caochangdi. Yet only months after its completion in 2010, the same authorities that had instigated its construction summarily demolished it on the pretext that it

Fig. 28 National Stadium, Beijing, 2002–08

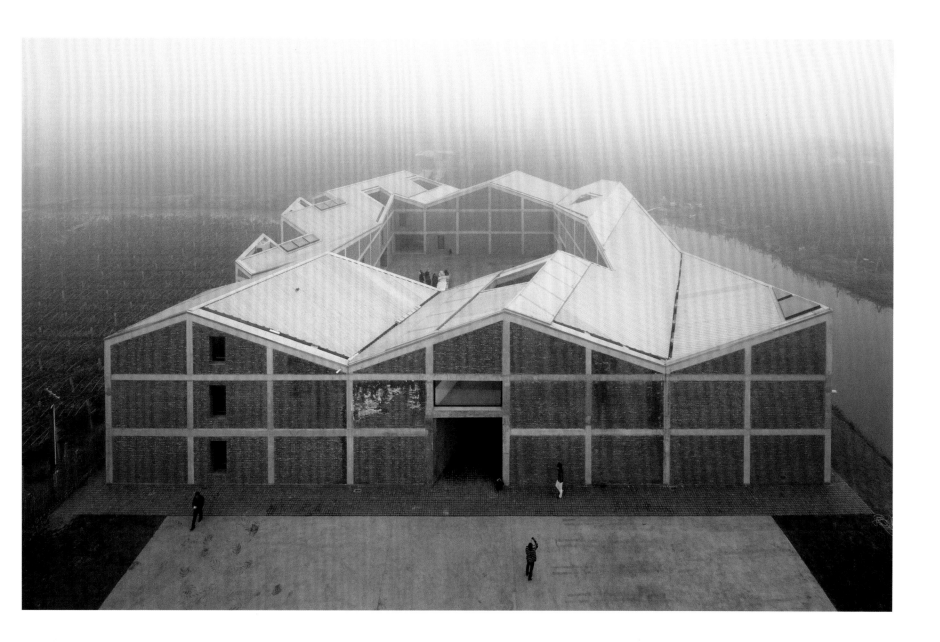

lacked proper permits; although, by that point, Ai's increasingly dissident status made clear that this was an act intended to demonstrate authority's ability to subdue dissenting voices through physical means. The artist's response was typically phlegmatic. Upon hearing of the demolition order, he sent the citizens of China an open invitation to attend a river-crab feast there, to celebrate the building's completion. As with the 3,000 porcelain crabs of *He Xie* (2011; cat. 18), the feast's theme punned on the use of the word for river crab as euphemistic internet

slang for censorship, due to its similarity to *héxié*, meaning 'harmonious', itself a reference to the Chinese Communist Party's goal of constructing a 'harmonious society'. Although house arrest precluded Ai's participation in the event, its attendance by hundreds of people from across the country solidified the Shanghai studio's brief physical presence within the collective memory. Alongside, *Souvenir from Shanghai* (2012; cat. 19) offers material evidence. Here, concrete and brick rubble recovered from the site is set against a timber bed-frame of the Qing

Dynasty, a juxtaposition that serves to place the work within the same critical framework as other pieces utilising historical fragments. Through these actions, Ai positions the studio, like China's iconic 'nail houses', as a symbol of political resistance, translated through art.

The theme of ruin and ruination is a potent image within Ai's work. Sometimes it is mythic, as in the constructed archaeology of the Neolithic Pottery Museum (2007; fig. 50), part of his Ai Qing Cultural Park project, or the supposedly re-excavated foundations of previous pavilions

Fig. 29 Shanghai Studio, Malu Town, Jiading district, eastern perspective, 2010

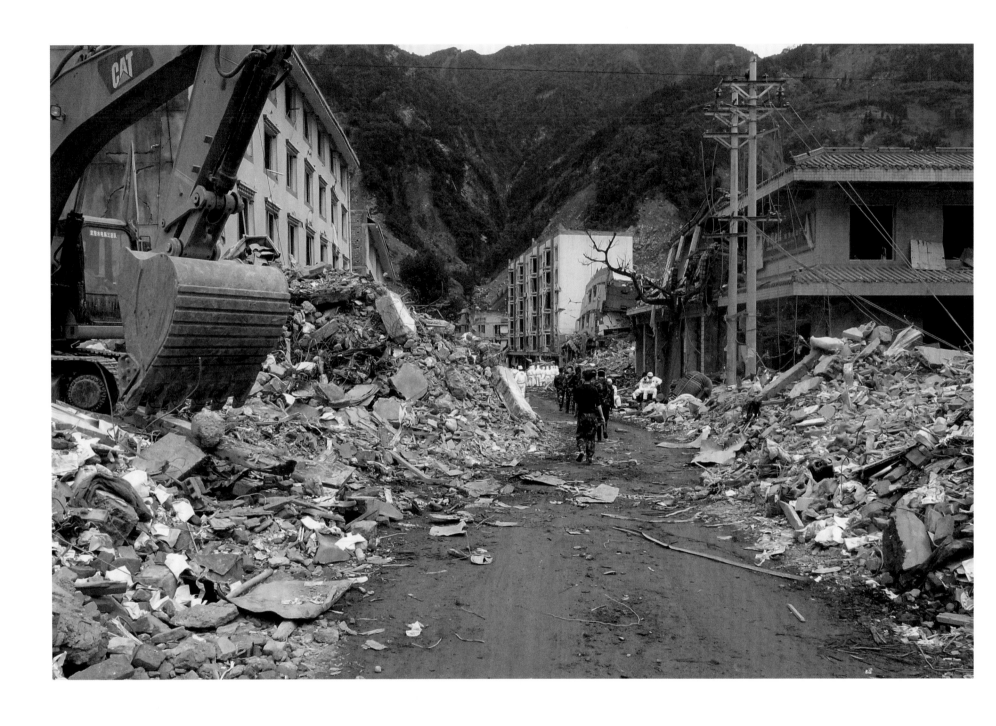

Fig. 30 Ai Weiwei, **Sichuan Earthquake Photographs**, 2008. Part of a series of photographs taken by Ai Weiwei at the earthquake disaster zone, May 2008

in his collaborative design for the Serpentine Pavilion (2012) in London, with architects Herzog & de Meuron. At other times, as in Shanghai, it becomes starkly real, a physical embodiment of memory, loss and futility that takes on deep social, political and cultural resonances. Nowhere does this happen with greater power or poignancy than in those pieces of work through which Ai confronted and exposed the tragedy of the 2008 Sichuan earthquake (fig. 30). While he may have abandoned the practice of architecture, these make clear his acute awareness of its power to embody and critique social and political structures and the consequences of their corruption. Asking himself 'How do I express such a historic and disastrous event simply and directly?'[39] he salvaged steel reinforcing bar (rebar) from collapsed school buildings across the region, the very material whose misuse the citizens' investigation he set up asserts to have been the principal reason why so many children lost their lives in the disaster. For the elegiac floor-structure *Straight* (2008–12; cat. 13) he had tonnes of this twisted, mangled bar laboriously straightened and stacked into an eerie, fissured landscape (see figs 31, 33). Newly readymade, as if pre-empting construction, these bars seem to collectively represent a culture of denial, until the accompanying list of 5,000 names transforms each one into a memorial for a lost child.

A sublime piece, its distillation of a complex and painstaking process of investigation, which overcame the resistance of a hostile regime to unearth the truth about the tragedy and the identities of its victims, positions it as a form of 'social sculpture'. This term, coined by Joseph Beuys, sought to name a type of art practice that takes place in the social realm, which requires social engagement for its completion

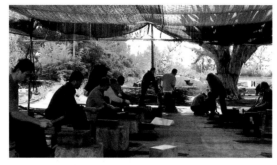
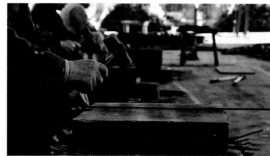
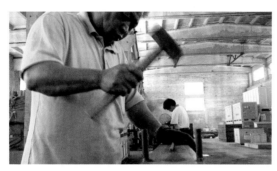
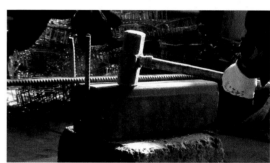
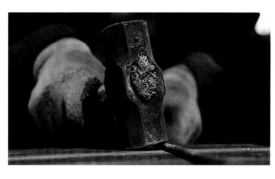
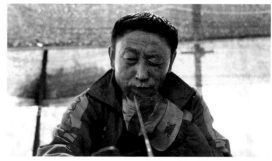
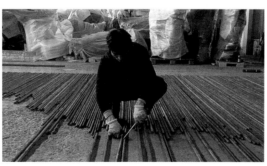
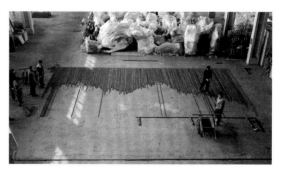

Fig. 31 Making **Straight**, 2008–12

and which seeks to transform society through the creative act. *Straight* uses the material of construction directly as the medium for such a process, but equally Ai's curation of the work of other architects could also be seen as a kind of social sculpture, in a country where uncensored dialogue and debate is so limited. 'Ordos 100' (2008; fig. 32), the project my practice took part in, revealed the artist as an engaging auteur. Flying in from every continent to spend time together in the deserts of Inner Mongolia, the one hundred architects felt reminiscent of the 1,001 Chinese citizens Ai invited to visit Kassel in Germany as part of *Fairytale* (2007; figs 55, 56), his installation for Documenta 12. While we were ostensibly there to design ostentatious 1,000 m² villas as part of a cultural quarter for a new city, it became clear that for Ai at least, the simple act of meeting and talking was the real focus of the project. The villas remain unbuilt but the international network of collaboration that emerged represents an ongoing cultural legacy.

Beyond architecture's role as a subject of Ai's work it provides the context within which he curates his art. As the Royal Academy exhibition demonstrates, Ai is intensely aware of the qualities and character of the spaces in which he is working and the effect of the placement of his works within them, making tangible for the viewer the latent orders, symmetries, scales and histories through which they respond to one another. In the Wohl Central Hall the placement of the intertwined bicycles of *Bicycle Chandelier* (2015; cat. 45) beneath the dome draws this representation of the heavens down to the viewer while enclosing a space that remains unreachable. The next gallery, lined in Ai's *Golden Age* wallpaper (2014; cat. 44), seems to remember the long-forgotten domesticity of Burlington House, with the classical enfilade of the building's plan establishing the calm disposition of each subsequent piece. Outside, the grove of fabricated timber trees that appear to have taken root in the Annenberg Courtyard (cat. 1) echoes both the house's former grounds and the gardens

of Chinese culture, creating in their constructed intricacy a poetic space of reflection on the relationship between things.

> Ai Qing, *Trees* (1940)
> *One tree, another tree,*
> *Each standing alone and erect.*
> *The wind and air*
> *Tell their distance apart.*
> *But beneath the cover of earth*
> *Their roots reach out*
> *And at depths that cannot be seen*
> *The roots of the trees intertwine.*

Like the trees in his father's poem, the many facets of Ai Weiwei's work and thought intertwine to form a complex whole, critically engaging an ever more complex world while remaining firmly grounded in the contingencies of material, making and the particularities of place. 'I actually never really separate those things: art, architecture, design or even curating,' he says 'to me they are just different angles or different ways to talk about the same things.'[40] Ai's buildings are a testament to the acuity of the artist's mind and eye. In turn, architecture's spatial, material presence and the processes of its production maintain a sustained influence upon his art. 'Architecture can also be silent,' he says, yet experience tells us, the viewers, that it remains deeply rooted in who he is and what he does.

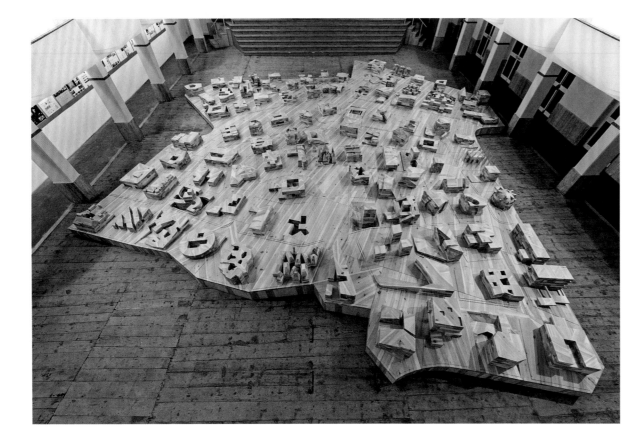

Fig. 32 Ai Weiwei, **Ordos 100**, 2011.
Pine wood, 15.11 x 13.57 x 0.8 m

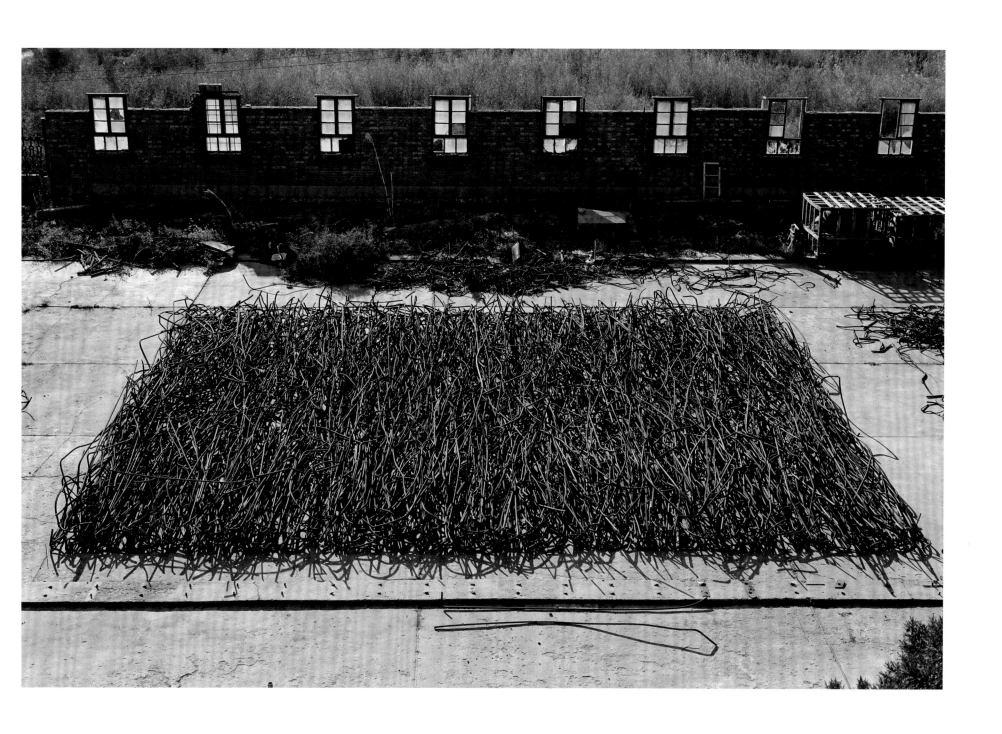

Fig. 33 Salvaged rebar at Left Right Studio, Beijing, 2011

CHRONOLOGY

ADRIAN LOCKE

1957

28 August: Ai Weiwei is born in Beijing. His father, Ai Qing (born Jiang Haicheng, 1910–1996; fig. 34), and mother, Gao Ying (b. 1933), are poets.

The Hundred Flowers Movement, instigated by the Communist Party of China (CPC) in 1956, encourages intellectuals to comment openly on the Communist regime. This is soon followed by the first wave of the Anti-Rightist Movement, during which the CPC arrests intellectuals who had been encouraged to voice their opinions during the Hundred Flowers Movement. A second wave follows two years later, in 1958.

Fig. 34 Ai Weiwei, one year old, with his father, Ai Qing, in Beijing, 1958

Figs 35, 37–40 Ai Weiwei, **New York Photographs, 1983–93**, C-prints, various dimensions

Fig. 35 (opposite) Ai Weiwei, In front of Duchamp's work, Museum of Modern Art, New York, 1987

1958–61

The Great Leap Forward, intended to shift China's economic base from dependence on traditional agriculture to a modern focus on industrialisation and collectivisation, causes the Great Famine, during which millions die of starvation.

1958

The CPC brands Ai Qing a 'Triple Criminal', i.e. against Party, state and country. He and his family are exiled to Beidahuang, Heilongjiang province, in the northeast of China near the border with North Korea.

1959

Ai Qing and his family are transferred to a military re-education camp in Shihezi, Xinjiang province (the Xinjiang Uyghur Autonomous Region) in the northwest of China.

1966–76

Chairman Mao announces the Great Proletarian Cultural Revolution, popularly known as the Cultural Revolution, as a means to reinvigorate a nationalist, Communist spirit and to eradicate perceived decadence among the populace. The Gang of Four – Jiang Qing (1914–1991), Zhang Chunqiao (1917–2005), Yao Wenyuan (1931–2005) and Wang Hongwen (1935–1992) – rise to dominate the CPC with Chairman Mao.

Ai Qing is sentenced to hard labour and forced to clean public lavatories; his family lives in a hole in the ground covered by brushwood. Gao Ying is away for long periods of time as she lobbies for Ai Qing to be rehabilitated.

1976

9 September: the death of Chairman Mao leads to Ai Qing's eventual rehabilitation, enabling him and his family to return to Beijing.

1978

The Beijing Spring, a brief relaxation of government restrictions under Deng Xiaoping, the new Chairman of the CPC, sees the emergence of the Democracy Wall, located at Xidan Junction (later moved to Ritan Park) on Chang'an Avenue, a major thoroughfare in Beijing. For the first time, members of the public can openly post views and air sentiments. The Chinese human-rights activist Wei Jingsheng posts 'The Fifth Modernisation' on the Democracy Wall, calling for democracy to be added to the CPC's list of 'Four Modernisations', namely agriculture, industry, national defence, and science and technology.

Following the reopening of art academies in China, Ai enters the Beijing Film Academy, where he studies animation. His fellow students in the cinematography department include Chen Kaige and Zhang Yimou.

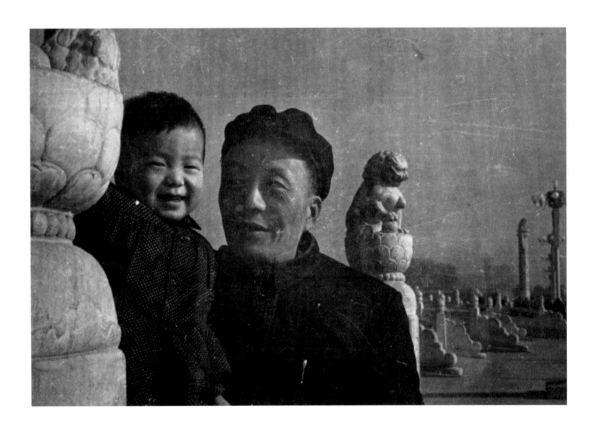

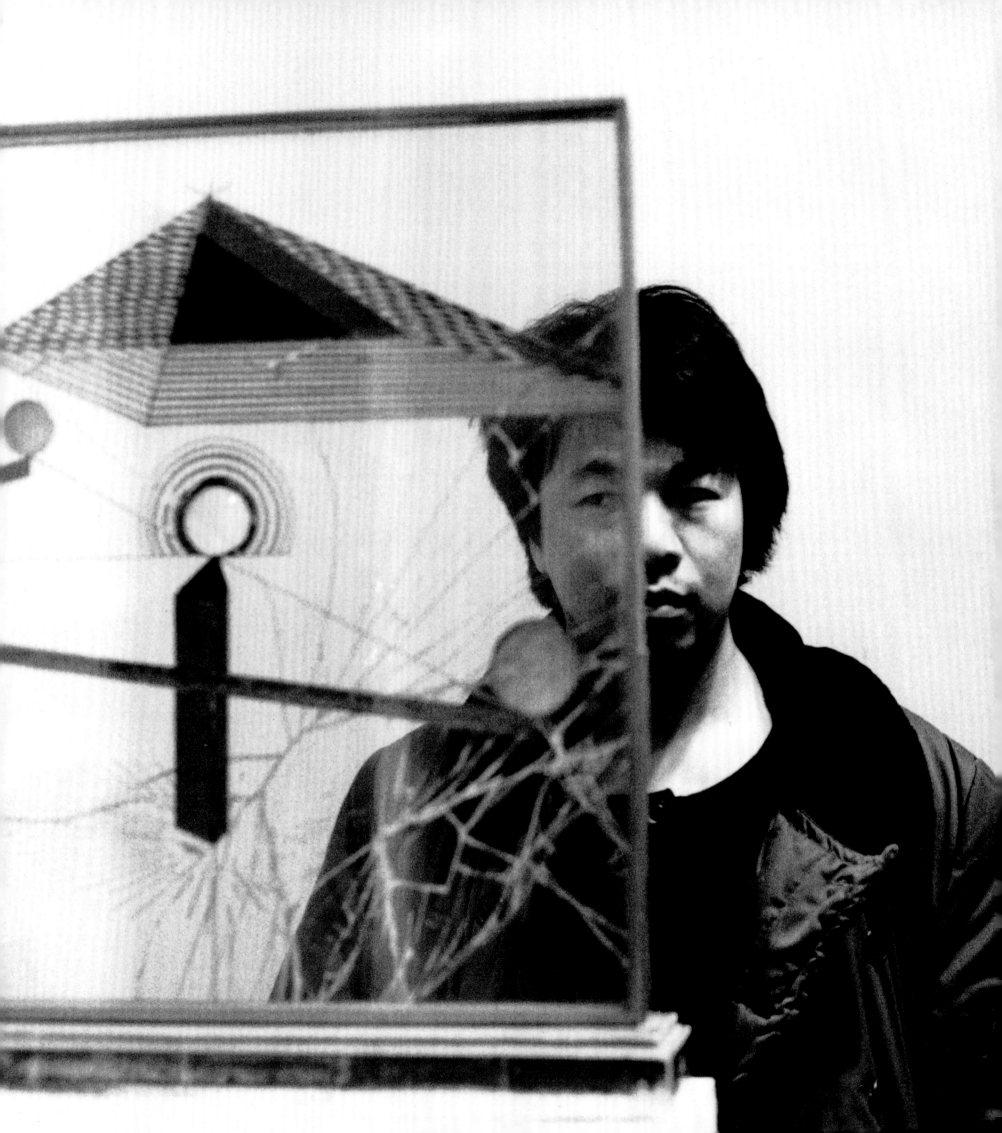

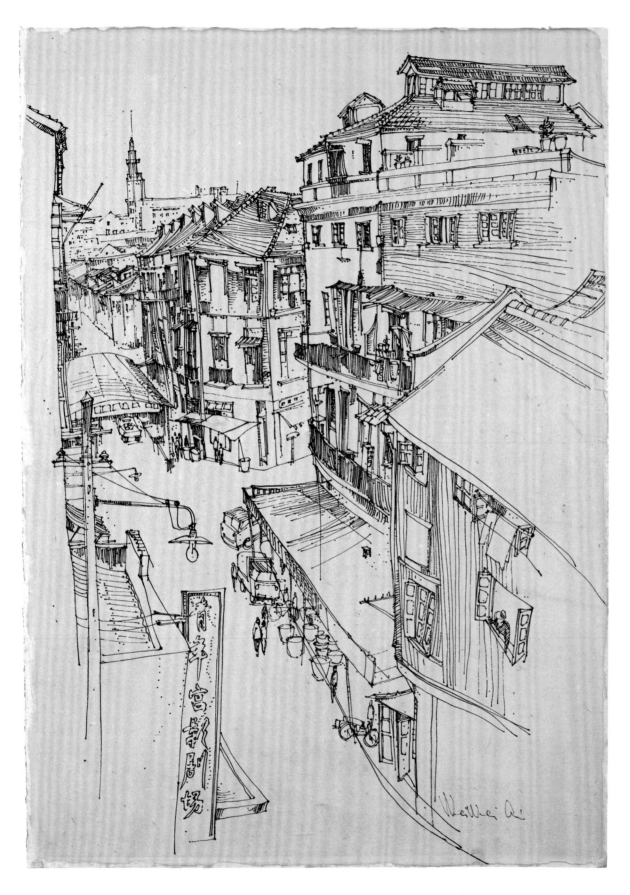

Fig. 36 Ai Weiwei, **Street in Shanghai**, 1979.
Pen and ink on paper, 53.3 x 38.1 cm. Christopher
Tsai Collection

1979

Two factory workers, Ma Desheng and Huang Rui, found the 'Stars' art collective. Ai is one of the original twelve signatories of the group, alongside Wang Keping and Qu Leilei.

27 September: the first Stars exhibition takes place on the railings outside the China Art Gallery (now the National Art Museum of China) in Beijing (fig. 10). After one day the exhibition is declared illegal by the authorities and after two days it is removed.

1 October: on the thirtieth anniversary of the foundation of the People's Republic of China members of the Stars collective march in protest from the Democracy Wall to the headquarters of the Beijing Municipal Party Committee on Tiananmen Square under a banner declaring 'We Demand Democracy and Artistic Freedom'.

23 November – 2 December: the authorities permit a second viewing of the Stars exhibition at Huafeng Studio, Beihai Park, Beijing.

1980

June/July: having not been recognised by either the Ministry of Culture or the Beijing Artists' Association, the Stars collective forms the 'Stars Painters Society' with twelve founding members: Ma Desheng, Huang Rui, Wang Keping, Yang Li, Yang Yiping, Qu Leilei, Mao Lizi, Bo Yun, Zhong Acheng, Shao Fei, Li Shuang and Ai Weiwei.

24 August – 7 September: the authorities permit the Stars Painters Society to mount a two-week exhibition at the China Art Gallery, Beijing.

1981

February: Ai moves to the USA. He stays initially in Philadelphia and then moves to Berkeley, studying English at the Universities of Pennsylvania and California in order to enter Parsons The New School for Design, Greenwich Village, New York.

1982

January: 'Ai Weiwei', his first solo exhibition, comprising thirty paintings made in China, takes place at the Asia Foundation, San Francisco.

December: Ai moves to New York, living initially in Long Island City in Queens, before moving to Brooklyn.

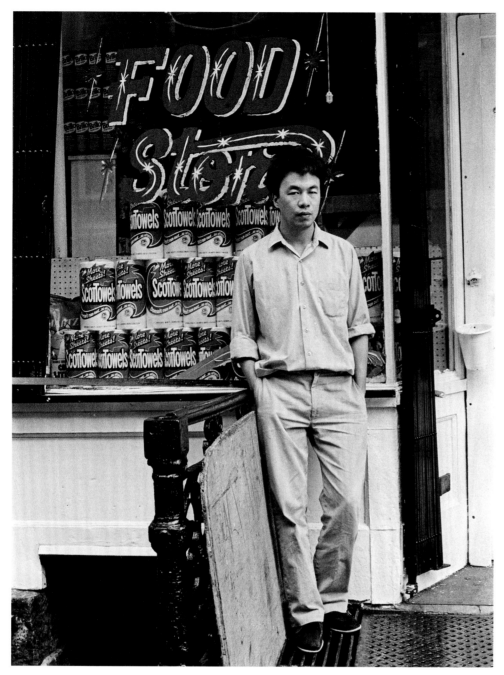

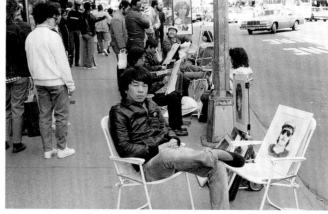

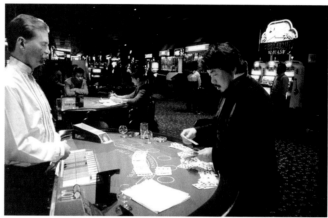

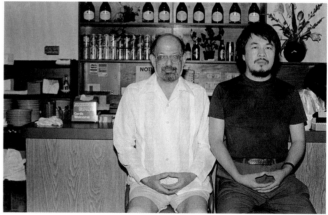

Fig. 37 (above) Ai Weiwei, Williamsburg, New York, 1983

Fig. 38 (right, top) Ai Weiwei, Portrait artist in Times Square, 1987

Fig. 39 (right, middle) Ai Weiwei, Setting up cards, Atlantic City, 1993

Fig. 40 (right, below) Ai Weiwei, Lower East Side restaurant, with Allen Ginsberg, 1988

1983

January: Ai enters Parsons, where he is tutored by, among others, Sean Scully, but drops out after six months. He also studies at the Art Students League of New York on West 57th Street under Richard Pousette-Dart, Bruce Dorfman and Knox Martin.

14 August: the last Stars exhibition, at Zixin Road Primary School, Beijing, curated by Ma Desheng, Huang Rui and Wang Keping, opens but is shut down by the authorities after five days.

Ai begins taking photographs, documenting his life in New York.

1985

Ai moves from Brooklyn to Manhattan, to an apartment on East 3rd Street in the Lower East Side, an area known as the East Village. He shares the apartment with various friends, among them Chen Kaige and the aspiring composer and conductor Tan Dun. Ai works as a portrait artist in Times Square (fig. 38) and regularly gambles in the casinos of Atlantic City to make a living (fig. 39). He befriends the Beat generation poet Allen Ginsberg (1926–1997) (fig. 40), whom his father had met in China in 1984.

QUESTIONS ARE OPINIONS

SEAN SCULLY

In 1983 I was teaching at Parsons School of Art in Manhattan. Every year there were two professors, and I was one of them. The class, which always had twenty-six students, was always divided in half, and due to the rise of Asia, nine of the twenty-six would be from the East. I would get them all on account of my patience and my universal use of the English language. So I would have nine from Asia and four from New York, and the other professor, who had a paucity of tolerance for people who speak slowly and think in four dimensions, had thirteen Americans; which seemed fair and just, since I was a party-crasher myself. The other professor's group were then free to engage in a self-referring festival of local in-jokes and the vernacular, while I laboured with the strange. I didn't mind though. I found it, on occasion, hypnotic and deeply tender. One of my strange ones was Ai Weiwei. He was a young, modestly immodest Chinese man, all the way from China.

At the outset, all the students had to make a painting. The others were in awe of the terminal perfection of Weiwei's piece. The students waited, expecting me to praise it and join them in their awe. However, I said that its smugly realised completion completed its death, thus making it, paradoxically, the worst painting I had ever seen. The ranking order in my class was cataclysmically reversed. And Ai Weiwei was the man who had stepped into an elevator whose cable had snapped on the penthouse floor, only to arrive physically unharmed, seconds later, in the sub-basement of the same building.

His brutality was very beautiful. Instead of arguing with me in English, in which he could never prevail, he simply threw away his paints.

Together, we made an agreement to study the history of the 'other' wing of art: conceptualisation. I don't practise it literally, I am too deeply attached to the pre-verbal profundity that painting believes it can incarnate. But I know it, sometimes I think better than painting, from the top of its head to its ingrown toenails.

Weiwei would arrive every week for a convivial chat, and I would drop in information on it here and there. From Breton to Duchamp to Kurt Schwitters's kick in the pants as people left his studio to Oppenheim's furry cup and on to the philosophical poetry of Beuys, the *Germania* of Hans Haacke. *Earthworks*. *The Broken Kilometer* and its parent, Manzoni's *Linea Lunga*. West Coast Video. Getting yourself shot. Getting yourself tied to a car. Up to my friend Peter Nadin, who used to do construction work, and then sign it. When my usefulness to Weiwei was exhausted, he said farewell. And I was sorry to see him go.

His head, now inhabited by Western thoughts of ego, assertion and fame, tilted slightly in my direction as we bade each other farewell. I imagined he would insinuate himself into the tightly woven fabric of Chinese or Asian society as my other Asian students have. But then he became famous and adored in Europe.

Thirty years later I arrived at his beautiful blue door outside Beijing. On the way, my driver got lost. I was taking photos with my iPhone. I found myself taking a photo of a house, which happened to have a young woman at the window, taking a photo of me taking a photo of her. She was laughing and so I joined in. Eventually, after this little adventure in the hinterland of Beijing, Weiwei and I embraced, closing the thirty-year space that had grown between us. We entered his room, and he told me why carpenters don't like to work with pine. Then we entered his studio, which is exactly the same size as mine in Germany: 10 metres by 20 metres, which, we agreed, is a human scale. Big, but not enormous.

I saw a big photograph of his, which put its hand on my heart, and I wanted it. And I still do. It is a tree made of trees that are not the same. As if the longing for unison is overthrown by the assertion of differentness. He said – miraculously, as only the grand of spirit can – that the work had come from my teaching ideas. My metaphor was the city. Things want to be together to complete our possible wholeness, and they are alike, but they are not the same. What is similar is also not. His metaphor is the tree. Like people, all trees want to be together: though we know that the birch, if it is able, will kill the oak. Our wholeness is at the end of our long road, and we are perpetual road-builders.

We took a nice limo to a posh Japanese restaurant. On the way we talked of our sons, who are both five. Once again, we were linked. By Oisin and by Lao, who have a play date in Beijing in April 2015. I was talking of children. I said I supported 200 poor children, and I was thinking of increasing this to 300. Though,

once taken on, one can never retreat, since a dependency is built. He said, so sweetly: 'I'll take the other hundred.' And true to his word, he did.

Now my friend Weiwei is separated from his son, who goes to school in Berlin, and lives with his mother. It is proven that boys suffer without their fathers. In 1949 we returned to London from Ireland, where I was born in 1945, and my father, who had refused to fight in the Second World War, was imprisoned in England for eight months. I was four years old when that happened to me; Weiwei's son Lao is five years old. This opened a space between my father and myself that closed only when I cared for him as he was dying. Though that was beautiful. Now I watch, with apprehension, the same film being played over again, at a different time, in a different place. We live in a world of endless sequels.

The world spins, and in imitation of it, we are in motion. So is China. Though Weiwei himself praises it, praises its extraordinary ability to lift up 300 million people from abject poverty.

Now Weiwei has an exhibition in London, one of the greatest cities in the world. Known for its tolerance and freedom, and where the police don't carry guns, which is in itself, unique as an achievement.

England, though, is also the country that partitioned China, and filled it with opium, in order to get at its riches, thus pushing it into a social and cultural abyss. The United States of America, the country in which I live and flourish, is the most incarcerated country on Earth. It is also the country where unrepentant police shoot little boys, point blank. Yet I live there. I speak against this, but this is breath against the steel of the military-industrial complex that owns America and has militarised the life of our great 'democracy'.

If we point the finger at everyone everywhere, we would need as many fingers as there are leaves in the forest. So let's not. And in any case, the coloniser is disqualified from pointing the finger at the colonised, on the grounds of hypocrisy.

Let art do its work. Art now has a transforming influence and authority that is new in its history, and was set up by the advent of the avant-garde in the twentieth century, when art became a free agent. Only fifty years ago homosexuality was illegal in the UK. Music and art have transformed the country. And laws always obey attitudes. That's what makes them change. And they will, everywhere they let us in.

That is the influence of art. Ai Weiwei has contributed a great humanism to conceptual art, with a deep and wide historical and political sweep. This is demonstrated so profoundly by *Stools* (2014). Over 6,000 Ming and Qing Dynasty wooden stools clearly bump into American monumental minimalism, though with a rough, weathered, historical weight added. Showing evidence of human use and passing lives, avoiding the possible sterility of the former, in favour of pathos and empathy. With bicycle saddles, Ai cares clearly about human scent, and how it is left on seats.

Weiwei and I seem to be paired in a magnetic friendship, contrapuntal and unbreakable. An old dad and an older dad. He faces west, and I east. He shows all over Europe, and I show all over China. We both come from embattled lineages. My grandfather, John Scully, hanged himself before the British Army could shoot him at dawn.

Weiwei is attracted to the fully blooming flower of democracy, and I to its open bud. I leave the final sentence to Henrik Ibsen, the great playwright, for whom James Joyce learned Norwegian: 'One of the qualities of liberty is that, as long as it is being striven after, it goes on expanding.'

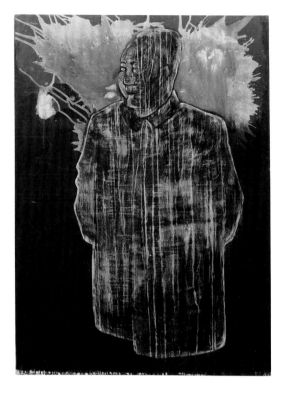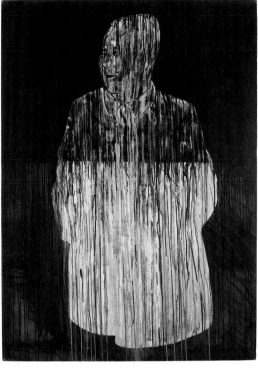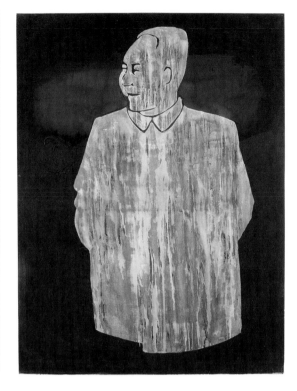

Fig. 41 (above) Ai Weiwei, **Mao I–III**, 1985. Acrylic on canvas, three panels, each 180 x 135 cm

Fig. 42 (below, left) Ai Weiwei, **Untitled**, 1986. Book with shoe, 16 x 43 x 24 cm

Fig. 43 (below, right) Ai Weiwei, **Safe Sex**, 1986. Raincoat, hanger, condom, 130 x 70 x 20 cm

He works on large-scale canvases (fig. 41) but abandons painting, beginning a series of works influenced by Dada and Duchamp that are often referred to as 'readymades' or sculptures (fig. 42). Ai describes them as 'paintings that were illusions of paintings – fake paintings if you like'.

1986

July: Ai participates in his first group exhibition outside China: 'Avant-garde Chinese Art: Beijing/New York', curated by Michael Murray at the City Gallery, New York.

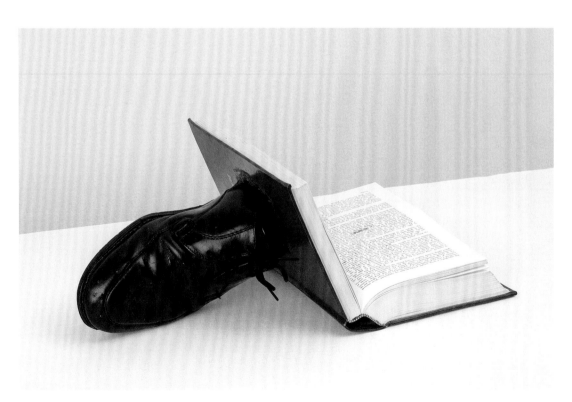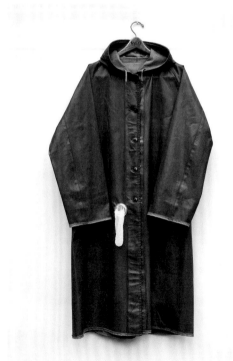

1987

'The Stars at Harvard: Chinese Dissident Art' takes place at the Fairbank Center for East Asian Research, Harvard University, Cambridge, MA.

January: 'The Stars: Ten Years', curated by Chang Tsong-zung (a.k.a. Johnson Chang), opens at Hanart TZ Gallery, Hong Kong. The exhibition travels to the Hanart Gallery, Taipei, in March.

September: 'China's New Expression' opens at the Municipal Gallery, New York.

1988

March: Ai's first solo exhibition in New York, 'Old Shoes – Safe Sex', takes place at Ethan Cohen's gallery Art Waves (fig. 43).

16 March: the first article on Ai – 'Ai Weiwei's Heart Belongs to Dada' by Sean Simon – is published in the New York journal *Artspeak*.

1989

15 April – 4 June: the student-led Democracy Movement's call for political reform leads to the occupation of Tiananmen Square in Beijing. Martial law is subsequently declared by the CPC. Troops violently disperse protesters, killing hundreds in the process, and sending shockwaves across the world. As a consequence, Ai joins in the international Solidarity for China movement and participates in eight days of hunger strikes in New York.

1993

The exhibition 'Fifteen Years of the Stars' takes place at the Tokyo Gallery.

On learning that his father is ill, Ai decides to return to Beijing. He says: 'I wasn't disappointed with America because I didn't have too many hopes for it. I went hoping to be an artist and in the end, I am still an artist' (Ai, Tancock et al. 2011, p. 33).

On his return to Beijing, Ai and his partner (later, his wife) the artist Lu Qing engage in 'Apartment Art', in which artists conceive and show often radical art in the privacy of their own homes. The term is coined by Gao Minglu. They are one of several couples of Chinese artists who have lived abroad to take part in this movement.

Fig. 44 Ai Weiwei, **Propaganda Poster**, 1993

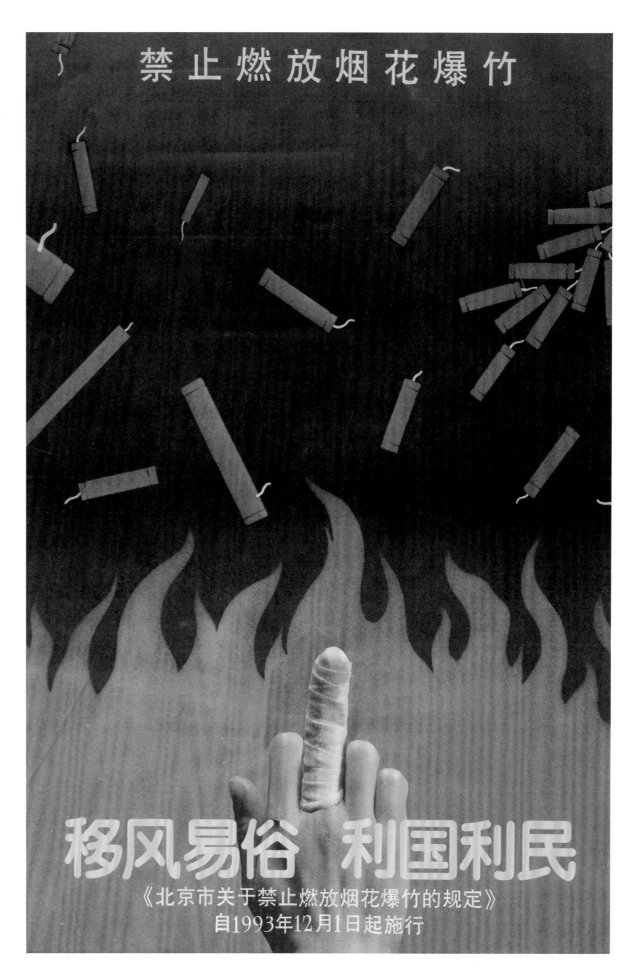

1994

Black Cover Book, edited by Ai and Feng Boyi, is published by Red Flag Book, Beijing. It is the first in a sequence of three books, all in editions of 3,000, and is followed by *White Cover Book* (1995), edited by Ai, and *Grey Cover Book* (1997), edited by Ai and Zhuang Hui (fig. 45). The books present new concepts and unrealised artistic projects by Ai and a number of fellow Chinese artists, and introduce the work of such influential Western artists as Marcel Duchamp, Jenny Holzer, Jeff Koons and Andy Warhol.

1995

Ai starts his *Study of Perspective* series of photographs (fig. 46).

January: he participates in his first group exhibition in Europe: 'Change – Chinese Contemporary Art', curated by Folke Edwards and Nils Olof Ericsson at the Göteborgs Konsthall.

Fig. 45 (above) **Black Cover Book** (1994), **White Cover Book** (1995) and **Grey Cover Book** (1997). Artist's books published by Tai Tei Publishing Company Limited, Hong Kong, each 22.9 x 18.2 cm

Fig. 46 (below) Ai Weiwei, **Study of Perspective – White House**, 1995–. Gelatin silver print, 38.9 x 59 cm. Acquired through the generosity of the Photography Council and the Contemporary Arts Council of The Museum of Modern Art, inv. 358.2008

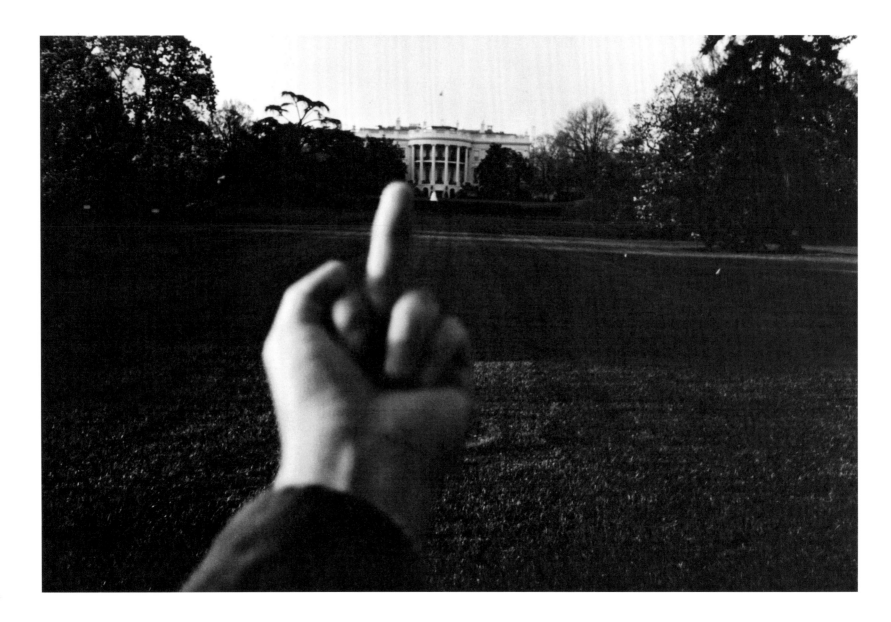

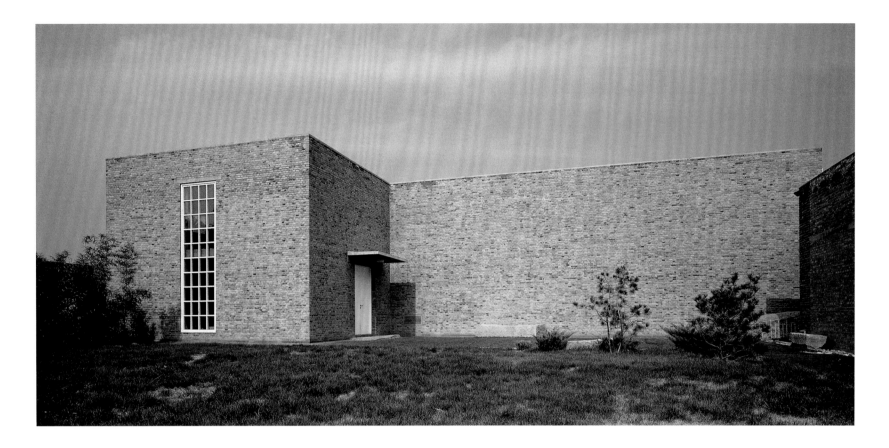

1996

5 May: Ai's father, Ai Qing, dies.

1997

Ai, Hans van Dijk (1946–2002) and Frank Uytterhaegen (1954–2011) found China Art Archives and Warehouse (CAAW) in Beijing, the first alternative space for exhibiting and cataloguing contemporary art in China.

1998

Ai serves as a jury member for the first Chinese Contemporary Art Awards, established by the Swiss collector Uli Sigg. The inaugural Best Artist prize is awarded to Zhou Tiehai.

1999

Ai designs and builds a studio and residence at Caochangdi, Chaoyang District, Beijing (fig. 47). He is the first artist to move into this area, which soon becomes a popular location for art galleries and artists' studios, and is known locally as 'the village'.

June: Ai participates in 'APERTO' at the 48th International Art Exhibition (Venice Biennale), directed by Harald Szeemann.

2000

Ai designs and builds China Art Archives and Warehouse at Caochangdi, Beijing.

4–20 November: Ai and the independent curator and critic Feng Boyi curate 'Fuck Off', an exhibition of the work of 46 emerging Chinese artists at Eastlink Gallery and a warehouse at 1133 West Suzhou River Road, Shanghai. The show runs parallel to the Third Shanghai Biennial, Shanghai Art Museum.

2002

Ai edits *Chinese Artists, Texts and Interviews: Chinese Contemporary Art Awards 1998–2002*, published by Timezone 8 Ltd, Hong Kong.

Fig. 47 (above) Ai Weiwei, Studio-house, Caochangdi, Beijing, 1999

Fig. 48 (below) Ai Weiwei, **Souvenir from Beijing**, 2002. Bricks from dismantled *hutong* houses and boxes made from iron wood (tieli wood) from dismantled temples of the Qing Dynasty (1644–1911), each 9.5 x 35.5 x 22.5 cm

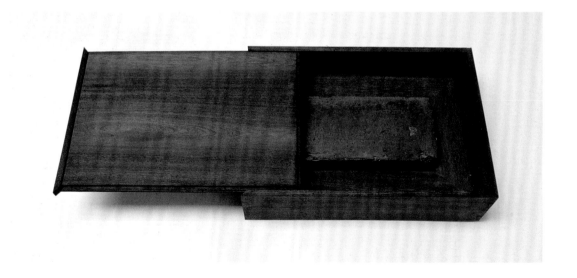

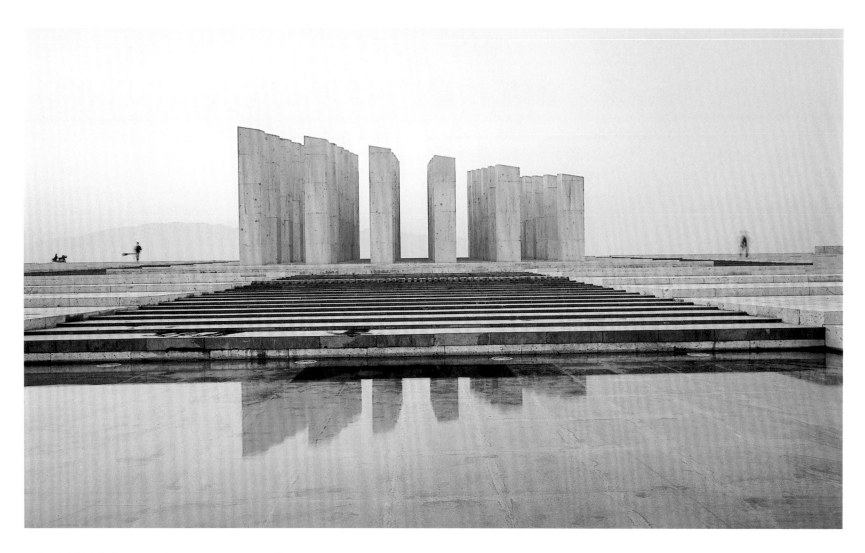

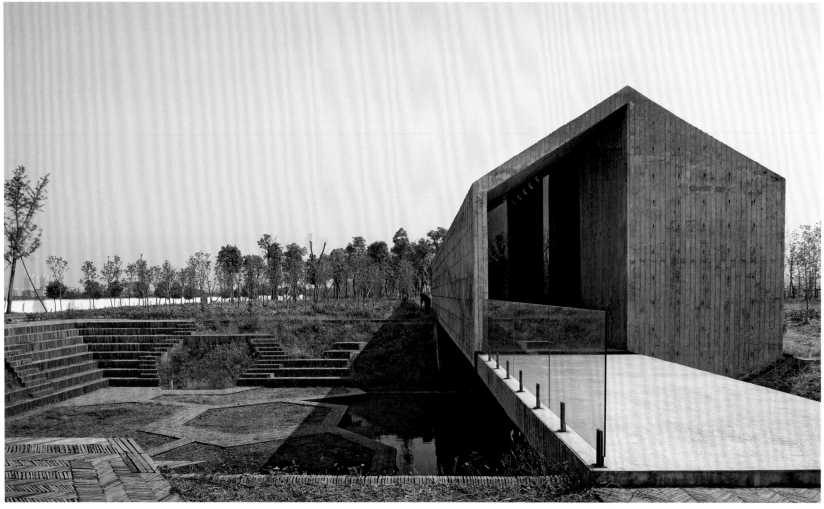

2003

Ai founds the architectural practice FAKE Design at Caochangdi, Beijing.

He is commissioned to work on the design of the National Stadium for the Beijing Summer Olympic Games (fig. 59) with the Swiss architects Jacques Herzog and Pierre de Meuron (Herzog & de Meuron).

He designs and builds the Ai Qing Memorial (fig. 49) at the Ai Qing Cultural Park, Jinhua, Zhejiang province.

November: 'Ai Weiwei', Ai's first solo exhibition in Europe, opens in Lucerne at Galerie Urs Meile.

2004

Ai curates the Jinhua Architecture Park in Jinhua, Zhejiang province, for which he designed the Neolithic Pottery Museum (fig. 50).

April: 'Ai Weiwei', his first major solo exhibition in Europe, is shown at the Kunsthalle Bern and the Caermersklooster – Provinciaal Centrum voor Kunst en Cultuur, Ghent.

September: Ai participates in 'Metamorph', the 9th International Architecture Exhibition (Venice Biennale of Architecture), directed by Kurt W. Forster.

September: His work is shown in 'Between Past and Future: New Photography and Video from China', curated by Wu Hung and Christopher Phillips at the Victoria and Albert Museum, London; the International Center of Photography and Asia Society, New York; the Smart Museum of Art, University of Chicago, and the Museum of Contemporary Art, Chicago; the Seattle Art Museum; the Haus der Kulturen der Welt, Berlin; and the Santa Barbara Museum of Art.

2005

Ai designs and builds Courtyard 104 (now the Galerie Urs Meile) and Courtyard 105, Caochangdi, Beijing, as well as a gallery and studio space for Pékin Fine Arts at 241 Caochangdi.

June: the Chinese Ministry of Culture establishes an official pavilion at the 51st International Art Exhibition (Venice Biennale).

September: with Bernhard Fibicher, Ai curates the exhibition 'Mahjong: Contemporary Chinese Art from the Sigg Collection' at the Kunstmuseum Bern, and the Hamburger Kunsthalle.

October: Ai posts the first of over 2,700 blog entries on sina.com.

November: Ai participates in 'Beyond', the 2nd Guangzhou Triennial, curated by Hou Hanru, Hans Ulrich Obrist and Guo Xiaoyan, at the Guangdong Museum of Art, Guangzhou City.

2006

Ai is speaker at the World Economic Forum Annual Meeting: 'Innovation and Design Strategy'.

May: Ai and Serge Spitzer (1951–2012) collaborate on the installation *Ghost Gu Coming Down the Mountain* (2005–06) for the exhibition 'Territorial: Ai Weiwei and Serge Spitzer' at the Museum für Moderne Kunst, Frankfurt-am-Main.

June: Ai participates in 'Zones of Contact', the 15th Biennale of Sydney, directed by Charles Merewether, at the Art Gallery of New South Wales (fig. 51).

September: Ai participates in 'Everywhere', the 5th Busan Biennale, directed by Manu D. Park, Busan Museum of Modern Art.

December: he participates in the 5th Asia Pacific Triennial of Contemporary Art – curated by a team from the Queensland Art Gallery – at the Gallery of Modern Art and the Queensland Art Gallery, Brisbane.

Fig. 49 (opposite, top) Ai Weiwei, **Ai Qing Memorial**, 2003. Ai Qing Cultural Park, Jinhua, Zhejiang province

Fig. 50 (opposite, below) Neolithic Pottery Museum, Jinhua Architecture Park, Jinhua, Zhejiang province, 2004–07

Fig. 51 (right) Ai Weiwei, **World Map**, 2006. Cotton and wood base, 100 x 800 x 600 cm. Installation shown at the 15th Biennale of Sydney at the Art Gallery of New South Wales

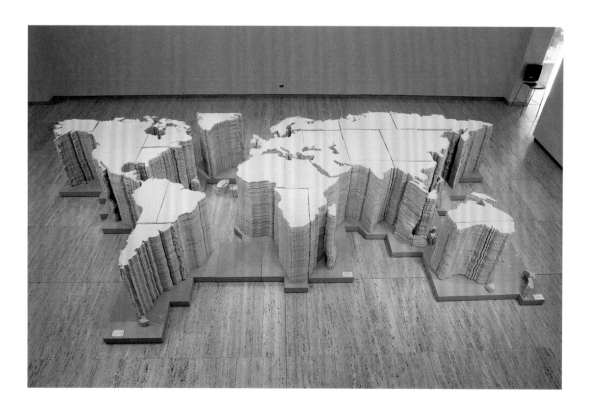

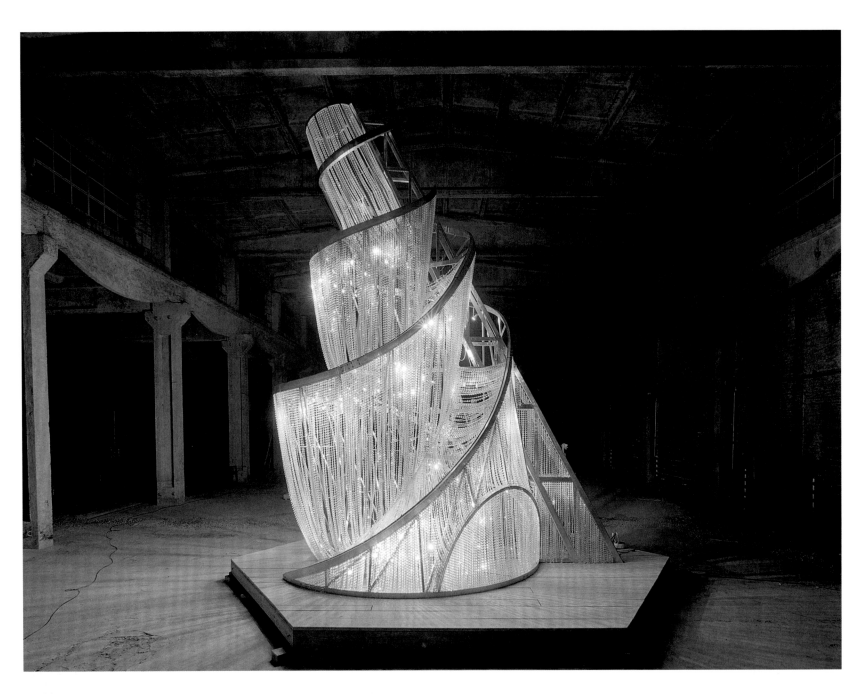

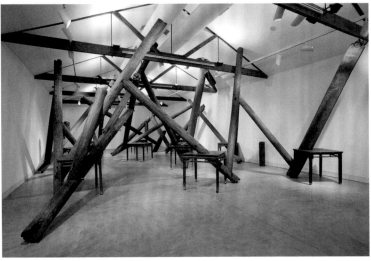

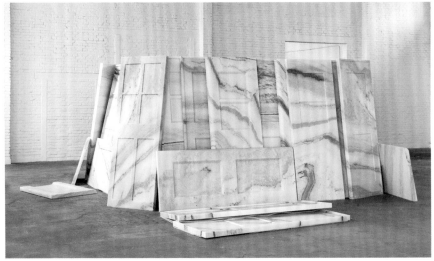

2007

March: Ai creates *Fountain of Light* (fig. 52) for 'The Real Thing: Contemporary Art from China', an exhibition at Tate Liverpool curated by Karen Smith, Xu Zhen and Simon Groom.

March: Ai participates in 'We Are Your Future', curated by Ethan Cohen and Juan Puntes as part of the 2nd Moscow Biennial of Contemporary Art, directed by Joseph Backstein.

May: Ai exhibits *Through* (2007–08; fig. 53) at the Sherman Contemporary Art Foundation, Sydney.

June: Ai presents *Fairytale* and *Template* at Documenta 12, Kassel. For *Fairytale* (figs 55, 56), he invites 1,001 Chinese citizens from across mainland China to travel to Germany in five groups, where they are lodged in a dormitory, complete with a makeshift kitchen. Some 3,000 people respond to Ai's original advertisement for participants on his website; his team arranges documentation and travel for the successful applicants. A condition of their involvement is that they take photographs and record texts during their stay in Kassel, saving these on USB memory sticks attached to their wrists. For many, this is their first experience of foreign travel. Ai also takes a photographic portrait of each participant. His sculpture *Template*, made of doors and windows salvaged from destroyed houses from the Ming (1368–1644) and Qing (1644–1911) dynasties, is installed but collapses during a storm. Ai decides that the work should remain in the shape that it assumed when it fell down.

Fig. 52 (opposite, top) Ai Weiwei, **Fountain of Light**, 2007. Steel and glass crystals on wooden base, 700 x 529 x 400 cm

Fig. 53 (opposite, left) Ai Weiwei, **Through**, 2007–08. Iron wood (tieli wood), tables, parts of beams and pillars from dismantled temples of the Qing Dynasty (1644–1911), 550 x 850 x 1380 cm. Installation at the Sherman Contemporary Art Foundation, Sydney

Fig. 54 (opposite, right) Ai Weiwei, **Monumental Junkyard**, 2007. Sixty marble doors, each approx. 210 x 80 x 6 cm. Installation at Galerie Urs Meile, Beijing. Courtesy of Galerie Urs Meile, Beijing

Fig. 55 (right) Ai Weiwei, **Fairytale**, Documenta 12, Kassel, 2007. 1,001 Chinese visitors, Gottschalk-Hallen, ladies dormitory, mixed media

Fig. 56 (overleaf) Ai Weiwei, **Fairytale**, Documenta 12, Kassel, 2007. 1,001 Qing Dynasty (1644–1911) wooden chairs, dimensions variable

Ai designs and builds the Three Shadows Photography Art Centre and the Red Brick Complex at Caochangdi, Beijing.

November: 'Origin Point: Star Group Retrospective Exhibition' is curated by Zhu Zhu at the Beijing Today Art Museum and the White Canvas Gallery, Nanjing.

November: the exhibition 'Ai Weiwei' opens at Galerie Urs Meile, Beijing–Lucerne, Lucerne (fig. 54).

2008

January: Ai receives a lifetime achievement award at the Chinese Contemporary Art Awards.

March: the authorities in Shanghai invite him to build a studio there in Malu Town, Jiading District, as part of an initiative to develop a cultural quarter in the area.

12 May: the Sichuan earthquake (sometimes referred to as the Wenchuan earthquake after its epicentre), measuring 8 on the Richter scale, devastates Sichuan province, killing some 90,000 people and displacing 5 million more.

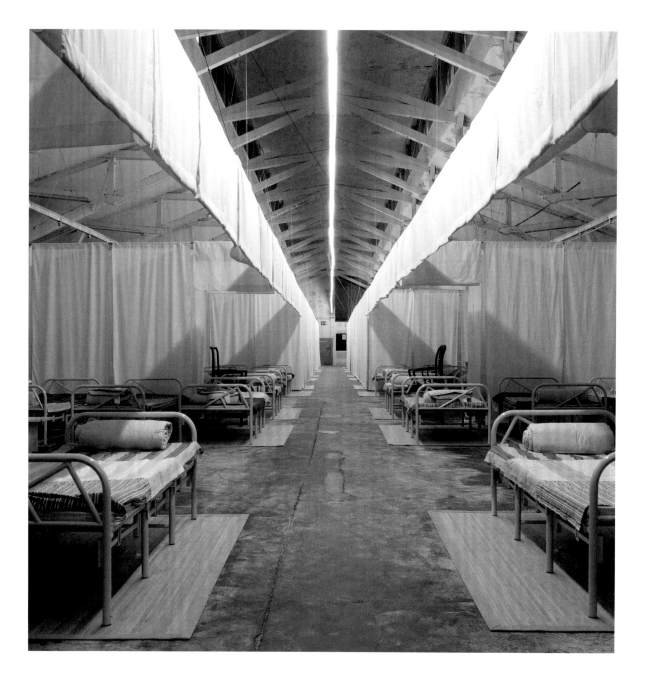

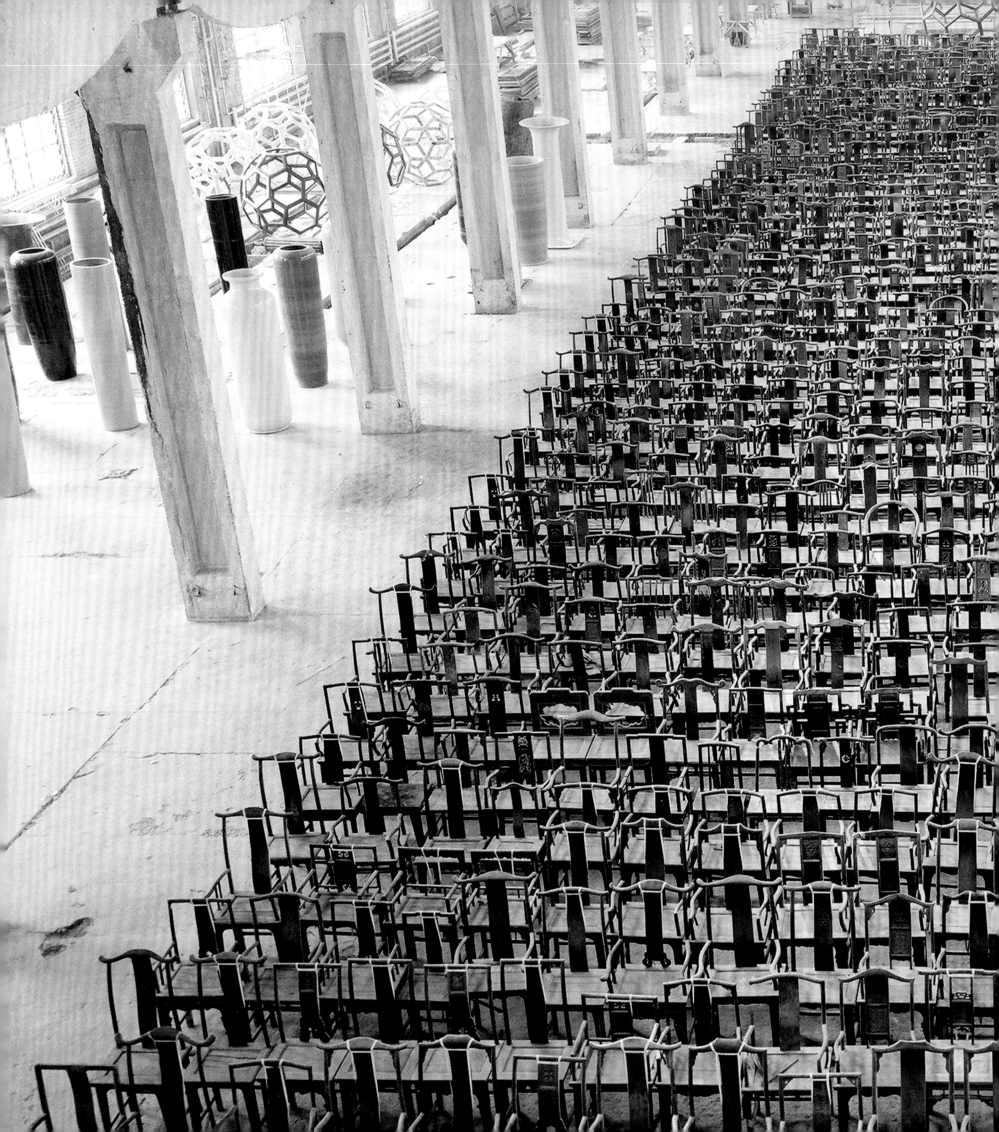

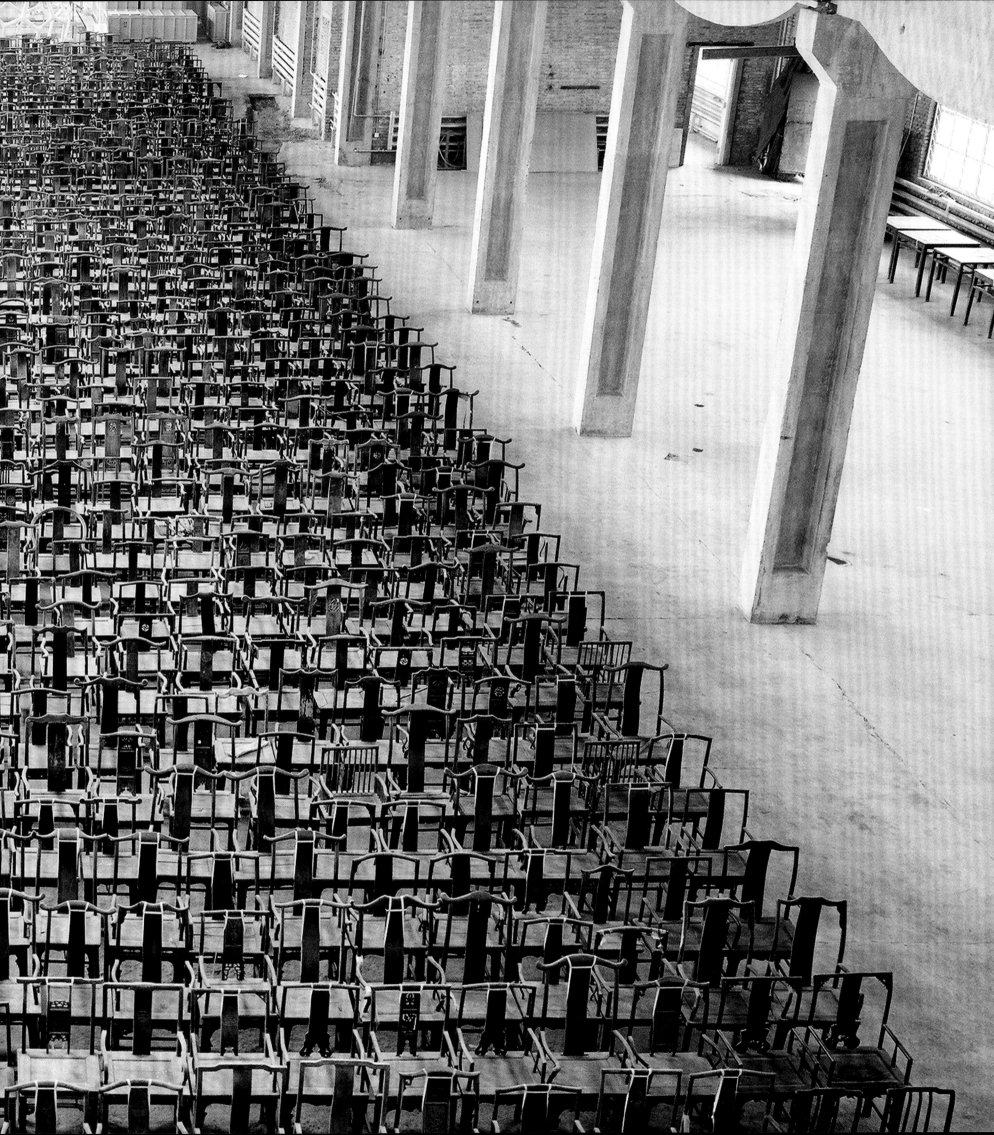

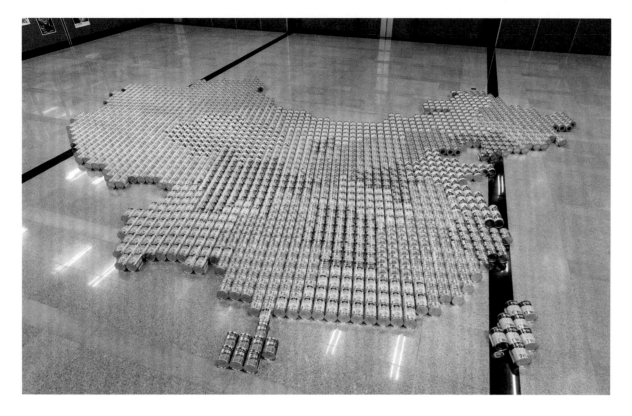

June: the National Stadium, Beijing, is officially opened.

July: the Sanlu baby-milk formula scandal emerges in Gansu province, northwest China, but cases are soon reported across the country. The scandal threatens to overshadow the success of the Beijing Olympics. Several babies die and hundreds of thousands more are hospitalised with industrial melamine poisoning. Ai later responds to the scandal with *Baby Formula* (2013; fig. 57).

September: Ai participates in 'Out There: Architecture Beyond Building' at the 11th International Architecture Exhibition (Venice Biennale of Architecture) (fig. 58), directed by Aaron Betsky, and in 'Made Up' at the 5th Liverpool Biennial, directed by Lewis Biggs.

October: 'Ai Weiwei', Ai's first solo exhibition in the UK, opens at the Albion Gallery, London.

October: an ambitious plan to create a new city, Ordos, in the coal-, oil- and gas-rich Ordos Basin in Inner Mongolia, is underwritten by the Chinese tycoon Cai Jiang through his companies Jiang Yuan Cultural and Creative Industrial Development Ltd and Jiang Yuan Water Engineering Ltd. Ai is invited to curate 'Ordos 100', bringing together 100 architects, selected by Herzog & de Meuron, from 27 countries to design and build 100 distinct 1,000 m² villas, each with a swimming pool (see fig. 32). Ai makes a video work, *Ordos 100* (2012), about the project.

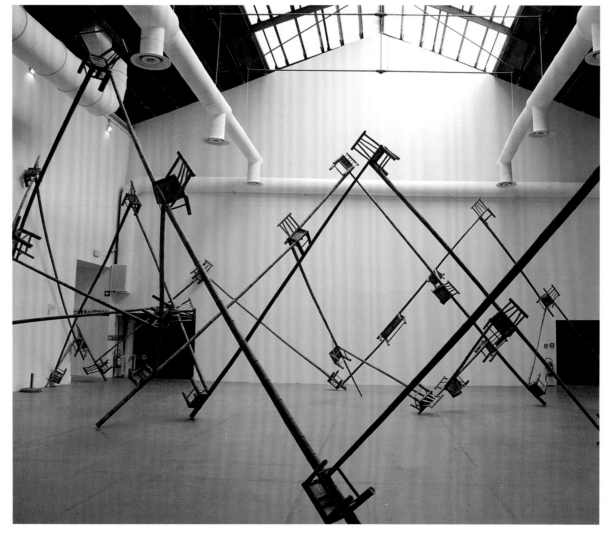

Fig. 57 (top) Ai Weiwei, **Baby Formula**, 2013. Installation of 1,800 tins of milk powder at the Sheung Wan Civic Centre, Hong Kong

Fig. 58 (left) Ai Weiwei with Jacques Herzog and Pierre de Meuron, **Installation for Venice Biennale**, 2008. Bamboo, 600 x 1,000 x 700 cm

Fig. 59 (opposite) National Stadium, Beijing, 2005–08

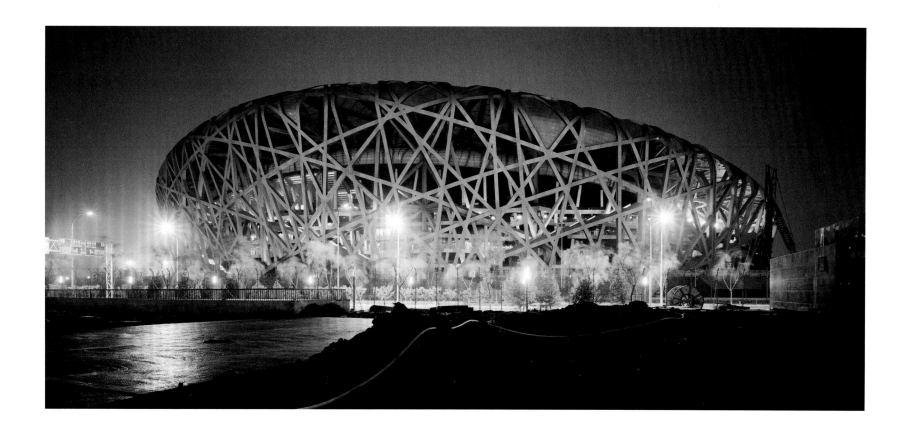

DOING THINGS TOGETHER

JACQUES HERZOG

When Pierre de Meuron and I look back at all the projects that we dreamed up, conceived and, in part, carried out with Ai Weiwei, we have no idea how they would have turned out without this 'combined effort'. Actually, we never really thought about it, nor did we do so during all the years of fruitful exchange with the painter Rémy Zaugg, with whom we also collaborated on many projects.

Our exchange with Weiwei is similar – not in terms of how long it has lasted or the number of projects we worked on, but in terms of the intensity of the time that we all invested. We did not look for this collaborative undertaking. There was no functional or artistic necessity for it – you might say that we found it or invented it. The same goes for the artist: he didn't look for us, he found us. We did not need each other.

It was only through the concrete time we spent together that this 'combined effort' became an indispensable experience for everyone involved. And it still is – including the current exchange with Weiwei for a combined installation in the Drill Hall of the Park Avenue Armory in New York.

Rémy Zaugg died in 2005 – that was a decade ago. For ten years we have no longer been able to meet with him, listen to him or forge ideas with him. He's gone, but he is still alive in us. There are all the shared projects, or rather their physical presence: texts, models and even buildings that everyone can see. But, above all, there's the time we spent together; it changed us and left an indelible stamp. There were times like that with Rémy and with Weiwei. The two artists never met but we always felt a kind of kinship between them. Maybe it was only because they both seduced Pierre and me and, conversely, we seduced them into investing more energy and spending more time with us than could possibly be sensible, economically speaking, in working on a concrete project.

We took endless trips through the French provinces with Rémy Zaugg, visiting dilapidated provincial museums and overly ambitious mayors – and envisioning projects on which we honed our ideas, although they had no prospect of success.

We travelled through the Chinese provinces for days with Ai Weiwei, also meeting with ambitious mayors, for instance in the city of Jinhua where Weiwei's father, the famous poet Ai Qing, was born. There we also forged ideas for big projects and visions of urban planning that would never have taken shape without this 'combined effort' while travelling. That has also left its mark, although our ideas never materialised because the mayor was no longer in office. But later, when Weiwei built his studio in Shanghai, he based it on the principles that the three of us had worked out for Jinhua. Pierre and I visited the almost finished studio with Weiwei shortly before the Chinese authorities had the impressive building demolished. The example of Weiwei's studio clearly showed us how Jinhua could have been a model city for urban planning in China. Everybody who saw the building also realised how exceptionally talented Ai is, not only as an artist but as an architect as well.

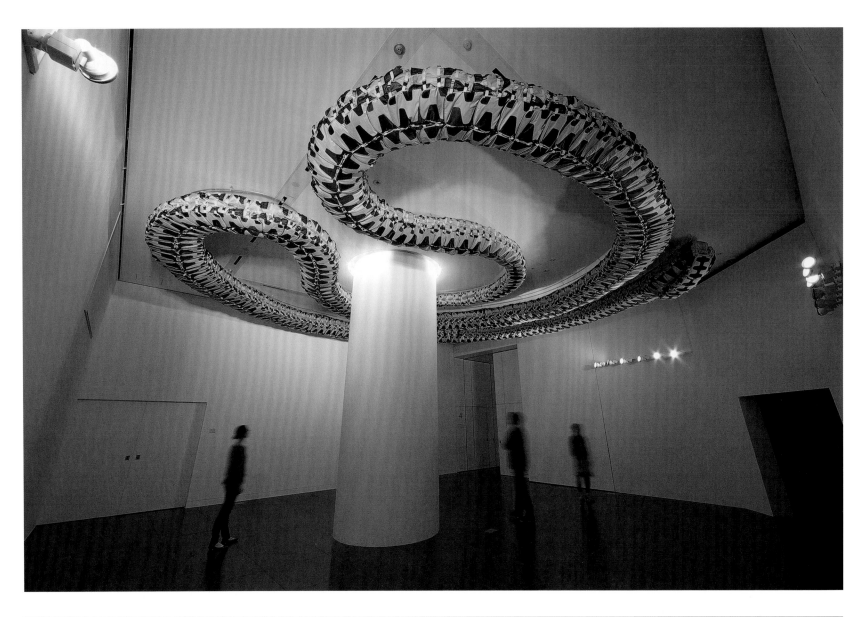

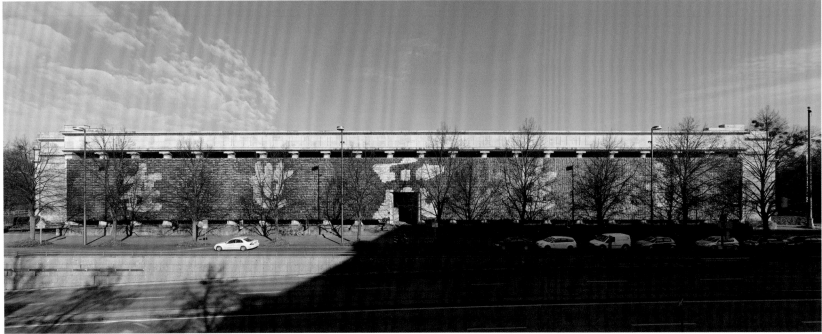

2009

Ai is ranked 43 in *The Art Review* 'Power 100'.

16 May: *Ai Weiwei*, the first monograph on the artist, written by Karen Smith, Hans Ulrich Obrist and Bernard Fibicher, is published by Phaidon Press, London.

29 May: the authorities shut down Ai's blog after he publishes names of casualties of the Sichuan earthquake, along with articles documenting the citizens' investigation into the disaster.

July: the exhibition 'Ai Weiwei: According to What?' is curated by Mami Kataoka at the Mori Art Museum, Tokyo (fig. 60).

12 August: Ai agrees to testify for the defence in the trial (at the Intermediate People's Court in Chengdu, Sichuan province) of Tan Zuoren, the activist who, with Xie Yuhui, formed the Citizens' Independent Investigative Report that investigated the collapse of school buildings during the Sichuan earthquake and published the findings online. Ai is attacked in his hotel room and prevented from testifying.

Fig. 60 (opposite, above) Ai Weiwei, **Snake Ceiling**, 2009. Installation at the Mori Art Museum, Tokyo. Courtesy Mori Art Museum, Tokyo

Fig. 61 (opposite, below) Ai Weiwei, **Remembering**, 2009, installation on the façade of the Haus der Kunst, Munich. Courtesy Ai Weiwei Studio. Detail of fig. 61 overleaf: photograph by Jens Weber, Munich

Fig. 62 (below) Ai Weiwei and Zuoxiao Zuzhou in an elevator as the police take them into custody, Chengdu, Sichuan province, 2009

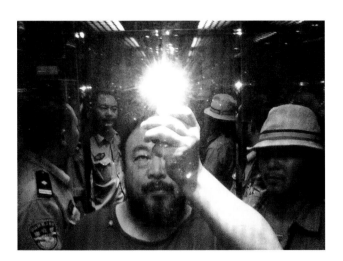

14 September: having travelled to Munich for the installation of the exhibition 'So Sorry', curated by Chris Dercon at the Haus der Kunst, Munich (fig. 61), Ai is hospitalised and has an emergency operation for a brain haemorrhage, an event he commemorates in *Brain Inflation* (2009; fig. 63).

October: Ai, Fan Di'an and Luc Tuymans curate 'The State of Things. Brussels/Beijing', at the Palais des Beaux-Arts (BOZAR), Brussels, and the National Art Museum of China, Beijing.

December: the site-specific installation 'Ai Weiwei. With Milk ___ find something everybody can use' is curated by Xavier Costa as part of the 'Pavilion Intervention' series at Mies van der Rohe's Barcelona Pavilion.

2010

Ai is ranked 13 in *The Art Review* 'Power 100'.

May: Ai collaborates with Vito Acconci on the installation *Acconci Studio + Ai Weiwei: A Collaborative Project*, for Para Site, Hong Kong.

September: he receives Das Glas der Vernunft (The Prism of Reason), the Kassel Citizen Award.

September: he exhibits *Circle of Animals* in 'There Is Always a Cup of Sea to Sail In' at the 29th Bienal de São Paulo, curated by Moacir dos Anjos and Agnaldo Farias, at the Parque Ibirapuera, São Paulo.

October: Ai's *Sunflower Seeds* is shown at Tate Modern, London, curated by Juliet Bingham, as part of the Unilever Turbine Hall Commissions (fig. 9).

October: the municipal government of Shanghai declares that Ai's studio in Malu Town, Jiading District, has been built without the requisite planning permission and condemns it. Ai invites the public via the internet to a party to celebrate the demolition of the studio.

5 November: Ai is placed under house arrest in Beijing in order to prevent him from attending the demolition celebration. At the party on 7 November the guests feast on river crabs. Over 1,000 people attend the event, which Ai commemorates in the video work *The Crab House* (2015; cat. 17).

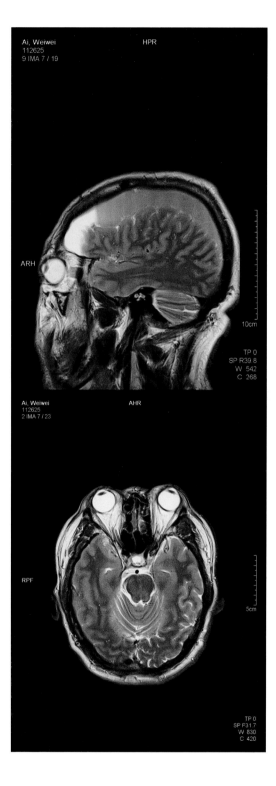

Fig. 63 (above) Ai Weiwei, **Brain Inflation**, 2009. Poster of MRI image showing Ai's cerebral haemorrhage, 200 x 100 cm

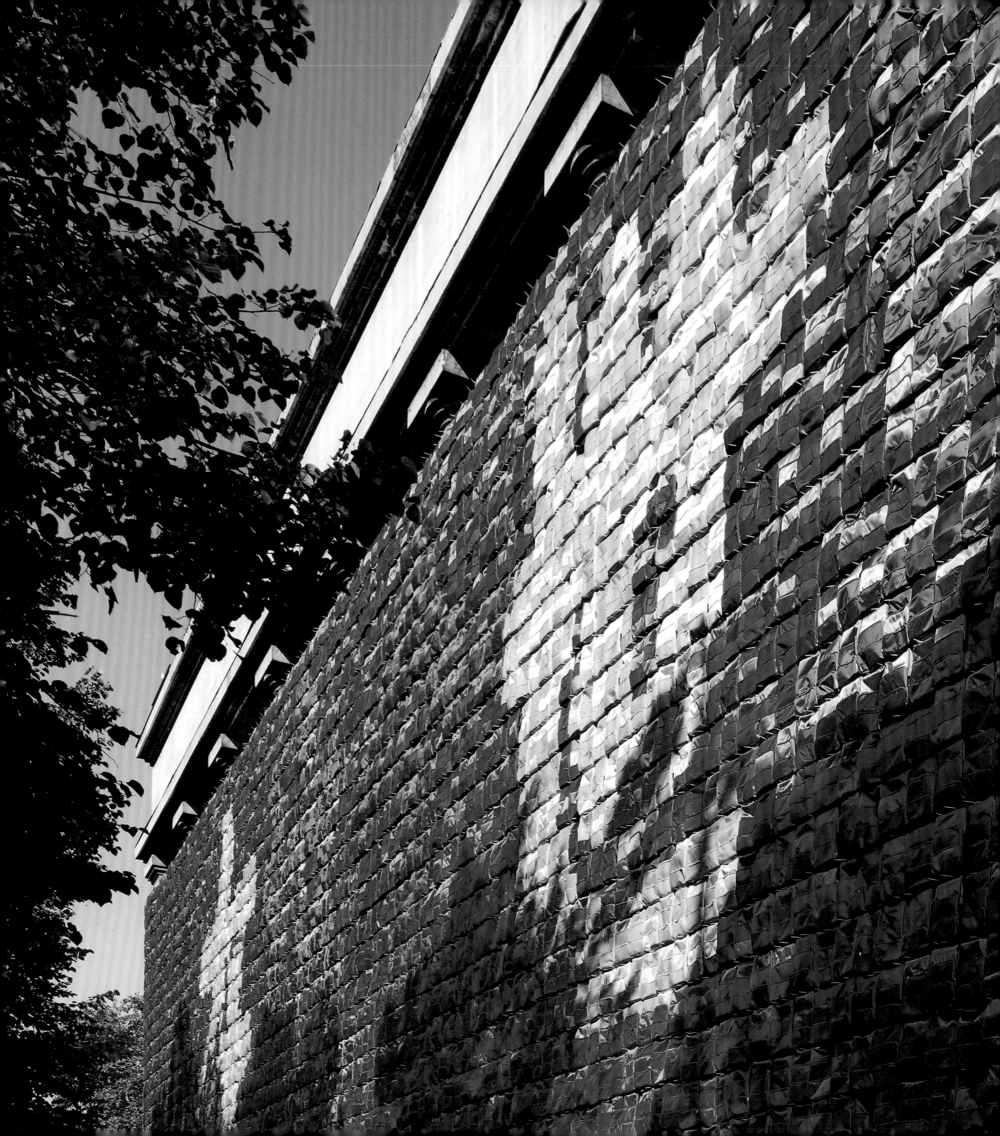

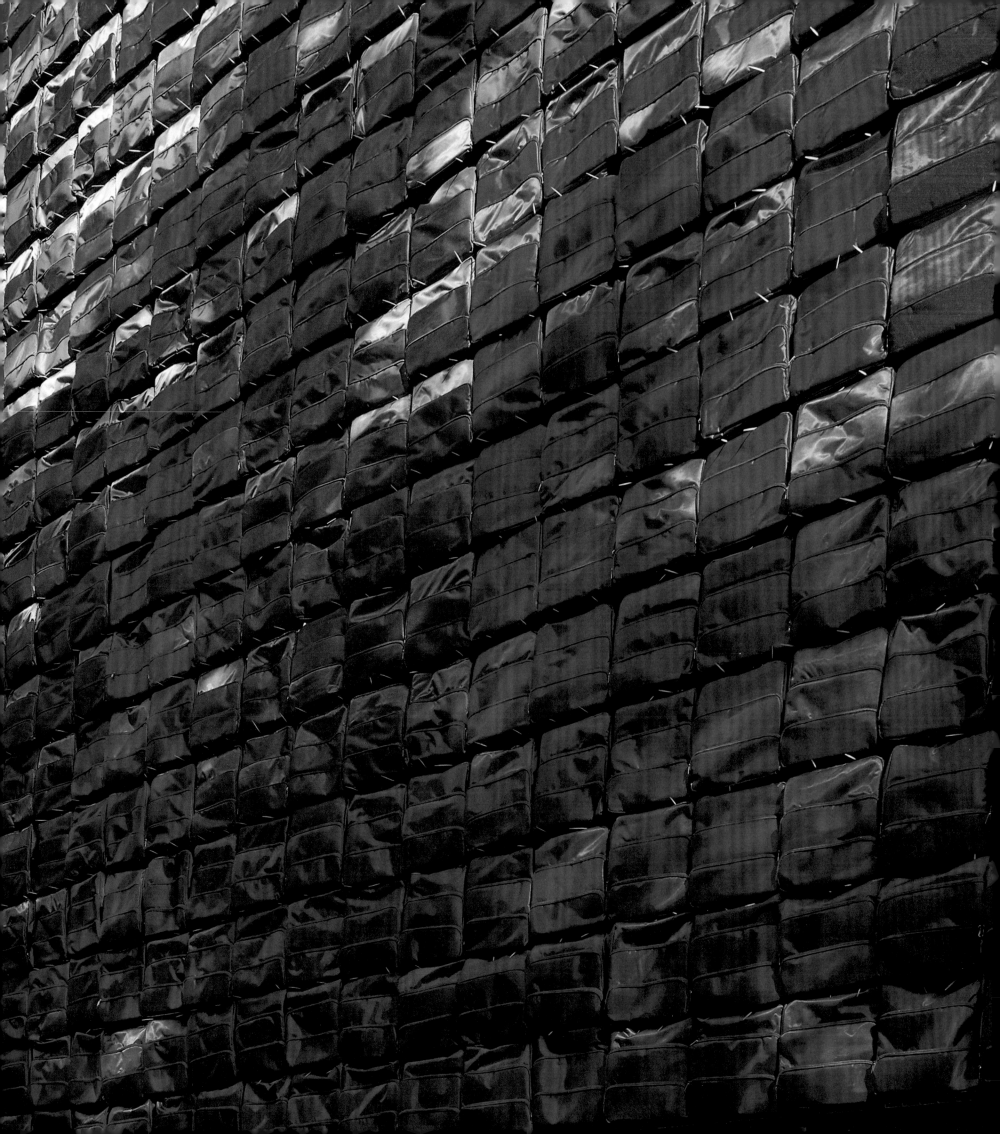

2011

Ai is ranked 1 in *The Art Review* 'Power 100' and named runner-up *TIME* Person of the Year.

January: 'Ai Weiwei: New York Photographs 1983–1993', curated by RongRong and inri, is shown at the Three Shadows Photography Art Centre at Caochangdi, Beijing, and the Asia Society, New York.

11 January: the municipal government of Shanghai demolishes Ai's studio in Malu Town, Jiading District.

March: *Ai Weiwei's Blog: Writings, Interviews and Digital Rants, 2006–2009*, edited by Lee Ambrozy, is published by MIT Press, Cambridge, MA.

3 April: Ai is arrested at Beijing Airport as he waits to board a flight to Taipei, where he is working on an exhibition. He is secretly detained for 81 days, kept in solitary confinement in a small padded cell accompanied at all times by two guards who are forbidden to speak to him.

20 April: Ai is appointed Visiting Professor of the Berlin University of the Arts.

Fig. 64 (below, left) Cover of *Dazed & Confused*, 2011. Photograph by Gao Yuan

Fig. 65 (below, right) Ai Weiwei, **Circle of Animals/Zodiac Heads**, 2012. Installation in the Edmond J. Safra Fountain Court, Somerset House, London, 2012

May: Ai is elected a member of the Akademie der Künste, Berlin.

21 May: during Ai's detention, the authorities accuse him of tax evasion through his company Fake Cultural Development Ltd, imposing back-taxes and fines totalling nearly £1.5 million to be paid within fifteen days. Following his release Ai contests the charges but is forbidden to appeal them. Public donations flood in to help him pay the fines; within ten days over £700,000 is raised. Committed to repaying these individuals, Ai produces a promissory note for each donation.

26 May: Ai is elected an Honorary Royal Academician by the Royal Academy of Arts, London.

22 June: Ai is released from detention but is kept under house arrest and prohibited from leaving Beijing for twelve months.

September: Ai is co-director, with Seung H-Sang, of the 4th Gwangju Design Biennale, 'Design Is Design Is Not Design'.

October: 'Dropping the Urn: Ceramic Works by Ai Weiwei' is inaugurated at the Victoria and Albert Museum, London. The exhibition is curated by Richard Torchia and Gregg Moore. It later travels to Arcadia University Art Gallery, Philadelphia; the Knoxville Museum of Art; and the Museum of Contemporary Craft, Portland.

October: 'Ai Weiwei: Absent', Ai's first exhibition in the Chinese-speaking world, takes place at the Taipei Fine Arts Museum.

November: the exhibition 'Ai Weiwei', curated by Anders Kold, opens at the Museum of Modern Art, Louisiana, Denmark, and then moves to the De Pont Museum of Contemporary Art, Tilburg, where it is curated by Hendrik Driessen.

2012

January: *Ai Weiwei: Never Sorry*, a documentary by the American filmmaker Alison Klayman (fig. 68), premieres at the Sundance Film Festival, Utah, and receives the Special Jury Prize for Spirit of Defiance.

9 February: Ai is elected an Honorary Fellow of the Royal Institute of British Architects, London.

3 April: *WeiweiCam*, a 24-hour online self-surveillance project of Ai's house and studio goes live. It is shut down by the authorities after 46 hours.

24 April: Ai is elected a Foreign Member of the Royal Swedish Academy of Arts, Stockholm, an event that coincides with the exhibition 'Ai Weiwei', at Magasin III, Stockholm, curated by Tessa Praun.

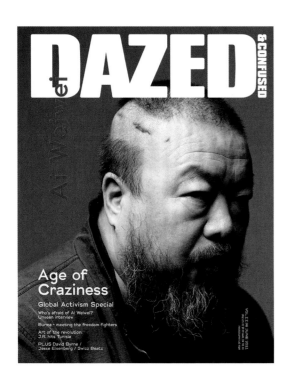

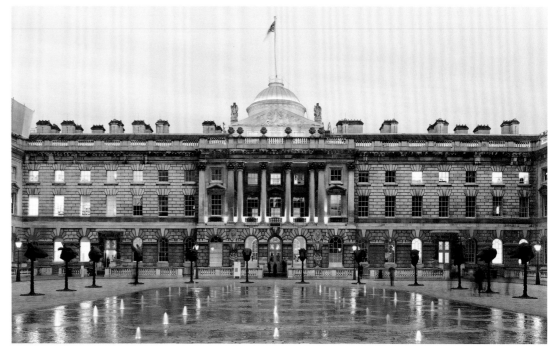

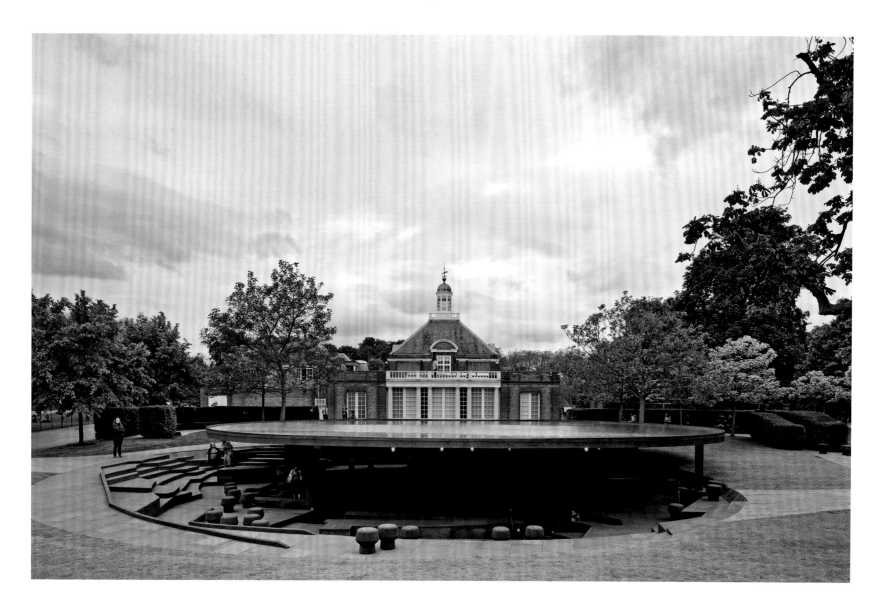

May: *Circle of Animals/Zodiac Heads* is exhibited in the Edmond J. Safra Fountain Court, Somerset House, London (fig. 65). The work has also been shown at Princeton, Mexico City, Chicago, Jackson, Cleveland, Miami, Toronto, Houston, Washington DC, Kiev, Taipei, Los Angeles, New York and São Paulo.

2 May: Ai receives the Cornell Capa Award from the International Center of Photography, New York.

9 May: alongside Aung San Suu Kyi and Manal al-Sharif, Ai receives the inaugural Václav Havel Prize for Creative Dissent from the Human Rights Foundation, New York.

June: Ai collaborates with Herzog & de Meuron on the design of the 12th Serpentine Gallery Pavilion, London (fig. 66).

21 June: Ai's house arrest is lifted.

September: the exhibition 'Art of Change: New Directions from China', curated by Stephanie Rosenthal, takes place at the Hayward Gallery, London.

October: the exhibition 'Ai Weiwei: According to What?', originally shown at the Mori Art Museum in Tokyo in 2009, becomes the first major exhibition of the artist's work in North America when it opens at the Hirshhorn Museum and Sculpture Garden, Washington DC. The show subsequently travels to the Indianapolis Museum of Art, the Art Gallery of Ontario, Toronto, the Pérez Museum of Art, Miami, and the Brooklyn Museum, New York.

18 October: Ai guest-edits the London-based journal the *New Statesman* (fig. 67). The periodical publishes an interview between Ai and the Chinese civil-rights activist Chen Guangcheng entitled 'Facts Have Blood as Evidence'.

Fig. 66 The 12th Serpentine Gallery Pavilion, designed by Herzog & de Meuron with Ai Weiwei, in front of the Serpentine Gallery, London, 2012. Universal Images Group

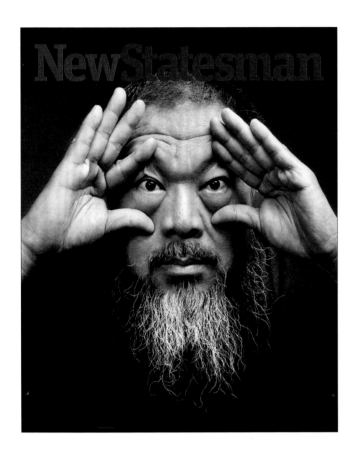
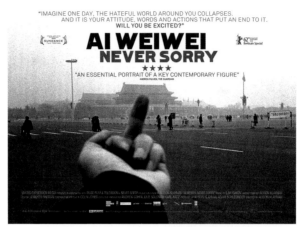
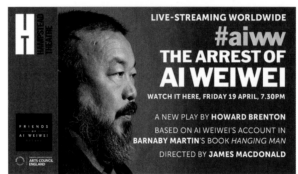
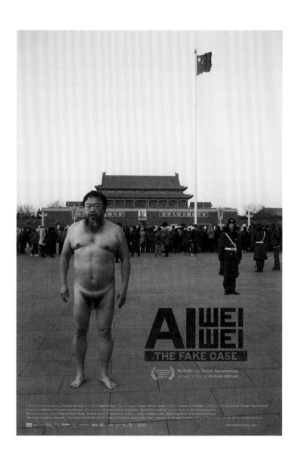

CITIZEN ARTIST

ANISH KAPOOR

The Citizen Artist is a condition thrown on us by the vagaries of our historical time and place. Weiwei has been unafraid to see this as a mission, a life's work. Many of us post-colonial artists have spent the last thirty years resisting the form given to artists from outside the western village.

We have shouted NO to the definition of art by origin.

NO to art labelled by ethnicity.

NO to the misjudgements of globalisation.

Yet Weiwei accepts that his is a Chinese art made and to be understood in a Chinese context.

The Citizen Artist has a conscience.

His is no mere agitprop; this is not the registering of an angry protest.

At its best, it is the recording of injustice. It is the acknowledgement that politics has aesthetic dimensions.

It is the declaration that shame is linked to beauty and that beauty and shame are both imminent.

Political rights have always been promised to us as something to be aspired to in the future.

Rights will come.

Freedom will be.

Ever forward.

Always to be.

Beauty in the future is never believable.

Beauty now.

All this puts the aesthetics of politics in a difficult place and we see that a good work of art must promote more than hope. Can a good work of art automatically claim ethical certainty or is it that ethics are imposed from outside?

Is a work of art morally innocent?

Intention is all in the act of art.

The Citizen Artist carries the burden of a conscience.

His art cannot run free in invention. He is always reminded of the politics of oppression and he must fear that should he be successful and politics change, his art will lose.

Weiwei is a courageous man. We danced Gangnam together in protest and in celebration. With two fingers to the politics of exclusion.

Citizen Artist do your work, I stand by your side.

Fig. 67 (opposite, left) Cover of *New Statesman*, 22 October 2012. Photograph by Gao Yuan for Ai Weiwei Studio

Fig. 68 (opposite, centre, top) **Ai Weiwei: Never Sorry**, 2012. Documentary film by Alison Klayman, poster by Artificial Eye. Collection of Larry Warsh

Fig. 69 (opposite, centre, below) **#aiww: The Arrest of Ai Weiwei**. Announcement of the live streaming of the play on 19 April 2013. Hampstead Theatre Collection

Fig. 70 (opposite, right) **Ai Weiwei: The Fake Case**, 2013. Documentary film by Andreas Johnsen. Denmark, International Film Circuit distribution

Fig. 71 (right) Ai Weiwei, **Forever**, 2013. 1,179 Forever bicycle frames, h. 10 m. Installation at the 55th Venice Biennale, 2013

Fig. 72 (right, below) Ai Weiwei, **Ye Haiyan's Belongings**, 2013. Installation at 'Ai Weiwei: According to What?', at the Brooklyn Museum of Art, New York

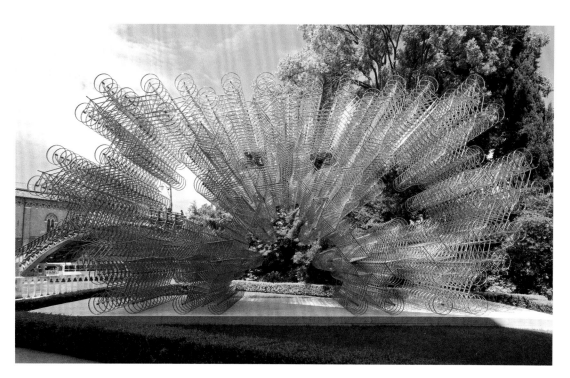

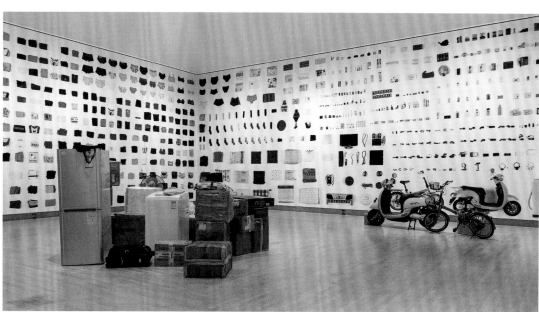

2013

11 April: *#aiww: The Arrest of Ai Weiwei* by the British playwright Howard Brenton (fig. 69) opens at the Hampstead Theatre, London.

May: the exhibition 'Fuck Off 2', curated by Ai, Feng Boyi and Mark Wilson, takes place at the Groninger Museum, Groningen.

May: Ai's *S.A.C.R.E.D.* (2012; cat. 43) is installed at the Chiesa di Sant'Antonin, Venice, in a parallel event to the 55th International Art Exhibition (Venice Biennale). *S.A.C.R.E.D.* is curated by Maurizio Bortolotti, as is an exhibition of Ai's new work at the Zuecca Project Space (fig. 71). Since his secret detention in 2011, Ai has been denied a passport by the Chinese authorities. In Ai's absence, his mother, Gao Ying, opens the exhibition.

16 May: Ai's response to the Sanlu baby-milk formula scandal, *Baby Formula* (2013; fig. 57), is included in 'A Journal of the Plague Year. Fear, Ghosts, Rebels. SARS, Leslie and the Hong Kong Story', curated by Cosmin Costinas and Inti Guerrero for Para Site, Hong Kong. As part of the exhibition, Ai's work is shown at the Sheung Wan Civic Centre Exhibition Hall in Hong Kong and then at Michael Janssen Gallery, Singapore.

21 May: Ai releases the music single and video 'Dumbass', a collaboration with the musician and artist Zuoxiao Zuzhou. An album, 'Divine Comedy', follows in June.

June: Ai participates in 'The Encyclopedic Palace', the 55th International Art Exhibition (Venice Biennale), curated by Massimiliano Gioni, Venice, presenting the installation *Bang* (2013; fig. 18), curated by Susanne Gaensheimer for the German Pavilion but installed in the French Pavilion.

17 June: Ai designs the cover of *TIME* magazine, New York.

September: with Seung H-Sang, Ai designs 'Anything, Something' at the 5th Design Biennale, Gwangju.

September: *Hanging Man: The Arrest of Ai Weiwei*, by the British journalist Barnaby Martin, is published by Faber & Faber, London.

20 November: *Ai Weiwei: The Fake Case*, a documentary by the Danish filmmaker Andreas Johnsen (fig. 70), premieres at the International Documentary Film Festival, Amsterdam.

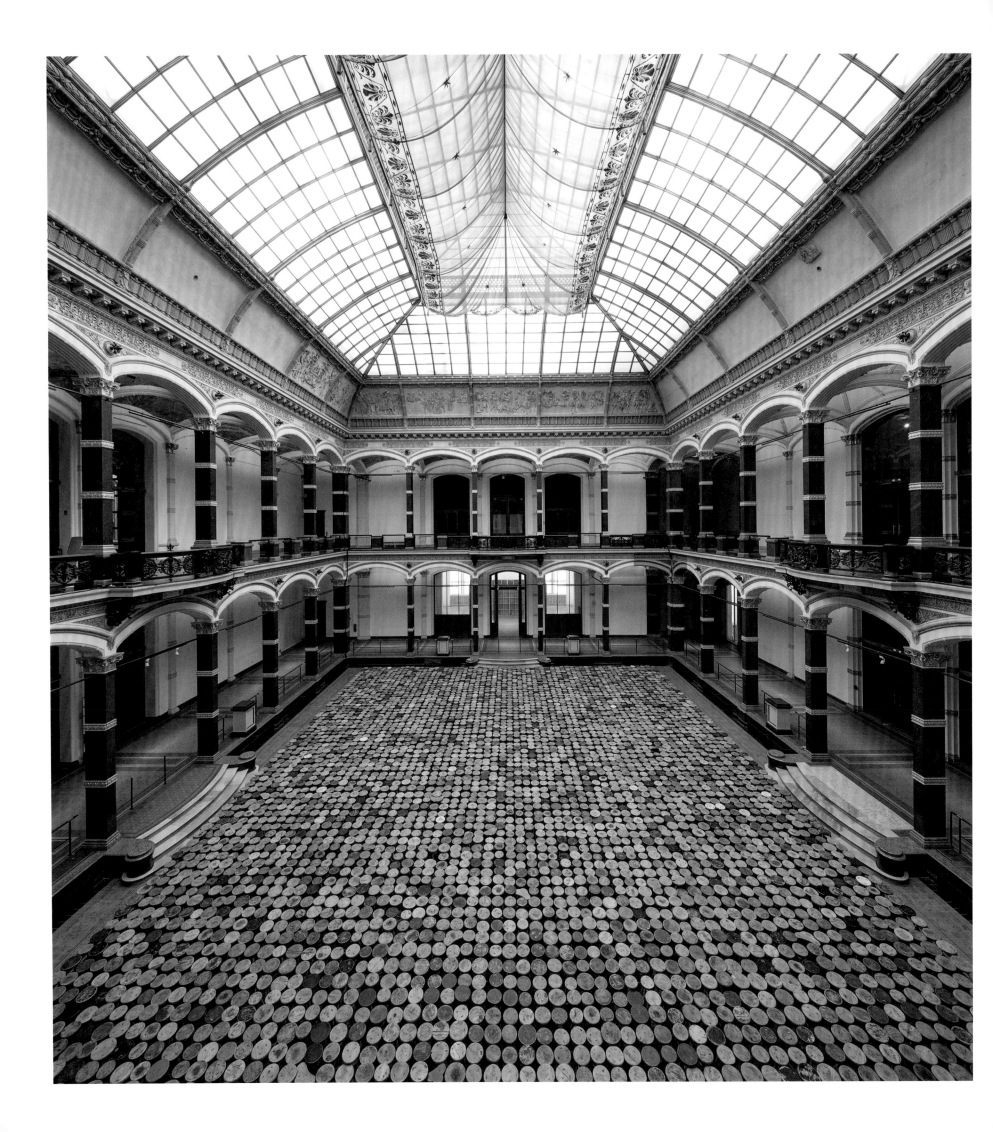

30 November: for the first time, Ai places fresh flowers in the basket of a bicycle outside his studio at Caochangdi, Beijing, as a symbol of defiance, an act he will carry out every day until his passport is returned and he has the freedom to travel outside mainland China (fig. 74).

2014

Ai's name is removed from the Chinese-language edition of *The Art Book*, published by Phaidon Press; he is replaced by the Italian Renaissance sculptor Agostino di Duccio (cat. 40).

March: Ai participates in 'Open Borders/ Crossroads Vancouver', the 3rd Vancouver International Sculpture Biennale, directed by Barrie Mowatt.

April: 'Ai Weiwei: Evidence', curated by Gereon Sievernich, takes place at the Martin-Gropius-Bau, Berlin (fig. 73).

May: the exhibition 'Ai Weiwei' is curated by Claire Lilley in the Chapel courtyard at the Yorkshire Sculpture Park, West Bretton (fig. 75).

May: Ai's name is omitted in the press release for the exhibition 'Hans van Dijk: 5,000 Names' at the Ullens Center for Contemporary Art, Beijing, commemorating the Dutch-born and Beijing-based curator Hans van Dijk, who died in 2002. The exhibition is curated by Marianne Brouwer with Philip Tinari and Defne Ayas.

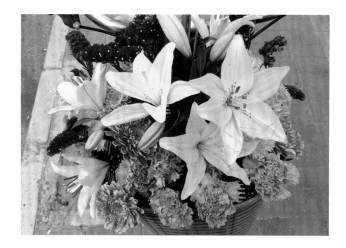

Fig. 73 Ai Weiwei, **Stools**, 2013. 6,000 antique stools, dimensions variable. Installation at Martin-Gropius-Bau, Berlin, 2014

Fig. 74 Flowers in the basket of the bicycle outside Ai's studio-house at Caochangdi, Beijing, 2013

Fig. 75 (overleaf) Ai Weiwei, **Iron Tree**, 2013. Iron, 628 x 710 x 710 cm. Chapel courtyard of the Yorkshire Sculpture Park, West Bretton

AI WEIWEI IN CHINA

CUI CANCAN

In May 2014 I witnessed Ai Weiwei's removal of his works from the exhibition 'Hans van Dijk: 5,000 Names', at the Ullens Center for Contemporary Art in Beijing. The incident occurred immediately before the opening; in fear of potential political reprisals, UCCA had self-censored its exhibition newsletter and omitted Ai's name from the list of participating artists. Ai refused to accept such enforced censorship of his shared memories with the curator Hans van Dijk, believing that the presence or absence of individuals and their works should not be determined by political views and values. His removal of his works was a protest against the long-standing and cosy acquiescence that existed between UCCA and the Chinese censors.

This incident was no aberration or one-off. The previous month, at '15 Years Chinese Contemporary Art Award (CCAA)' at the Power Station of Art in Shanghai, despite the fact that Ai had himself been both a judge and a winner of the award, the Shanghai authorities issued an order that prohibited the exhibition of his works. Without raising any protest or expressing any doubts about this, all the artists Ai had nominated for the award accepted the censors' decision and left Ai to face his political predicament alone.

Since his detention in 2011, Ai has become a politically sensitive figure in China. He still cannot travel overseas, his passport having been confiscated by the Chinese government; until this year his works have not been shown in exhibitions in mainland China and all mention and discussion of his circumstances have been banned from the Chinese media. Ai has been a non-existent person in Chinese society. Facing omnipresent censorship and constraints, he nevertheless perseveres in his quest to ask the fundamental questions that China faces, attempting to draw attention to and improve individual people's circumstances. Here in China, Ai has combined the purpose and form of his works with the reality of his own situation.

Communication is a fundamental element of art. If a work receives wide attention and circulation, it can, perhaps, be considered a meaningful and good piece, though what it communicates is another complicated issue. Even when an exhibition is well curated and presented, facing censors' revisions, an artist's withdrawal from participation in order to insist on their belief in freedom of speech can be a powerful method of communication.

Through his actions and deeds, Ai has turned his protests into a substantial part of reality, and thus his life experiences lead his art. Although he doesn't know in which direction this route will lead him, it is clear that no matter his destination, he will never abandon or avoid the reality he faces, and his existence will always be connected to his communication with us. When his art reaches a wide audience, no matter how much he sacrifices, his attitude and his views certainly benefit the public and Chinese society and beyond, as he uses art to express his unapologetic character and to establish the modern and free context for expression that China has never embraced.

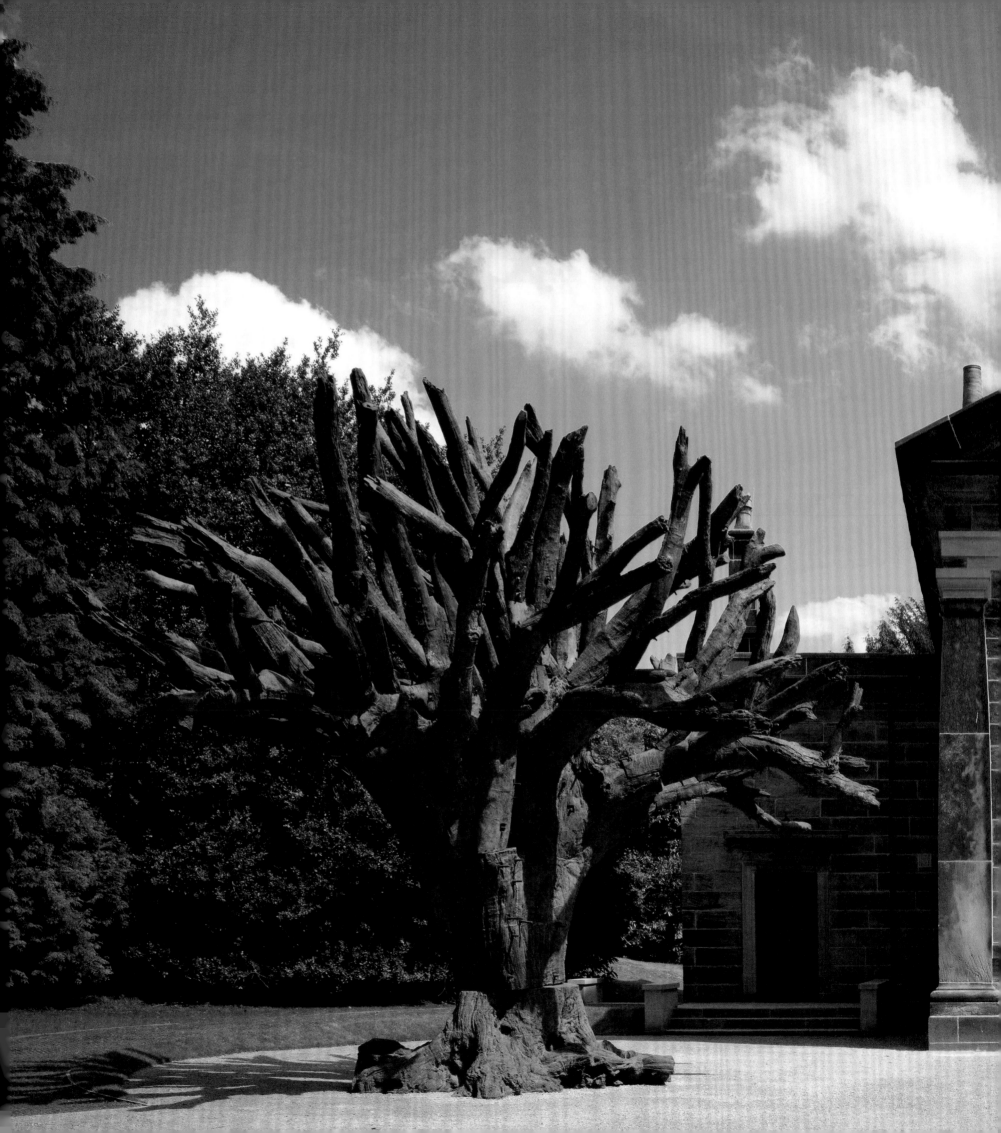

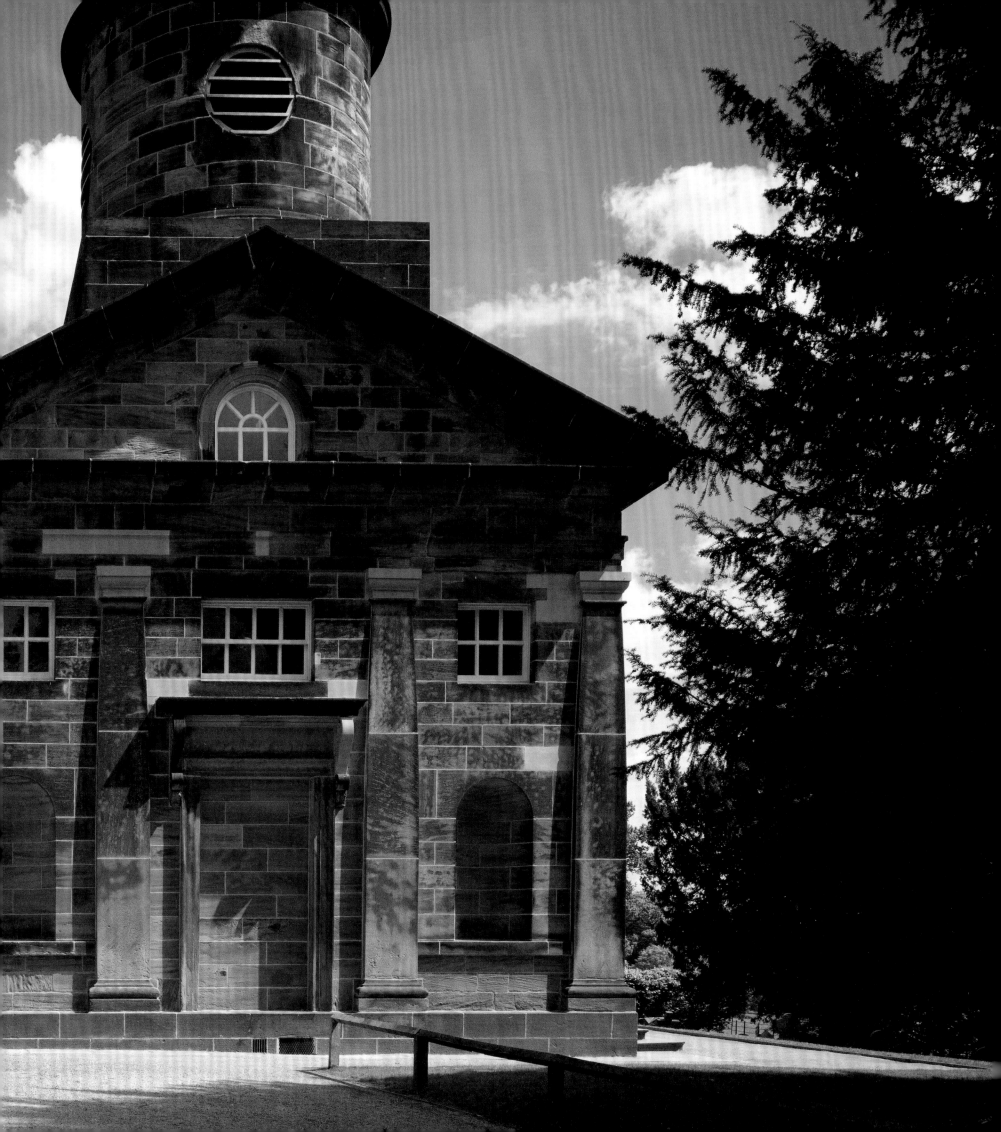

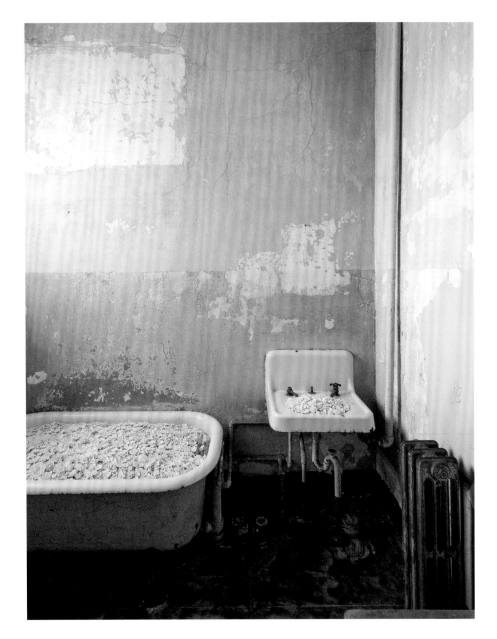

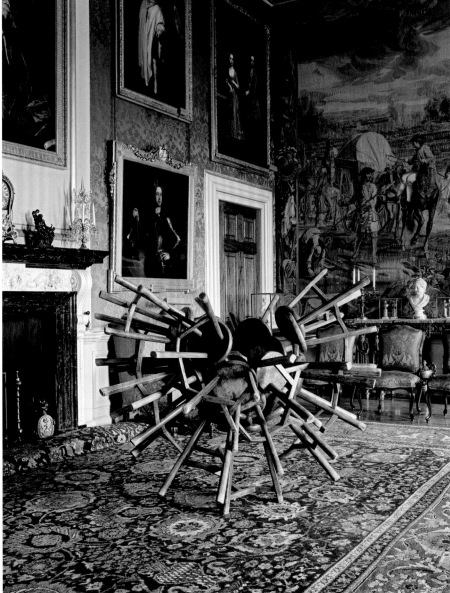

June: *Ai Weiwei*, a large-format monograph edited by Hans Werner Holzwarth, is published by Taschen, Cologne. The book is available in two limited editions: nos 1–100, signed by Ai, are wrapped in a silk scarf and come with a marble stand designed by the artist, and nos 101–1,000 are wrapped in a silk scarf.

July: Ai's name is removed from the exhibition '15 Years China Contemporary Art Award', curated by Li Xianting, Liu Lili, Li Zhenhua and Lars Nittve at the Power Station of Art, Shanghai.

July: 'Ai Weiwei, To Be Found', curated by Sebastian Cichocki, takes place as the sixth edition of the Bródno Sculpture Park, Warsaw.

August: 'Leeum 10th Anniversary Exhibition: Beyond and Between', curated by Hyesoo Woo, at the Samsung Museum of Art, Seoul, features Ai's installation *Tree*.

September: '@Large: Ai Weiwei on Alcatraz', curated by Cheryl Haines, takes place on the former penitentiary island of Alcatraz in San Francisco Bay (fig. 76).

October: 'Ai Weiwei at Blenheim Palace', curated by Michael Frahm, takes place at the ancestral home of the Duke and Duchess of Marlborough, Woodstock, Oxfordshire (fig. 77). The exhibition includes *Circle of Animals/Zodiac Heads: Gold*, previously exhibited at San Diego, Montreal, East Hampton, Dallas, Moscow, Berlin, Palm Springs and Skovvej.

Fig. 76 (above, left) Ai Weiwei, **Blossom**, 2014. Installation detail at Alcatraz Hospital

Fig. 77 (above, right) Ai Weiwei, **Grapes**, 2011. 27 antique stools from the Qing Dynasty (1644–1911), 167 x 174 x 140 cm. Installation at Blenheim Palace, Woodstock

November: Ai curates 'Everything Is Under Control' at the Copenhagen International Documentary Film Festival, Copenhagen.

November: 'Ai Weiwei: On the Table' is curated by Rosa Pera at the Palacio de la Virreina, Barcelona.

2015

April: Ai and Jacob Appelbaum, the American independent computer security researcher and hacker, collaborate on an artwork for Rhizome's Seven on Seven Conference, 'Empathy and Disguise', which takes place on 2 May at the New Museum, New York.

May: Ai participates in 'All the World's Futures', the 56th International Art Exhibition (Venice Biennale), curated by Okwui Enwezor, for the Iraq Pavilion.

May: Ai participates in 'Go East: The Gene and Brian Sherman Contemporary Asian Art Collection', curated by Suhanya Raffel, at the Art Gallery of New South Wales.

May: Ai shares the Amnesty International Ambassador of Conscience Award with the American singer-songwriter and civil-rights activist Joan Baez.

June: Ai's installation *Think Different (How to Hang Workers' Uniforms)* is included in the fifth OpenArt Biennial in Örebro, curated by Feng Boyi and Lars Johnson.

6 June: 'Ai Weiwei', curated by Cui Cancan, opens at Galleria Continua, Beijing, in co-ordination with Tang Contemporary Art Center.

July: *Still Life* (1993–2000; fig. 13) is included in 'Four Decades of Chinese Art', curated by M+ at the Whitworth Art Gallery, Manchester.

22 July: the Chinese authorities return Ai's passport (figs 78, 79).

September: Ai participates in 'Une Brève histoire de l'avenir', an intervention in the galleries of the Musée du Louvre, Paris, curated by Jean de Loisy and based on the 2006 book of the same title by Jacques Attali.

September: 'Ai Weiwei', curated by Erja Pusa and Heli Harni, opens at the Helsinki Art Museum.

September: *Forever*, one of Ai's bicycle sculptures, is exhibited in the City of London, part of the fifth 'Sculpture in the City' event.

Fig. 78 (below, left) Ai with his returned passport, 22 July 2015

Fig. 79 (below, right) The bicycle outside Ai's studio-house, without flowers, following the return of his passport

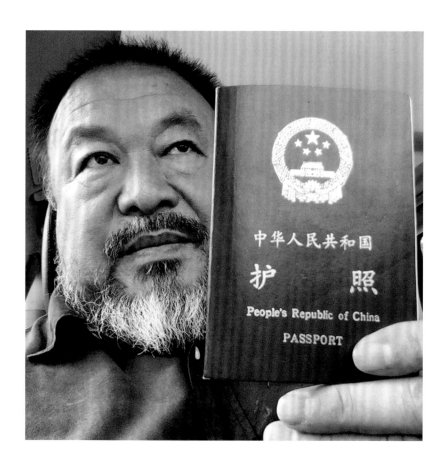

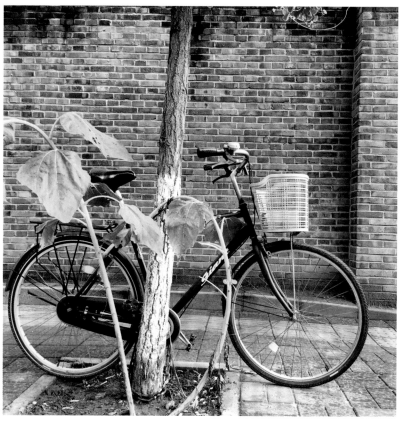

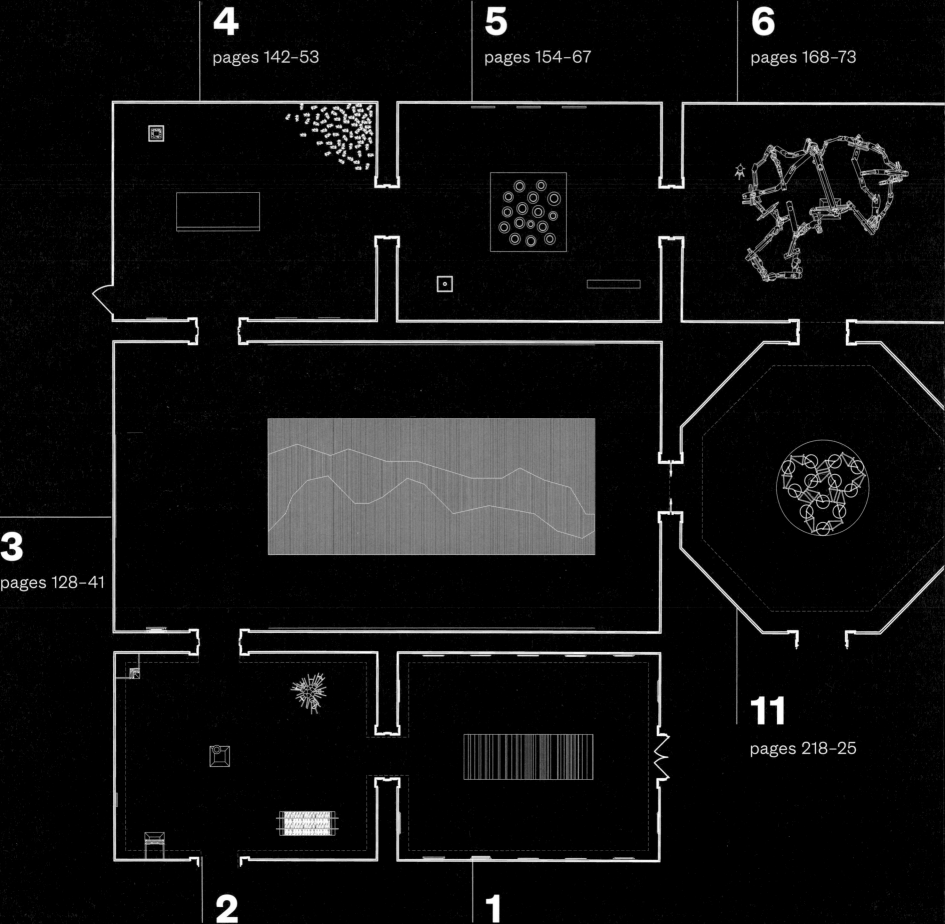

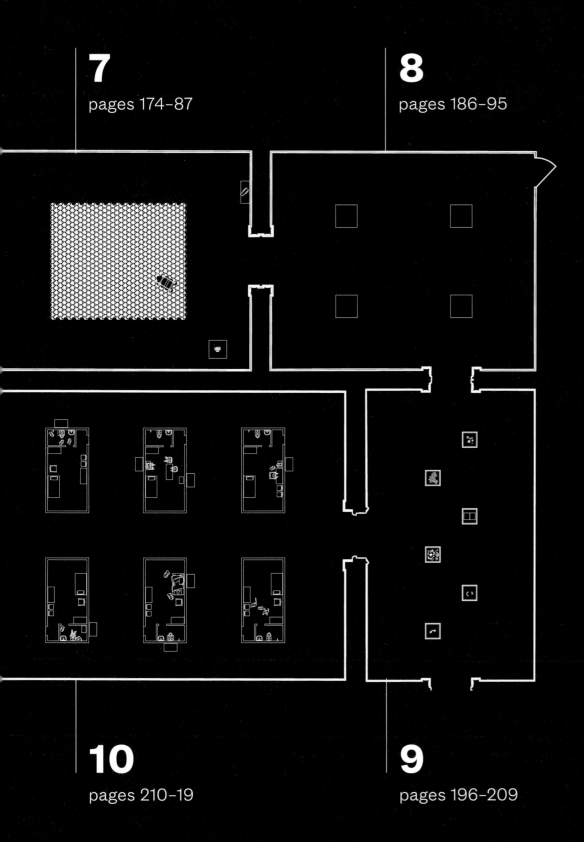

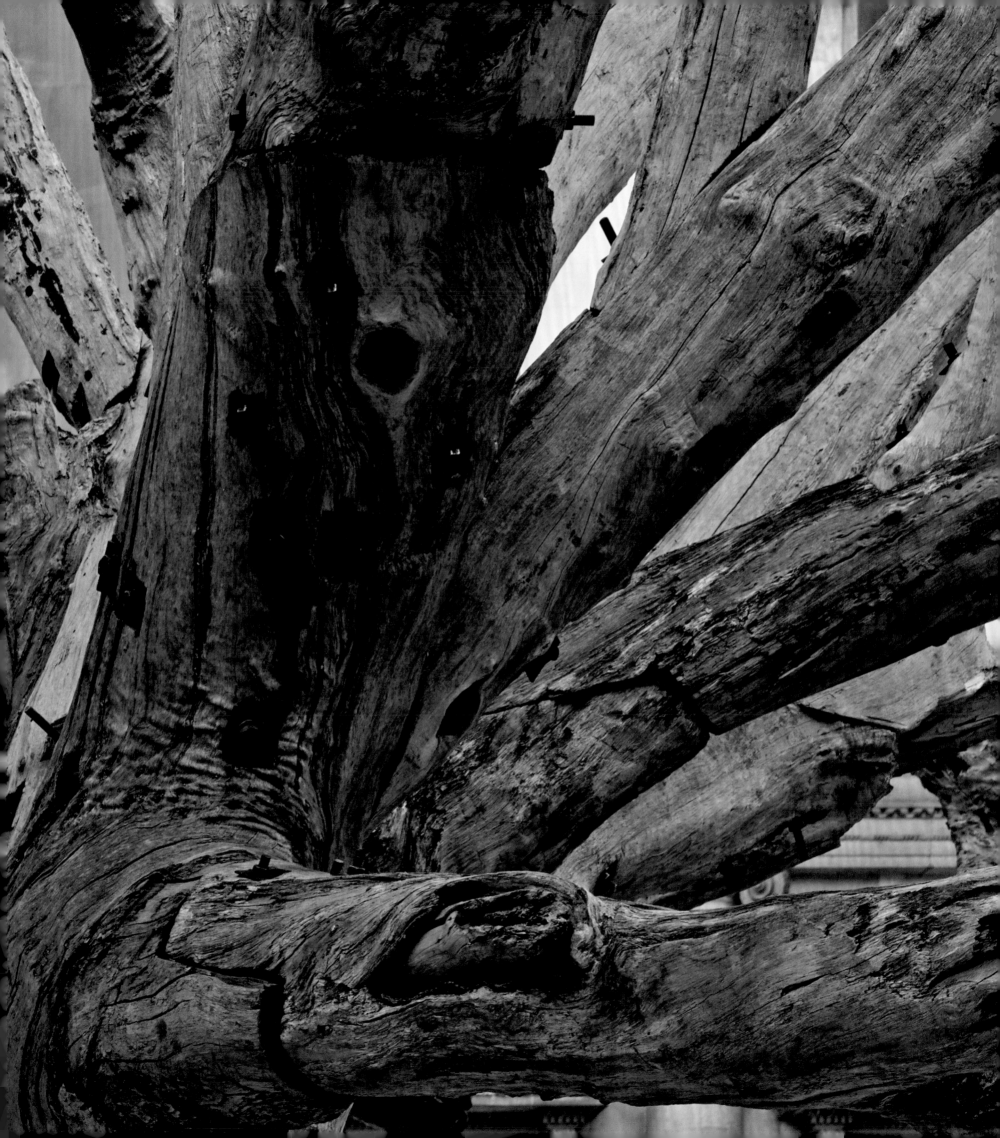

ANNENBERG COURTYARD

Ai Weiwei began his ongoing series *Tree* in 2009; the eight-part work in the Royal Academy's Annenberg Courtyard is the largest to date. In order to create each element, Ai purchases parts of dead trees, collected on the mountains of southern China and sold in the markets of Jingdezhen, Jiangxi province, and has them transported to his studio in Beijing. During a process lasting several months, these disparate parts – whether root, trunk or branch – are painstakingly pieced together by skilled carpenters using traditional hidden mortise-and-tenon joints to create 'complete' trees. As Ai says, 'It's just like trying to imagine what the tree looked like.' Industrial steel nuts and bolts are then added to reinforce the structure, apparently rendering these wooden joints superfluous, and provoking an uncomfortable tension between the visible and the invisible, the refined and the unrefined. These artificial constructions have been interpreted as a commentary on the Chinese nation, in which geographically and culturally diverse peoples have been brought together to form 'One China' in a state-sponsored policy aimed at protecting and promoting China's sovereignty and territorial integrity.

The marble couch placed within the grove of trees recalls the sculpture of Chairman Mao seated in an armchair that occupies the antechamber of his mausoleum in Tiananmen Square, Beijing. They also reference the Ming Dynasty (1368–1644) vogue for fashioning commonplace objects from luxurious materials, which resulted in items that served no practical use, but emphasised the wealth and power of the rulers of Imperial China.

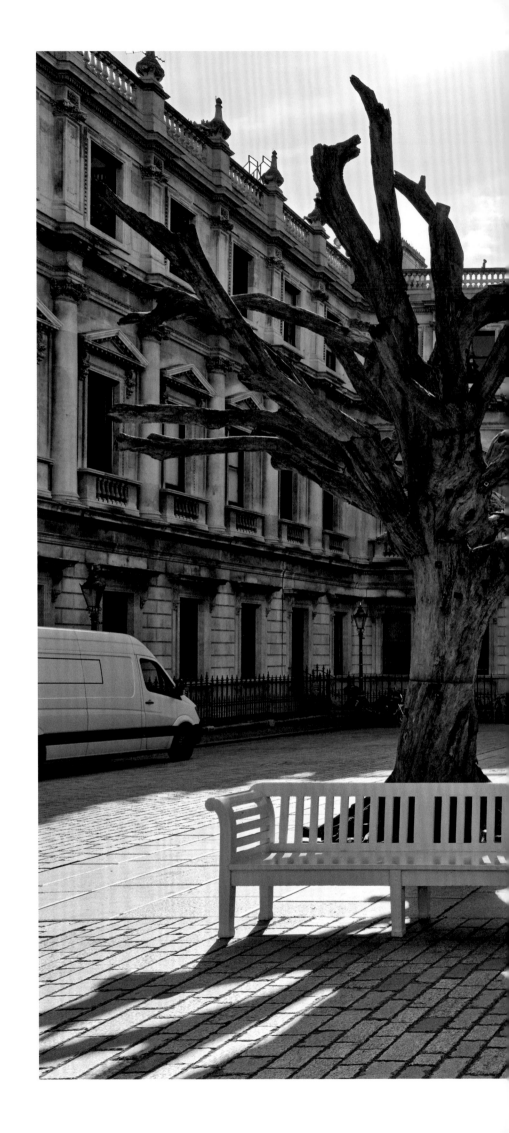

1

Tree, 2009–10, 2015

Tree sections and steel, dimensions variable

Courtesy of Ai Weiwei Studio

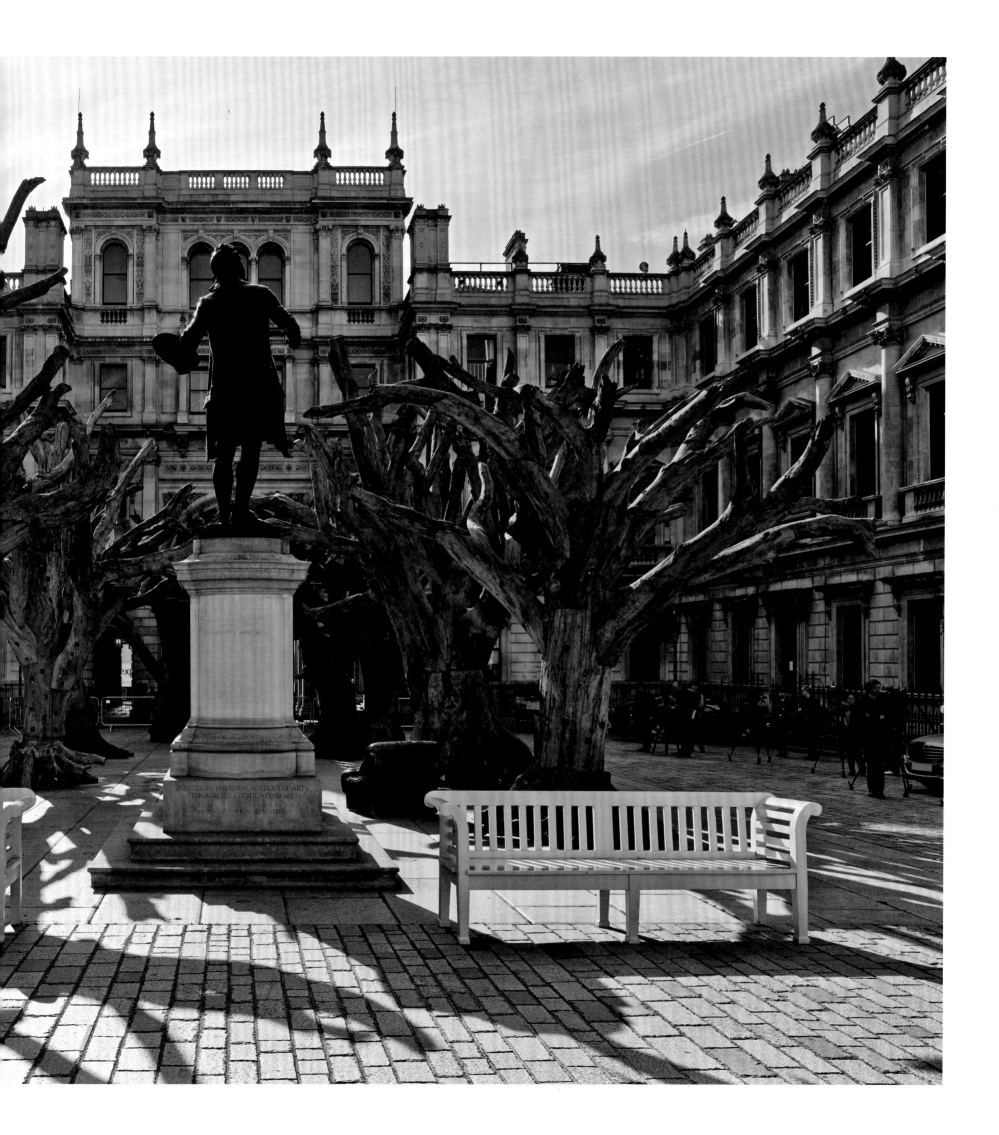

ERECTED BY THE ROYAL ACADEMY OF ARTS
THROUGH THE LEIGHTON FUND 1931

2

Marble Couch, 2011

Marble, 95 x 92 x 85 cm

Courtesy of Ai Weiwei Studio

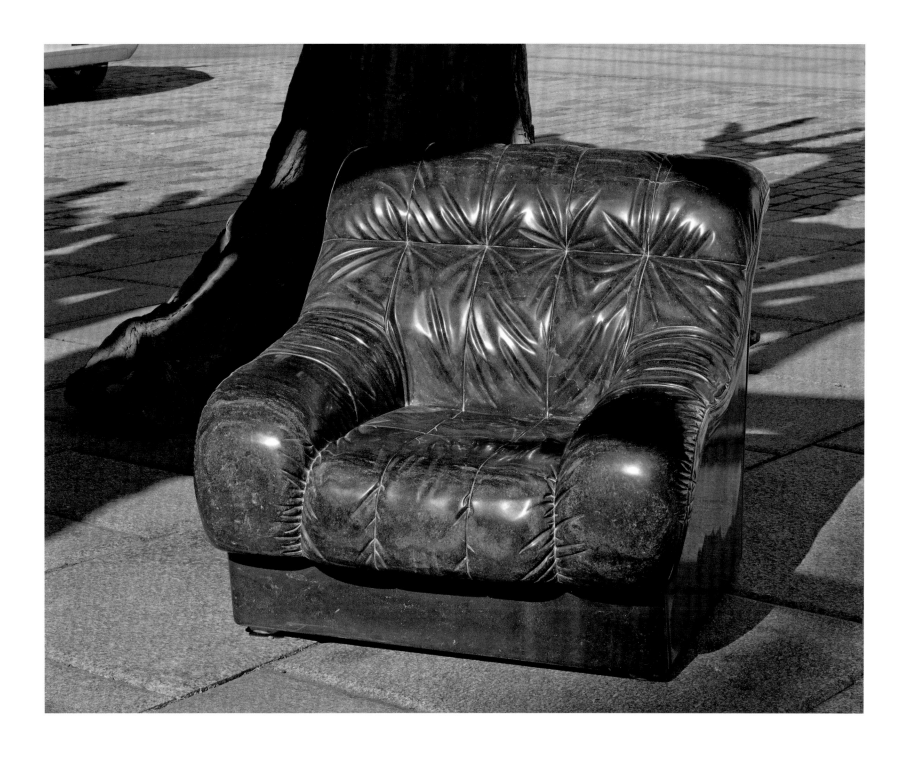

1

In Imperial China, the hardwood tieli (*Mesua ferrea*) – commonly known as iron wood for its hardness and durability – was favoured for the construction of timber-framed buildings and furniture. On his return to China in 1993 Ai began purchasing reclaimed tieli timbers from temples of the Qing Dynasty (1644–1911) that were being dismantled to make way for the rapid development and expansion of the principal cities. Keen to promote traditional methods of carpentry that were fast becoming obsolete in a country driven by technological advances and mass production, Ai conceived the idea of challenging the skill of carpenters by asking them to produce three-dimensional maps of China, often but not always including the islands of Hainan and Taiwan. These carpenters use hidden mortise-and-tenon joints to create works without recourse to nails, screws or glue.

Bed is part of a series that presents China as a three-dimensional map, making the country look as though it has been rolled out and laid flat like a mattress.

Ai has also created maps of China in cotton, milk-formula cans and porcelain. *Untitled* (cat. 4), made of cast aluminium, is his latest exploration of this subject. Fourteen of the forty-four pieces that comprise the entire work are seen here; they mirror the contours of the map of China seen in *Bed*, each presented as a unique empty roundel or frame.

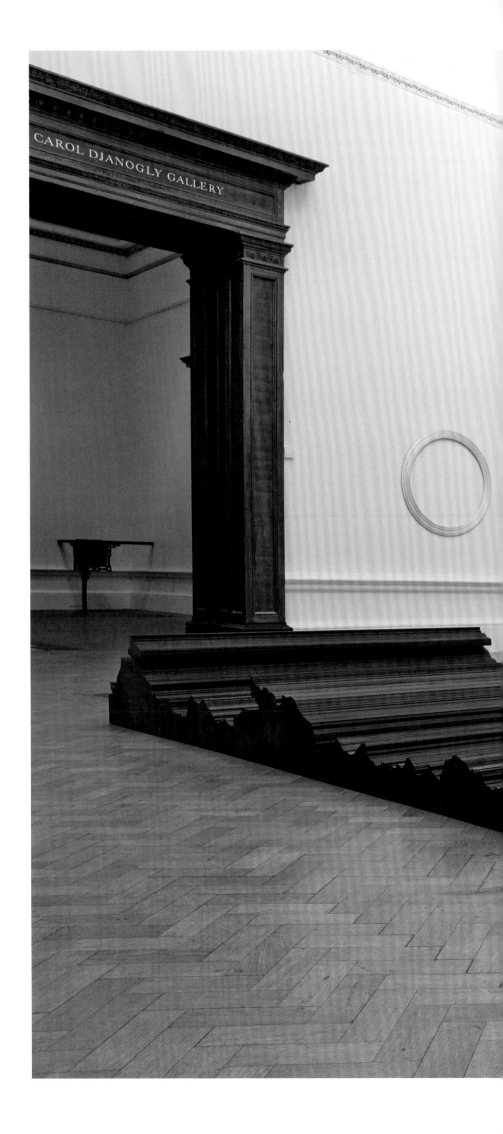

3

Bed, 2004

Iron wood (tieli wood) from dismantled temples of the Qing Dynasty (1644–1911), 200 x 600 cm

Courtesy of Ai Weiwei Studio

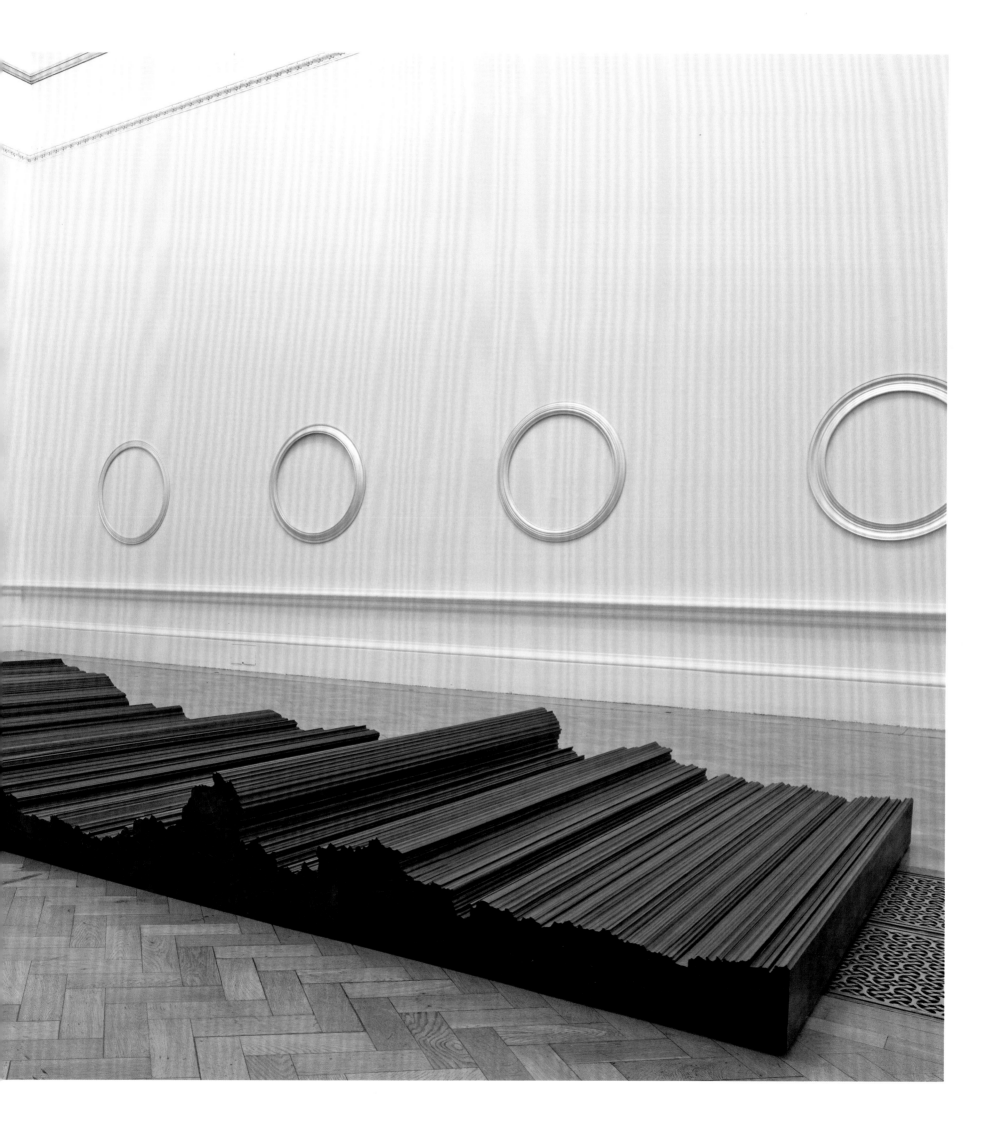

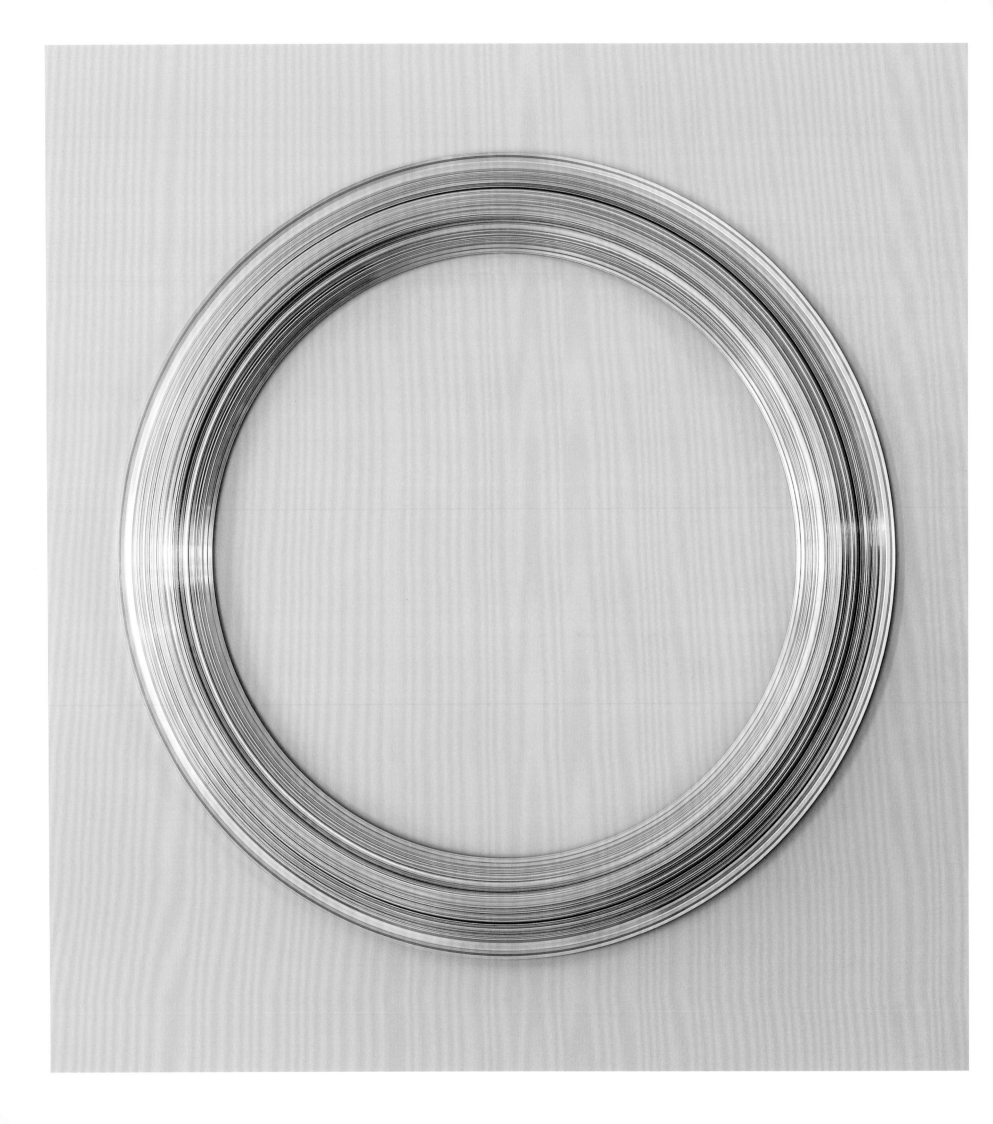

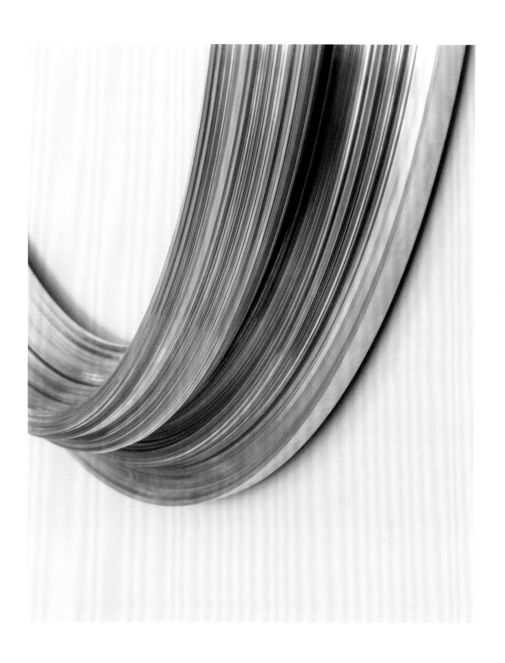

4

Untitled, 2014

Aluminium, each 100 x 100 x 11 cm, 14/44 displayed

Courtesy of Ai Weiwei Studio

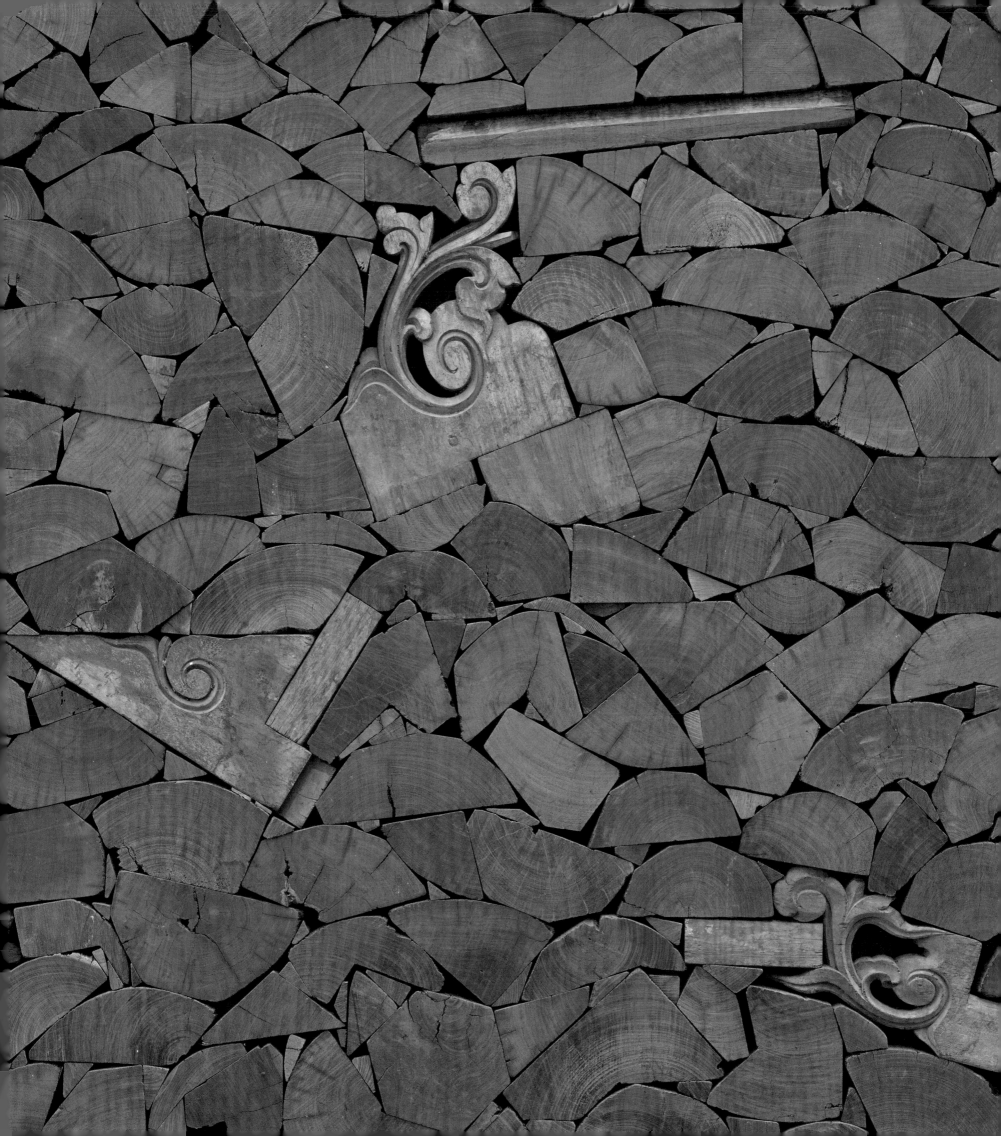

2

Among the first works Ai made on his return to China in 1993 was the Furniture series, of which *Table with Two Legs on the Wall* was the earliest piece. For Ai, the cabinetmakers' skilful and apparently invisible interventions, including maintaining the integrity of the surface patina, are fundamental to the success of these works, which are intended to be as true as possible to the Ming and Qing Dynasty originals, despite their bizarre reconfigurations. Ai subverts the objects' original purpose to render them impractical yet aesthetically appealing. *Grapes*, for instance, which is made with 27 Qing Dynasty stools, defies gravity with its acrobatic composition and minimal contact with the ground. Consequently it becomes, in Ai's words, a 'useless object'.

Ai acknowledges *Table and Pillar* as the most important single work to emerge from this group.

Many technical challenges were overcome to create this apparently simple conjunction of an architectural column and a Qing Dynasty table.

Kippe is made from offcuts of the salvaged tieli timbers that were used to produce the larger work *Fragments* (cat. 24). The offcuts are precisely stacked, like firewood, between a set of parallel bars that Ai reclaimed from his Zuoyou studio in Beijing, a former tractor factory that had belonged to the government. Such factories were obliged to provide workers with an area for physical exercise comprising such equipment as a single bar, parallel bars, a basketball hoop and a ping-pong table. In German the word 'Kippe' refers to the initial spring action used to mount the parallel bars from the ground; it can also be used to describe something that is finely balanced.

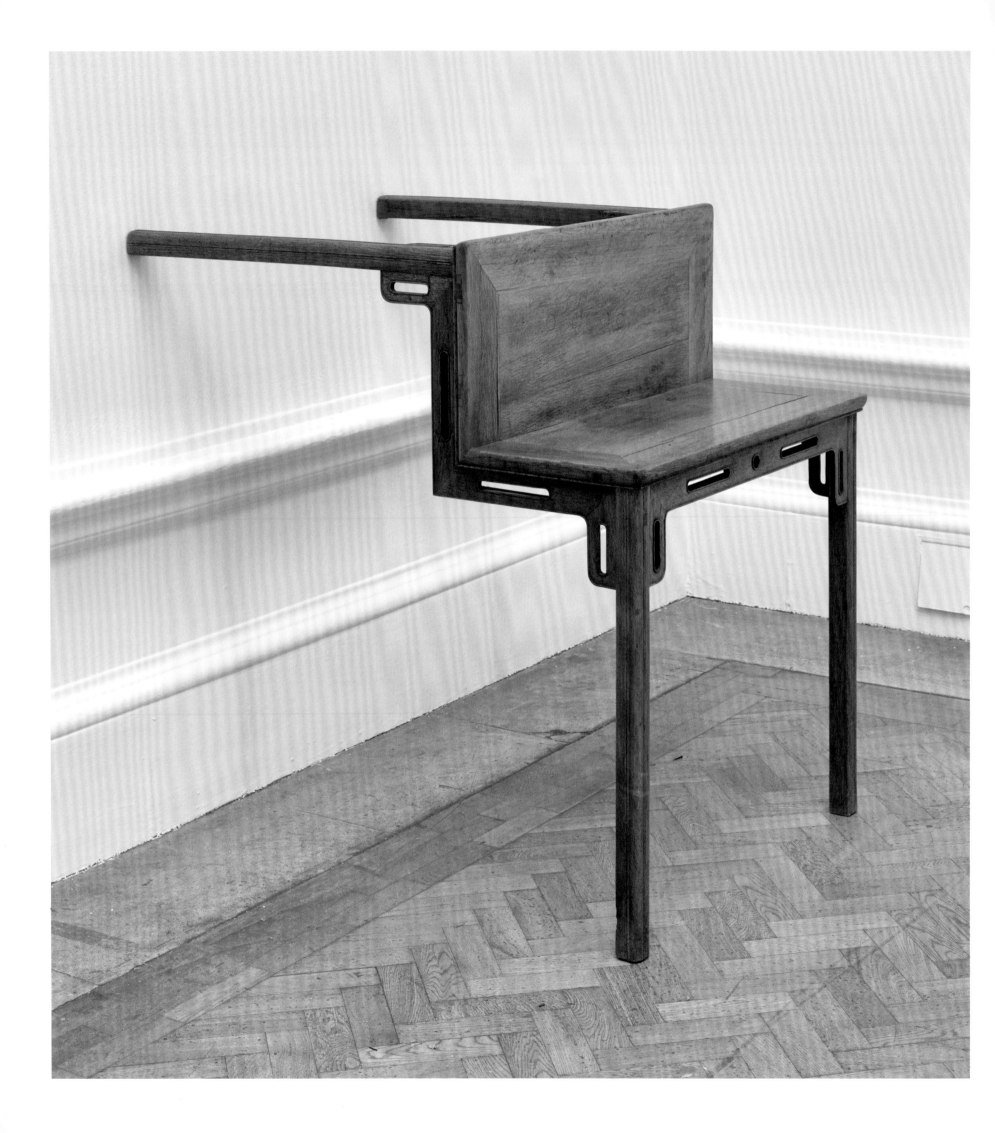

5

Table with Two Legs on the Wall, 1997

Table from the Qing Dynasty (1644–1911), 120 x 90 x 120 cm

Courtesy of Ai Weiwei Studio

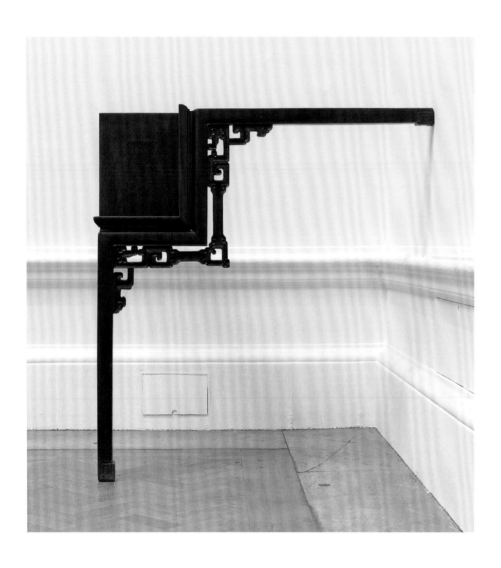

6

Table with Three Legs, 2011

Table from the Qing Dynasty (1644–1911), 117 x 81 x 169 cm

Courtesy of Ai Weiwei Studio

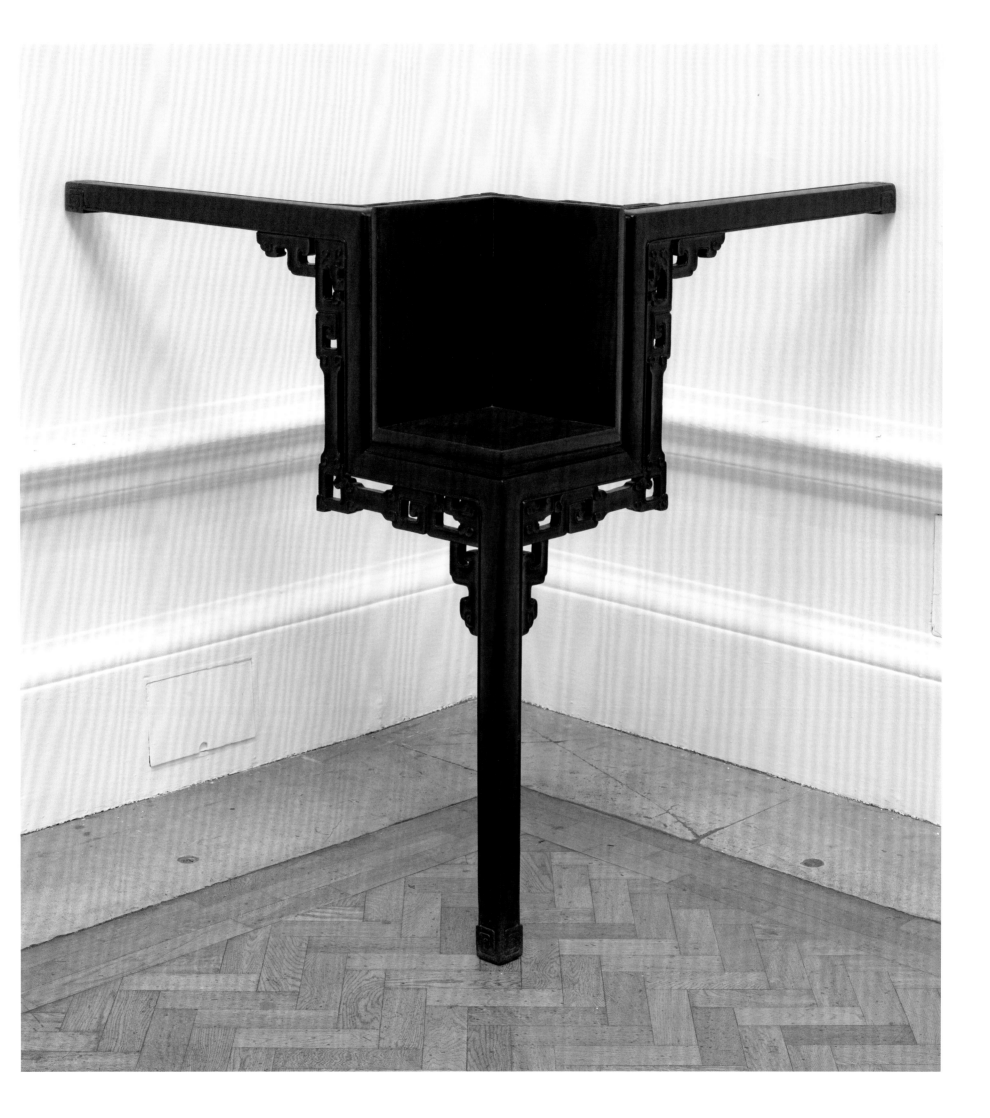

7

Grapes, 2010

27 wooden stools from the Qing Dynasty (1644–1911),
148 x 196 x 188 cm

Courtesy of Ai Weiwei Studio

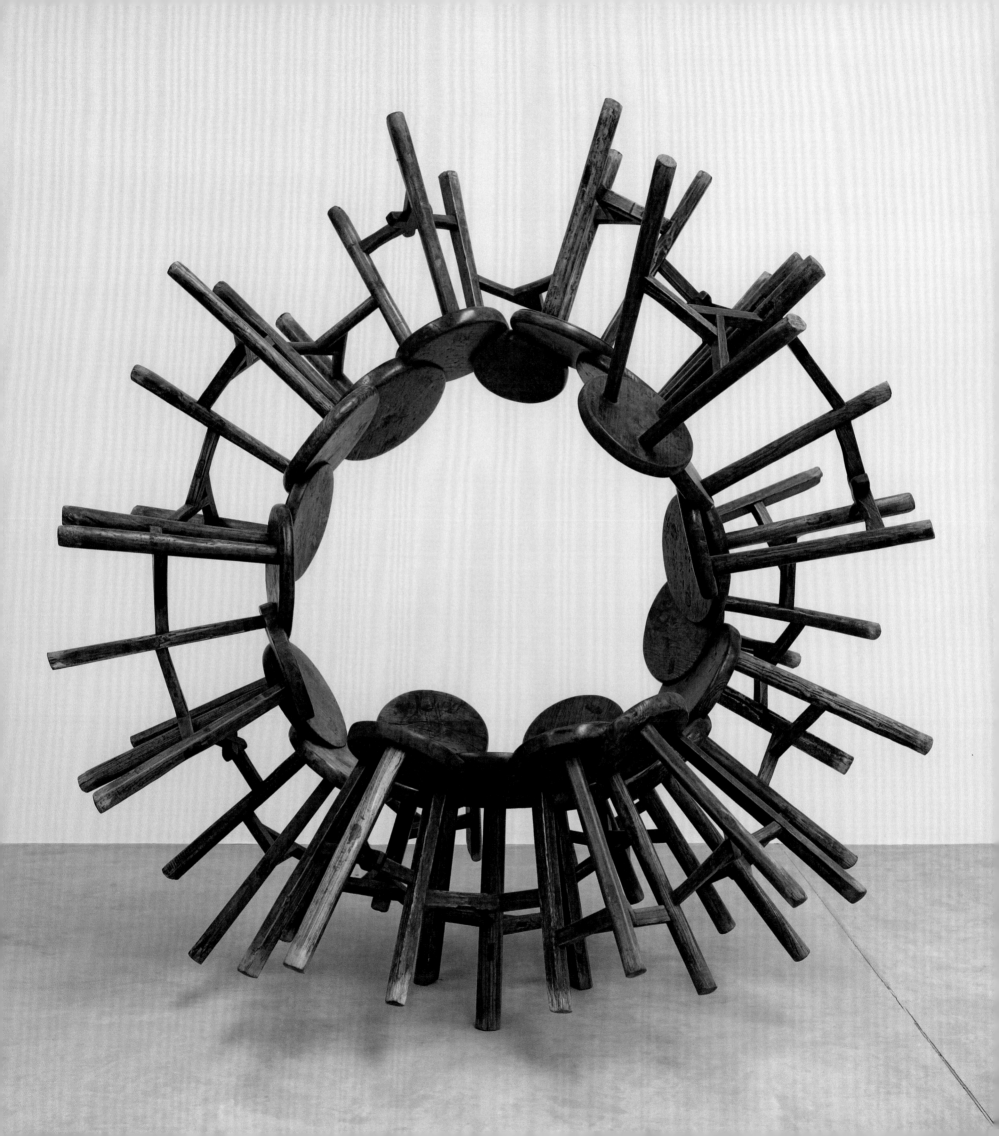

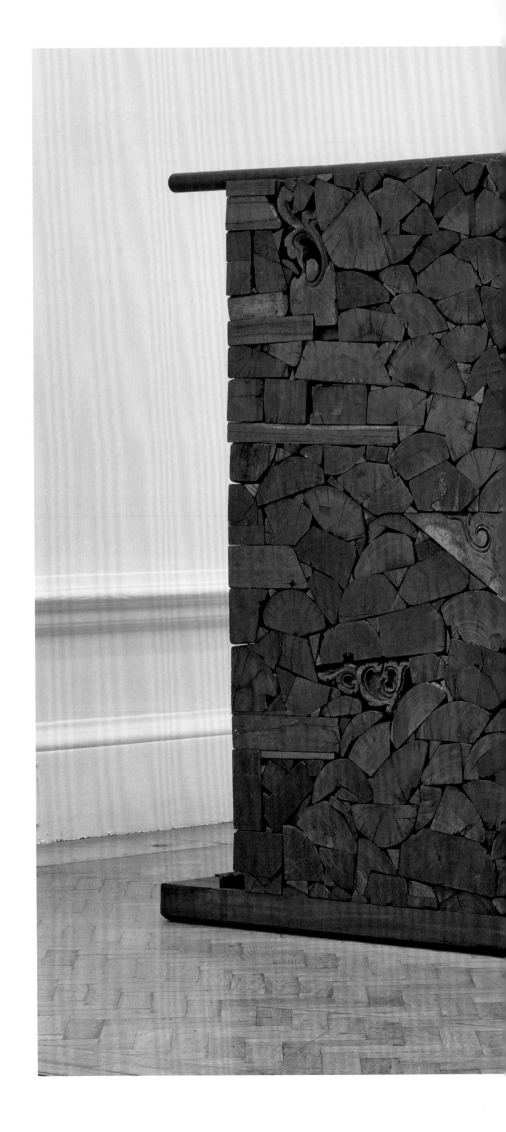

8 (production views overleaf)

Kippe, 2006

Iron wood (tieli wood) from dismantled temples of the Qing Dynasty
(1644–1911) and iron parallel bar, 182 x 286 x 104 cm

Collection of Honus Tandijono

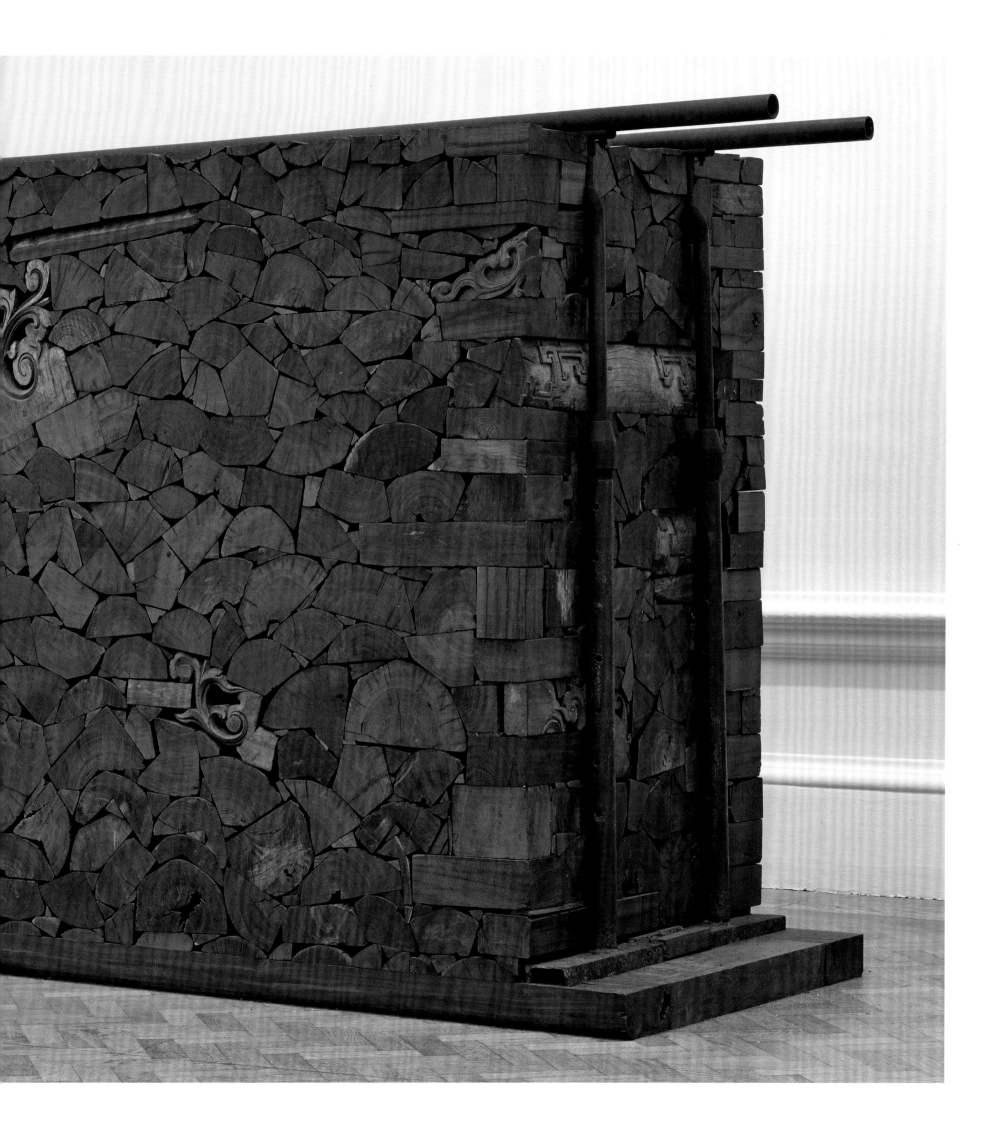

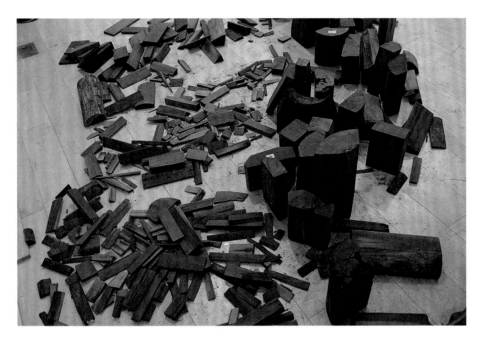
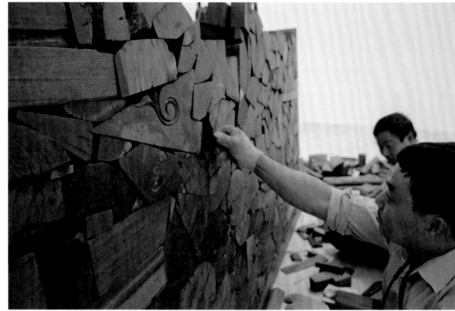
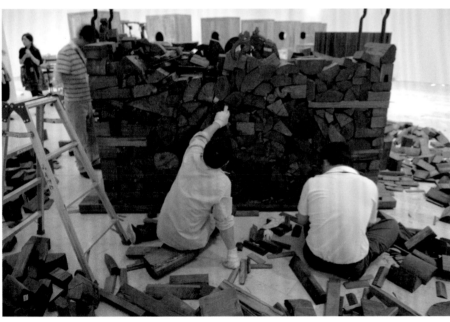
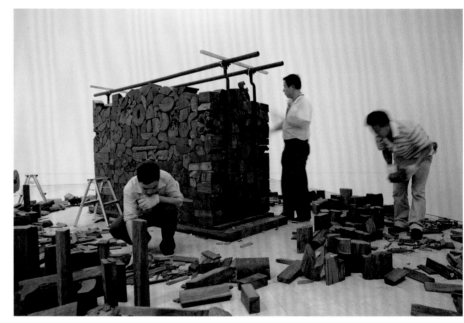

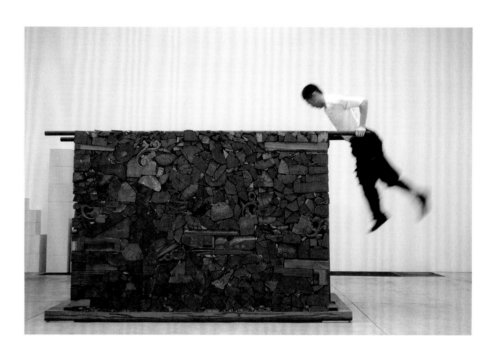

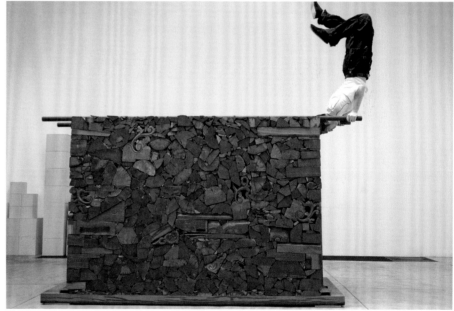

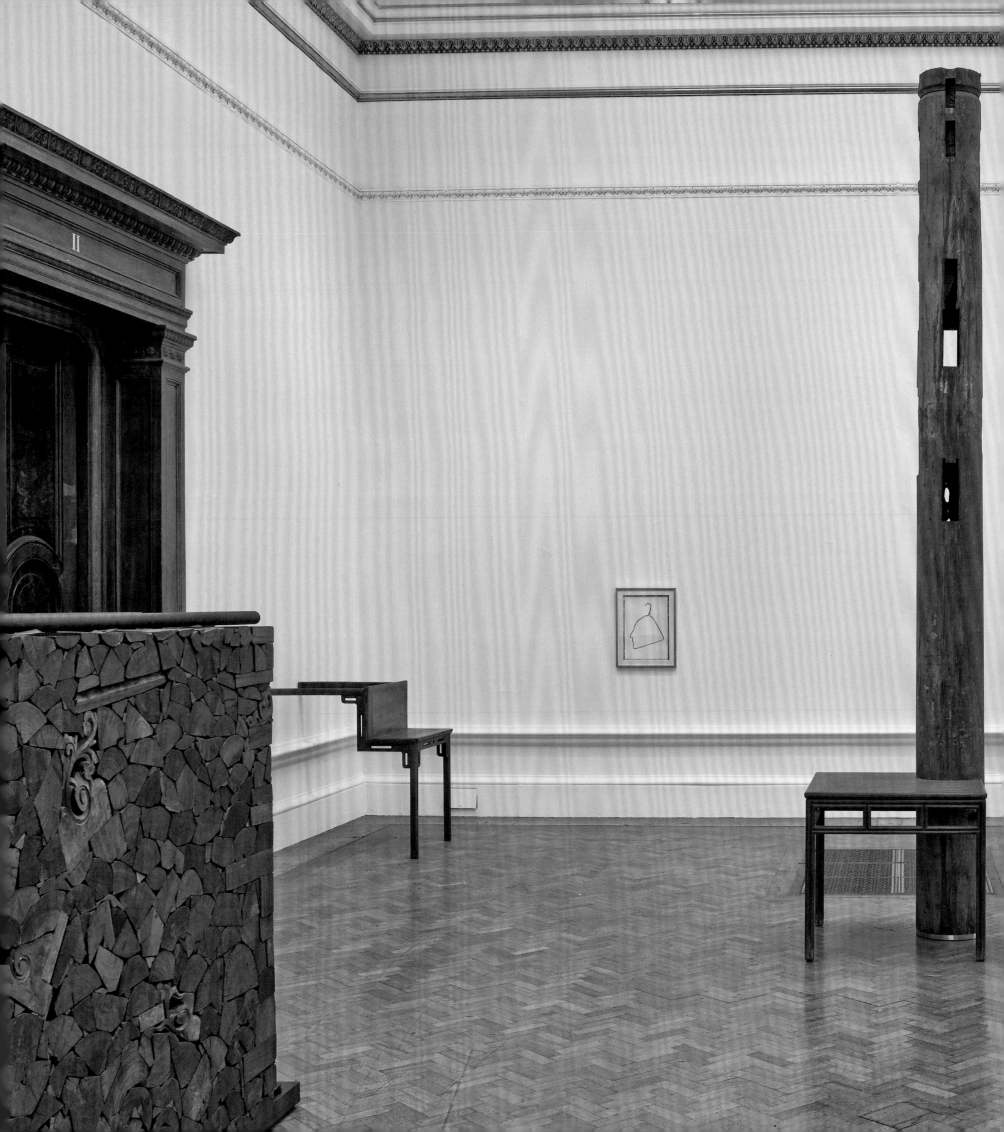

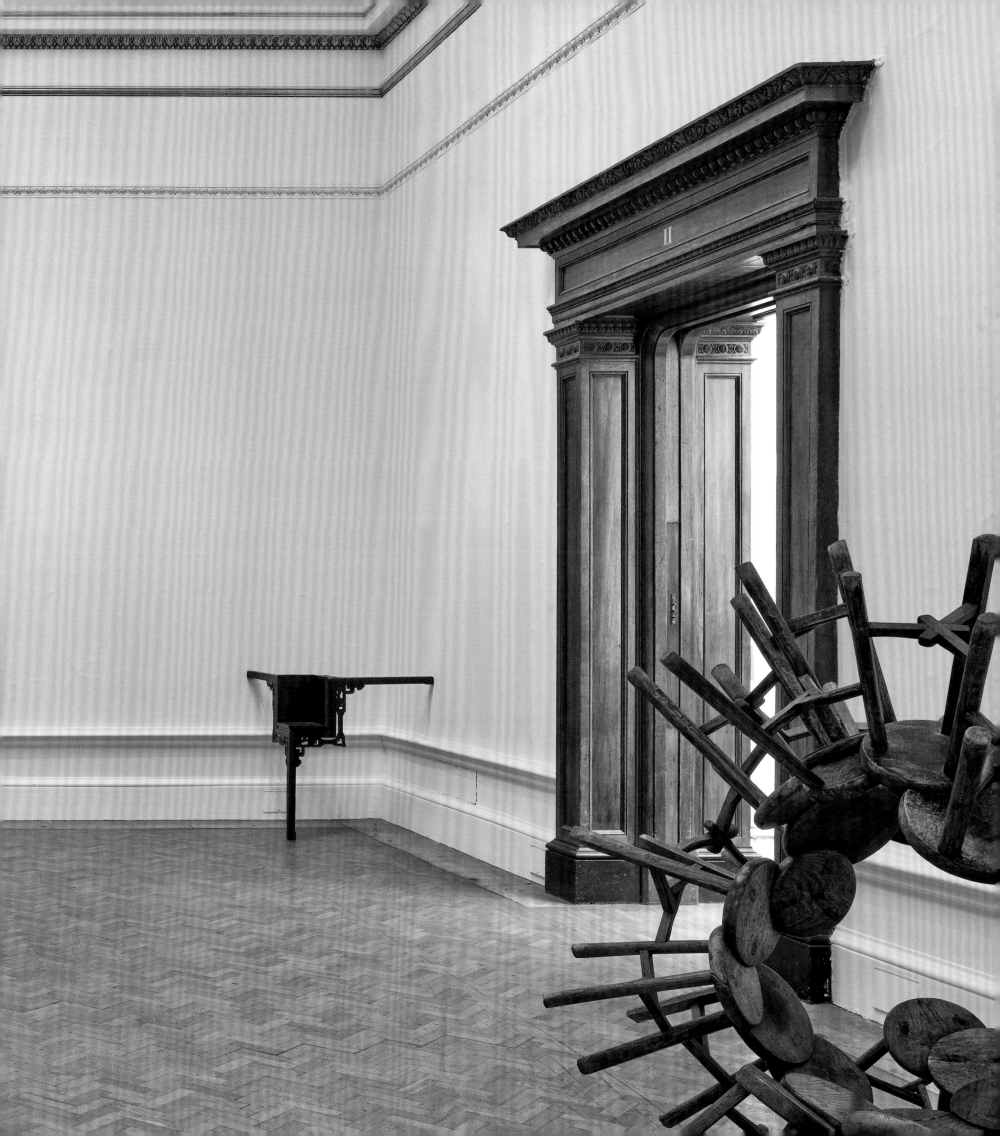

9 (previous pages, centre)

Table and Pillar, 2002

Table and pillar from dismantled temple of the Qing Dynasty (1644–1911), 460 x 90 x 90 cm

Tate, London. Purchased with funds provided by the Asia Pacific Acquisitions Committee, 2008

10

Hanging Man, 1985

Metal clothes hanger with frame, 66 x 50 cm

Courtesy of Ai Weiwei Studio

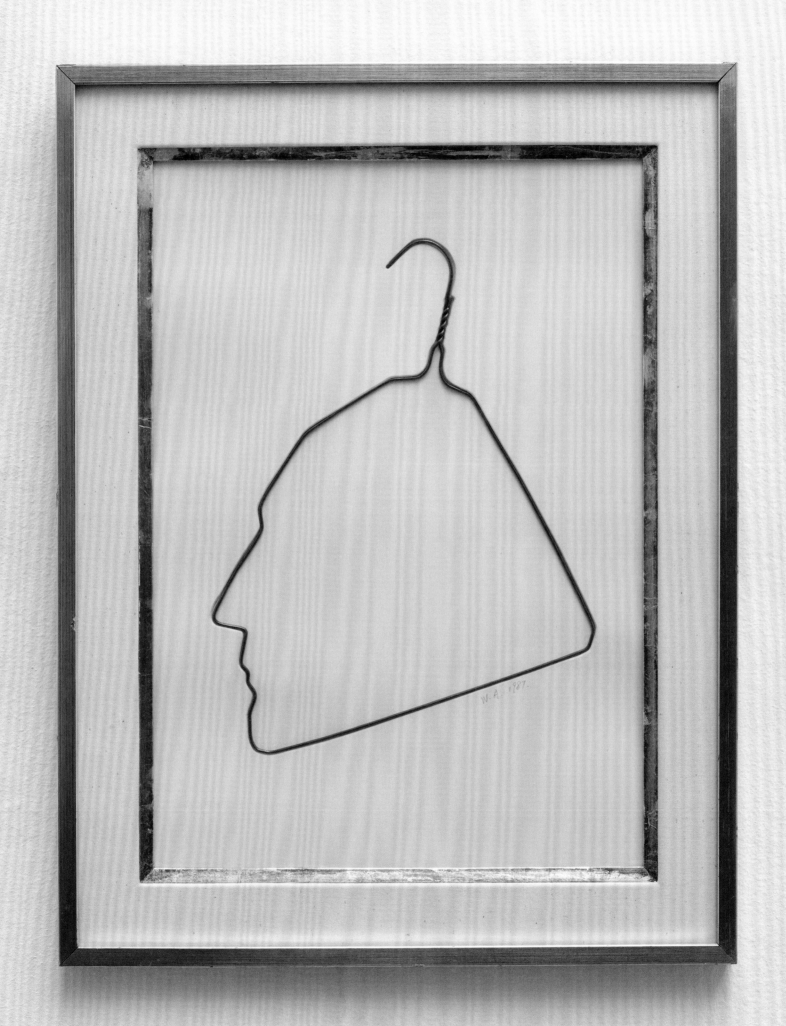

3

At 2.28 pm on 12 May 2008 a powerful earthquake caused extensive damage and significant loss of life in the Sichuan province of south-western China. Some twenty schools collapsed, killing more than five thousand students. Despite considerable and sustained harassment from the police, Ai and a number of others established a citizens' investigation with the aim of recording the names of all the victims of the collapsed schools, information that was not forthcoming from the authorities.

Ai based a number of works, including several films, on the earthquake and its impact on the families of the victims. The most significant is *Straight* (2008–12), which can be seen both as a memorial and an abiding reminder of the substandard and hasty construction methods used for building state schools. In China, government buildings are notoriously badly built and their materials commonly referred to as 'tofu-dreg', i.e. porous and flimsy like the remnants from making bean curd. The disproportionately high number of fatalities among school children was blamed on corrupt local officials who had compromised on building materials for personal gain.

Following the earthquake Ai clandestinely purchased bent and twisted rebar – the steel reinforcing bars used in the construction of concrete structures – that had been earmarked for recycling. He had 150 tonnes of this scrap metal transported to his studio in Beijing, where it was painstakingly straightened by hand and returned to its original pre-construction and pre-earthquake state.

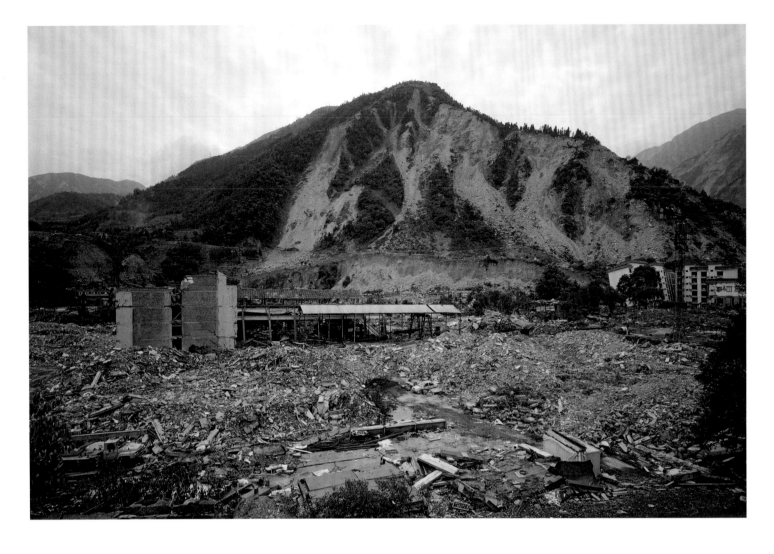

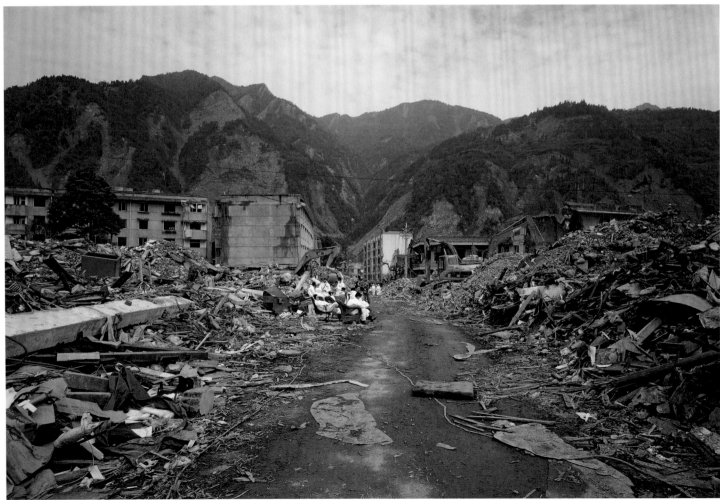

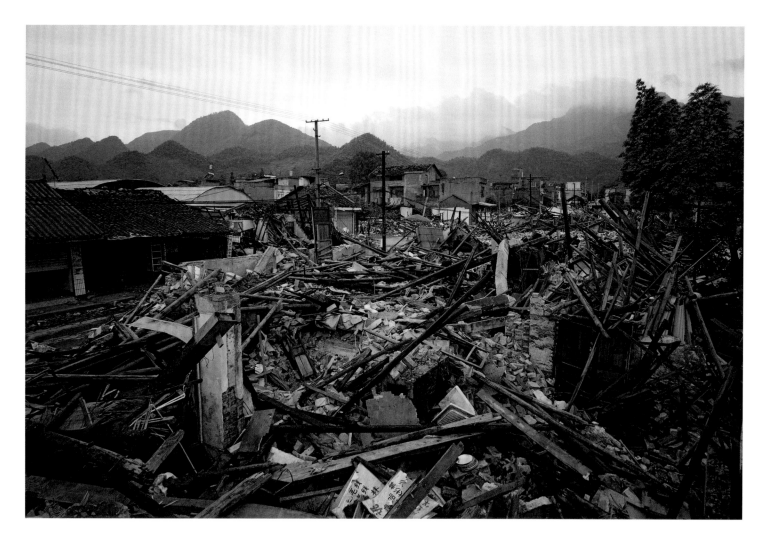

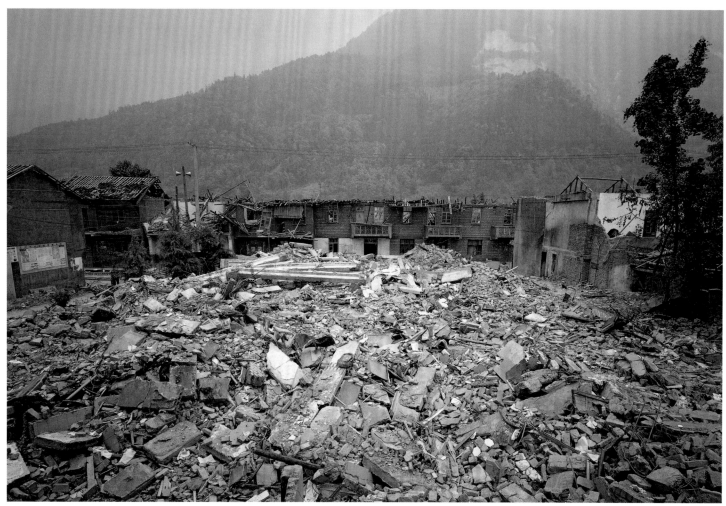

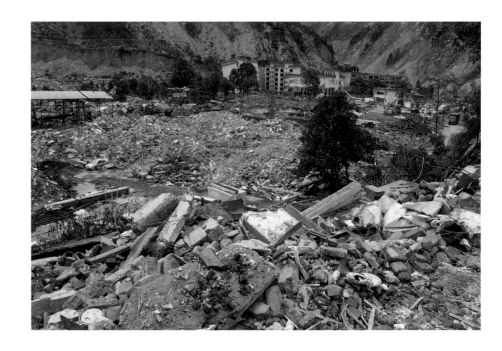

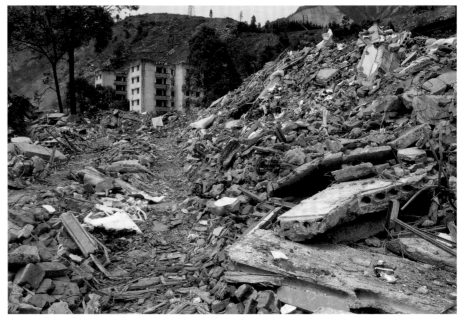

11 (pages 130–33)

Sichuan Earthquake Photographs, 2008

Black-and-white and colour photographic prints, each 50 x 75 cm

Courtesy of Ai Weiwei Studio

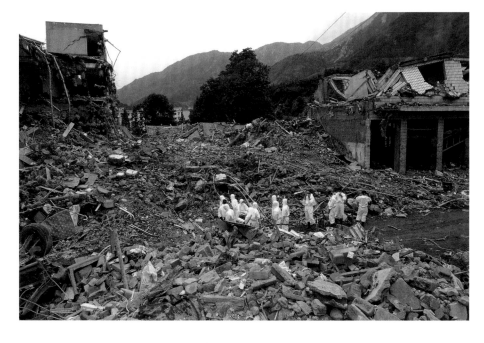

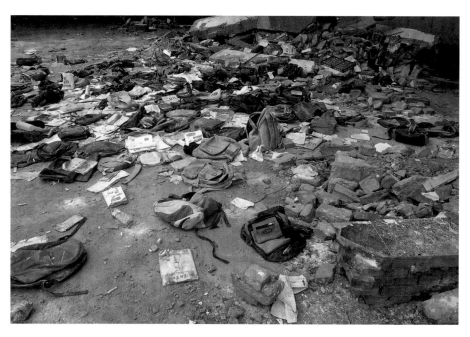

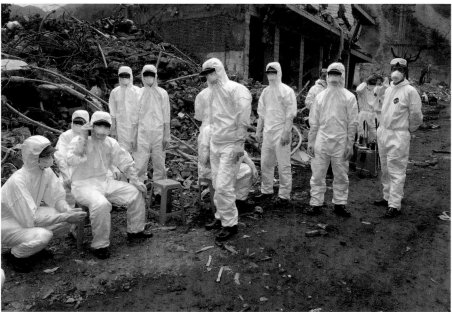

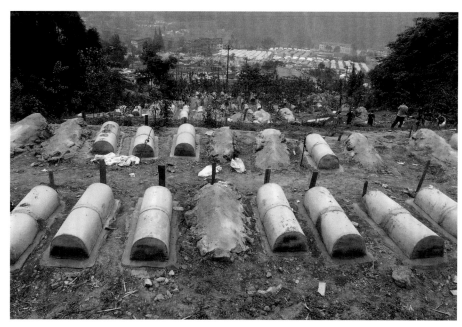

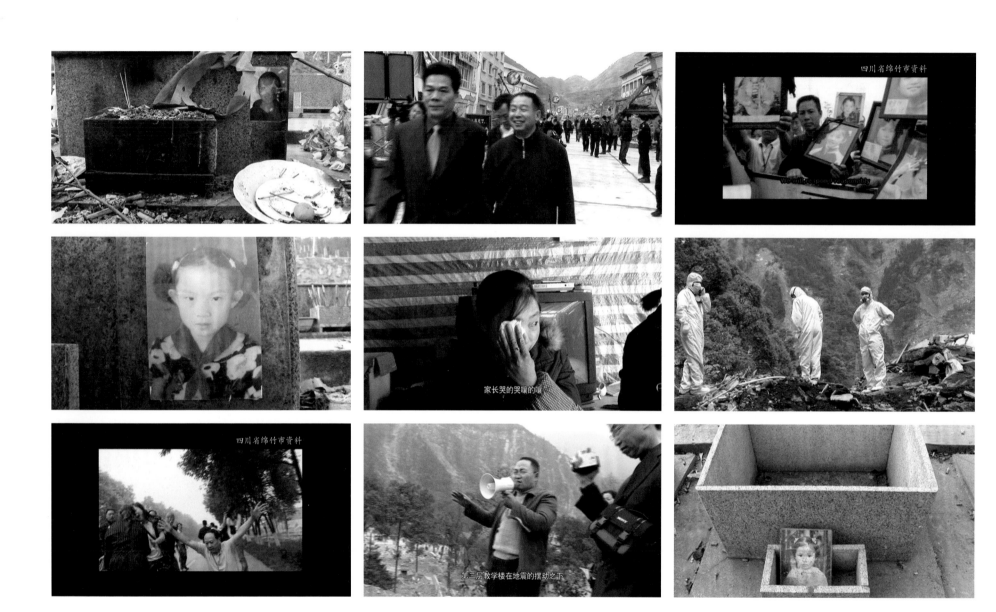

12

Straight, 2015

Film, duration 16 minutes

Courtesy of Ai Weiwei Studio

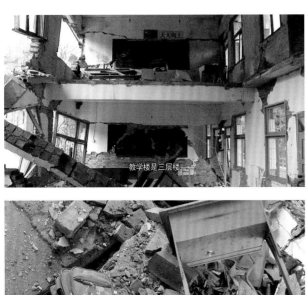

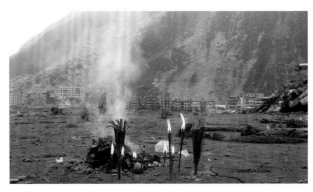

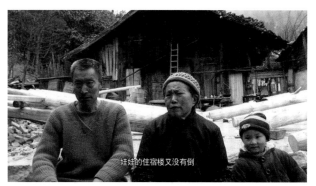

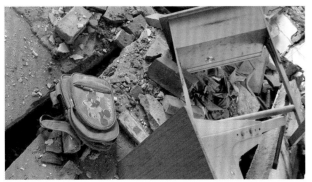

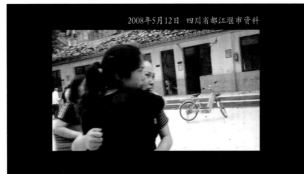

2008年5月12日　四川省都江堰市资料

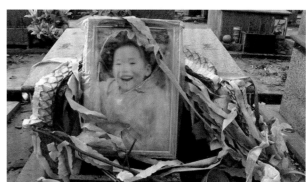

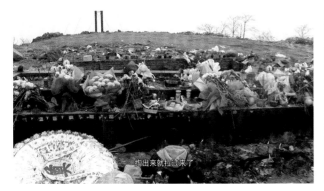

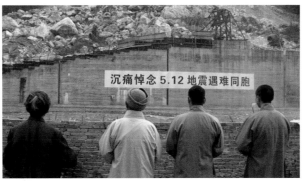

沉痛悼念5.12地震遇难同胞

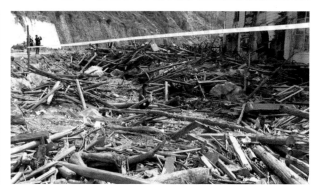

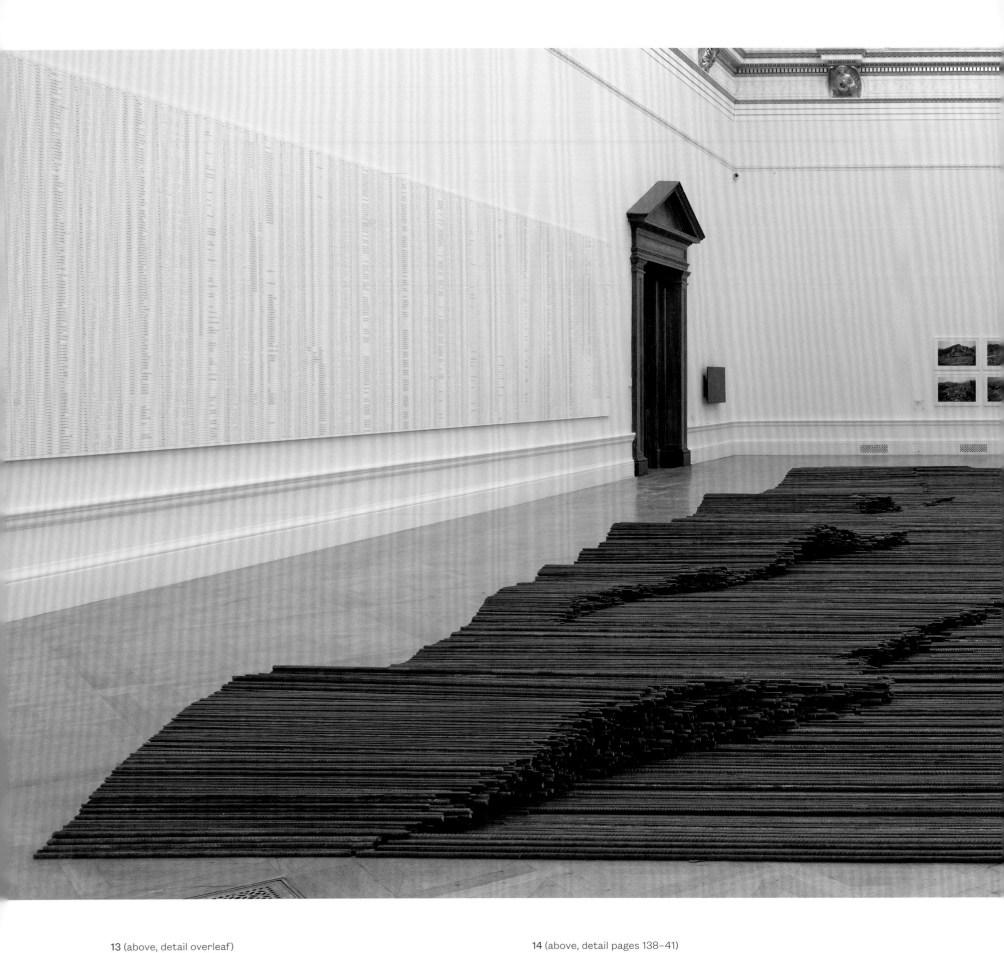

13 (above, detail overleaf)

Straight, 2008–12

Steel reinforcing bars, 1200 x 600 cm

Courtesy of Ai Weiwei Studio

14 (above, detail pages 138–41)

Names of the Student Earthquake Victims
Found by the Citizens' Investigation, 2008–11

Black-and-white print, dimensions variable

Courtesy of Ai Weiwei Studio

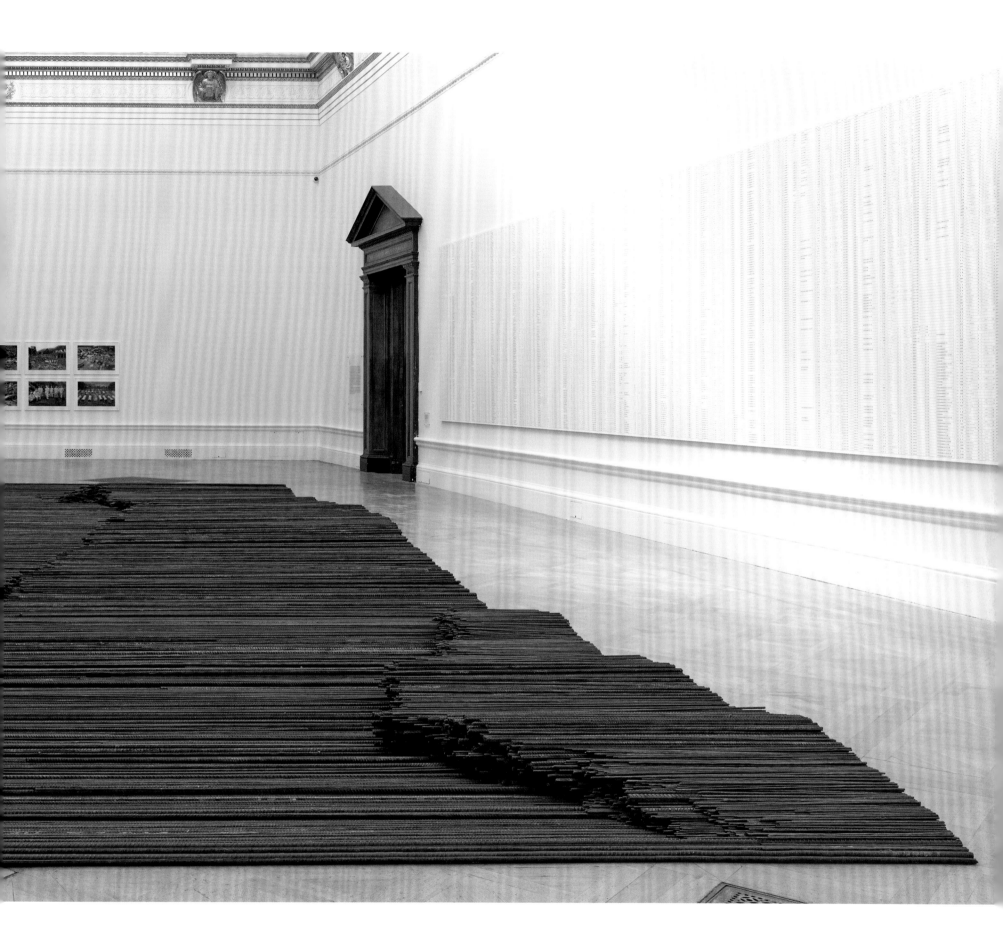

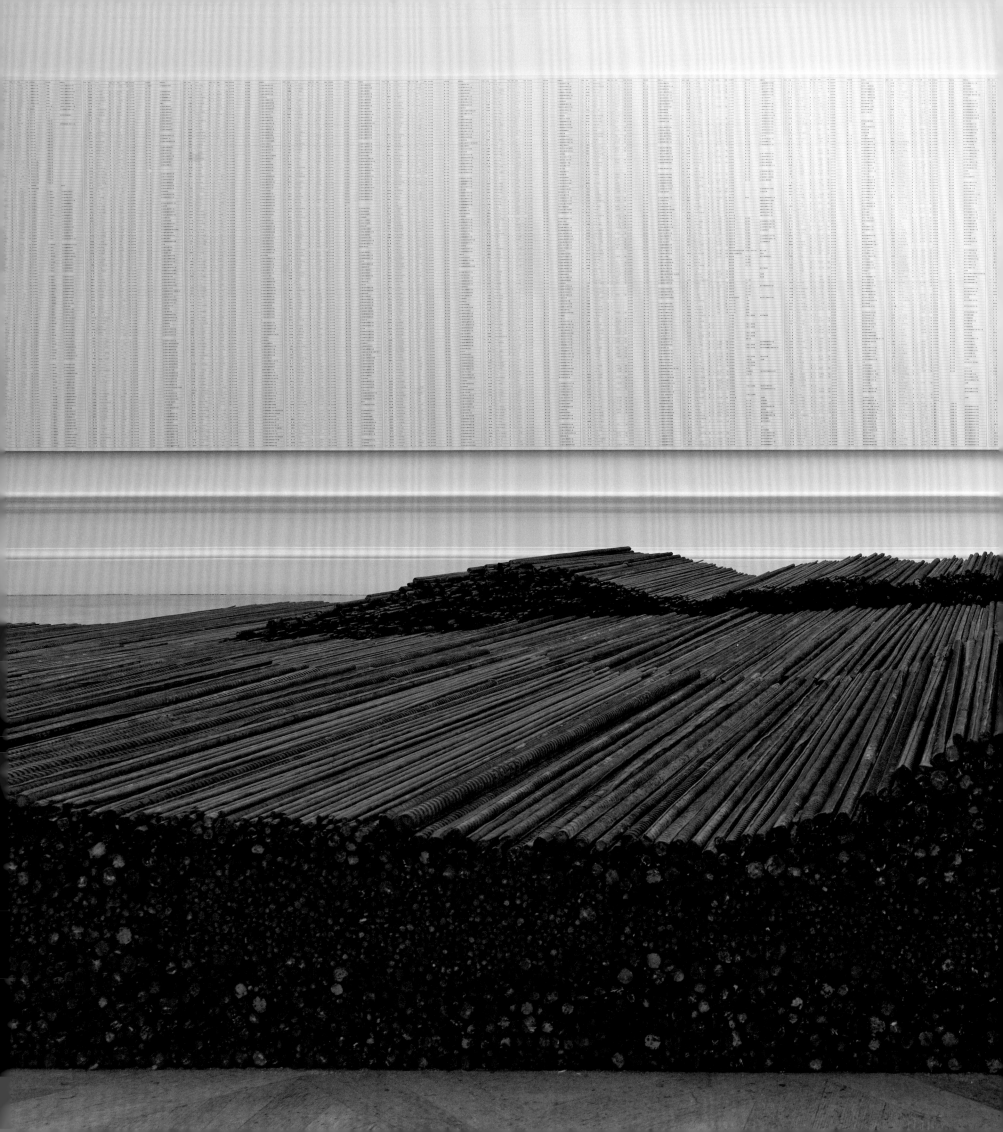

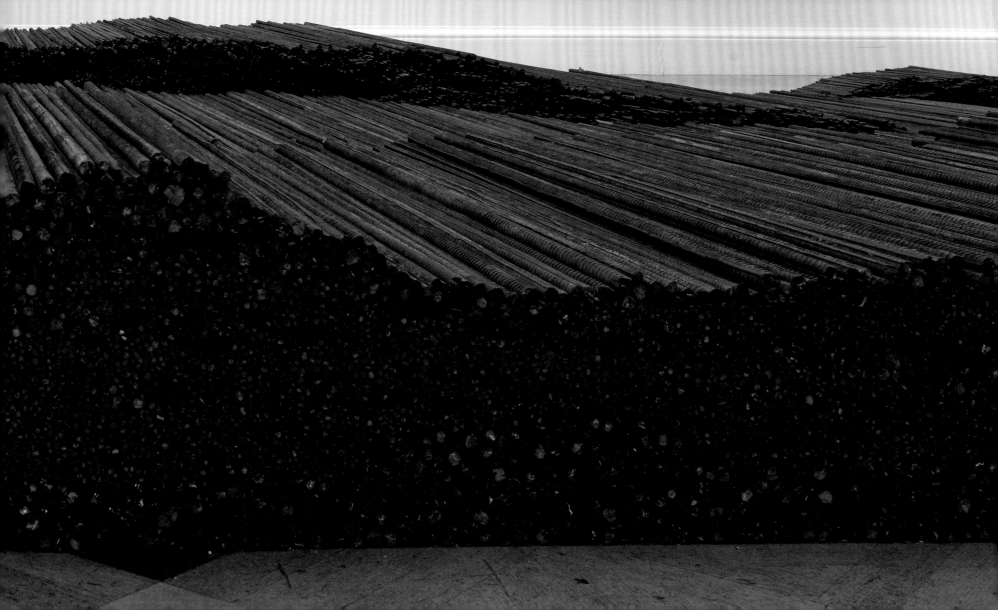

17岁	东汽中学	高二一班	东汽二磨具
19岁	东汽中学	高二一班	绵竹市遵道镇龙凤村4组
18岁	东汽中学	高二一班	绵竹市汉旺镇五居委
	东汽中学	高二一班	绵竹市土门镇新乐村5组
	东汽中学	高二一班	绵竹市拱星镇百灵村4组
18岁	东汽中学	高二一班	绵竹市武都镇白果村13组
18岁	东汽中学	高二一班	绵竹市九龙镇清泉村2组
	东汽中学	高二一班	绵竹市汉旺镇群列村6组
18岁	东汽中学	高二一班	绵竹市土门镇石团4组
18岁	东汽中学	高二一班	绵竹市板桥镇金星村8组
17岁	东汽中学	高二一班	绵竹市土门镇白鹤村
17岁	东汽中学	高二一班	绵竹市土门镇14大6组
18岁	东汽中学	高二一班	绵竹市土门镇天宝村11组
17岁	东汽中学	高二一班	东汽实业公司
	东汽中学	高二一班	绵竹市广济镇8大12组
19岁	东汽中学	高二一班	绵竹市东北镇天河村2组
18岁	东汽中学	高二一班	绵竹市汉旺镇牛鼻村3组
18岁	东汽中学	高二一班	绵竹市兴隆镇川木村2组
17岁	东汽中学	高二一班	绵竹市汉旺镇东汽中学
	东汽中学	高二一班	绵竹市孝德镇金土村14组
19岁	东汽中学	高二一班	绵竹市齐天镇六大队1组
18岁	东汽中学	高二一班	绵竹市遵道镇2大1组
	东汽中学	高二一班	绵竹市东北镇
18岁	东汽中学	高二一班	绵竹市孝德镇洪拱村9组
	东汽中学	高二一班	绵竹市兴隆镇桥楼村4组
18岁	东汽中学	高二一班	东汽建安公司
18岁	东汽中学	高二一班	绵竹市拱星镇
18岁	东汽中学	高二一班	绵竹市剑南镇
18岁	东汽中学	高二一班	绵竹市广济镇4大2组
17岁	东汽中学	高二一班	绵竹市天池镇乡天池村
	东汽中学	高二一班	东汽
18岁	东汽中学	高二一班	绵竹市西南镇3大1组
17岁	东汽中学	高二一班	绵竹市板桥镇2大2组
	东汽中学	高二一班	东汽
18岁	东汽中学	高二二班	绵竹市拱星镇家乐村4组
18岁	东汽中学	高二二班	绵竹市什镇地7大1
18岁	东汽中学	高二二班	绵竹市土门镇林堰村5组
17岁	东汽中学	高二二班	绵竹市孝德镇苦葛村15组34#
18岁	东汽中学	高二二班	绵竹市九龙镇双同村
18岁	东汽中学	高二二班	绵竹市广济镇6大9组
18岁	东汽中学	高二二班	绵竹市拱星镇2大1组
	东汽中学	高二二班	绵竹市土门镇新乐村7组
	东汽中学	高二二班	绵竹市汉旺镇
18岁	东汽中学	高二二班	绵竹市玉泉镇永林村
	东汽中学	高二二班	绵竹市拱星镇2大4组
18岁	东汽中学	高二二班	绵竹市汉旺镇七大队9队
	东汽中学	高二二班	东汽铸造分厂
	东汽中学	高二二班	东汽主机一分厂
18岁	东汽中学	高二二班	绵竹市西南镇醒狮村7组
18岁	东汽中学	高二二班	绵竹市广济镇1大7组
18岁	东汽中学	高二二班	绵竹市九龙镇5大3组
18岁	东汽中学	高二二班	绵竹市兴隆镇安仁村1组
18岁	东汽中学	高二二班	绵竹市西南镇4大3
18岁	东汽中学	高二二班	绵竹市遵道镇马跪村4组
18岁	东汽中学	高二二班	绵竹市土门镇天宝村5组
18岁	东汽中学	高二二班	绵竹市东北镇1大5组
17岁	东汽中学	高二二班	绵竹市汉旺镇大柏林村1组
19岁	东汽中学	高二二班	绵竹市清道镇
18岁	东汽中学	高二二班	绵竹市汉旺镇13村7组
18岁	东汽中学	高二二班	
	东汽中学	高二二班	绵竹市观鱼镇火石村4组
	东汽中学	高二二班	绵竹市拱星镇五大1组
18岁	东汽中学	高二二班	绵竹市拱星镇5大1组
17岁	东汽中学	高二二班	绵竹市孝德镇大乘村
	东汽中学	高二二班	绵竹市清平镇元保村1组
18岁	东汽中学	高二二班	绵竹市拱星镇3大6组
18岁	东汽中学	高二二班	绵竹市孝德镇4大1
19岁	东汽中学	高二二班	绵竹市孝德镇豪照村3组
	东汽中学	高二二班	绵竹市东汽镇锻垫检查站
19岁	东汽中学	高二二班	绵竹市剑南镇仿古社区5居委6组316号
18岁	东汽中学	高二二班	绵竹市孝德镇万源村2组
17岁	东汽中学	高二二班	东汽主机一分厂
17岁	东汽中学	高二二班	绵竹市九龙镇白玉村15组
17岁	东汽中学	高二三班	绵竹市土门镇鹿角村4组
	东汽中学	高二三班	绵竹市玉镇泉玉江村9组
19岁	东汽中学	高二三班	绵竹市孝德镇石桥1组
17岁	东汽中学	高二三班	绵竹市玉泉镇旗署公村2组
	东汽中学	高二三班	东汽
	东汽中学	高二四班	绵竹市清平镇磷矿
18岁	东汽中学	高二四班	绵竹市汉旺镇板房
	东汽中学	高二四班	绵竹市孝德镇妙相村9组
19岁	东汽中学	高二四班	绵竹市孝德镇高兴村（寄住）
18岁	东汽中学	高二四班	绵竹市板桥镇八一村4组

1135	何　川	He Chuan	男	M	10/12/89	19岁	东汽中学	高二五班	绵竹市孝德镇茶店子
1136	胡秋云	Hu Qiuyun	女	F	9/20/90	18岁	东汽中学	高二五班	绵竹市板桥镇白杨村15组
1137	黄登峰	Huang Dengfeng	男	M	5/11/90	18岁	东汽中学	高二五班	绵竹市富新镇圣庵村7组
1138	江志冬	Jiang Zhidong	男	M	1/3/91	17岁	东汽中学	高二五班	绵竹市广济中村8组
1139	姜　陈	Jiang Chen	男	M	10/4/90	18岁	东汽中学	高二五班	兴绵竹市隆镇5大6组
1140	蒋英英	Jiang Yingying	女	F	1/28/90	18岁	东汽中学	高二五班	绵竹市齐福镇洪拱村4组46号
1141	廖　雪	Liao Xue	女	F	12/5/90	18岁	东汽中学	高二五班	绵竹市土门镇珊瑚村6组
1142	刘　东	Liu Dong	男	M	9/1/90	18岁	东汽中学	高二五班	绵竹市什地镇双瓦村4组
1143	潘　丽	Pan Li					东汽中学	高二五班	绵竹市清平镇伐木厂
1144	邱　琴	Qiu Qin	女	F	4/5/90	18岁	东汽中学	高二五班	绵竹市土门镇罗云村15组
1145	汪　兵	Wang Bing	男	M	11/26/89	19岁	东汽中学	高二五班	绵竹市富新镇三会村1组
1146	吴　剑	Wu Jian	男	M	8/31/90	18岁	东汽中学	高二五班	绵竹市拱星镇红旗村1组
1147	杨力维	Yang Liwei	男	M	7/12/91	17岁	东汽中学	高二五班	东汽焊接
1148	杨镇宇	Yang Zhenyu	男	M	12/14/90	18岁	东汽中学	高二五班	东汽协作处
1149	叶德权	Ye Dequan	男	M	3/4/91	17岁	东汽中学	高二五班	绵竹市玉泉镇信用社
1150	尹　杨	Yin Yang	男	M	1990-	18岁	东汽中学	高二五班	
1151	尹泽阳	Yin Zeyang	男	M	5/12/90	18岁	东汽中学	高二五班	绵竹市东北镇玉马村3组
1152	昝龙锐	Zan Longrui	男	M	1/16/91	17岁	东汽中学	高二五班	绵竹市土门镇罗荣4组
1153	赵　凡	Zhao Fan	男	M	7/14/89	19岁	东汽中学	高二五班	绵竹市齐天镇1大5组
1154	朱　勇	Zhu Yong	男	M	8/25/91	17岁	东汽中学	高二五班	绵竹市孝德镇洪孝村
1155	安加全	An Jiaquan	男	M	10/25/89	19岁	东汽中学	高二六班	绵竹市汉旺镇板桥村12大1组
1156	戴正啸	Dai Zhengxiao	男	M	6/15/90	18岁	东汽中学	高二六班	绵竹市九龙镇五大村1组
1157	邓　敏	Deng Min	男	M	7/2/91	17岁	东汽中学	高二六班	绵竹市玉泉镇桂花村3组
1158	邓　强	Deng Qiang	男	M	6/2/90	18岁	东汽中学	高二六班	绵竹市兴隆镇桥楼村3组
1159	何关香	He Guanxiang	女	F			东汽中学	高二六班	绵竹市玉泉镇3大3
1160	黄云涛	Huang Yuntao	男	M	8/13/91	17岁	东汽中学	高二六班	绵竹市观鱼镇范存村
1161	江任轩	Jiang Renxuan	男	M	3/4/91	17岁	东汽中学	高二六班	绵竹市遵道镇新田村5组
1162	姜启龙	Jiang Qilong					东汽中学	高二六班	绵竹市广济镇新和村16组
1163	李长清	Li Changqing	男	M	6/8/90	18岁	东汽中学	高二六班	绵竹市兴隆镇广灵村20组
1164	李　鸽	Li Ge	女	F	5/1/91	17岁	东汽中学	高二六班	绵竹市汉旺镇天池煤矿
1165	李　薇	Li Wei	女	F	3/25/91	17岁	东汽中学	高二六班	绵竹市孝德镇苦葛村2组
1166	林　鹏	Lin Peng	男	M	8/29/90	18岁	东汽中学	高二六班	绵竹市西南镇金泉村6组
1167	刘述平	Liu Shuping	男	M	1/30/91	17岁	东汽中学	高二六班	绵竹市土门镇名堰村15组
1168	罗庆峰	Luo Qingfeng	男	M	9/10/89	19岁	东汽中学	高二六班	绵竹市齐天镇2大1
1169	邱佩悦	Qiu Peiyue	女	F	11/6/90	18岁	东汽中学	高二六班	绵竹市武都镇
1170	王登丽	Wang Dengli	女	F	4/28/89	19岁	东汽中学	高二六班	绵竹市拱星镇1大4组
1171	王海燕	Wang Haiyan	女	F	8/15/90	18岁	东汽中学	高二六班	绵竹市清平镇元保村2组
1172	向兴宁	Xiang Xingning					东汽中学	高二六班	东汽机电公司
1173	萧　魁	Xiao Kui					东汽中学	高二六班	
1174	徐　涛	Xu Tao	男	M	12/3/90	18岁	东汽中学	高二六班	绵竹市孝德镇金星村6组
1175	许　进	Xu Jin	男	M	1/14/91	17岁	东汽中学	高二六班	绵竹市广济镇一大3组
1176	杨建威	Yang Jianwei	男	M	7/23/90	18岁	东汽中学	高二六班	绵竹市遵道镇龙凤村2组
1177	杨万飞	Yang Wanfei	男	M	6/11/90	18岁	东汽中学	高二六班	绵竹市孝德镇茶店子村8组
1178	杨祯芮	Yang Zhenrui	女	F	10/12/90	18岁	东汽中学	高二六班	绵竹市玉泉镇1大1组
1179	张明建	Zhang Mingjian	男	M	9/8/90	18岁	东汽中学	高二六班	绵竹市兴隆镇六大9组
1180	周欢欢	Zhou Huanhuan	女	F	9/22/90	18岁	东汽中学	高二六班	绵竹市兴隆镇广平村
1181	马明壮	Ma Mingzhuang	男	M	1991-	17岁	东汽中学	高三	汉旺镇
1182	边　楠	Bian Nan	女	F	8/31/90	18岁	东汽中学	高三一班	绵竹市汉旺镇东汽精铸车间风电事业部
1183	冯志生	Feng Zhisheng	男	M	1989-	19岁	东汽中学	高三一班	绵竹市遵道镇马跪村1组
1184	李　玲	Li Ling				18岁	东汽中学	高三一班	绵竹市孝德镇金星村
1185	廖小丽	Liao Xiaoli	女	F	8/14/89	19岁	东汽中学	高三一班	绵竹市西南镇金隆村3组
1186	刘　琴	Liu Qin	女	F	1989-	19岁	东汽中学	高三一班	
1187	罗　燕	Luo Yan	女	F			东汽中学	高三一班	绵竹市绵远镇吉兆村14组
1188	甯丽君	Ning Lijun					东汽中学	高三一班	绵竹市清平镇元建村2组
1189	唐　芬	Tang Fen	女	F	3/23/89	19岁	东汽中学	高三一班	绵竹市玉泉镇6大3组
1190	周文超	Zhou Wenchao	女	F	2/18/90	18岁	东汽中学	高三一班	东汽中学
1191	陈正东	Chen Zhengdong	男	M	10/29/89	19岁	东汽中学	高三二班	绵竹市兴隆镇广灵村9组
1192	伏　雪	Fu Xue	女	F	1989-	19岁	东汽中学	高三二班	
1193	李小佳麟	Li Xiaojialin	女	F	6/30/89	19岁	东汽中学	高三二班	绵竹市东北镇天齐村7组
1194	胡　珊	Hu Shan	女	F	3/28/89	19岁	东汽中学	高三三班	
1195	安　棋	An Qi	女	F	4/6/88	20岁	东汽中学	高三五班	绵竹市汉旺镇武都村2组
1196	陈甜甜	Chen Tiantian	女	F			东汽中学	高三五班	绵竹市清平镇磷矿
1197	陈宇航	Chen Yuhang	男	M	4/5/90	18岁	东汽中学	高三五班	东汽物资管理处
1198	樊　静	Fan Jing	女	F	9/8/90	18岁	东汽中学	高三五班	绵竹市富新镇8大7组
1199	付元忠	Fu Yuanzhong	男	M	1989-	19岁	东汽中学	高三五班	绵竹市清平镇
1200	何　璐	He Lu	女	F	1/15/90	18岁	东汽中学	高三五班	东汽物资管理处
1201	姜　剑	Jiang Jian	男	M	10/8/88	19岁	东汽中学	高三五班	绵竹市五都镇板房50栋3单元10号
1202	刘　梦	Liu Meng	女	F	10/22/88	20岁	东汽中学	高三五班	东汽工业公司
1203	刘兴环	Liu Xinghuan	女	F		18岁	东汽中学	高三五班	绵竹市天池镇
1204	刘　英	Liu Ying	女	F		19岁	东汽中学	高三五班	绵竹市汉旺镇泉新村10组
1205	马倩茹	Ma Qianru	女	F	6/28/89	19岁	东汽中学	高三五班	绵竹市齐天镇4大2
1206	邱宝龙	Qiu Baolong	男	M	6/23/89	19岁	东汽中学	高三五班	绵竹市汉旺镇凌法村
1207	邱　雷	Qiu Lei	男	M	9/30/88	20岁	东汽中学	高三五班	绵竹市绵远镇西村15组
1208	任　婷	Ren Ting	女	F	6/7/89	19岁	东汽中学	高三五班	绵竹市兴隆镇安仁村7组
1209	孙红梅	Sun Hongmei	女	F	1/7/89	19岁	东汽中学	高三五班	绵竹市汉旺镇2大队
1210	孙亚莉	Sun Yali	女	F	10/4/89	19岁	东汽中学	高三五班	绵竹市板桥镇1大8组
1211	唐　宇	Tang Yu	女	F	3/7/90	18岁	东汽中学	高三五班	东汽储运
1212	向　雅	Xiang Ya	女	F	6/12/89	19岁	东汽中学	高三五班	绵竹市清平乡（清平磷矿）
1213	肖　睿	Xiao Rui	男	M	10/27/89	19岁	东汽中学	高三五班	
1214	赵文海	Zhao Wenhai			1989-	19岁	东汽中学	高三五班	东汽动力分厂
1215	朱晓蛟	Zhu Xiaojiao	女	F	12/3/89	19岁	东汽中学	高三五班	绵竹市汉旺镇
1216	车小强	Che Xiaoqiang	男	M			东汽中学		绵竹市五福镇7大8组
1217	刘　刚	Liu Gang					东汽中学		绵竹市拱星镇泉乐村3组

1259	王小雪	Wang Xiaoxue	女	F	2/12/96	12岁	富新二
1260	肖正学	Xiao Zhengxue	男	M	1998-	10岁	富新二
1261	徐紫玲	Xu Ziling	女	F	7/1/98	10岁	富新二
1262	余　欢	Yu Huan	女	F	5/19/98	10岁	富新二
1263	张　佳	Zhang Jia	女	F	5/8/98	10岁	富新二
1264	张　敏	Zhang Min	女	F	9/30/97	11岁	富新二
1265	张万鑫	Zhang Wanxin	男	M	5/27/98	10岁	富新二
1266	张珍玲	Zhang Zhenling	女	F	10/4/97	11岁	富新二
1267	郑晓亚	Zheng Xiaoya	女	F	5/26/98	10岁	富新二
1268	左　豪	Zuo Hao	男	M	9/14/97	11岁	富新二
1269	陈　坤	Chen Kui	男	M	1997-	11岁	富新二
1270	丁丹妮	Ding Danni	女	F	8/14/96	12岁	富新二
1271	巩　豪	Gong Hao	男	M	1997-	11岁	富新二
1272	江　瑶	Wang Yao	女	F	7/13/97	11岁	富新二
1273	景明清	Jing Mingqing	女	F	11/24/96	11岁	富新二
1274	黎　婷	Li Ting	女	F	1997-	11岁	富新二
1275	李　欢	Li Huan	女	F	1997-	11岁	富新二
1276	李思琦	Li Siqi	女	F	1/21/96	12岁	富新二
1277	刘　超	Liu Chao	女	F	4/1/96	12岁	富新二
1278	刘子宇	Liu Ziyu	男	M	6/28/97	11岁	富新二
1279	马科明	Ma Keming	男	M	1/14/96	12岁	富新二
1280	沈思铭	Shen Siming	男	M			富新二
1281	汪　露	Wang Lu	女	F	8/16/95	13岁	富新二
1282	王龙志	Wang Longzhi	男	M	12/2/96	12岁	富新二
1283	王　永	Wang Yong	男	M	1997-	11岁	富新二
1284	熊　欣	Xiong Xin	女	F	6/1/97	11岁	富新二
1285	叶小曼	Ye Xiaoman	女	F	8/20/96	12岁	富新二
1286	张秋月	Zhang Qiuyue	女	F	10/17/96	12岁	富新二
1287	张玉萍	Zhang Yuping	女	F	12/19/96	12岁	富新二
1288	周玉娇	Zhou Yujiao	女	F	4/27/96	12岁	富新二
1289	白　玲	Bai Ling	女	F	10/10/96	11岁	富新二
1290	董　文	Dong Wen	女	F	1996-	12岁	富新二
1291	冯　俊	Feng Jun	男	M	1997-	11岁	富新二
1292	付　豪	Fu Hao	男	M	1996-	12岁	富新二
1293	贺素华	He Suhua	女	F	1995-	13岁	富新二
1294	黄　滤	Huang Hu	女	F	4/17/97	11岁	富新二
1295	景兴波	Jing Xingbo	男	M	4/22/97	11岁	富新二
1296	兰　婪	Lan Lan	女	F	1997-	11岁	富新二
1297	黎　佳	Li Jia	女	F	1997-12-	11岁	富新二
1298	李　超	Li Chao	男	M	1996-	12岁	富新二
1299	刘佳玉	Liu Jiayu	女	F	10/16/96	12岁	富新二
1300	刘湘玲	Liu Xianglin	女	F	3/11/97	11岁	富新二
1301	刘新月	Liu Xinyue	女	F	10/19/97	11岁	富新二
1302	彭鑫怡	Peng Xinyi	女	F	11/29/96	12岁	富新二小
1303	桑　蕊	Sang Rui	女	F	1997-	11岁	富新二小
1304	桑兴鹏	Sang Xingpeng	男	M	1997-	11岁	富新二小
1305	沈　伟	Shen Wei	女	F	10/4/96	12岁	富新二小
1306	王　露	Wang Lu	女	F	4/22/96	12岁	富新二小
1307	杨　婷	Yang Ting	女	F	12/26/96	12岁	富新二小
1308	杨　伟	Yang Wei	男	M	6/19/96	12岁	富新二小
1309	叶师师	Ye Shishi	女	F	3/10/96	12岁	富新二小
1310	张　涛	Zhang Tao	男	M	4/6/97	11岁	富新二小
1311	毕月星	Bi Yuexing	女	F	9/23/95	13岁	富新二小
1312	陈顺航	Chen Shunhang	男	M	9/30/96	12岁	富新二小
1313	陈紫薇	Chen Ziwei	女	F	11/10/99	12岁	富新二小
1314	杜　皓	Du Hao	男	M	7/4/96	12岁	富新二小
1315	黄　强	Huang Qiang	男	M	3/15/96	12岁	富新二小
1316	黄晴峰	Huang Qingfeng	男	M	10/26/95	13岁	富新二小
1317	吉庆朕	Ji Qingzhen	男	M	1995-	13岁	富新二小
1318	李　敏	Li Min	女	F	1996-	12岁	富新二小
1319	刘　涛	Liu Tao	男	M	12/20/96	12岁	富新二小
1320	卢　英	Lu Ying	女	F	6/27/95	13岁	富新二小
1321	蒲　红	Pu Hong	女	F	1996-	12岁	富新二小
1322	宋　辉	Song Hui	男	M	7/5/95	13岁	富新二小
1323	王　程	Wang Cheng	女	F	4/23/95	13岁	富新二小
1324	吴　凡	Wu Fan	女	F	3/30/96	12岁	富新二小
1325	杨　丹	Yang Dan	女	F	7/3/95	13岁	富新二小
1326	杨贵云	Yang Guiyun	男	M	1996-	12岁	富新二小
1327	杨　坤	Yang Kun	男	M	10/6/95	13岁	富新二小
1328	张　菊	Zhang Ju	女	F	7/11/95	13岁	富新二小
1329	张　琪	Zhang Qi	男	M	3/16/95	13岁	富新二小
1330	张　怡	Zhang Yi	女	F	9/9/95	13岁	富新二小
1331	陈　龙	Chen Long	女	F	1995-	13岁	富新二小
1332	陈园园	Chen Yuanyuan	女	F	1996-	12岁	富新二小
1333	丁　鹏	Ding Peng	男	M	1996-	12岁	富新二小
1334	丁云涛	Ding Yuntao	男	M	1995-	13岁	富新二小
1335	付　锐	Fu Rui	女	F	1996-	12岁	富新二小
1336	郭　玲	Guo Ling	女	F	3/26/95	13岁	富新二小
1337	郭　霜	Guo Shuang	女	F	6/27/95	12岁	富新二小
1338	胡寿莲	Hu Shoulian	女	F	9/10/95	13岁	富新二小
1339	景明春	Jing Mingchun	女	F	1/14/96	12岁	富新二小
1340	李玉冠	Li Yuguan	男	M	1996-	12岁	富新二小
1341	卢　倩	Lu Qian	女	F	1996-	12岁	富新二小

年级班级	住址
年级二班	绵竹市什地镇
年级二班	绵竹市富新镇普胜村二组
年级二班	绵竹市富新镇常明村三组
年级一班	绵竹市富新镇普明村一组
年级一班	绵竹市什地镇
年级一班	绵竹市五福镇友助村二组
年级一班	绵竹市五福镇友助村三组
年级一班	绵竹市富新镇普胜村二组
年级一班	绵竹市五福镇二三六队（普胜六组）
年级一班	绵竹市富新镇普胜村四组
年级一班	绵竹市富新镇友助村六组
年级一班	绵竹市富新镇普胜村三组
年级一班	绵竹市什地镇
年级一班	
年级一班	绵竹市富新镇普明村四组
年级一班	绵竹市富新镇茅坝村三组
年级一班	绵竹市富新镇友助村三组
年级一班	绵竹市富新镇友助村六组
年级一班	绵竹市富新镇杜林村二组
年级二班	绵竹市富新镇杜林村二组
年级二班	绵竹市富新镇普胜村四组
年级二班	绵竹市富新镇永丰村一组
年级二班	绵竹市富新镇杜林村八组
年级二班	绵竹市富新镇永丰村六组
年级二班	绵竹市富新镇普胜村六组
年级二班	绵竹市富新镇普胜村一组
年级二班	绵竹市富新镇常明村二组
年级二班	绵竹市齐天镇
年级二班	绵竹市齐天镇
年级二班	绵竹市富新镇荣华社区
年级二班	绵竹市什地镇
年级二班	绵竹市富新镇永丰村六组
年级二班	绵竹市富新镇永丰村三组
年级二班	绵竹市富新镇普胜村七组
年级二班	绵竹市富新镇普胜村四组
年级二班	绵竹市富新镇杜林村五组
年级二班	绵竹市富新镇友助村六组
年级二班	绵竹市富新镇荣华社区
年级一班	绵竹市富新镇杜林村五组
年级一班	绵竹市富新镇友助村六组
年级一班	绵竹市富新镇荣华社区
年级一班	绵竹市富新镇永丰村一组
年级一班	绵竹市五福镇
年级一班	绵竹市富新镇常明村三组
年级一班	绵竹市富新镇杜林村六组
年级一班	绵竹市富新镇普胜村二组
年级一班	节能厂
年级一班	绵竹市富新镇杜林村五组
年级一班	绵竹市富新镇友助村二组
年级一班	绵竹市富新镇永丰村二组
年级一班	绵竹市富新镇常明村三组
年级一班	绵竹市富新镇永丰村四组
年级二班	绵竹市五福镇茅坝村八组
年级二班	绵竹市富新镇友助村五组
年级二班	绵竹市富新镇永丰村六组
年级二班	绵竹市富新镇友助村六组
年级二班	绵竹市富新镇友助村四组
年级二班	绵竹市富新镇花泉村二组
年级二班	绵竹市富新镇常明村二组
年级二班	绵竹市富新镇常明村二组
年级二班	绵竹市富新镇普胜村五组
年级二班	绵竹市富新镇常明村四组
年级二班	绵竹市什地镇
年级二班	绵竹市富新镇普胜村五组

序号	姓名	拼音	性别		出生日期	年龄	学校	年级班级	住址
1384	杨丁泙	Yang Dingping	男	M	1997-	11岁	汉昌春蕾小学	五年级二班	安县黄岛乡入伍4组
1385	杨洋	Yang Yang	男	M	6/4/96	12岁	汉昌春蕾小学	五年级二班	安县汉昌东风村12队
1386	钟丽	Zhong Li	女	F	1998-	10岁	汉昌春蕾小学	五年级二班	
1387	刘仁税	Liu Renzhu	女	F	6/18/90	18岁	汉昌初级中学		
1388	杨双	Yang Shuang	男	M	1/24/92	16岁	汉昌初级中学	09级1班	绵竹市汉旺镇
1389	袁倩倩	Yuan Qianqian	女	F	2/7/90	18岁	汉昌初级中学		绵竹市汉旺镇
1390	王珊	Wang Shan	女	F	7/13/86	22岁	汉旺镇职业学校		
1391	刘东东	Liu Dongdong	男	M	2001-	7岁	汉旺镇中心小学	一年级一班	
1392	夏苗君	Xia Miaojun	女	F	2001-	7岁	汉旺镇中心小学	一年级一班	
1393	张雨龙	Zhang Yulong	男	M	8/31/01	7岁	汉旺镇中心小学	一年级一班	
1394	郑强	Zheng Qiang	男	M	2001-	7岁	汉旺镇中心小学	一年级一班	
1395	邱宇轩	Qiu Yuxuan	男	M	12/2/00	8岁	汉旺镇中心小学	一年级一班	
1396	李成智	Li Chengzhi	男	M	1999-	9岁	汉旺镇中心小学	三年级三班	
1397	刘雅	Liu Ya	女	F	1996-	12岁	汉旺镇中心小学	三年级四班	
1398	唐鑫	Tang Xin	男	M	1995-	13岁	汉旺镇中心小学	三年级四班	
1399	朱悦	Zhu Yue	女	F	1999-	9岁	汉旺镇中心小学	三年级四班	
1400	杨岚	Yang Lan	女	F	1997-	11岁	汉旺镇中心小学	四年级二班	
1401	夏仁杰	Xia Renjie	男	M	1998-	10岁	汉旺镇中心小学	四年级二班	
1402	曹俊杰	Cao Junjie	男	M	1998-	10岁	汉旺镇中心小学	四年级三班	
1403	陈璐	Chen Lu	女	F	9/5/98	10岁	汉旺镇中心小学	四年级三班	
1404	陈婉娇	Chen Wanjiao	女	F	10/17/98	10岁	汉旺镇中心小学	四年级三班	
1405	陈煜薇	Chen Yuwei	女	F	12/28/98	10岁	汉旺镇中心小学	四年级三班	
1406	杜峰	Du Feng	男	M	1998-	10岁	汉旺镇中心小学	四年级三班	
1407	谷月雯	Gu Yuewen	女	F	5/18/98	10岁	汉旺镇中心小学	四年级三班	绵竹市青义镇东街9户3号406
1408	何志伟	He Zhiwei	男	M	1998-	10岁	汉旺镇中心小学	四年级三班	
1409	李春娟	Li Chunjuan	女	F	4/14/97	11岁	汉旺镇中心小学	四年级三班	
1410	李显荣	Li Xianrong	男	M	6/20/98	10岁	汉旺镇中心小学	四年级三班	绵竹市汉旺镇片区28栋4单元8号
1411	刘鑫	Liu Xin	男	M	3/9/97	11岁	汉旺镇中心小学	四年级三班	
1412	罗利虎	Luo Lihu	男	M	1998-	10岁	汉旺镇中心小学	四年级三班	
1413	罗新冰	Luo Xinbing	男	M	11/29/97	11岁	汉旺镇中心小学	四年级三班	绵竹市汉旺镇板房区9号5栋5单元4号
1414	欧婷丹	Ou Tingdan	女	F	11/1/98	10岁	汉旺镇中心小学	四年级三班	绵竹市孝德镇
1415	潘宇	Pan Yu	男	M	1998-	10岁	汉旺镇中心小学	四年级三班	
1416	谭思宇	Tan Siyu	女	F	1998-5-	10岁	汉旺镇中心小学	四年级三班	
1417	王晨	Wang Chen	男	M	11/2/97	11岁	汉旺镇中心小学	四年级三班	
1418	吴欣柯	Wu Xinke	女	F	1998-	10岁	汉旺镇中心小学	四年级三班	
1419	肖何	Xiao He	男	M	10/28/97	11岁	汉旺镇中心小学	四年级三班	绵竹市马尾镇板房区12栋5单元3号
1420	薛依琳	Xue Yilin	女	F	1998-	10岁	汉旺镇中心小学	四年级三班	
1421	严艺洋	Yan Yiyang	男	M	10/3/97	11岁	汉旺镇中心小学	四年级三班	绵竹市马尾镇板房区52栋5单元2号
1422	杨丹妮	Yang Danni	女	F	1998-	10岁	汉旺镇中心小学	四年级三班	
1423	杨楠锋	Yang Nanfeng	男	M	11/7/97	11岁	汉旺镇中心小学	四年级三班	绵竹市汉旺镇河南路
1424	杨怡	Yang Yi	女	F	1998-	10岁	汉旺镇中心小学	四年级三班	
1425	张毅	Zhang Yi	男	M	9/24/97	11岁	汉旺镇中心小学	四年级三班	
1426	张钰林	Zhang Yulin	女	F	5/19/98	10岁	汉旺镇中心小学	四年级三班	
1427	张玥	Zhang Yue	女	F	2/11/98	10岁	汉旺镇中心小学	四年级三班	绵竹市汉旺镇天池集团板房36栋4单元4号
1428	杜金琼	Du Jinqiong	女	F	1998-	10岁	汉旺镇中心小学	四年级四班	
1429	杜静	Du Jing	女	F	5/25/98	10岁	汉旺镇中心小学	四年级四班	
1430	何怡轩	He Yixuan	男	M	1998-	10岁	汉旺镇中心小学	四年级四班	
1431	雷汉林	Lei Hanlin	男	M	9/28/97	11岁	汉旺镇中心小学	四年级四班	绵竹市汉旺镇武都板房126#4-4
1432	刘雅文	Liu Yawen	女	F	1997-	11岁	汉旺镇中心小学	四年级四班	
1433	罗雨晴	Luo Yuqing	女	F	3/24/98	10岁	汉旺镇中心小学	四年级四班	
1434	庞博文	Pang Bowen	男	M	1998-	10岁	汉旺镇中心小学	四年级四班	
1435	谭志敏	Tan Zhimin	女	F	1998-	10岁	汉旺镇中心小学	四年级四班	
1436	张长兴	Zhang Changxing	男	M	1998-	10岁	汉旺镇中心小学	四年级四班	
1437	张田亮	Zhang Tianliang	男	M	1998-	10岁	汉旺镇中心小学	四年级四班	
1438	赵兰馨	Zhao Lanxin	女	F	3/27/98	10岁	汉旺镇中心小学	四年级四班	绵竹市汉旺镇天池集团板房22栋2单元8号
1439	陈璐	Chen Lu	女	F	1997-	11岁	汉旺镇中心小学	五年级一班	
1440	邓辉	Deng Hui	男	M	1997-	11岁	汉旺镇中心小学	五年级一班	
1441	胡佩佩	Hu Peipei	女	F	1997-	11岁	汉旺镇中心小学	五年级一班	
1442	李俊	Li Jun	男	M	6/24/96	12岁	汉旺镇中心小学	五年级一班	绵竹市汉旺镇汉新社区126栋五单元
1443	李双	Li Shuang	女	F	1997-	11岁	汉旺镇中心小学	五年级一班	
1444	谢易杰	Xie Yijie	男	M	1997-	11岁	汉旺镇中心小学	五年级一班	
1445	杨敏	Yang Min	女	F	1997-	11岁	汉旺镇中心小学	五年级一班	
1446	何恬	He Tian	女	F	1997-	11岁	汉旺镇中心小学	五年级二班	
1447	黄兰蕊	Huang Lanrui	女	F	1997-	11岁	汉旺镇中心小学	五年级二班	
1448	黎星	Li Xing	男	M	1997-	11岁	汉旺镇中心小学	五年级二班	
1449	刘雪婷	Liu Xueting	女	F	12/29/96	11岁	汉旺镇中心小学	五年级二班	
1450	罗慧玲	Luo Huiling	女	F	1997-	11岁	汉旺镇中心小学	五年级二班	
1451	尹邦仪	Yin Bangyi	男	M	12/29/97	11岁	汉旺镇中心小学	五年级二班	汉旺镇顺河南段3号
1452	赵莉	Zhao Li	女	F	1997-	11岁	汉旺镇中心小学	五年级二班	
1453	朱睿	Zhu Rui	女	F	1997-	11岁	汉旺镇中心小学	五年级二班	
1454	陈留林	Chen Liulin	男	M	1/16/97	11岁	汉旺镇中心小学	五年级三班	绵竹市汉旺镇板房区16栋5单元
1455	陈佩	Chen Pei	女	F	1997-	11岁	汉旺镇中心小学	五年级三班	
1456	邓艾瑾	Deng Aijin	女	F	1997-	11岁	汉旺镇中心小学	五年级三班	
1457	何秀频	He Xiupin	女	F	5/23/97	11岁	汉旺镇中心小学	五年级三班	绵竹市汉旺镇天池煤矿
1458	蒋东	Jiang Dong	男	M	3/26/95	13岁	汉旺镇中心小学	五年级三班	绵竹市汉旺镇方大区
1459	刘辉	Liu Hui	女	F	1997-	11岁	汉旺镇中心小学	五年级三班	
1460	刘爽	Liu Shuang	男	M	1997-	11岁	汉旺镇中心小学	五年级三班	
1461	石磊	Shi Lei	男	M	1997-	11岁	汉旺镇中心小学	五年级三班	
1462	孙浩	Sun Hao	男	M	1997-	11岁	汉旺镇中心小学	五年级三班	
1463	唐鑫	Tang Xin	男	M	1997-	11岁	汉旺镇中心小学	五年级三班	
1464	王熙	Wang Xi	男	M	9/30/96	12岁	汉旺镇中心小学	五年级三班	
1465	杜雪	Du Xue	女	F	1997-	11岁	汉旺镇中心小学	五年级四班	

序号	姓名	拼音	性别		出生日期	年龄	学校	年级班级
1508	肖宇涵	Xiao Yuhan	男	M	3/11/03	5岁	红白幼儿园	幼儿园
1509	周禄豪	Zhou Luhao	男	M	3/4/03	5岁	红白幼儿园	幼儿园
1510	周艺鑫	Zhou Yixin					红白幼儿园	幼儿园
1511	方红阳	Fang Hongyang					红白中心学校	学前班
1512	房宇	Fang Yu					红白中心学校	学前班
1513	何蕊月	He Ruiyue	女	F	2001-	7岁	红白中心学校	学前班
1514	黄茜	Huang Xi					红白中心学校	学前班
1515	黄杨	Huang Xi	男	M	2002-2-29	6岁	红白中心学校	学前班
1516	林箱箱	Lin Koukou					红白中心学校	学前班
1517	林磊	Lin Lei					红白中心学校	学前班
1518	刘鑫耀	Liu Xinyao					红白中心学校	学前班
1519	谢菁	Xie Jing	女	F	9/15/02	6岁	红白中心学校	学前班
1520	杨西孟	Yang Ximeng					红白中心学校	学前班
1521	郑莎	Zheng Sha	女	F	12/27/02	6岁	红白中心学校	学前班
1522	方垚	Fang Yao			8/9/01	7岁	红白中心学校	一年级
1523	黄磊	Huang Lei					红白中心学校	一年级
1524	廖文熙	Liao Wenxi	男	M	4/22/00	8岁	红白中心学校	一年级
1525	林峰	Lin Feng	男	M	7/23/01	7岁	红白中心学校	一年级
1526	王洋	Wang Yang					红白中心学校	一年级
1527	易思潼	Yi Sitong					红白中心学校	一年级
1528	张辉磊	Zhang Huilei	男	M	4/13/01	7岁	红白中心学校	一年级
1529	李进飞	Li Jinfei					红白中心学校	二年级
1530	李菁	Li Jing					红白中心学校	二年级
1531	赵昌齐	Zhao Changqi					红白中心学校	二年级
1532	赵昌睿	Zhao Changrui	男	M	2000-	8岁	红白中心学校	二年级
1533	李清	Li Qing					红白中心学校	二年级二班
1534	陈毅	Chen Yi	男	M	9/12/98	10岁	红白中心学校	三年级一班
1535	方若华	Fang Ruohua	男	M	8/8/99	9岁	红白中心学校	三年级一班
1536	黎晓林	Li Xiaolin					红白中心学校	三年级一班
1537	李文俊	Li Wenjun	男	M	1998-	10岁	红白中心学校	三年级一班
1538	李祥	Li Xiang					红白中心学校	三年级一班
1539	李小兵	Li Xiaobing					红白中心学校	三年级一班
1540	李亚男	Li Yanan					红白中心学校	三年级一班
1541	毛全兴	Mao Quanxing					红白中心学校	三年级一班
1542	米小雨	Mi Xiaoyu	男	M	7/11/98	10岁	红白中心学校	三年级一班
1543	谢宇池	Xie Yuchi	女	F	1/1/99	9岁	红白中心学校	三年级一班
1544	邢远豪	Xing Yuanhao					红白中心学校	三年级一班
1545	徐梦怡	Xu Mengyi	女	F	9/23/99	9岁	红白中心学校	三年级一班
1546	易鑫月	Yi Xinyue	女	F	2/17/99	9岁	红白中心学校	三年级一班
1547	冯瑶	Feng Yao	女	F	1999-	9岁	红白中心学校	三年级二班
1548	李彤灿阳	Li Tongcanyang	男	M	8/12/98	10岁	红白中心学校	三年级二班
1549	李宇竹	Li Yuzhu	女	F	2/3/99	9岁	红白中心学校	三年级二班
1550	聊沅	Liao Yuan					红白中心学校	三年级二班
1551	王阳	Wang Yang	男	M	7/18/98	10岁	红白中心学校	三年级二班
1552	谢天航	Xie Tianhang	男	M	1/6/99	10岁	红白中心学校	三年级二班
1553	张鹏	Zhang Peng					红白中心学校	三年级二班
1554	赵雪莲	Zhao Xuelian	女	F	1999-	9岁	红白中心学校	三年级二班
1555	赵玉贝	Zhao Yubei	男	M	4/6/99	9岁	红白中心学校	三年级二班
1556	朱婷	Zhu Ting	女	F	5/18/98	10岁	红白中心学校	三年级二班
1557	冯斯琪	Feng Siqi	女	F	2/2/98	10岁	红白中心学校	四年级一班
1558	赖九钰	Lai Jiuyu	女	F	1/2/98	10岁	红白中心学校	四年级一班
1559	宋沛昱	Song Peiyu	男	M	8/4/98	10岁	红白中心学校	四年级一班
1560	唐小宇	Tang Xiaoyu	男	M	6/18/97	11岁	红白中心学校	四年级一班
1561	王若宇	Wang Ruoyu	女	F	9/27/97	11岁	红白中心学校	四年级一班
1562	赵馨	Zhao Xin	女	F	1998-		红白中心学校	四年级一班
1563	赵萱	Zhao Xuan	女	F	1/29/98	10岁	红白中心学校	四年级一班
1564	周子琪	Zhou Ziqi	男	M	8/5/98	10岁	红白中心学校	四年级一班
1565	陈娅	Chen Ya					红白中心学校	四年级二班
1566	冯帅	Feng Shuai	男	M	6/10/97	11岁	红白中心学校	四年级二班
1567	郭婷	Guo Ting					红白中心学校	四年级二班
1568	何佳霖	He Jialin	女	F	5/18/98	10岁	红白中心学校	四年级二班
1569	姜兴宇	Jiang Xingyu					红白中心学校	四年级二班
1570	罗一鸿	Luo Yihong					红白中心学校	四年级二班
1571	叶启红	Ye Qihong	女	F	9/19/97	11岁	红白中心学校	四年级二班
1572	张珏	Zhang Jue	女	F	2/2/98	10岁	红白中心学校	四年级二班
1573	赵泓全	Zhao Hongquan	男	M	8/30/97	11岁	红白中心学校	四年级二班
1574	郑锋	Zheng Feng					红白中心学校	四年级二班
1575	周黎	Zhou Li	女	F	1/20/98	10岁	红白中心学校	五年级一班
1576	陈军	Chen Jun	男	M	1996-	12岁	红白中心学校	五年级一班
1577	陈美	Chen Mei					红白中心学校	五年级一班
1578	陈庆	Chen Qing					红白中心学校	五年级一班
1579	陈英杰	Cheng Yingjie	男	M	11/9/96	12岁	红白中心学校	五年级一班
1580	冯丹	Feng Dan					红白中心学校	五年级一班
1581	梁思悟	Liang Siwu					红白中心学校	五年级一班
1582	廖翠	Liao Cui	女	F	1996-3-		红白中心学校	五年级一班
1583	肖航	Xiao Hang					红白中心学校	五年级一班
1584	肖帅鑫	Xiao Shuaixin	男	M	1/10/97	11岁	红白中心学校	五年级一班
1585	谢周星	Xie Zhouxing					红白中心学校	五年级一班
1586	杨思建	Yang Sijie	男	M	8/27/97	11岁	红白中心学校	五年级一班
1587	张辉璐	Zhang Huilu	女	F	7/11/96	12岁	红白中心学校	五年级一班
1588	张梦琪	Zhang Mengqi	女	F	6/28/97	11岁	红白中心学校	五年级二班

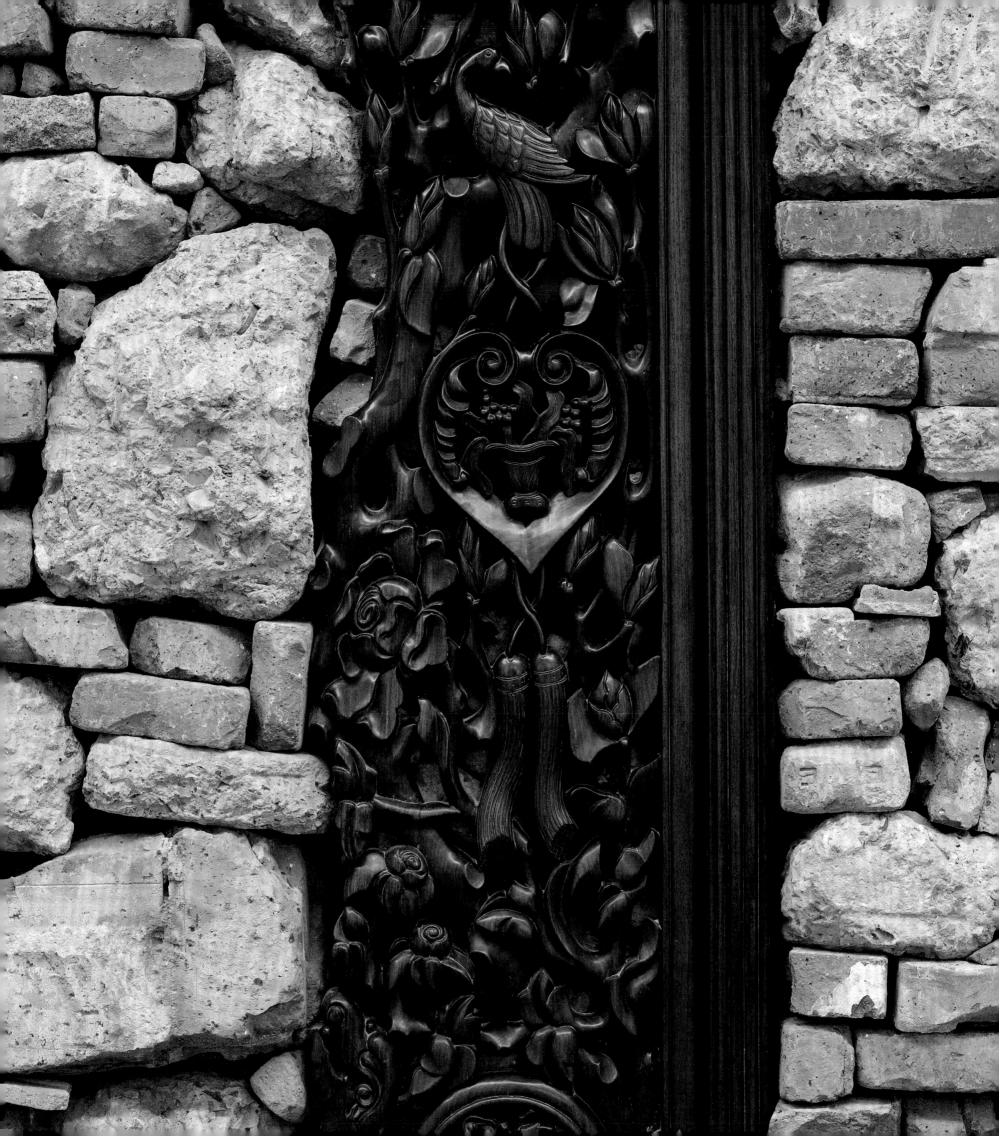

4

In 1999 Ai built a studio-house of his own design at Caochangdi, which was then on the outskirts of Beijing. A number of artists and commercial galleries soon followed, turning this former agricultural village into a successful art district. In 2008 the municipal authorities in Shanghai, keen to replicate the success of Caochangdi, invited Ai to build a studio in Malu Town, Jiading district, at their cost.

As requested, Ai designed and arranged the construction of this new studio, which was completed in October 2010. The federal authorities then countermanded the agreement and ordered the building to be demolished on the pretext that Ai had not gained the requisite planning permission. On 7 November Ai placed an open invitation on the internet, encouraging supporters to attend a lunch during which they would feast on river crabs to commemorate both the completion of the new building and its imminent demolition. The Chinese word for river crabs, *He Xie*, is a homonym for 'harmonious', a word much used in government propaganda, but which has lately become internet slang for censorship.

Although Ai was placed under house arrest and prevented from being at the lunch in person, some 800 guests attended. The studio was razed to the ground on 11 January 2011. Despite the authorities' attempts to prevent Ai accessing the site during the demolition he managed to procure some of the original building materials to make *Souvenir from Shanghai*.

15

Shanghai Studio Model, 2011

Wood, 45 x 41 x 9.5 cm

Courtesy of Ai Weiwei Studio

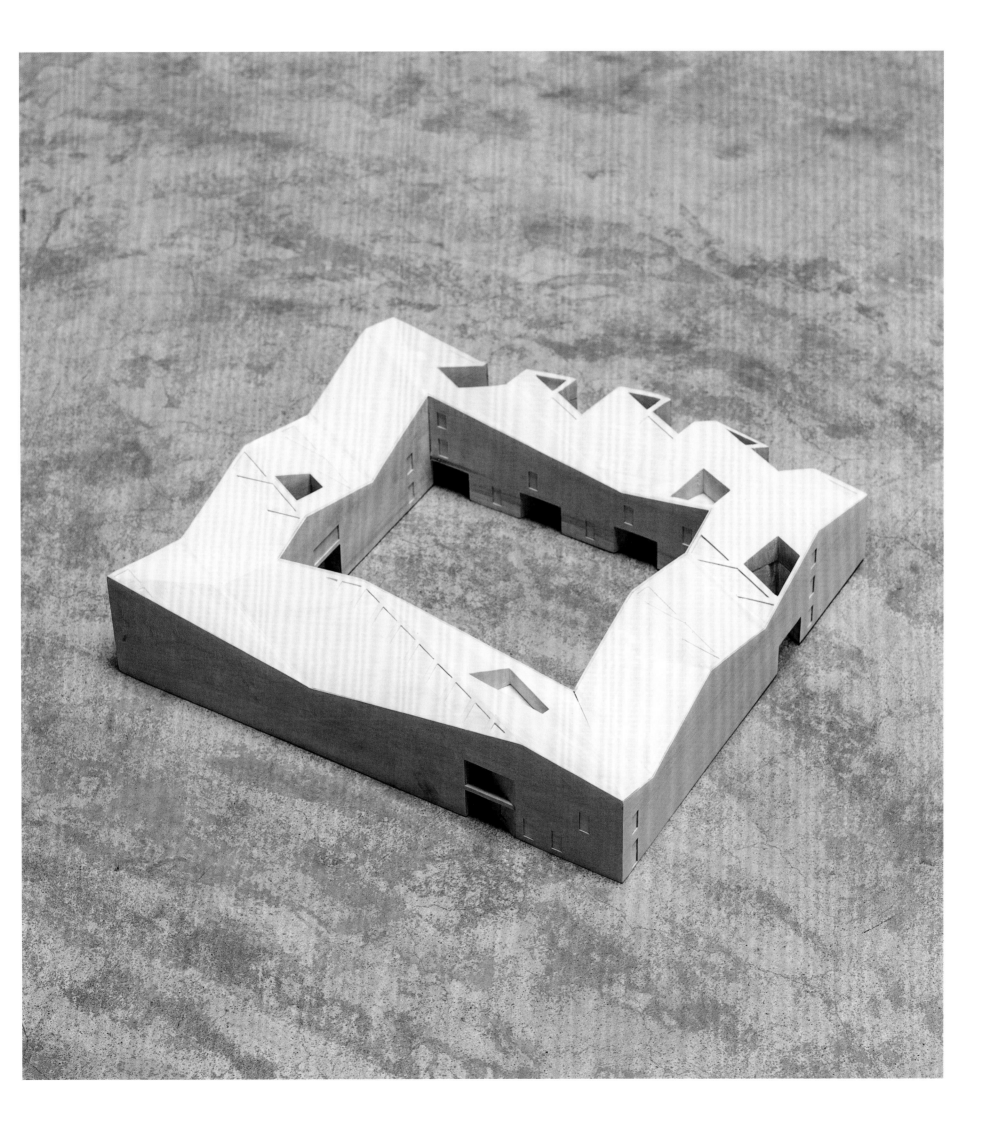

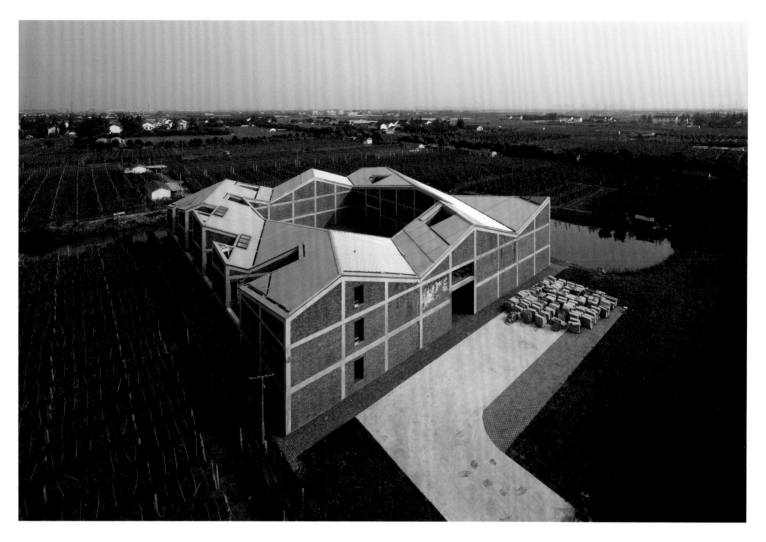

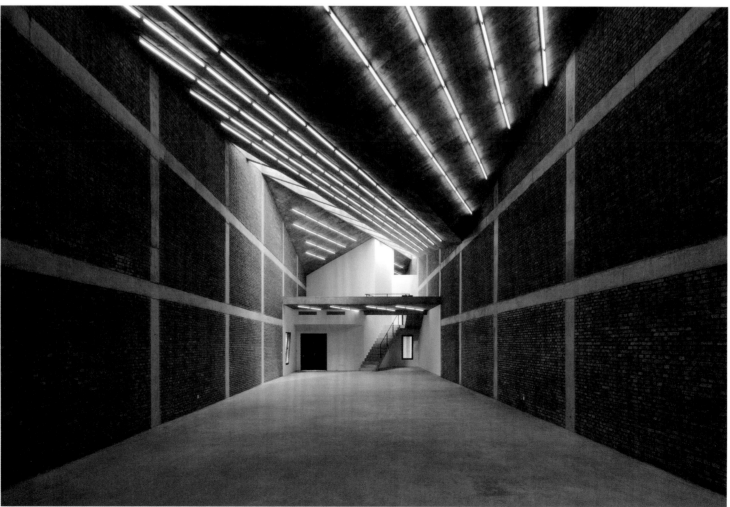

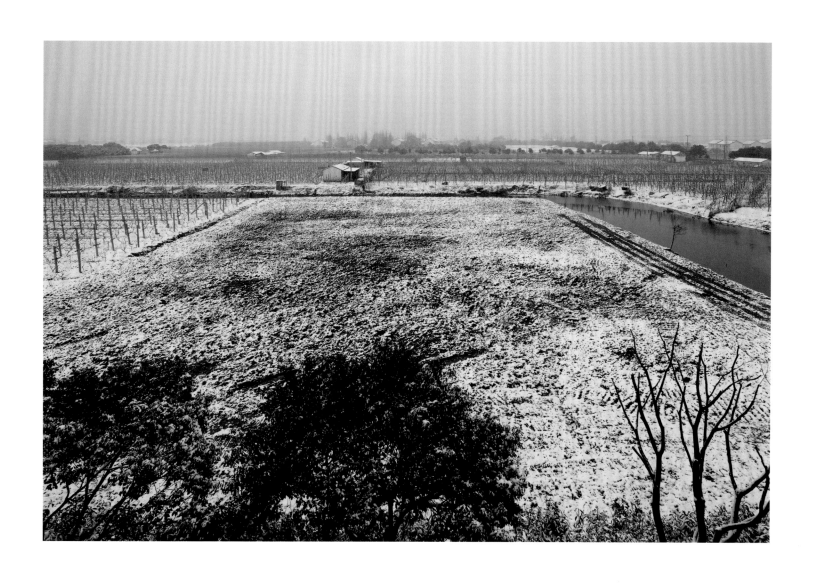

16

Shanghai Studio (Jiading Malu), 2010–11

Colour photographic prints, 50 x 75 cm

Courtesy of Ai Weiwei Studio

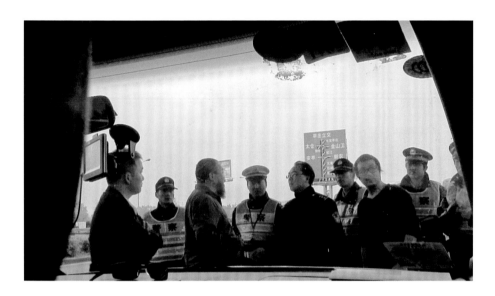

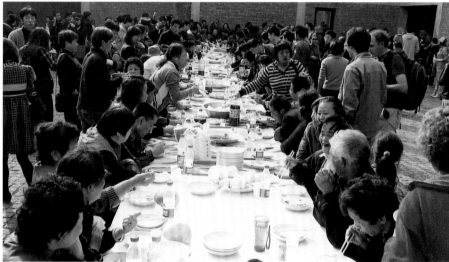

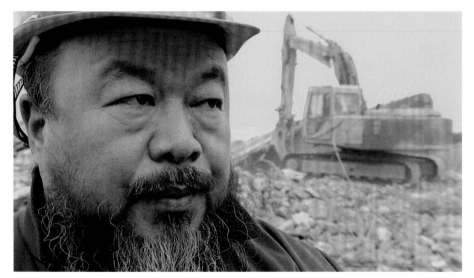

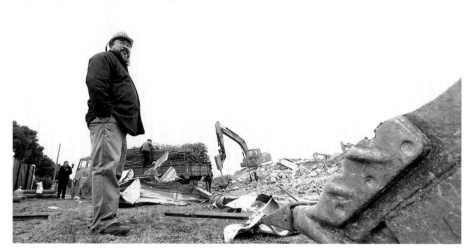

17

The Crab House (He xie fang zi), 2015

Video, duration 21 minutes 45 seconds

Courtesy of Ai Weiwei Studio

18 (overleaf)

He Xie, 2011

Porcelain, 3,000 pieces, each 5 x 25 x 10 cm

Courtesy of Ai Weiwei Studio

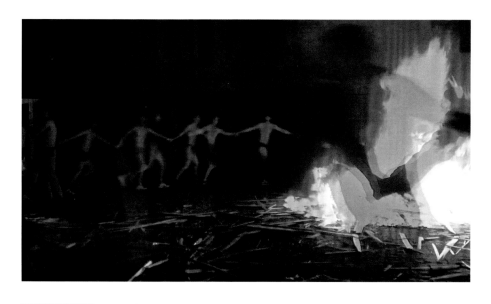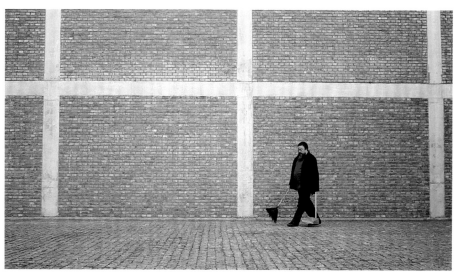
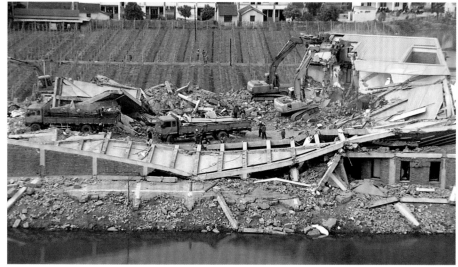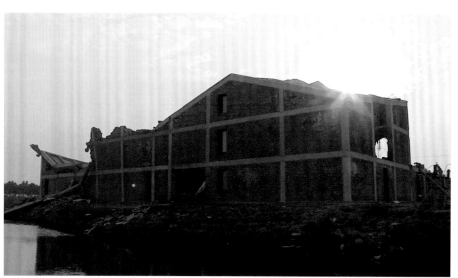

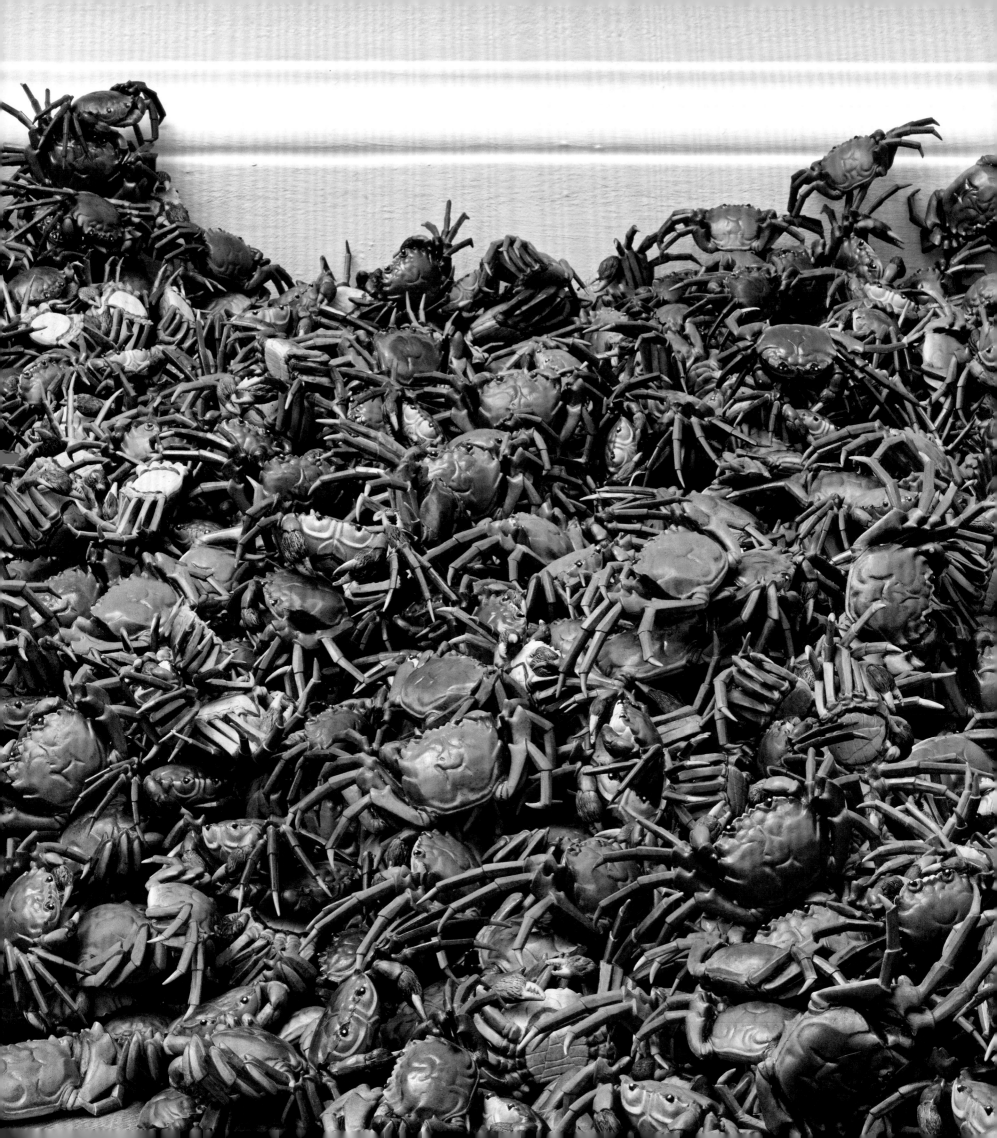

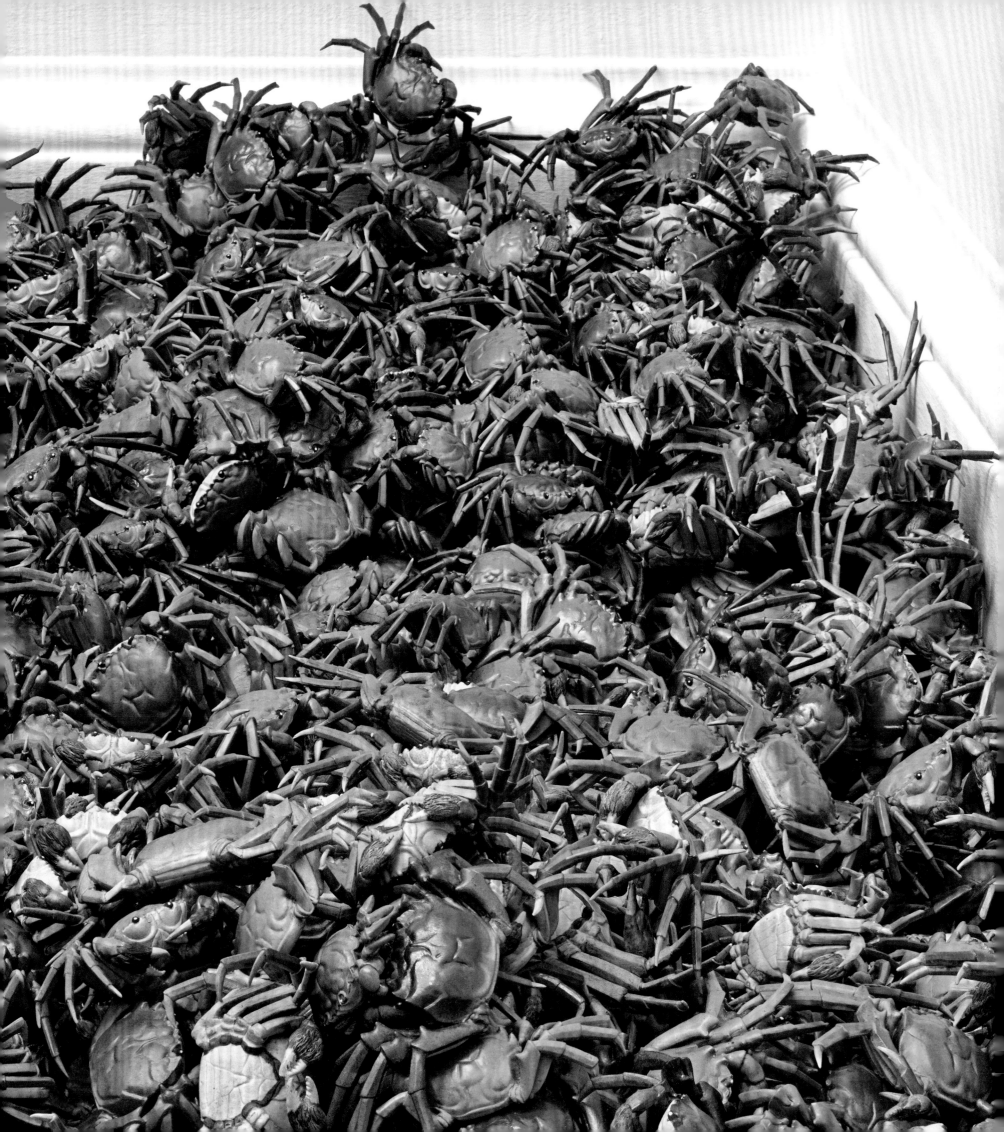

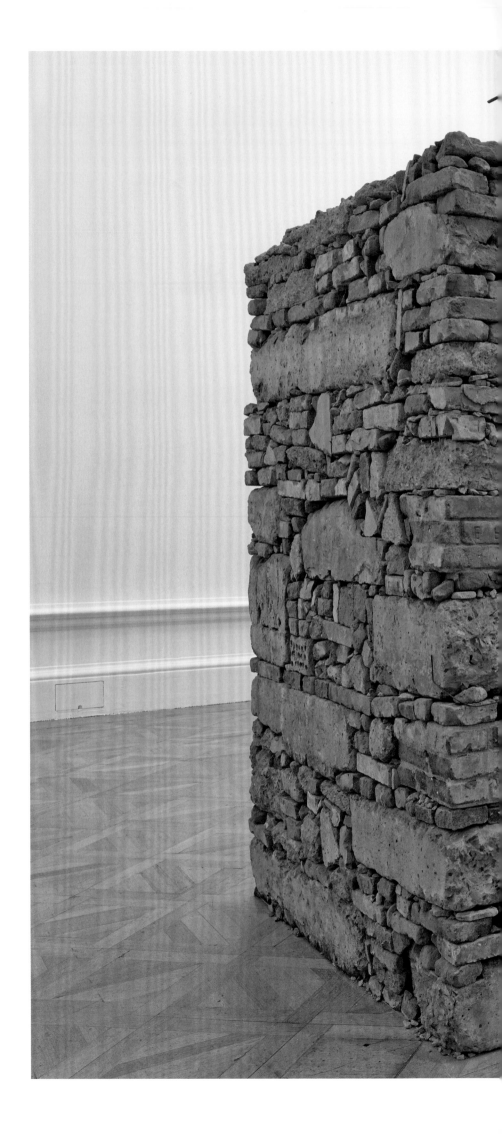

19

Souvenir from Shanghai, 2012

Concrete and brick rubble from the artist's destroyed Shanghai studio, set in a wooden frame, 380 x 170 x 260 cm

Courtesy of Ai Weiwei Studio

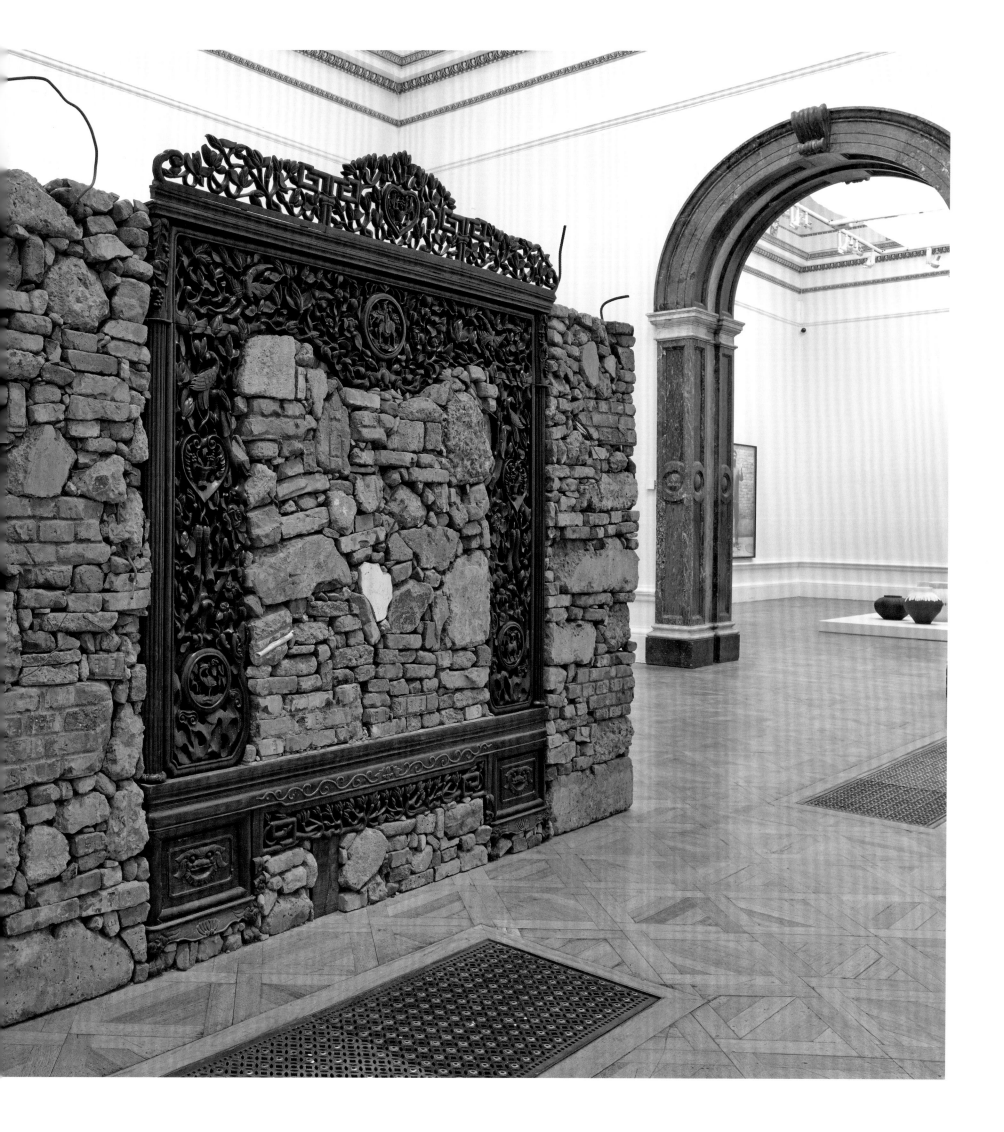

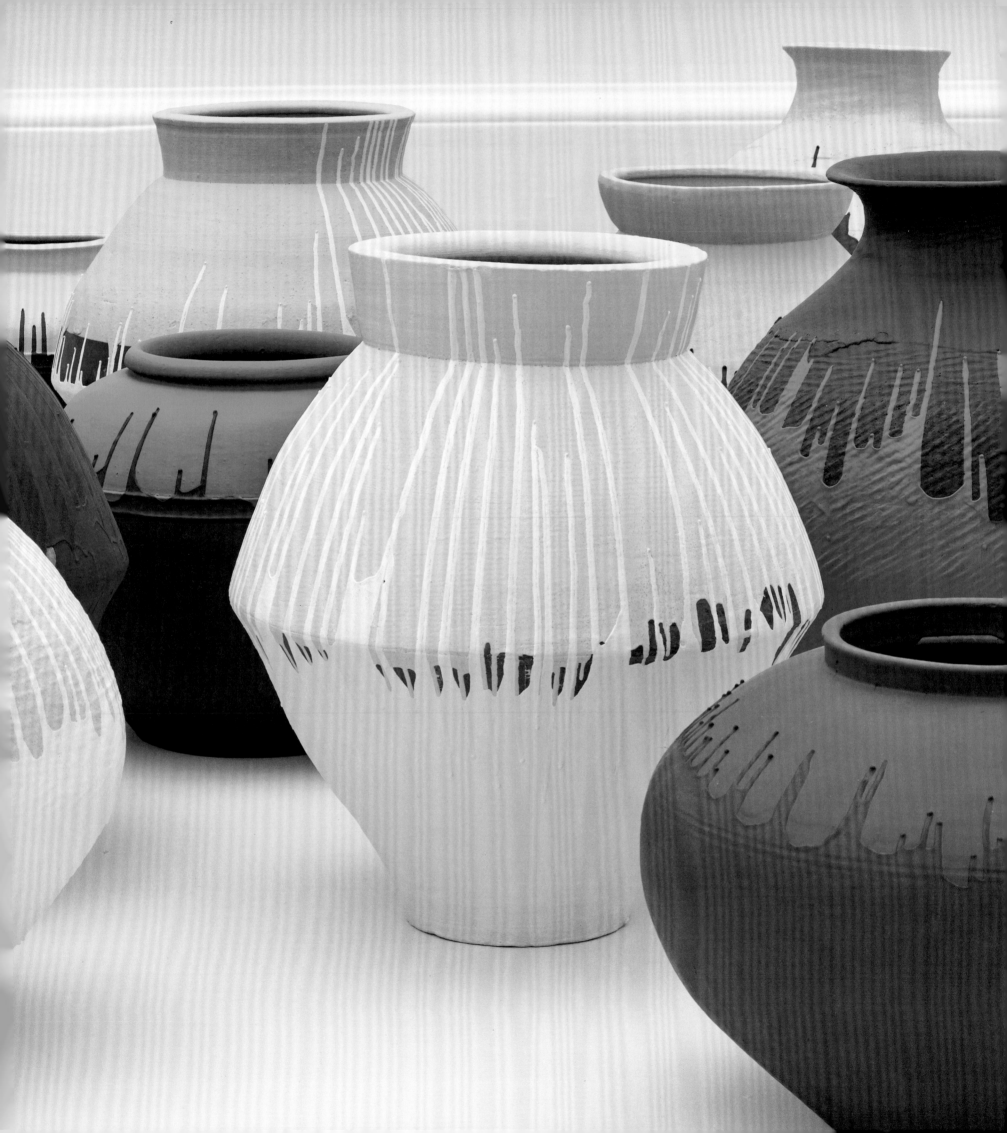

5

Since his return to China in 1993 Ai has systematically engaged with ceramics. He purchases historic vessels, ranging from Neolithic pottery to Qing Dynasty porcelain, in markets and from antique dealers. These are grouped and classified by period and style before his interventions. Ai is very conscious that markets are full of fakes being sold as originals, and that only experts can distinguish between them. The creation of forgeries interests him since the same skills and traditions used to create the originals are used to create modern versions. The question of authenticity is, therefore, central to this body of work. By extension, he is also interested in value: is a Neolithic vase dipped in paint or ground to dust more valuable as a contemporary artwork than it was as an original? In China, which is so marked by rapid change and development, Ai exposes the tension between old and new.

Ai produced the first *Coca Cola Vase* in his ongoing series in 1994. The logo of the ubiquitous soft drink is emblazoned across the vase, blurring notions of history and global branding.

In *Dropping a Han Dynasty Urn* he overtly refers to the wilful destruction of China's historic buildings and antique objects that took place in the decade following Chairman Mao's instigation of the Cultural Revolution in 1966. Ai's impassive face in the photograph can also be seen as a reference to the lack of protection given by the authorities to the historic fabric of many of China's cities, sacrificed in pursuit of economic development.

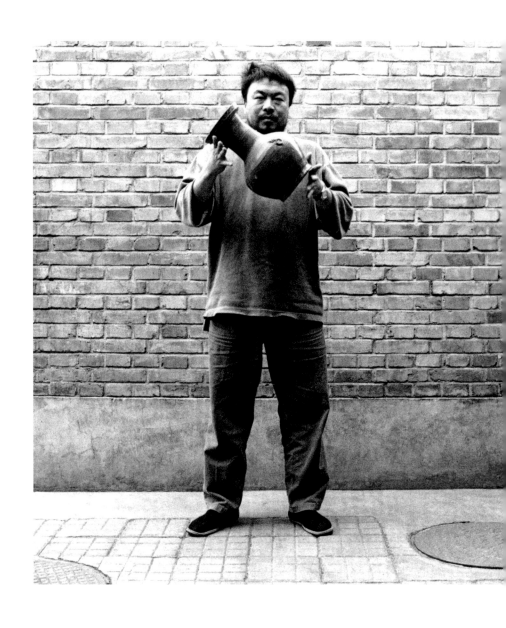

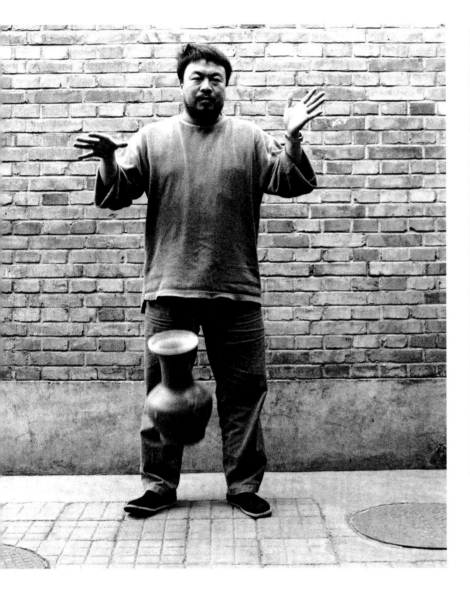
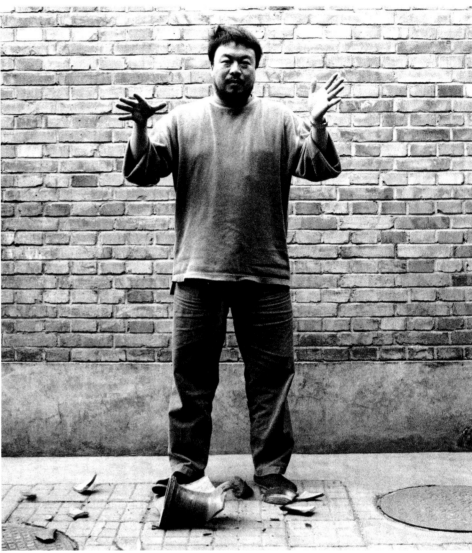

20

Dropping a Han Dynasty Urn, 1995

Triptych of black-and-white prints, each 199.9 x 180 cm

Courtesy of Ai Weiwei Studio

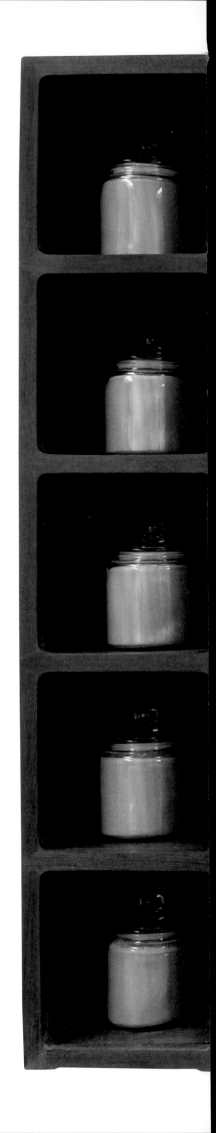

21

Dust to Dust, 2008

Thirty glass jars with powder from ground Neolithic pottery
(5000–3000 BC), wooden shelving, 200 x 240 x 36 cm

Collection of Larry Warsh

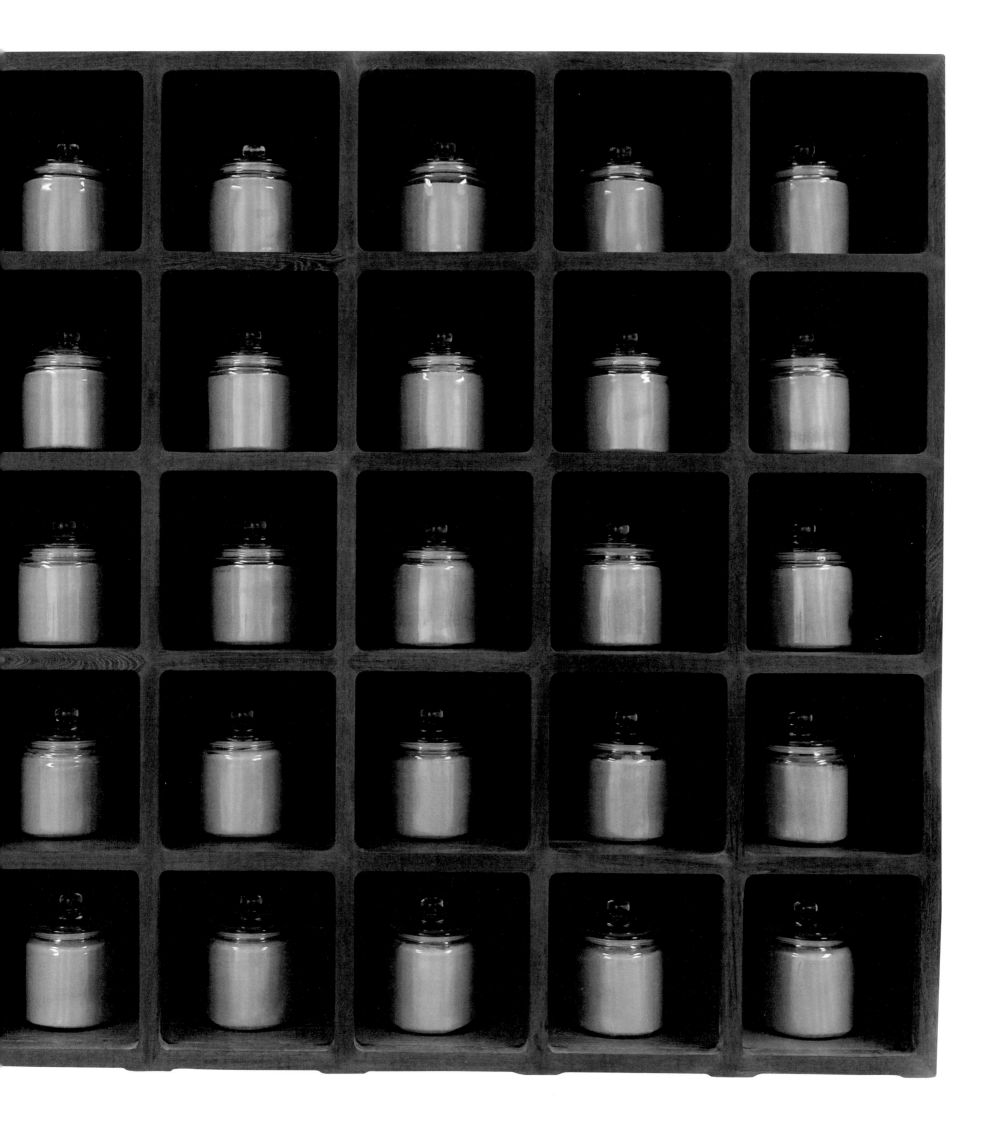

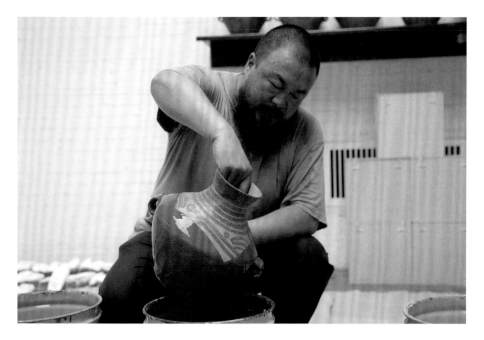
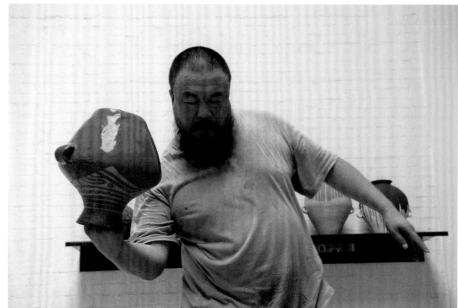
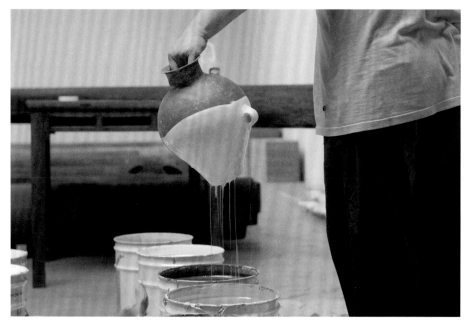
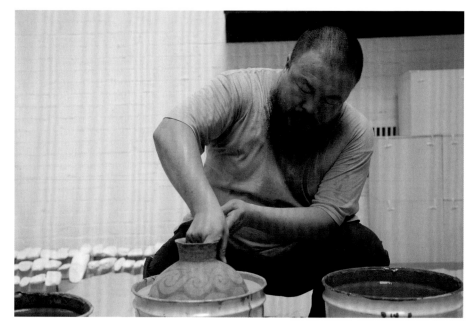

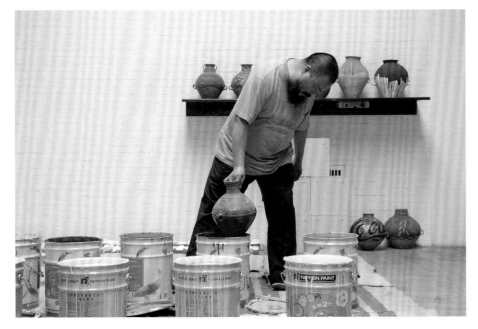

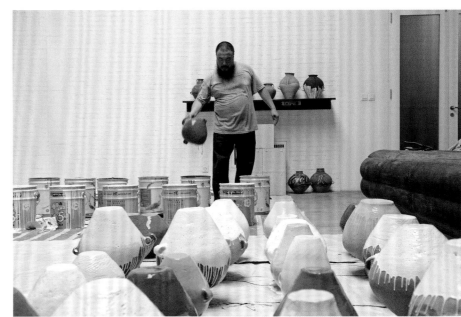

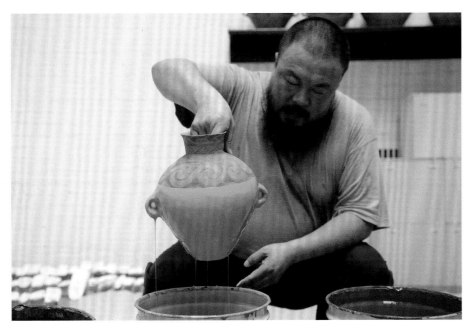

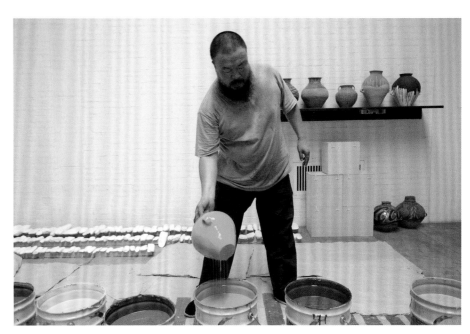

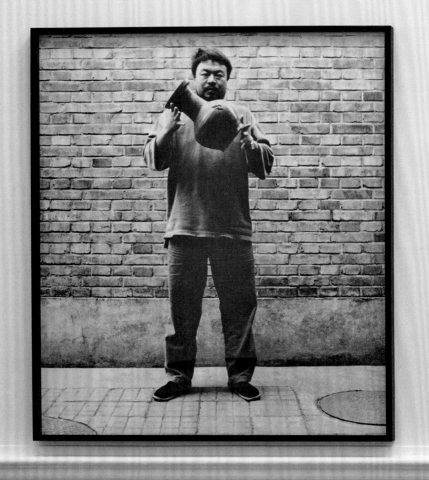
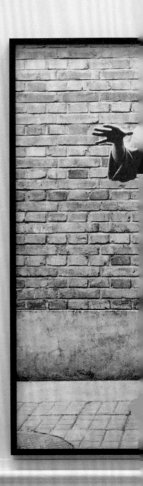
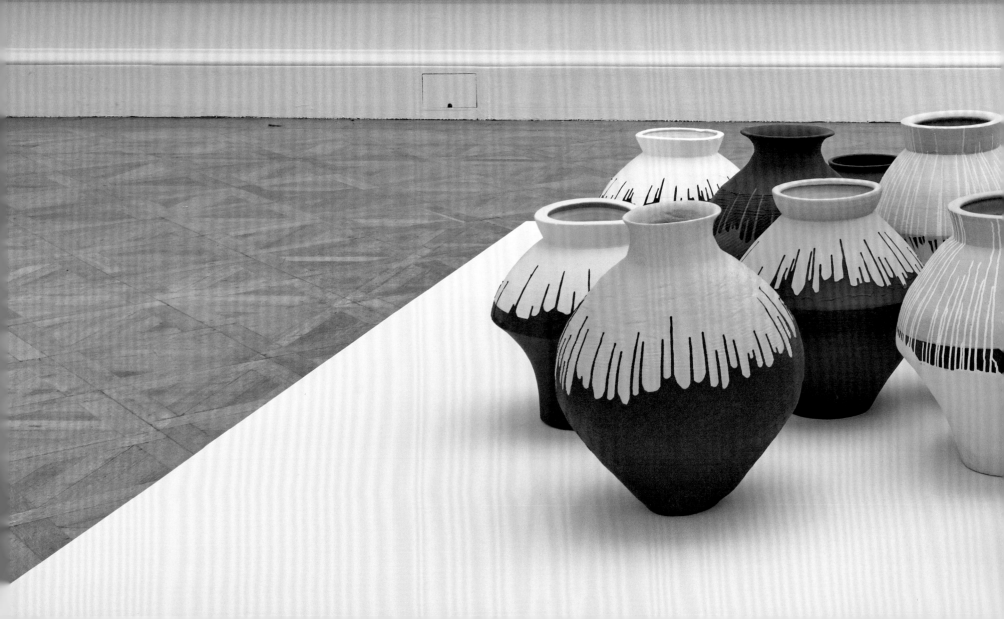

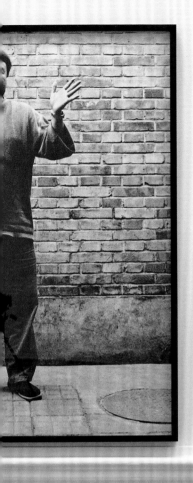
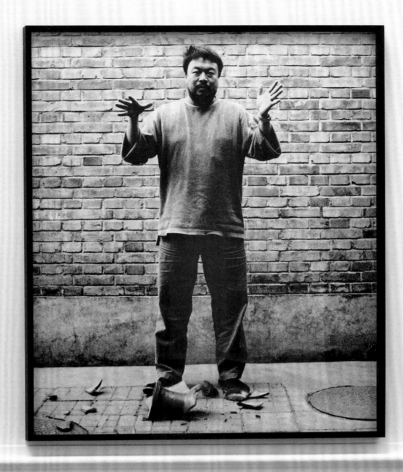
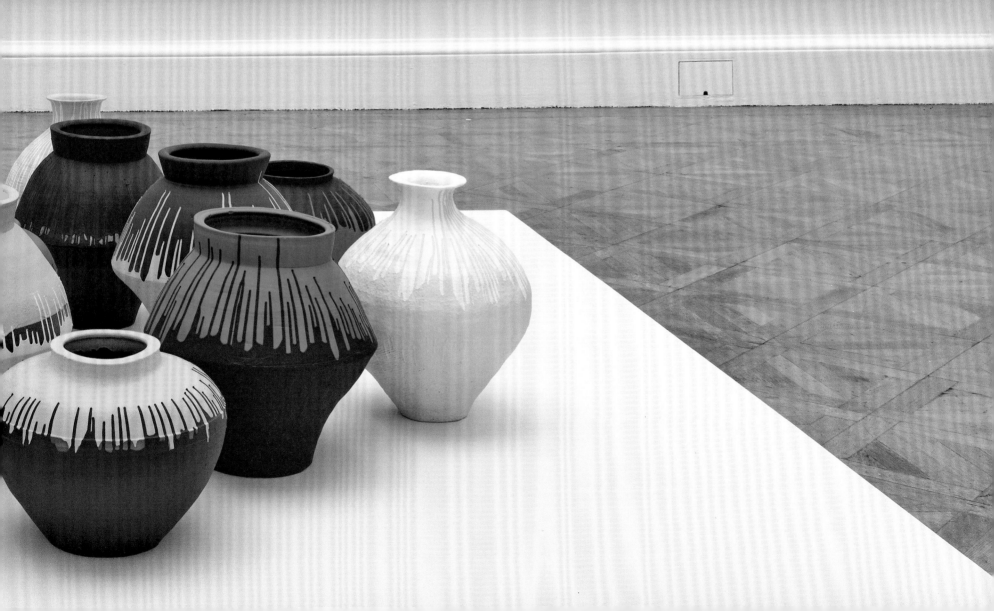

22 (previous pages; production views pages 160–61)

Coloured Vases, 2015

Twelve Han Dynasty (206 BC – 220 AD) and four Neolithic (5000–3000 BC) vases with industrial paint, dimensions variable

Private collection, Private collection, Collection of Lisa and Danny Goldberg

23 (production views overleaf)

Coca Cola Vase, 2014

Han Dynasty (206 BC – 220 AD) vase with paint, 42 x 42 x 35 cm

Courtesy of Ai Weiwei Studio

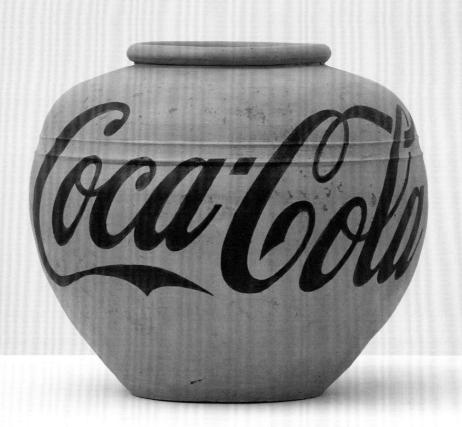

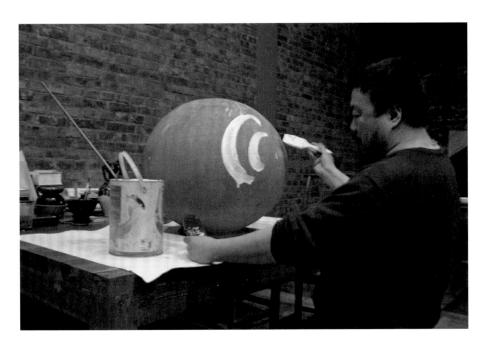
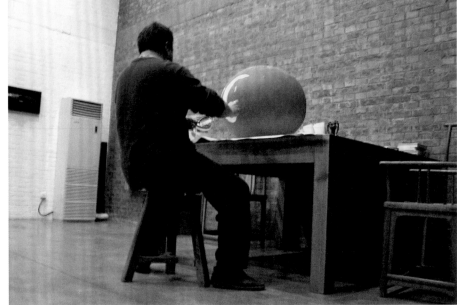

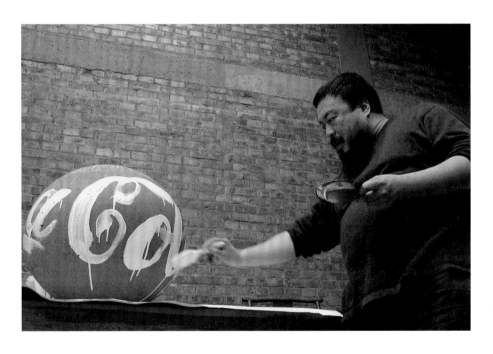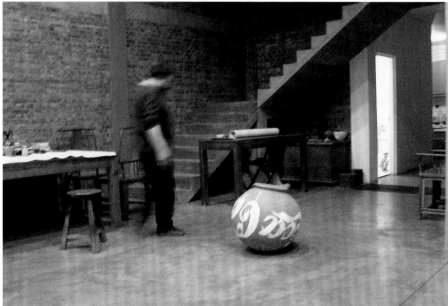

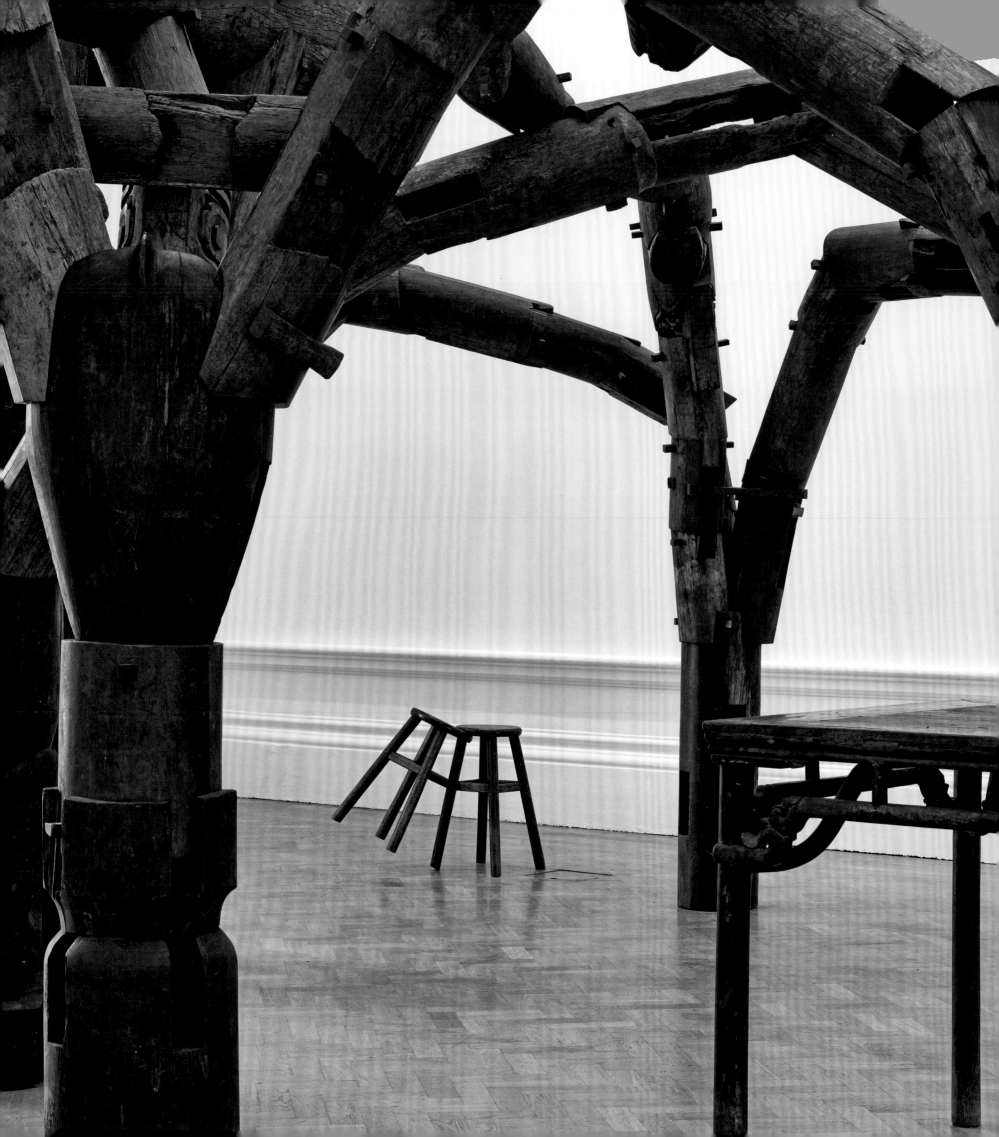

6

One of Ai's most ambitious sculptures, *Fragments* is an amalgamation of his Furniture and Map series. Created using architectural salvage from four temples and items of furniture from the Ming and Qing Dynasties, the work at first appears to be a random construction made from unrelated objects. As Ai says: 'Everything is misfit and connected wrongly.' Yet when it is seen from above – a physical impossibility within the gallery – the timber frame is revealed as a map of China including Taiwan (represented by the conjoined stools).

The sculpture can be traversed, allowing the visitor obliviously to permeate the borders of China and cross the country freely, much as tourists do when they visit, in a way that Chinese citizens cannot. The different geographic and ethnographic identities of the country are rendered immaterial and China is presented as a skeleton. Despite its robust construction, this skeletal form suggests an inherent fragility that can be seen as a commentary on the concept of 'One China', the state-sponsored policy aimed at protecting and promoting China's sovereignty and territorial integrity.

Offcuts of the salvaged timbers used to make *Fragments* were kept and used to create *Kippe* (cat. 8).

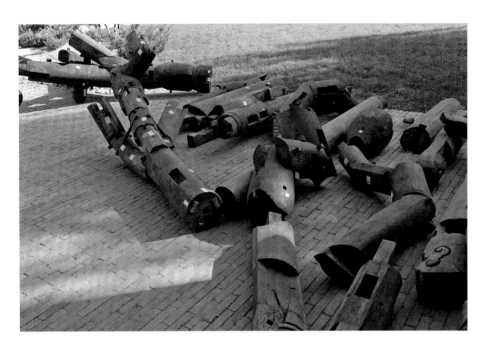

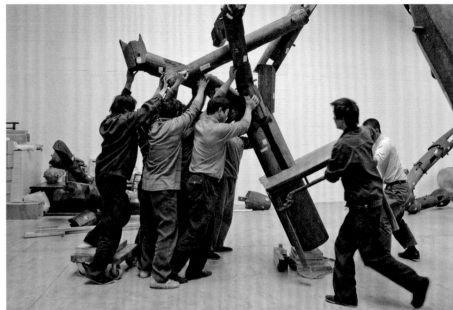

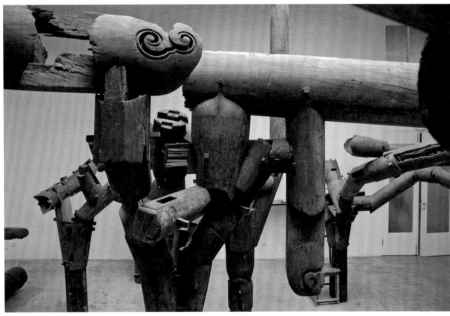

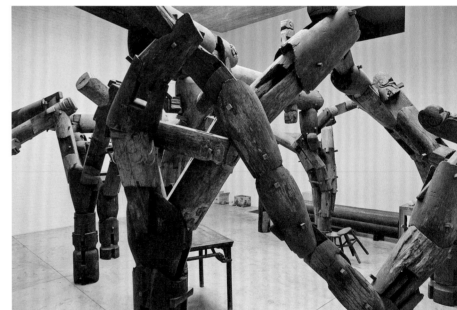

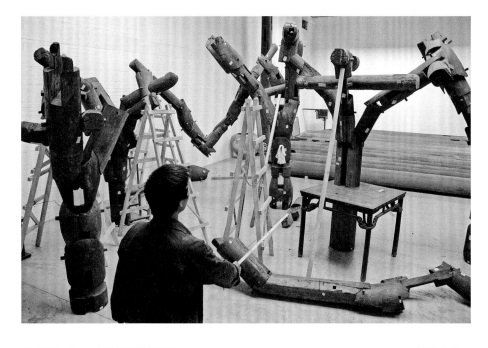

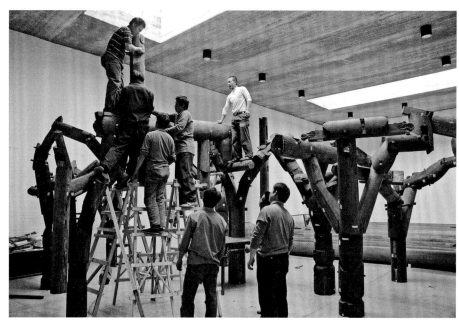

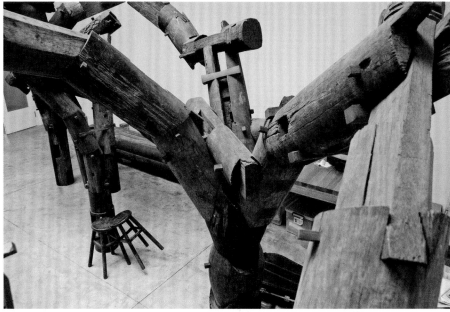

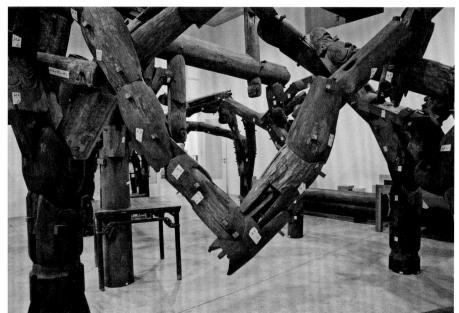

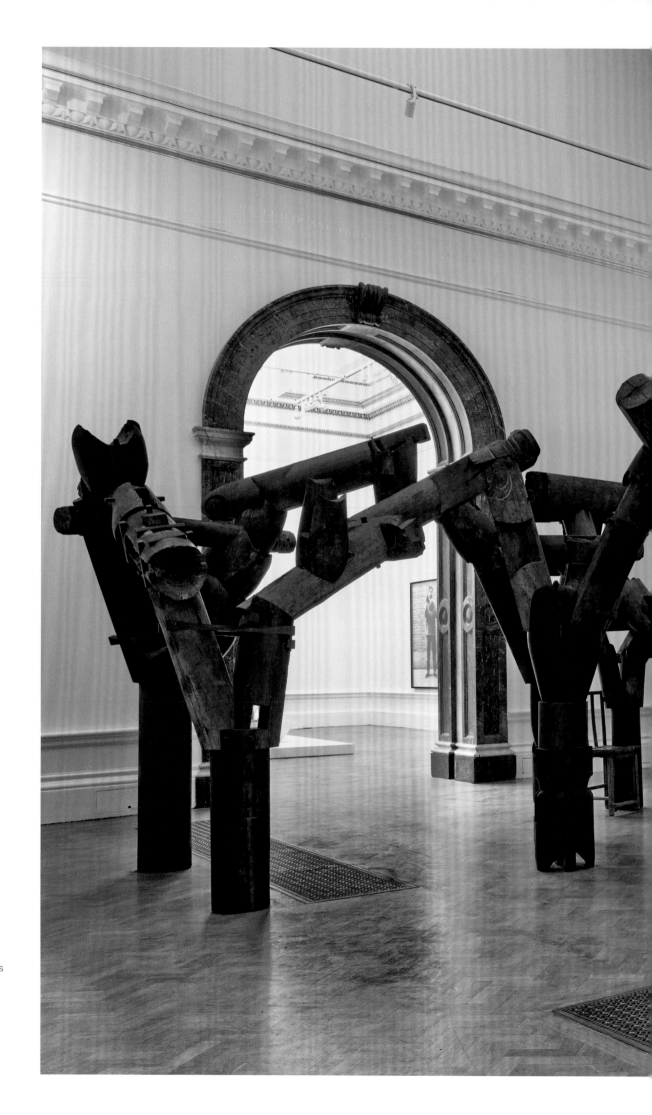

24 (production views previous pages)

Fragments, 2005

Iron wood (tieli wood) table, chairs, parts of beams and pillars from dismantled temples of the Qing Dynasty (1644–1911), 500 x 850 x 700 cm

M+ Sigg Collection, Hong Kong. By donation

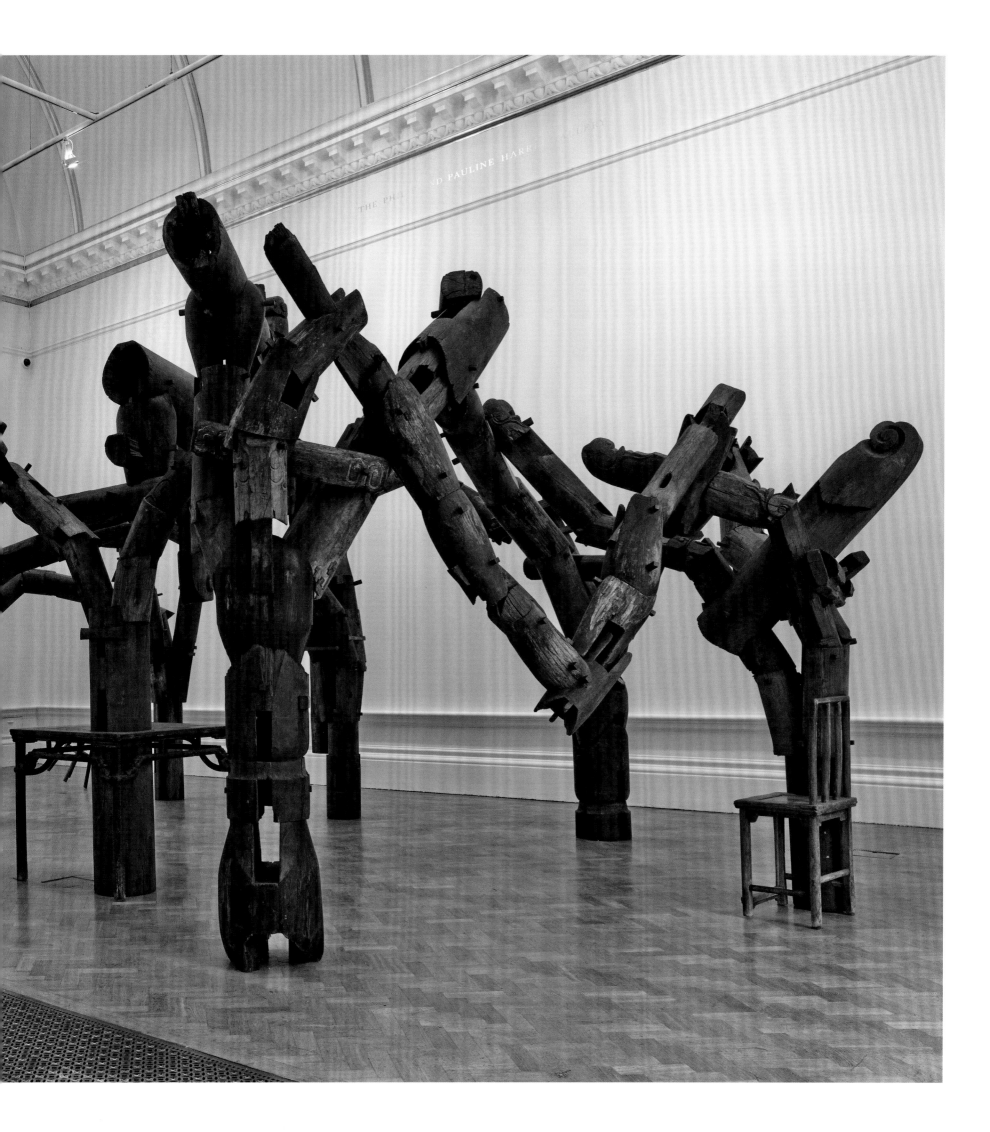

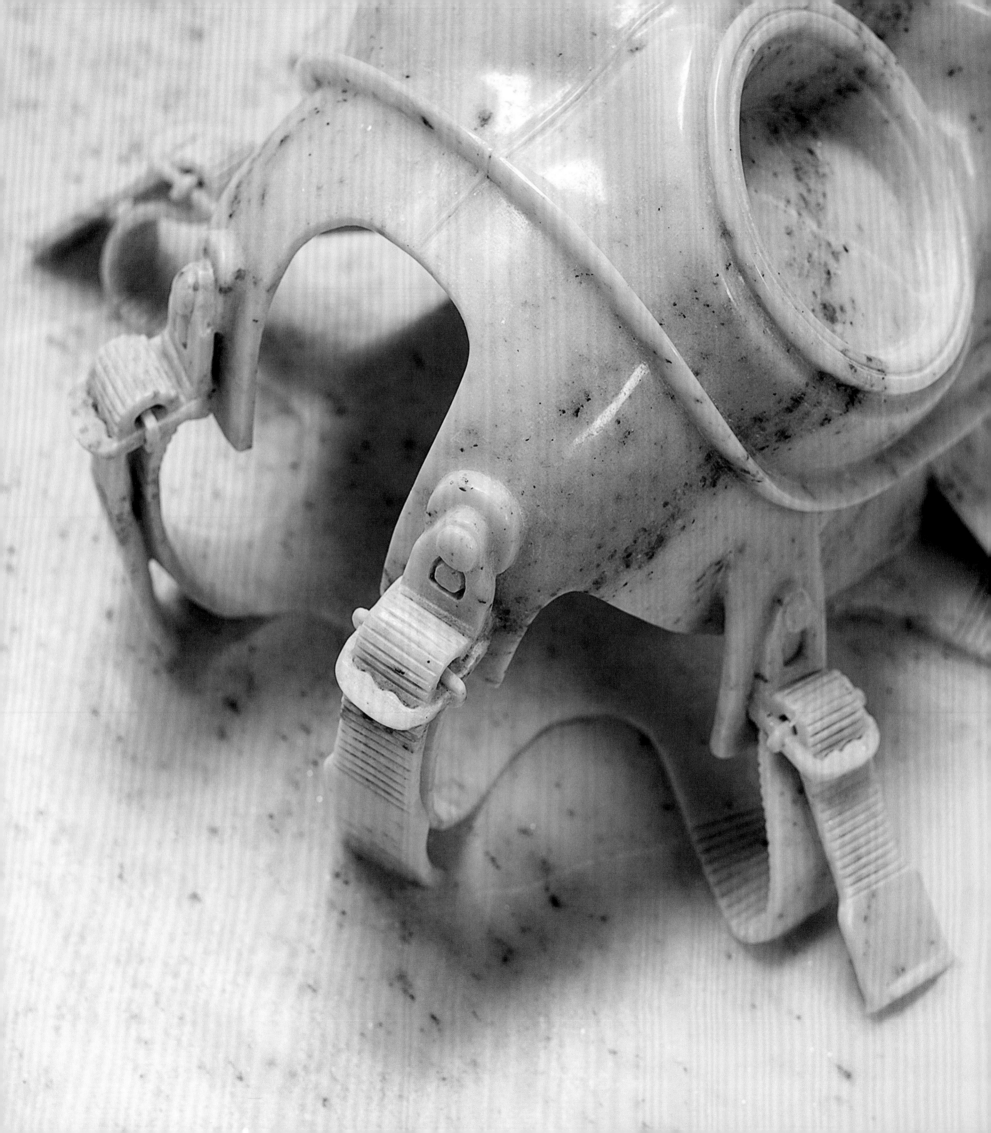

7

In China, as in many countries, marble is symbolic of wealth and power, and the material has historic associations with both Imperial and Communist China. Some years ago Ai purchased an interest in the Dashiwo Quarry in Fangshan, where white marble has been quarried for hundreds of years. Marble from Dashiwo was used in the construction of the Forbidden City between 1406 and 1420 and, more recently, in the creation of Chairman Mao's mausoleum in Tiananmen Square following his death in 1976.

Ai has everyday objects sculpted manually in marble, pushing the limits of this brittle material's tolerance as well as the skill of his stonemasons. In choosing to use a material associated with China's imperial past and the immortalisation of Mao Zedong, Ai has turned these household objects into monuments on a domestic scale that commemorate moments in his life as well as reflecting on Chinese society.

The surveillance camera is a copy of the twenty placed around his studio-house to monitor his every movement. The gas mask is a stark reminder of the thousands of children who suffer serious respiratory illnesses or die every year from the polluted atmosphere of Beijing. *Cao* has many interpretations: for instance, the word is slang for 'grass roots', in the sense of the lower levels of society, as well as being a widely used substitute for a swear word on the internet.

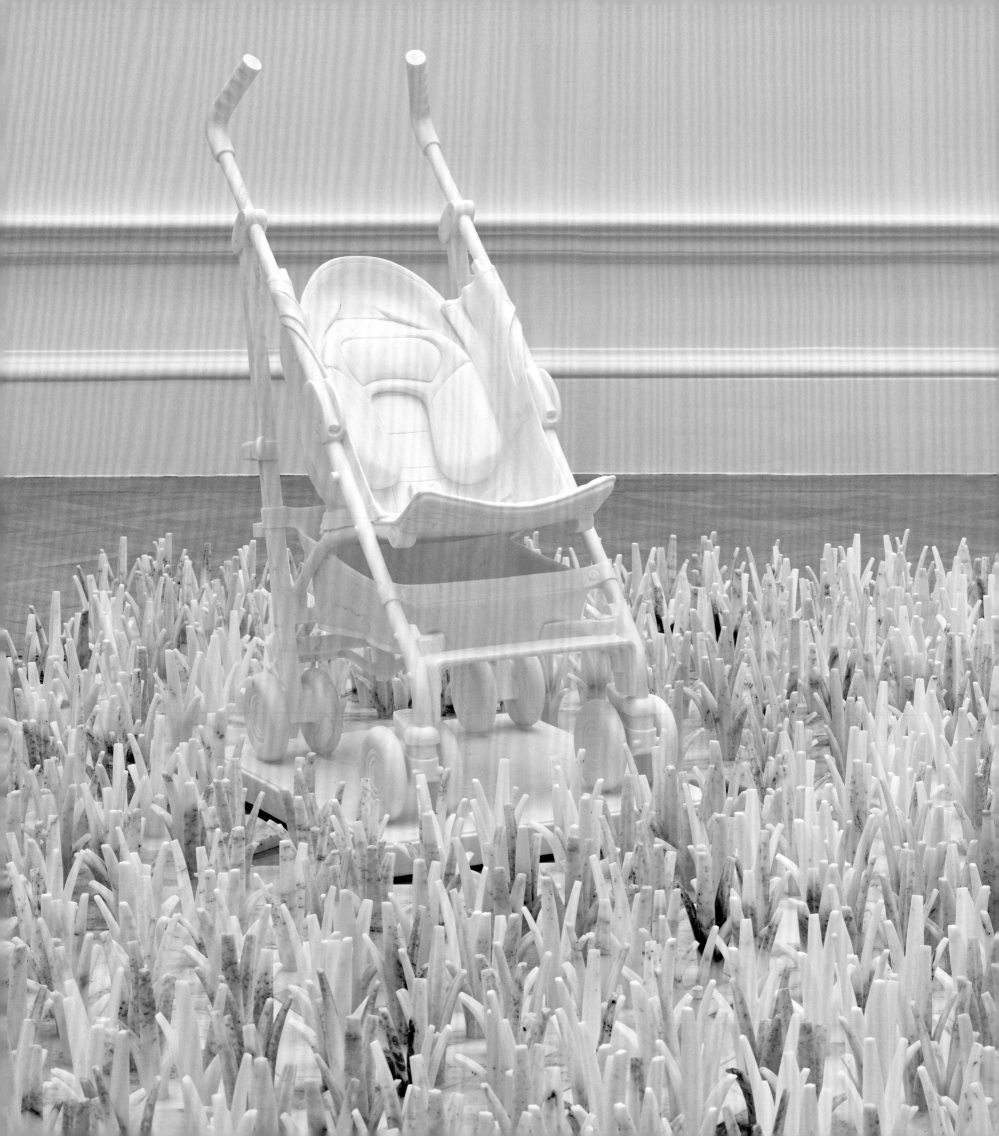

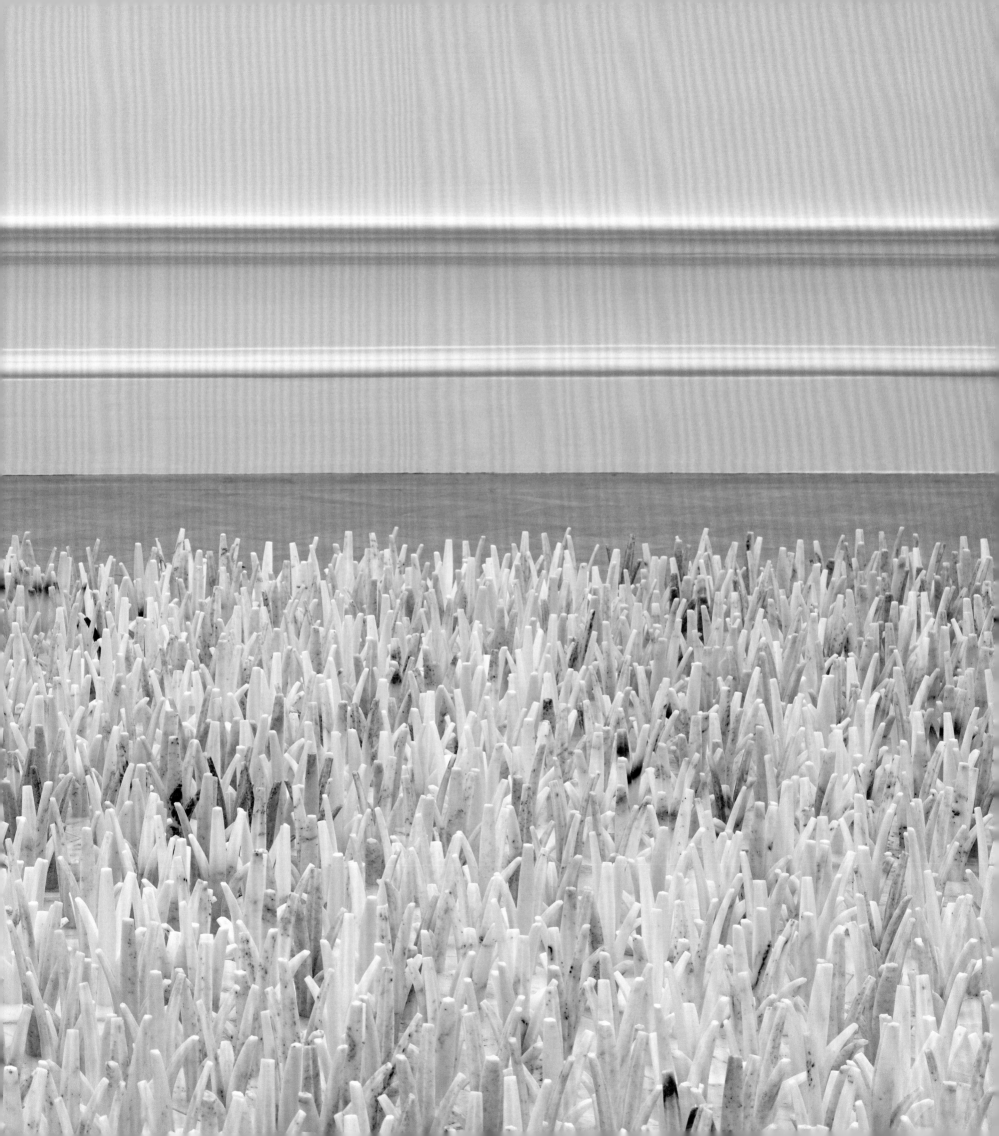

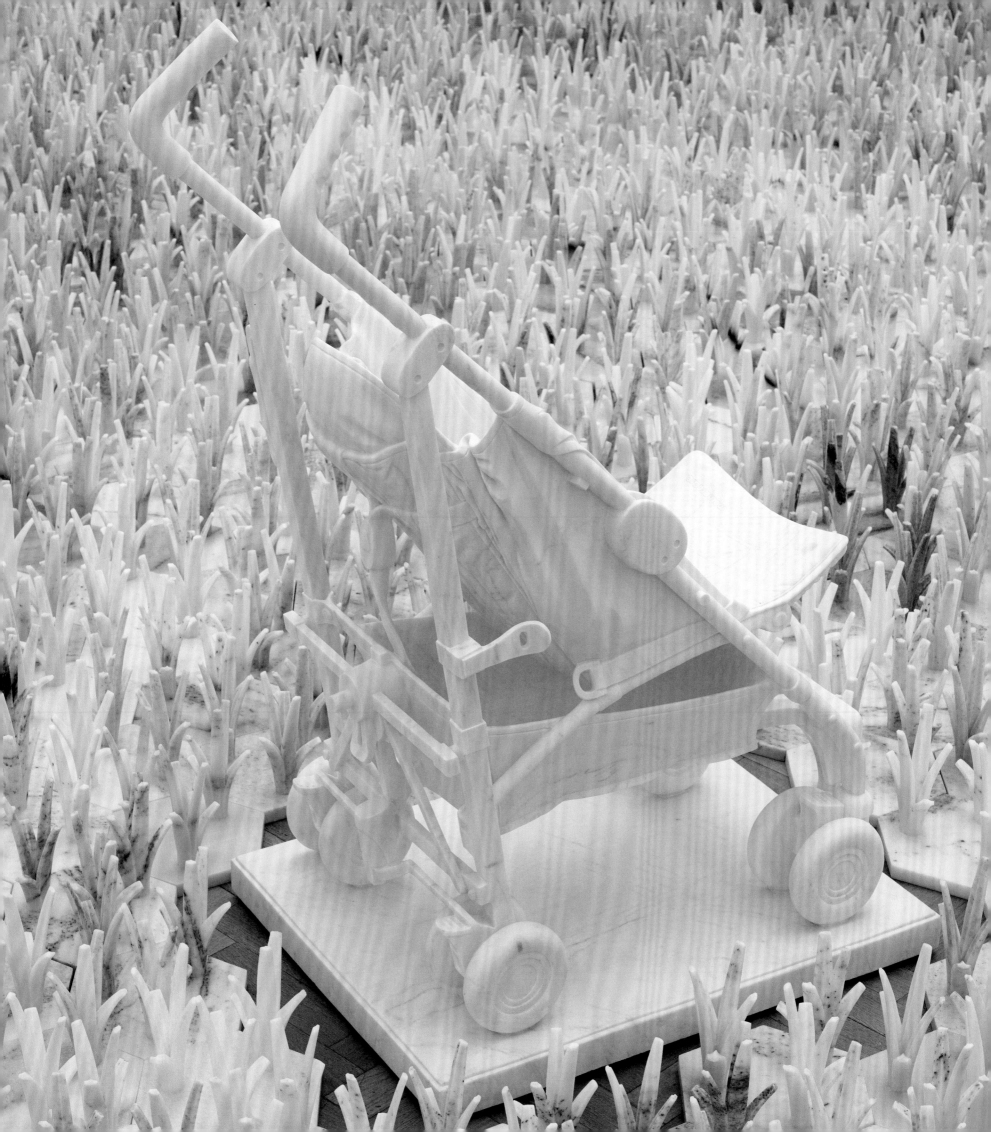

25 (opposite and previous pages)
Cao, 2014
Marble, 770 pieces, each 20 x 22 x 25 cm
Courtesy of Ai Weiwei Studio

26 (opposite and previous pages)
Marble Stroller, 2014
Marble, 115 x 87 x 49 cm
Courtesy of Ai Weiwei Studio

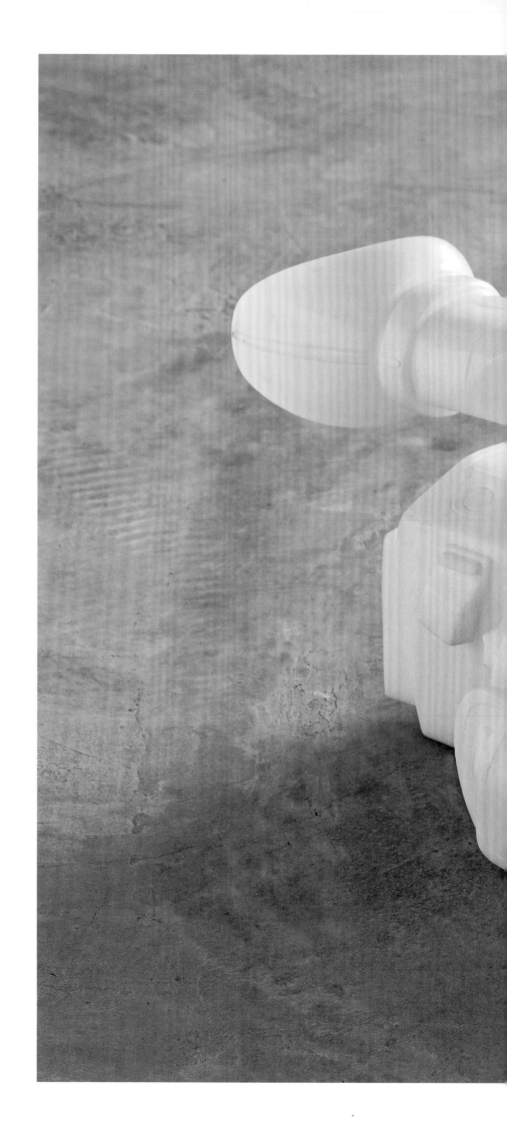

27
Video Recorder, 2010
Marble, 43 x 19 x 19 cm
Courtesy of Ai Weiwei Studio

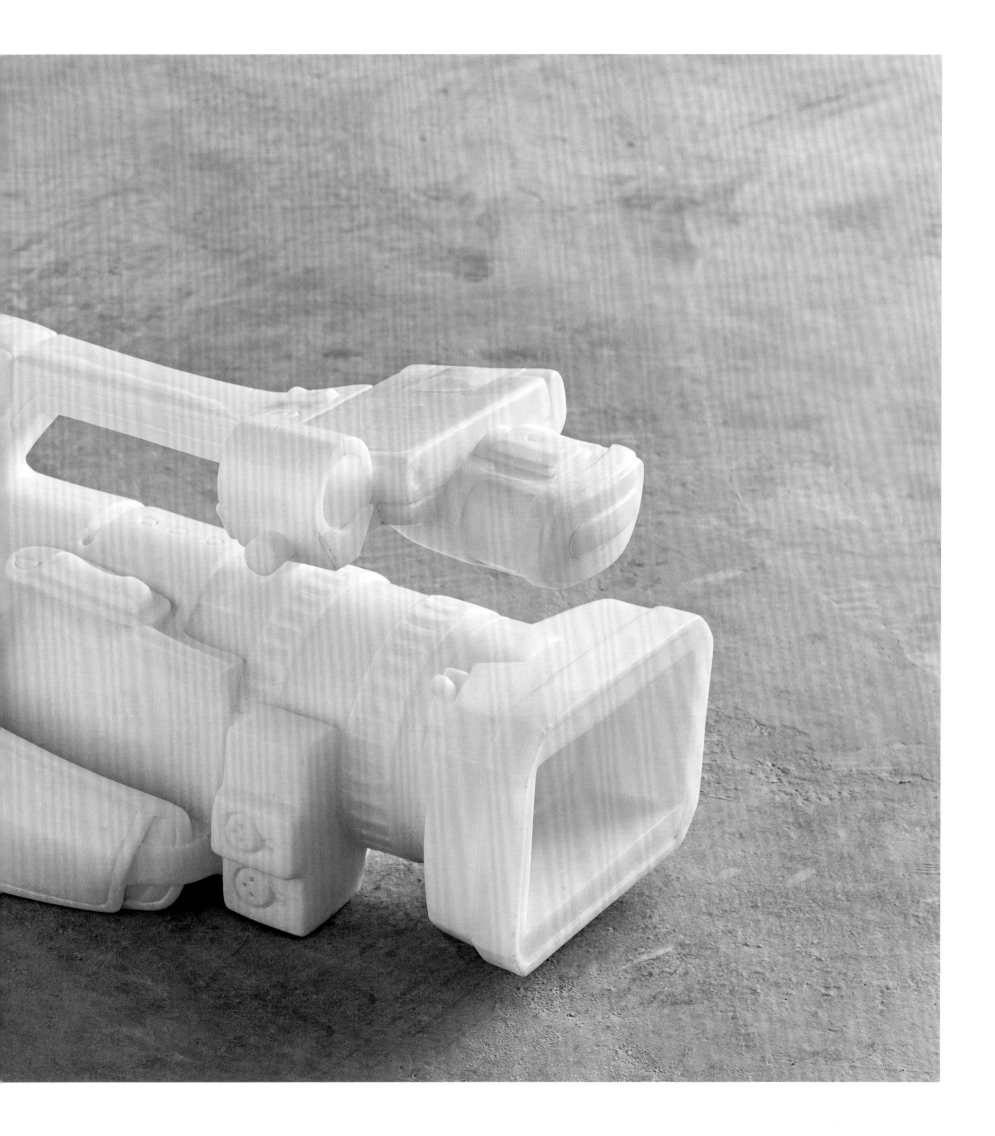

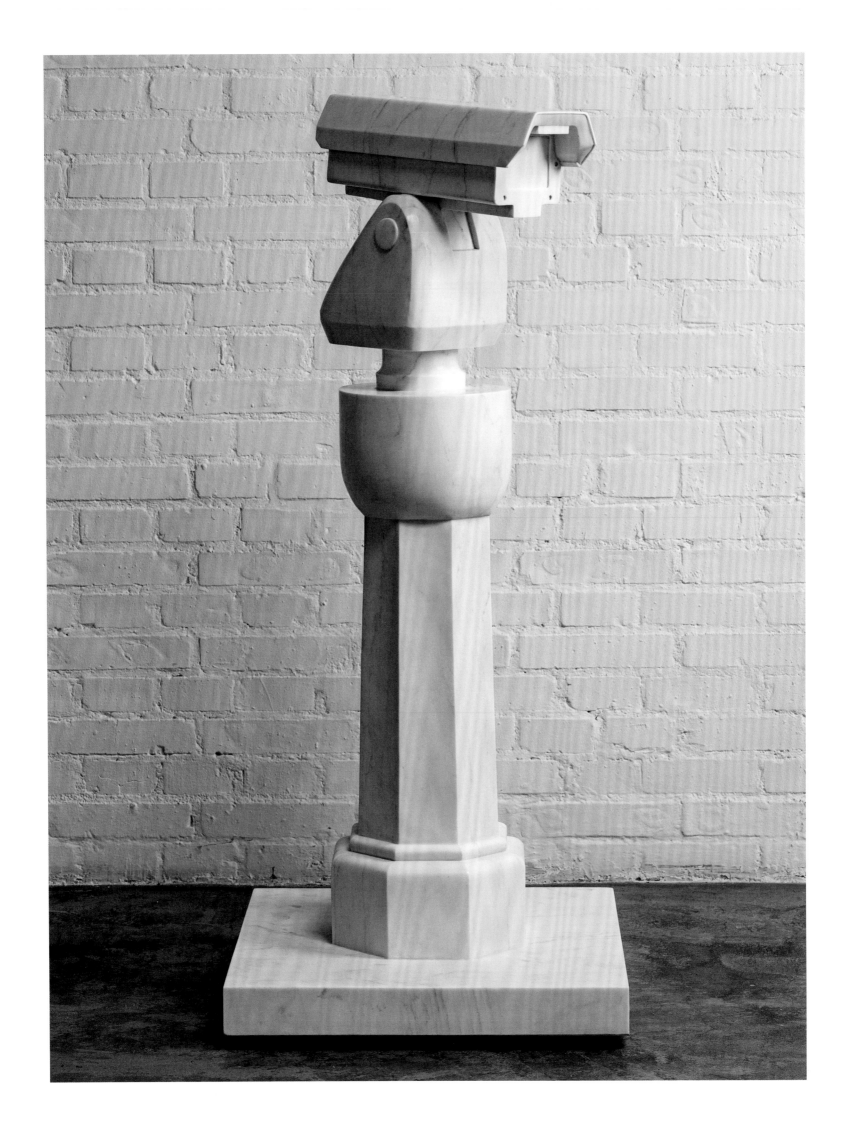

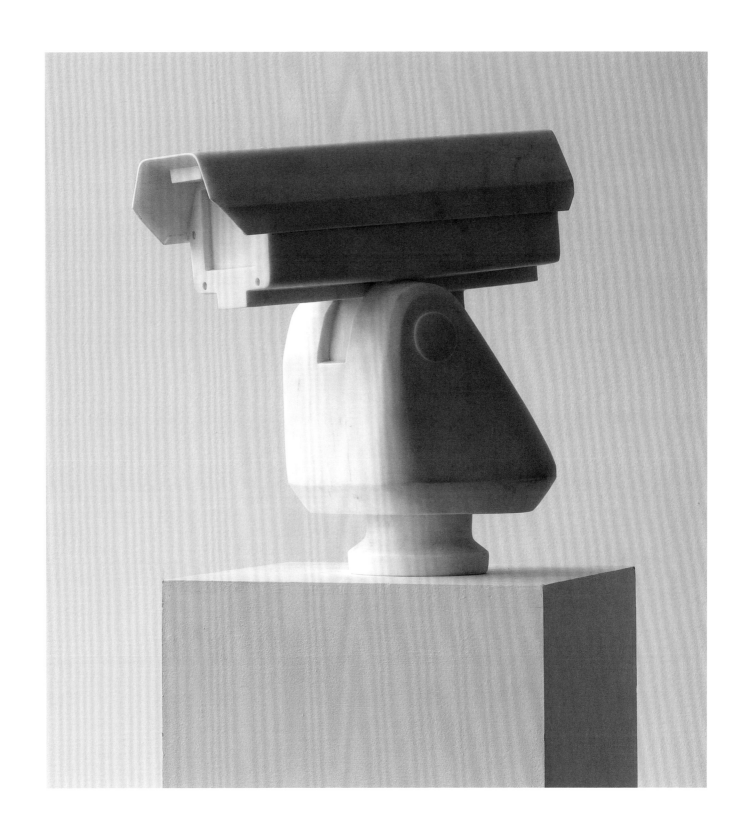

28 (opposite)
Surveillance Camera and Plinth, 2015
Marble, 52 x 52 x 117.5 cm
Courtesy of Ai Weiwei Studio

29 (above)
Surveillance Camera, 2010
Marble, 39.2 x 39.8 x 19 cm
Courtesy of Ai Weiwei Studio

30
Mask, 2013
Marble, 30 x 80 x 80 cm
Courtesy of Ai Weiwei Studio

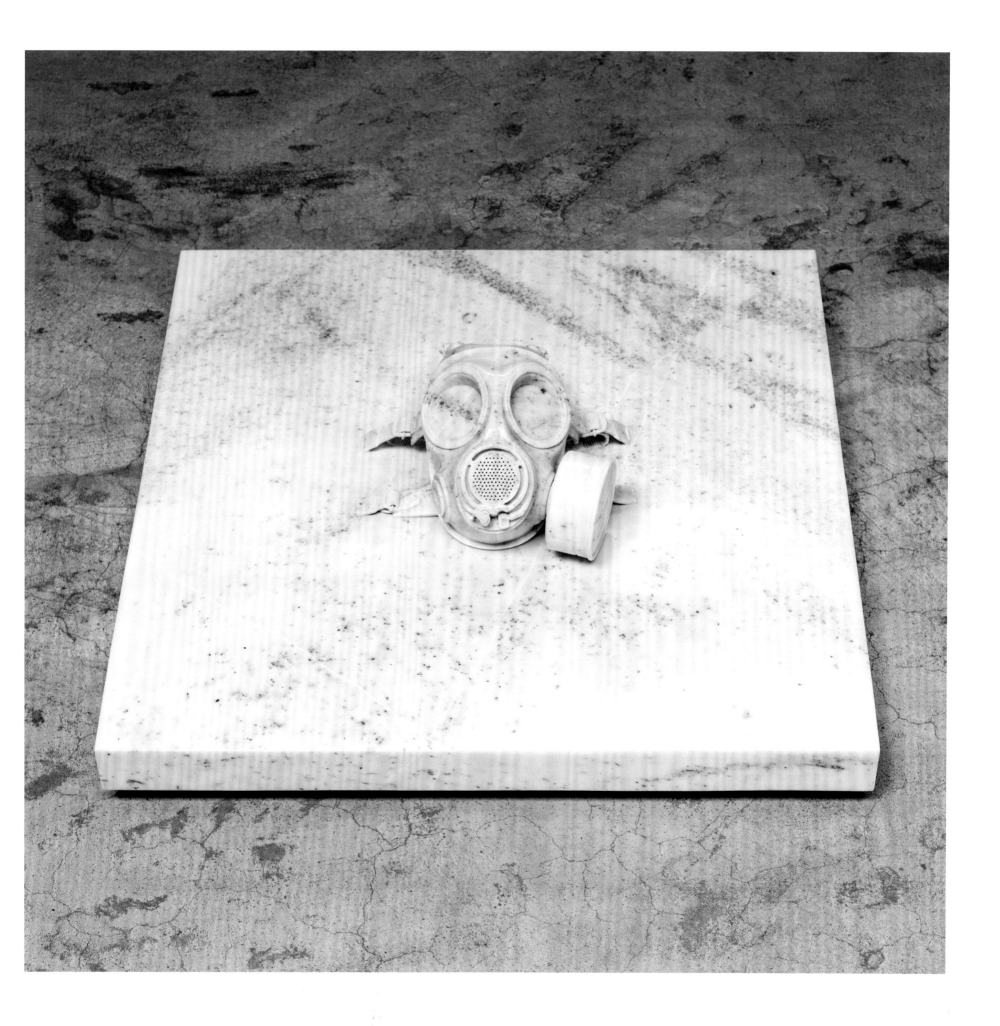

8

In these works Ai has combined his interest in form and volume with his respect for materials and traditional Chinese craftsmanship to create a series of cubes with sides of one metre. Cubic metres are universally used to measure quantity, for example when ordering concrete or timber. The measure is temporary or transient since the material loses its cubic form as soon as it is turned into something else during construction of a building. Ai, however, makes the cubic metre permanent by choosing different materials in which he creates objects of the same size but with very different properties. These cubes can also be seen as an expression of Ai's interest in minimalism, a feature of his architecture. His choice of material and surface texture gives them a distinctive Chinese identity. *Cube in Ebony* references a small box that Ai's father gave him. Its scale and surface texture are amplified to such an extent that the object becomes impractical. Yet it still requires the same skill of the craftsman, and the quantity of material used in its manufacture makes it an object of unimaginable opulence.

Treasure Box is a monumental version of a traditional Chinese puzzle box with a series of hidden parts that have to be manipulated in order to open the box successfully. The large scale of Ai's version, with its exquisite marquetry, makes it impossible for one person to open it. When unlocked it reveals a wealth of compartments, each finished to the highest standard.

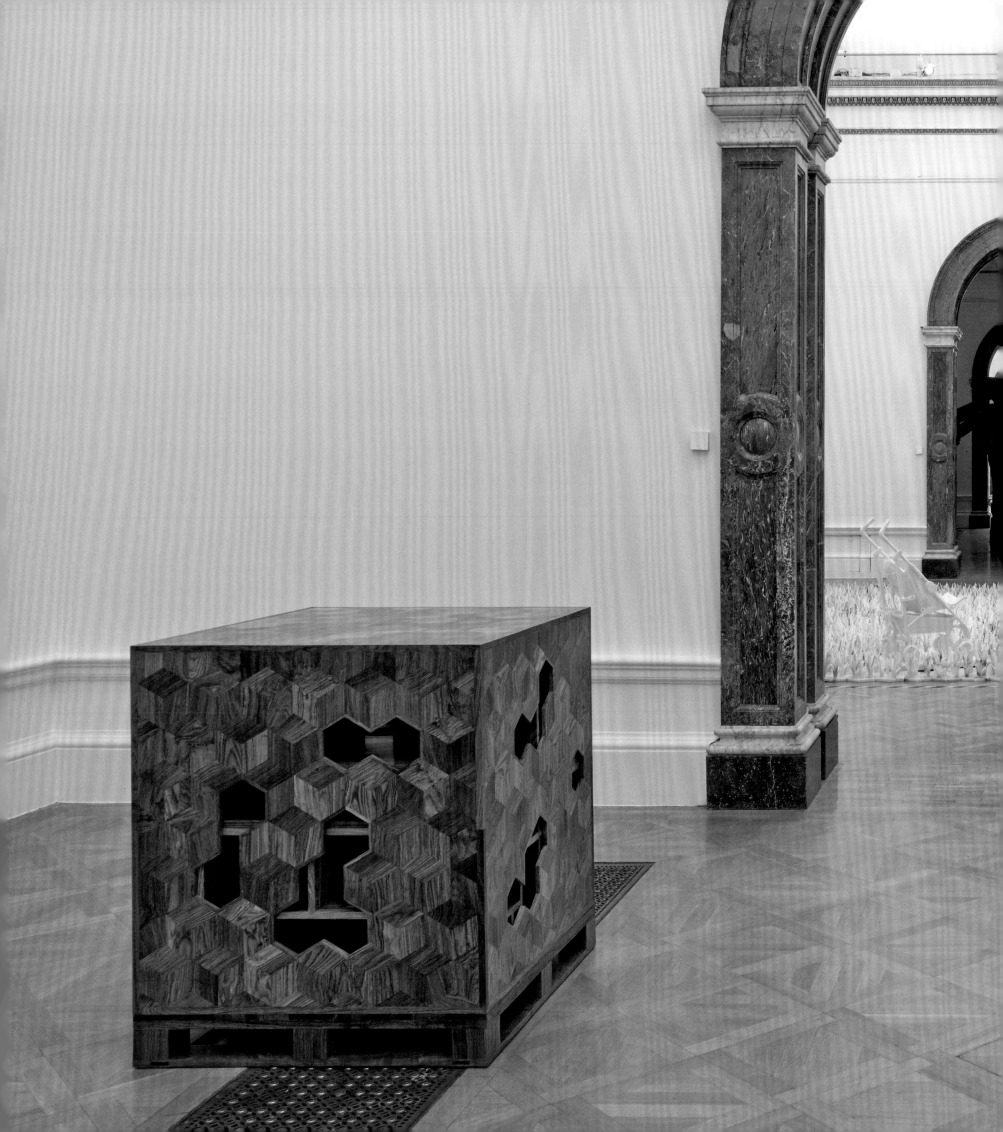

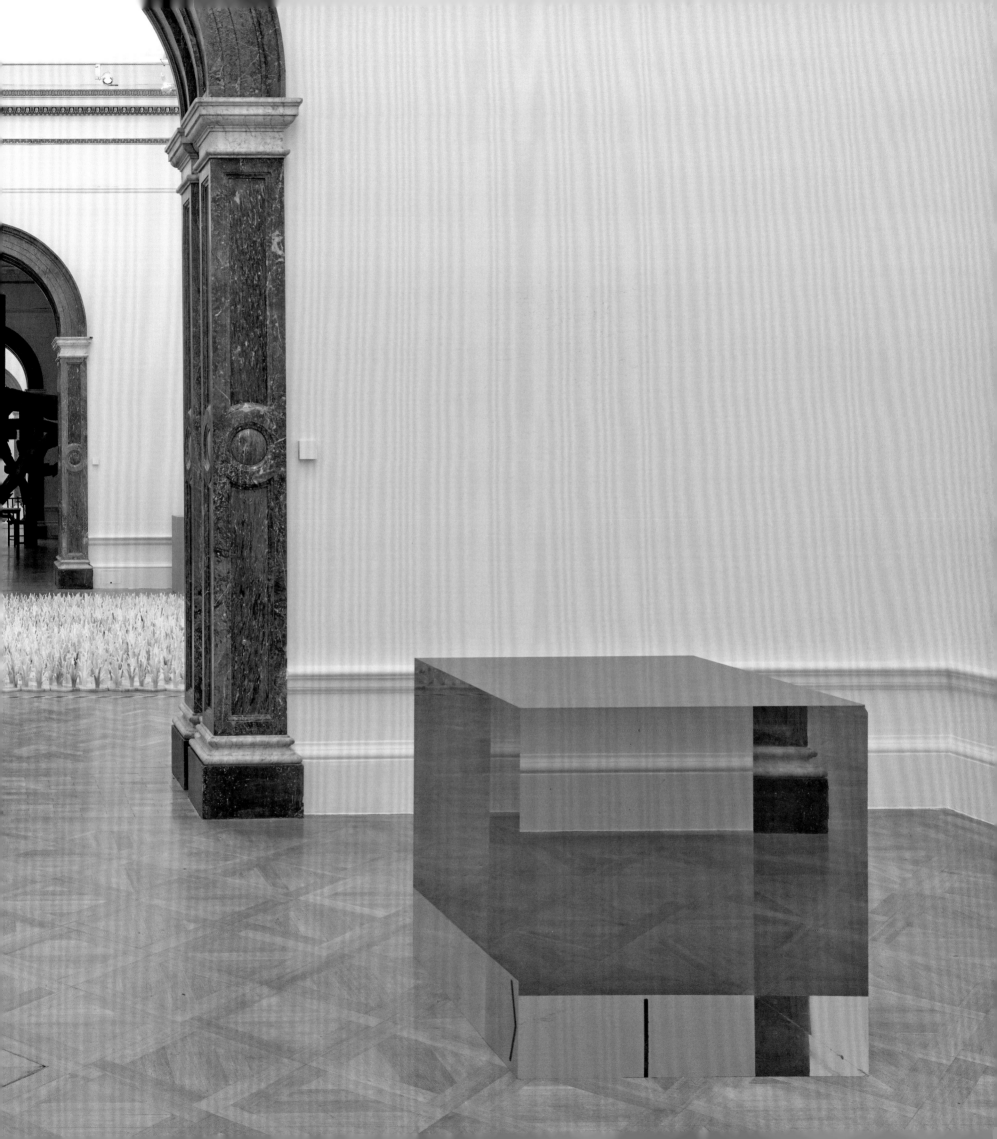

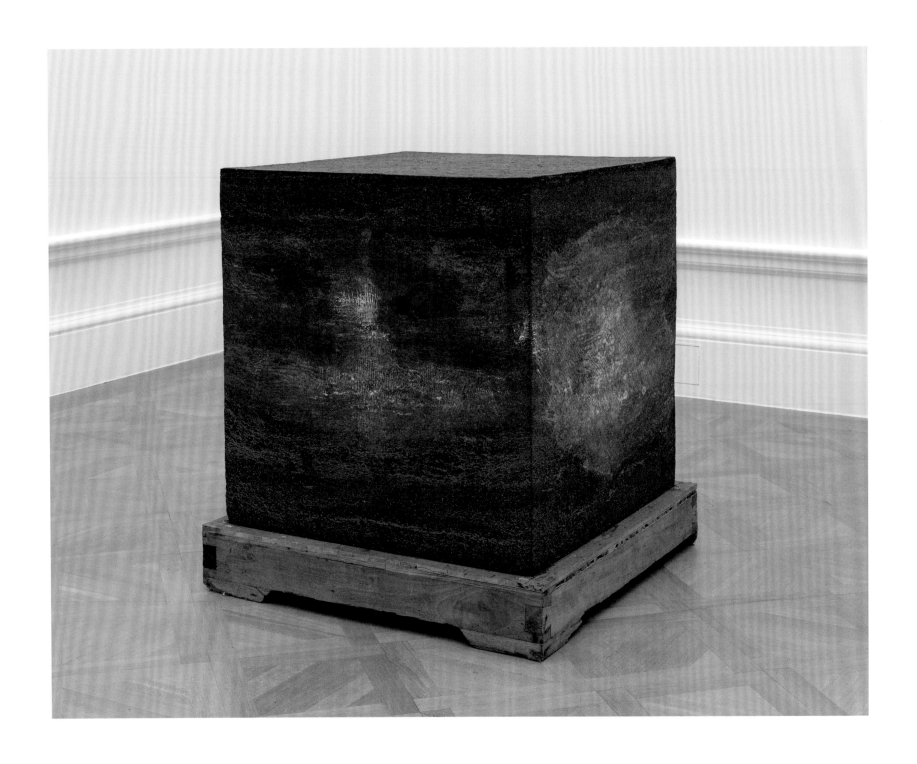

31

Ton of Tea, 2008

One ton of compressed tea, 100 x 100 x 100 cm

Courtesy of Ai Weiwei Studio

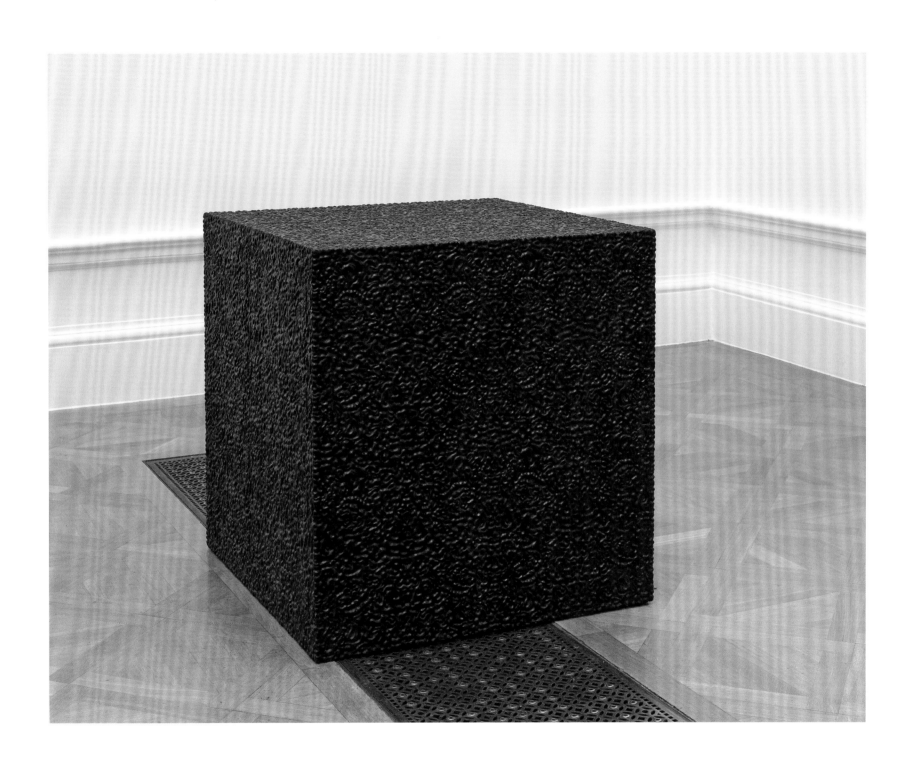

32
Cube in Ebony, 2009
Rosewood, 100 x 100 x 100 cm
Courtesy of Ai Weiwei Studio

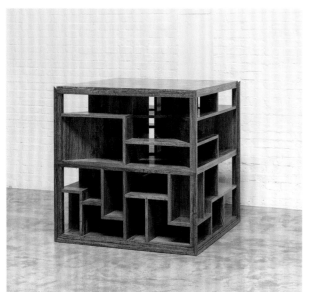 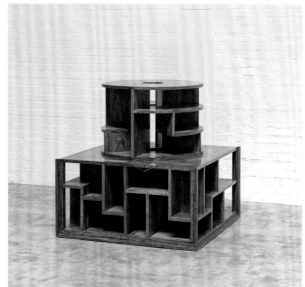 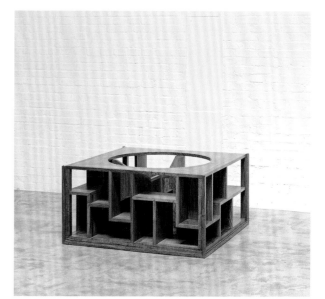

33

Treasure Box, 2014

Huali wood, 100 x 100 x 100 cm

Courtesy of Ai Weiwei Studio

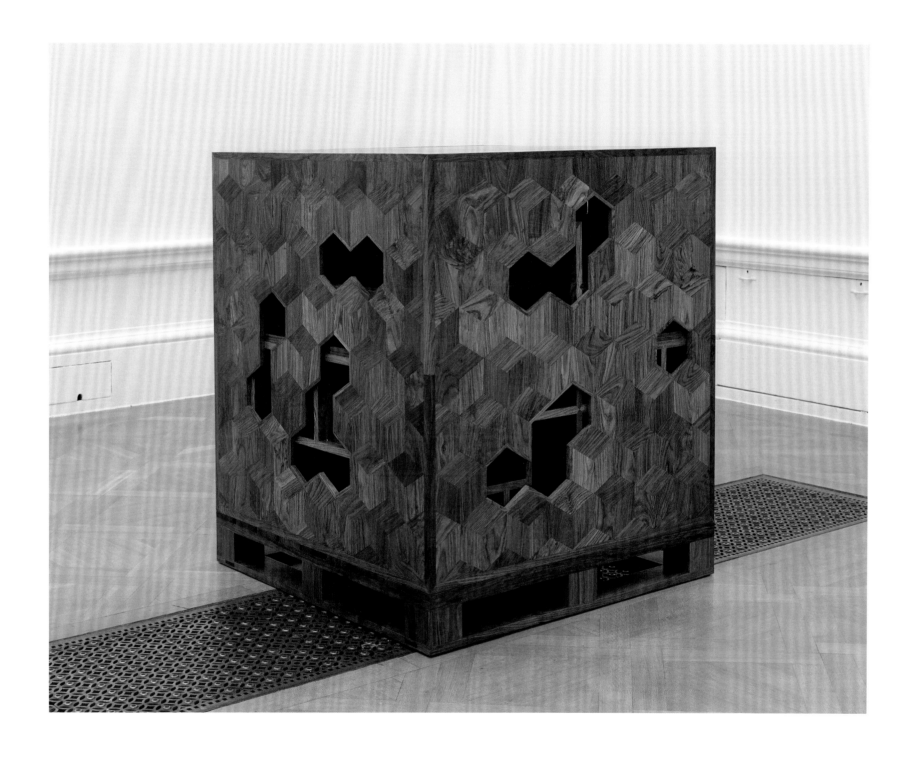

34

Crystal Cube, 2014

Crystal, 100 x 100 x 100 cm

M. Neil Wong Hou-Lianq

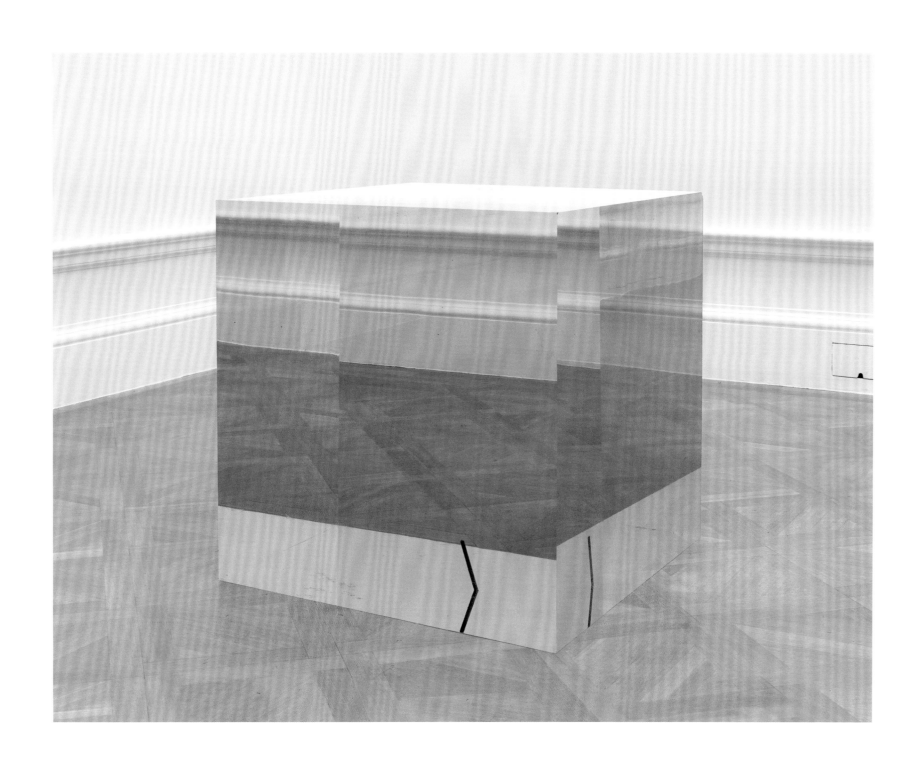

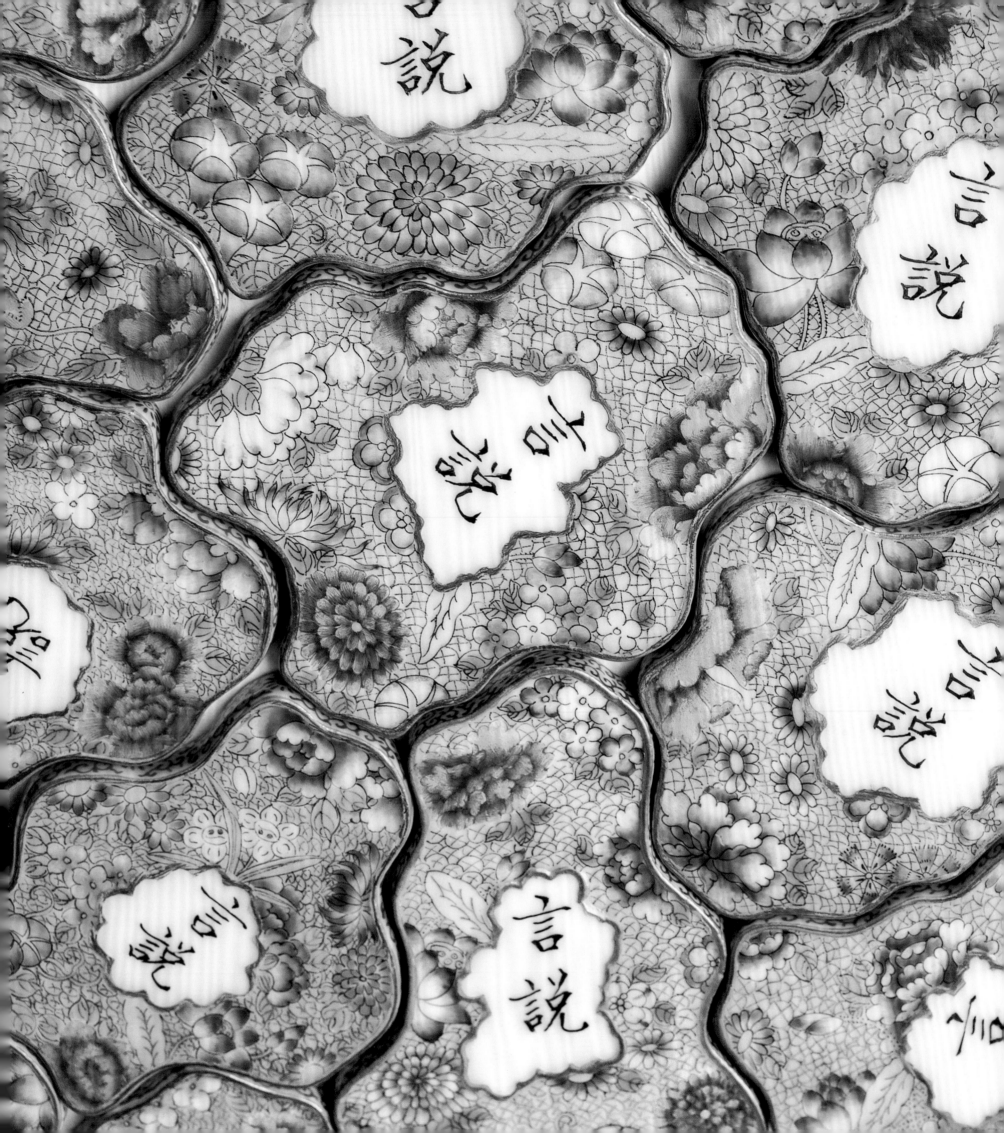

9

Ai has produced a group of exquisite showcases mimicking those found either in museums or in boutiques in which desirable objects of high value are typically displayed. Here, however, he has subverted their anticipated contents. Despite the richness of their materials and their superb levels of craftsmanship, the works in these showcases refer to human-rights abuses, lack of freedom of speech and state censorship as well as more playful objects such as sex toys and cosmetic containers.

A pair of handcuffs carved from a single piece of jade refers to Ai's secret detention in 2011. In the Chinese edition of *The Art Book* Ai is replaced by the Italian Renaissance sculptor Agostino di Duccio, in response to state censorship. A set of bones recovered clandestinely from a former work camp in north-western China – the region where Ai's father, the poet Ai Qing, was interred and where many intellectuals lost their lives during the brutal regime of Chairman Mao – is meticulously re-created in porcelain. A number of individual porcelain pieces, each decorated with the slogan 'Free Speech', collectively form a map of China. They are based on traditional pendants of various materials that bore a family's name and served as markers of status and good-luck charms for the wearer.

The wallpaper, featuring a raised middle finger arranged in a decorative geometric pattern, references two previous works by Ai: *Marble Arm* (2007), a disembodied arm and extended finger carved in white marble, and *Study of Perspective* (1995–; fig. 46), a series of photographs Ai has taken of himself raising his middle finger – an internationally recognised gesture of contempt – at buildings and monuments such as the White House and Tiananmen Square.

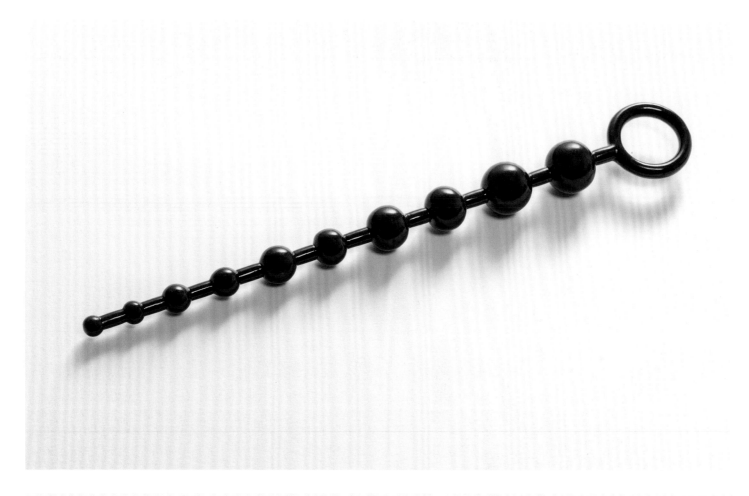

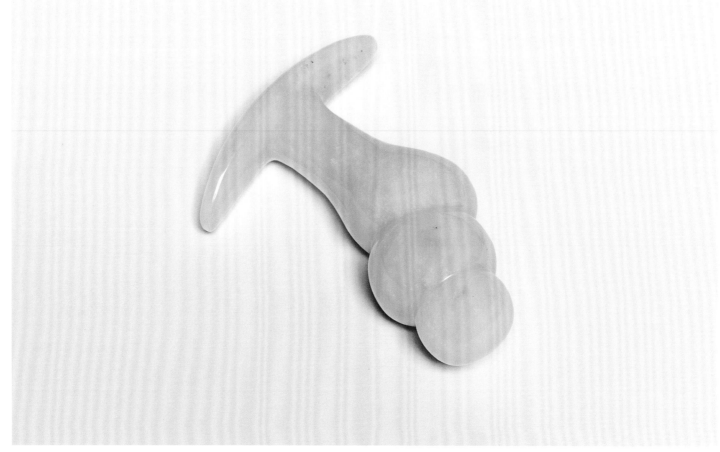

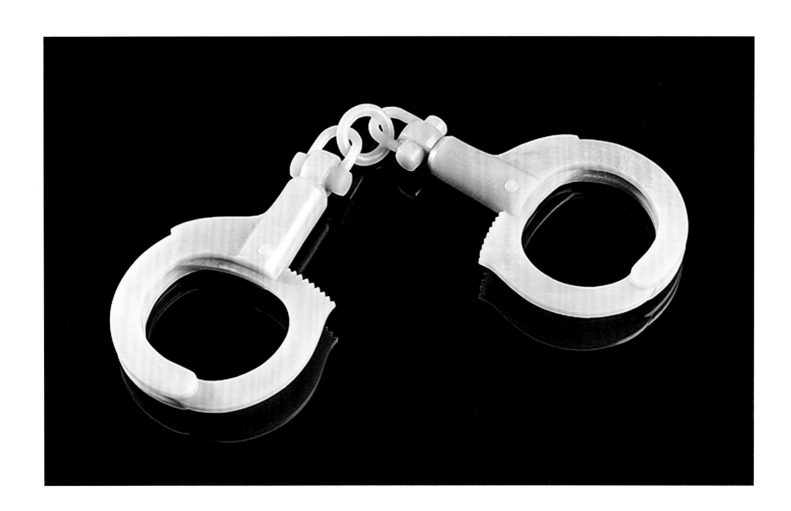

35
Sex Toy, 2014
Jade, 32 x 4.8 x 3 cm
Courtesy of Ai Weiwei Studio

36
Sex Toy, 2014
Jade, 11 x 8 x 3.5 cm
Courtesy of Ai Weiwei Studio

37
Handcuffs, 2011
Jade, 0.7 x 26 x 8 cm
Courtesy of Ai Weiwei Studio

38

Cosmetics, 2014

Jade, seven pieces, dimensions variable

Courtesy of Ai Weiwei Studio

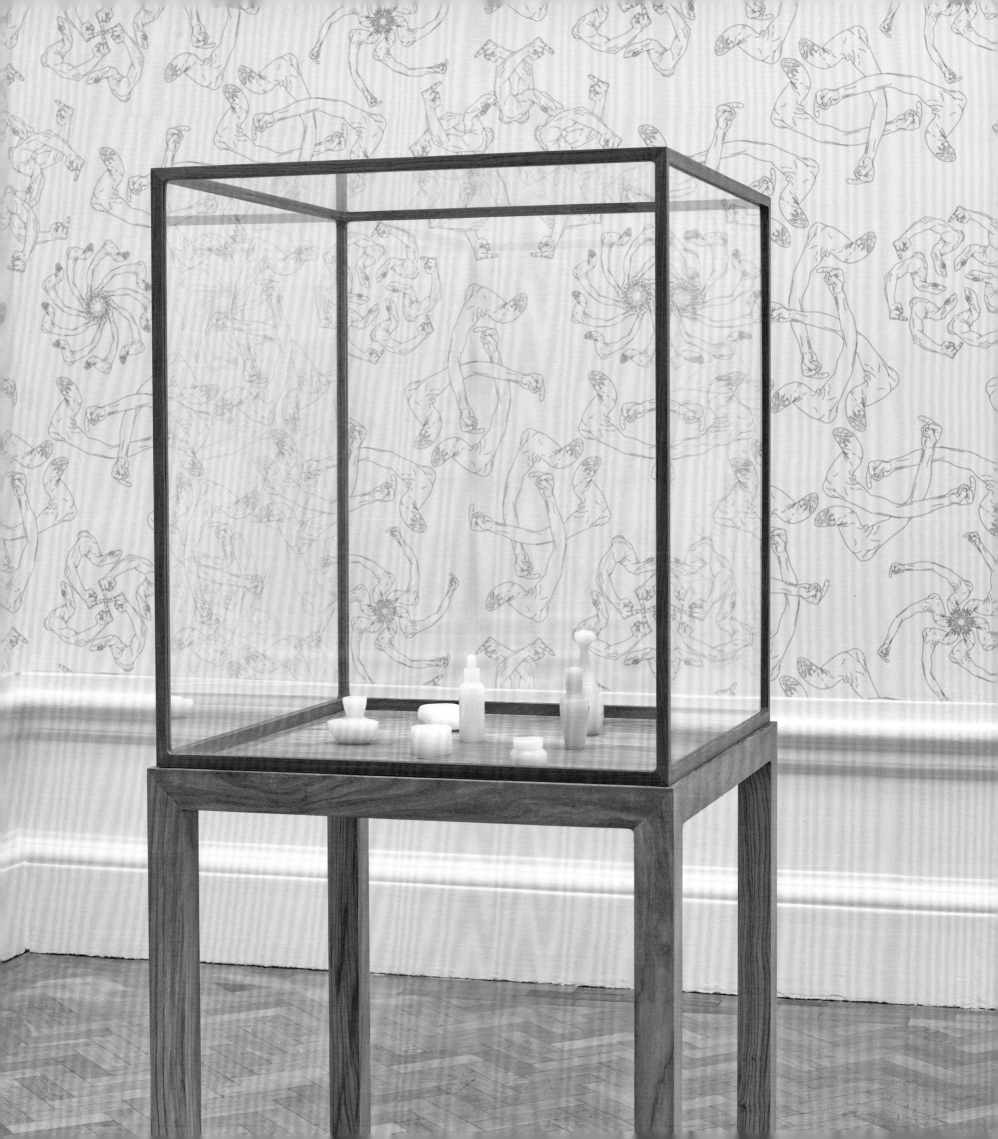

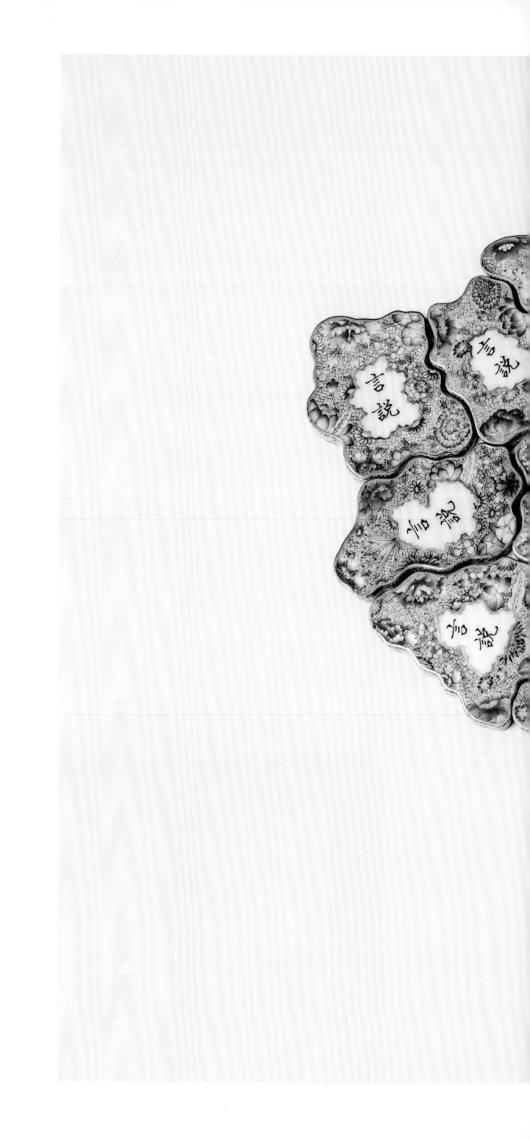

39

Free Speech Puzzle, 2014

Hand-painted porcelain in Qing Dynasty imperial style,
32 pieces, 51 x 41 x 0.8 cm

Courtesy of Ai Weiwei Studio

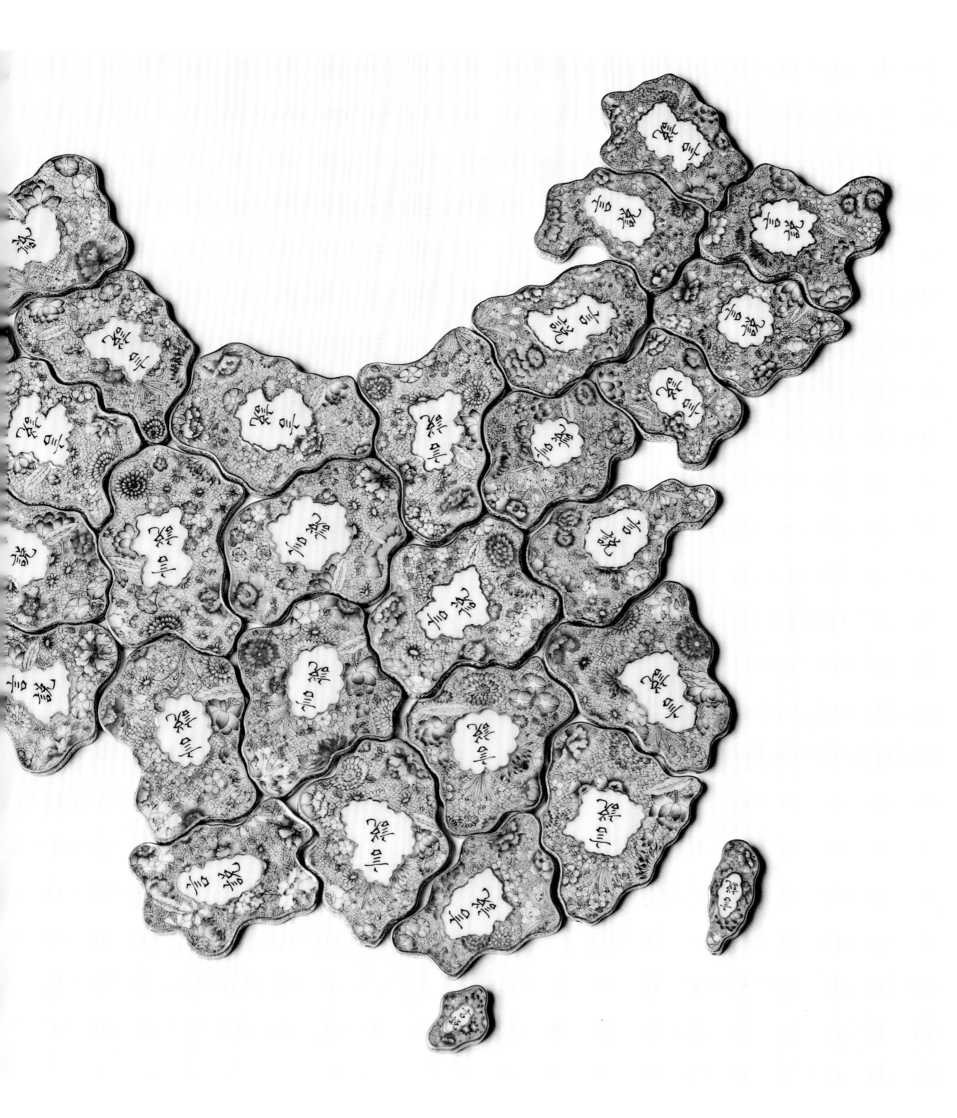

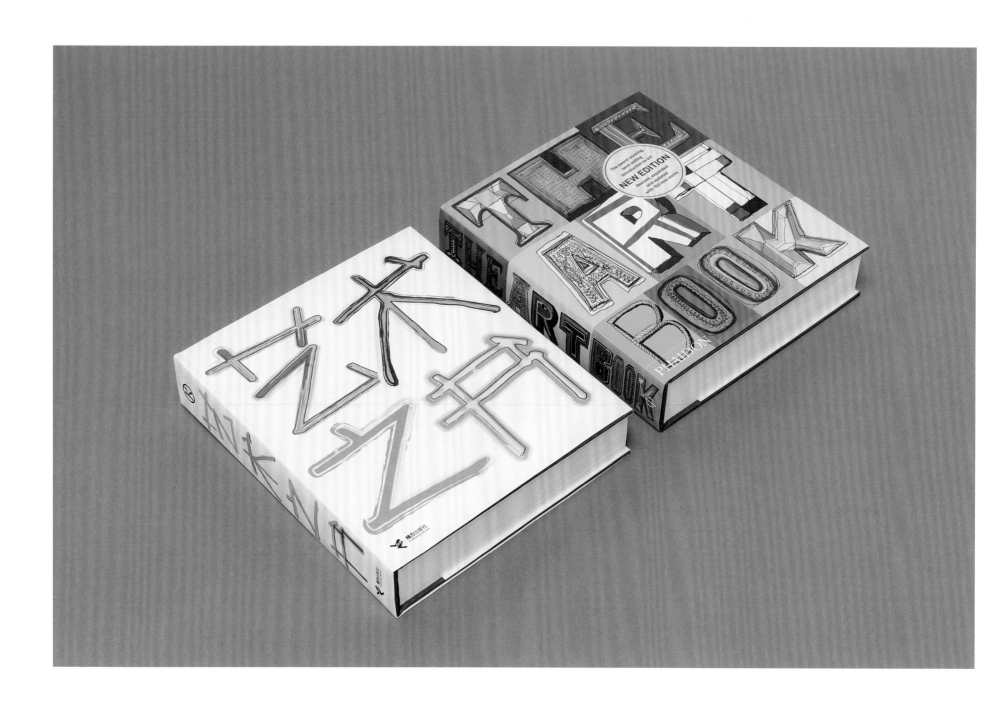

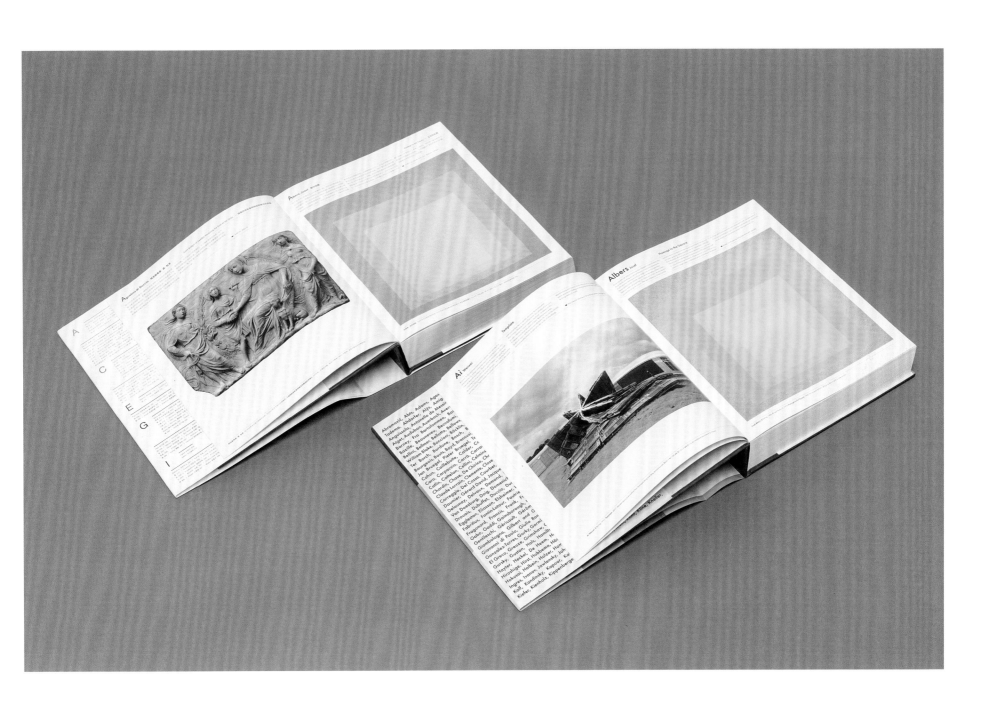

40

The Art Book, 2014

Two hardback books edited by Phaidon Press, each 29 x 26 x 5.7 cm

Courtesy of Ai Weiwei Studio

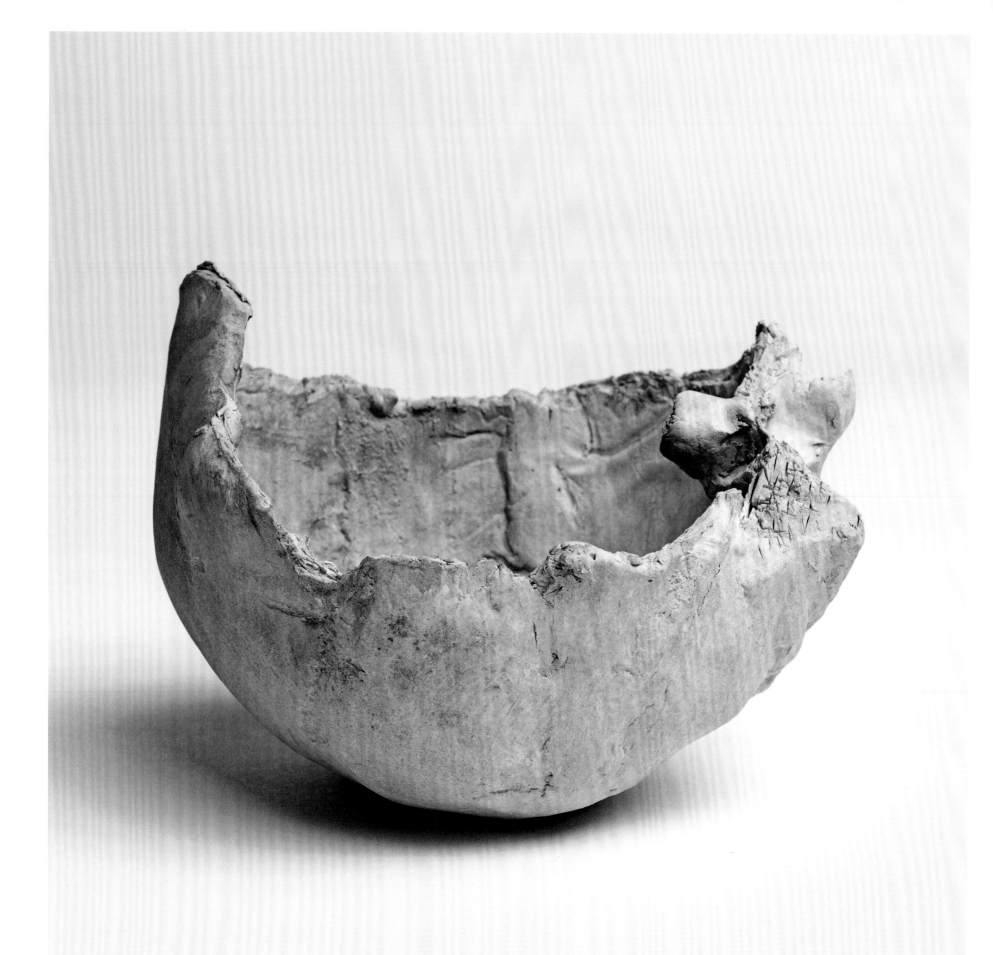

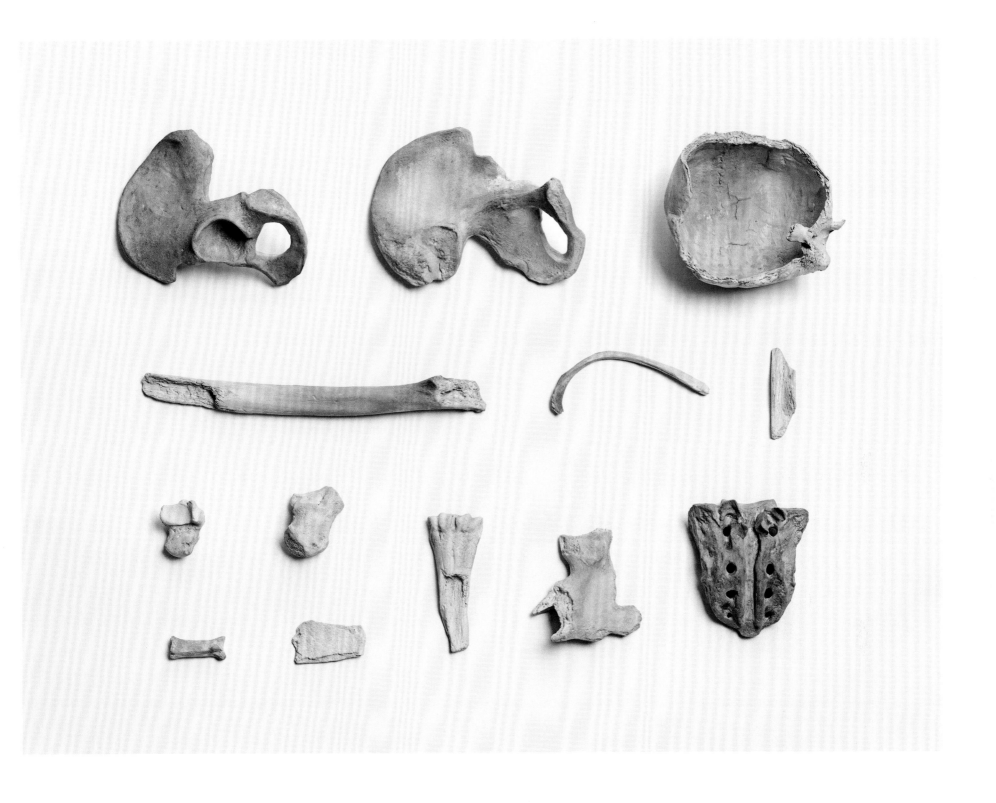

41

Remains, 2015

Porcelain, thirteen pieces, dimensions variable

Courtesy of Ai Weiwei Studio

42

Finger, 2014

Black-and-white wallpaper, dimensions variable

Courtesy of Ai Weiwei Studio

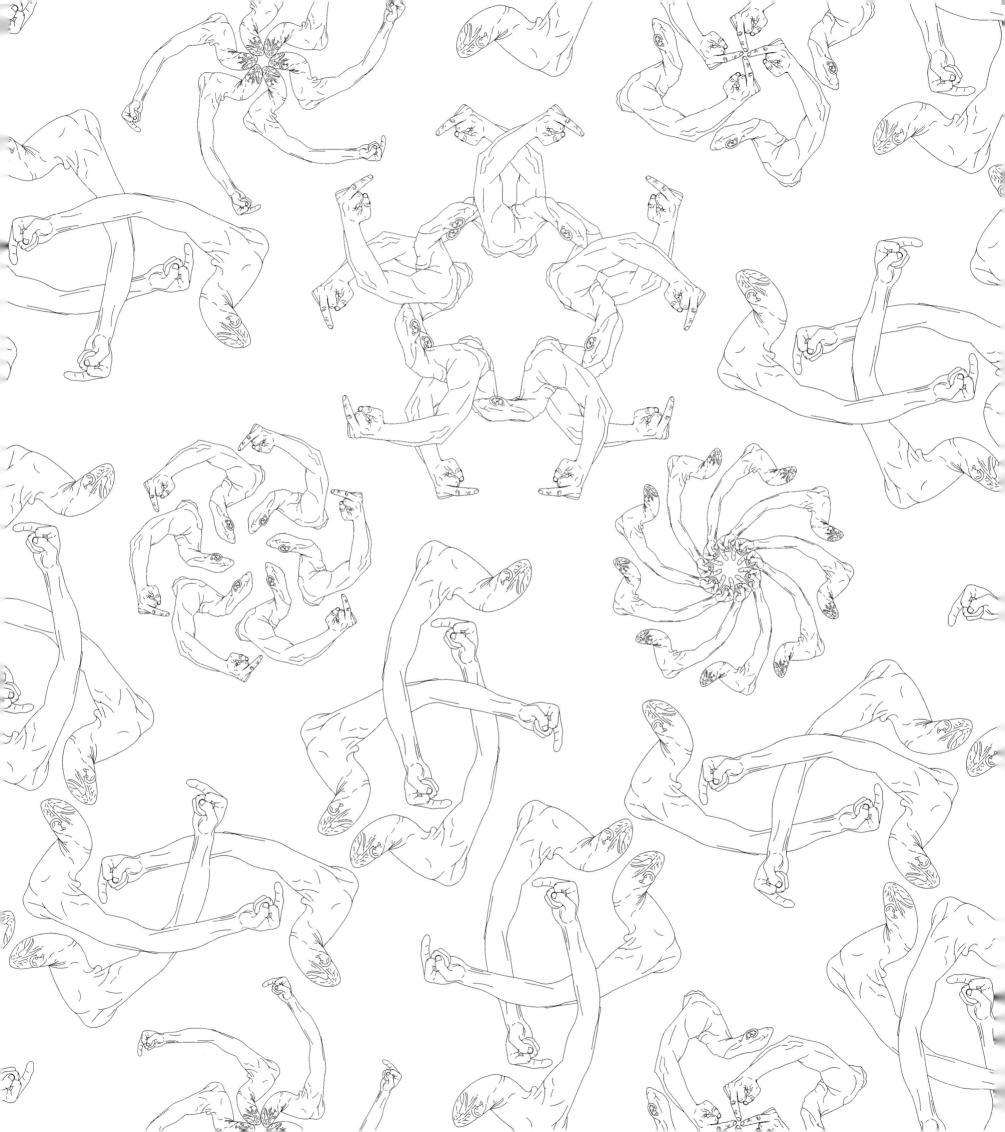

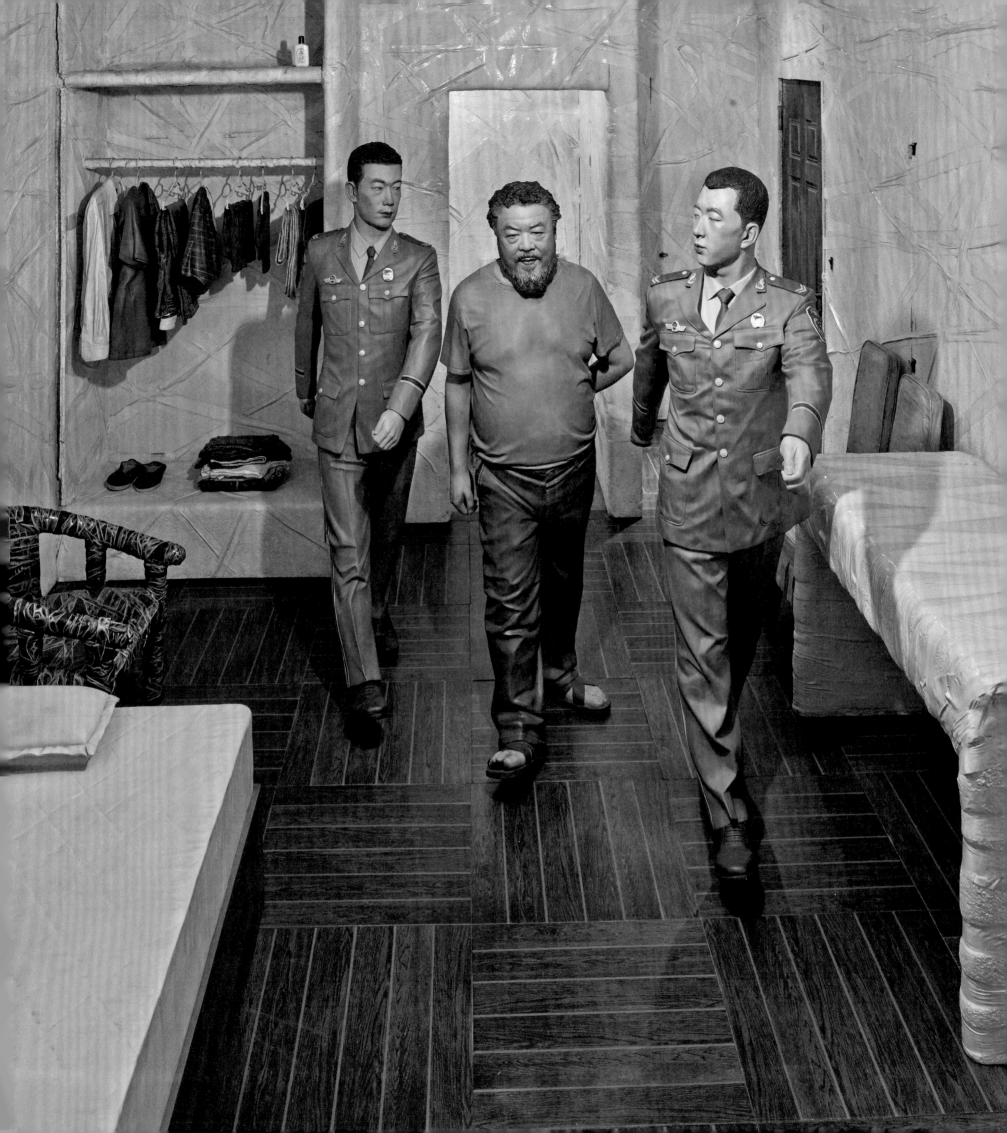

10

On Sunday 3 April 2011 Ai was arrested at Beijing airport as he prepared to board a flight to Taipei. He was illegally detained at a secret location for 81 days. Handcuffed for the first 30 days, he was accompanied 24 hours a day by two guards who were forbidden to communicate with him. The only source of ventilation for his windowless room was a small wall fan.

Ai memorised every detail of the cell, whose walls and every piece of whose furniture were wrapped in plastic. On his release on 22 June 2011 he was forbidden to discuss his incarceration and was placed on parole for twelve months; in addition to this his passport was withheld. Despite this restriction Ai re-created six models of his cell, all half actual size, and populated them with figures of himself engaged in different activities under the watchful eyes of his guards. The dioramas of *S.A.C.R.E.D.* reveal how degrading Ai's detention was and leave little doubt that the intense and claustrophobic experience he underwent was designed to break his spirit and discourage him from publically challenging the Chinese authorities.

Following his release Ai was formally charged with tax evasion, and was denied the right to defend himself in court. The authorities fined him nearly £1.5 million and gave him 15 days to pay. The public offered their unsolicited support by giving him money towards settling the tax demand. Some threw donations over the wall of his studio compound while others contributed online. Ai responded with *I.O.U.*, a work in which he wrote promissory notes to each of these 30,000 donors. These notes were in turn scanned and turned into wallpaper.

The wallpaper work *Golden Age* is decorated with the Twitter logo, a pair of handcuffs and a surveillance camera, all presented in gold, referencing Ai's interest in social media and the curtailment of his personal freedom by the authorities.

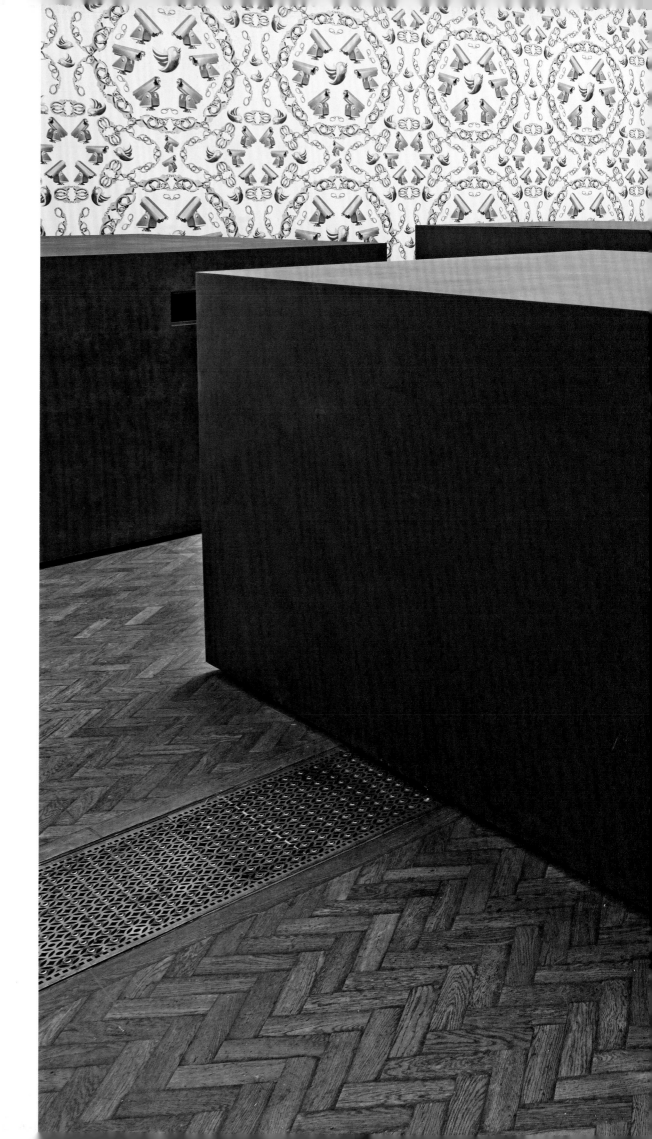

43 (details overleaf)

S.A.C.R.E.D., 2012

Six-part work composed of six dioramas –
Supper, Accusers, Cleansing, Ritual, Entropy,
Doubt – in fibreglass, iron, oxidised metal, wood,
polystyrene, sticky tape, each 377 x 198 x 153 cm

Courtesy of Ai Weiwei Studio and Lisson Gallery

44 (detail pages 216–17)

Golden Age, 2014

Wallpaper in gold, dimensions variable

Courtesy of Ai Weiwei Studio

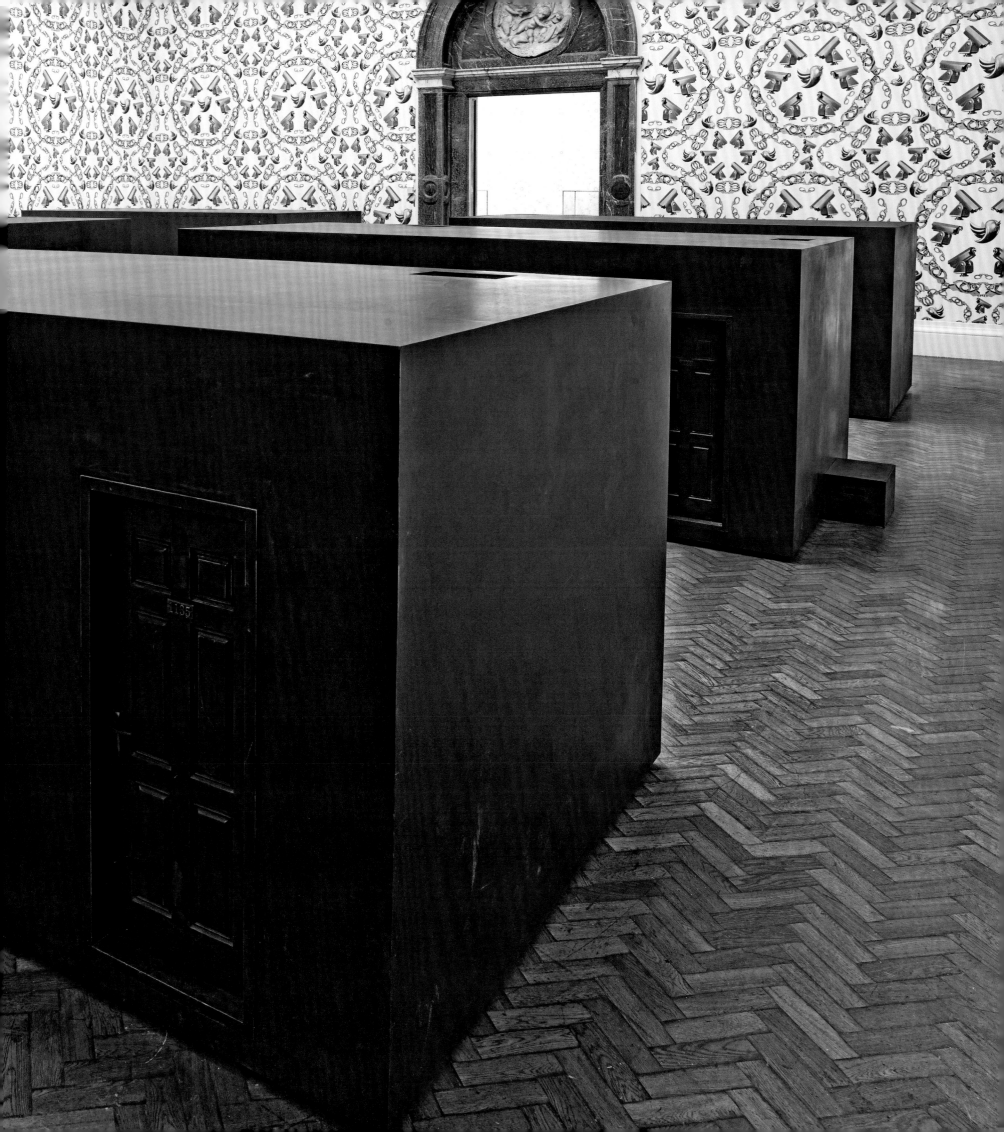

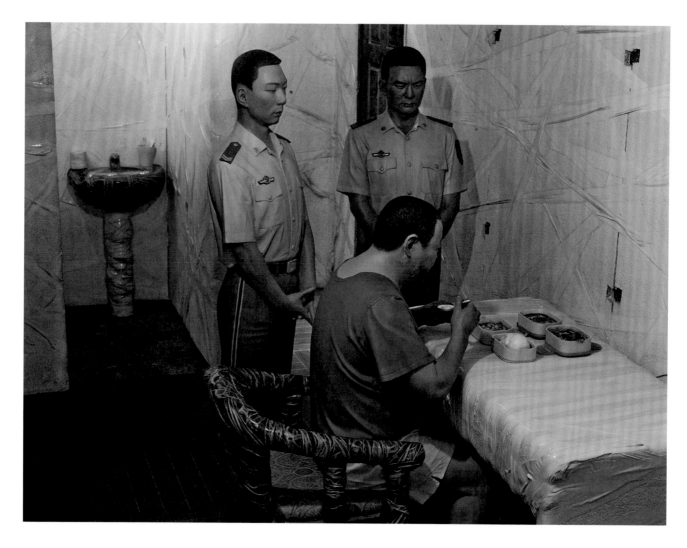

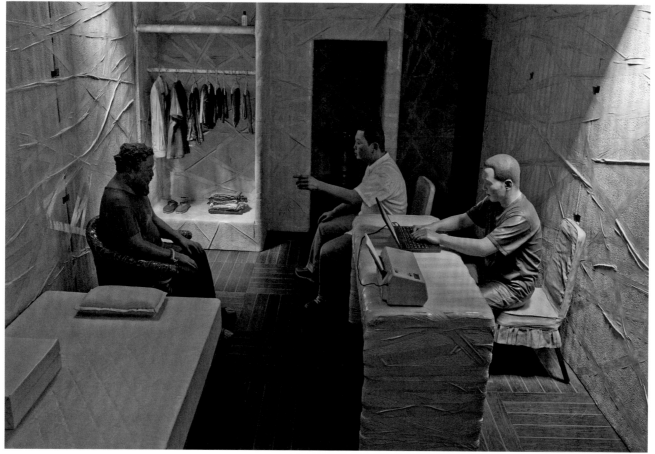

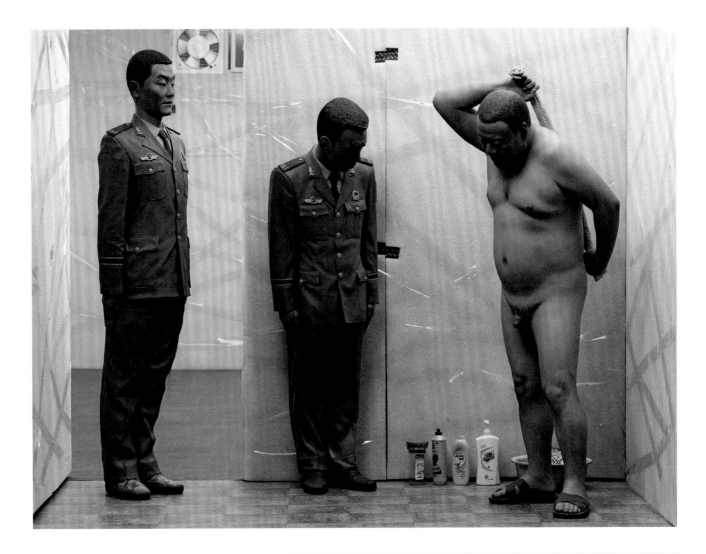

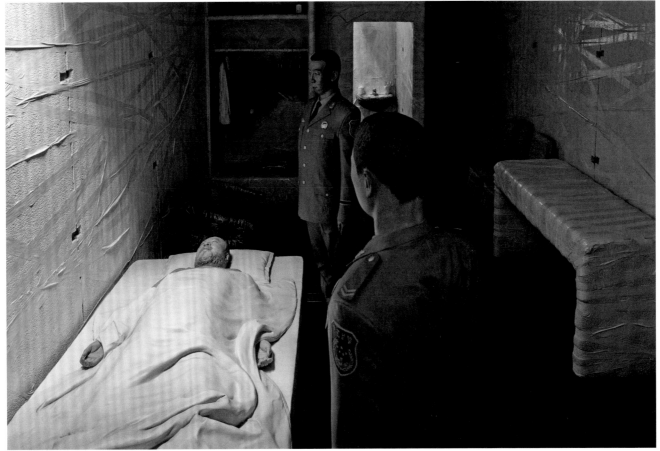

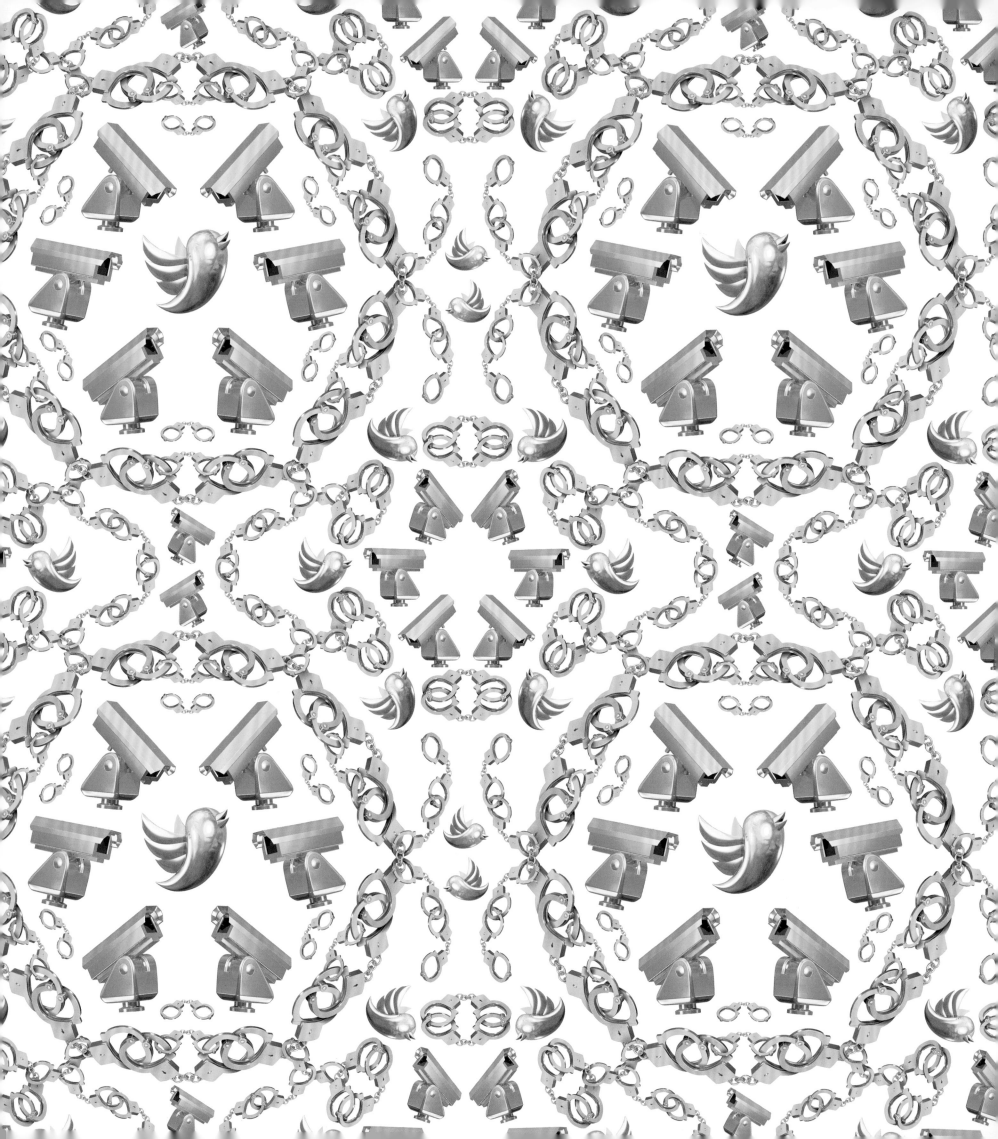

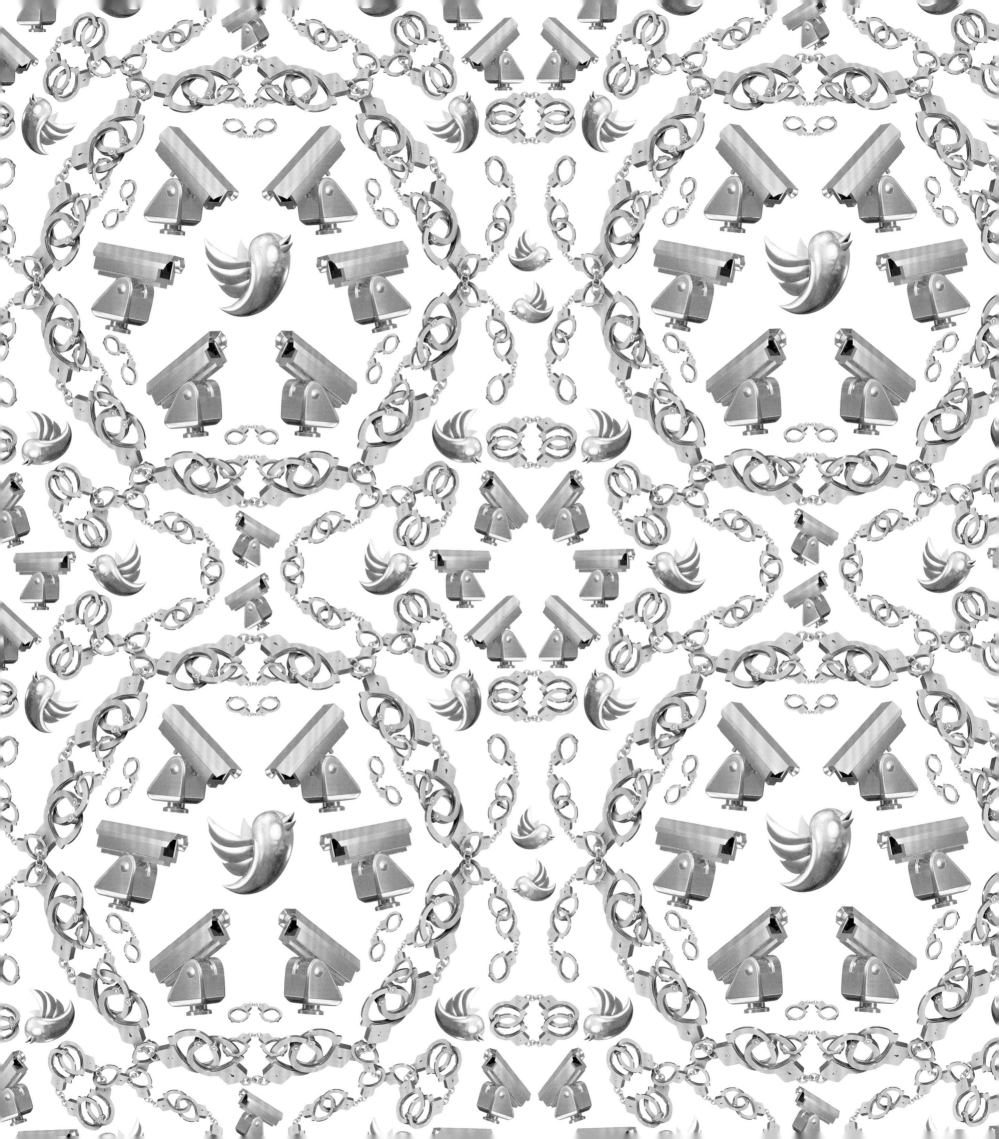

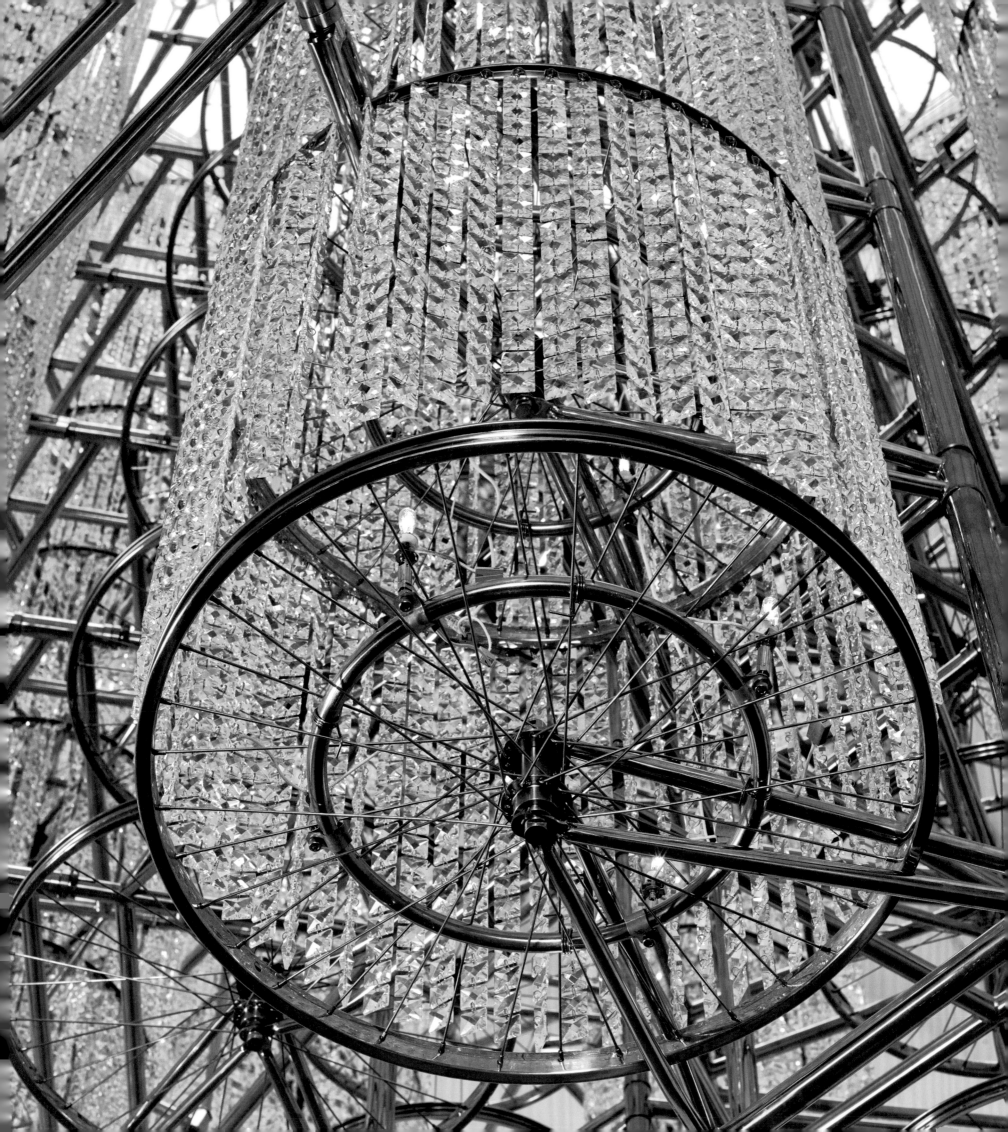

11

Ai first began working with chandeliers in 2002: 'I became interested in light as an object: both the object that gives off light, but also the form the light creates by itself in the illumination that it creates, and how illumination alters the surrounding environment.' Ai's point of reference was the grand chandelier of the vast Great Hall of the People in Tiananmen Square; he even sourced his crystals from the same place, in Zhejiang province.

At around the same time as he made his first chandelier work, Ai began creating sculptures and installations with bicycles. When collecting kindling as a boy, he used to ride a Forever bicycle, a Chinese brand, first produced in 1940,

synonymous with the mass transportation of the urban workforce before cars became widely available: 'My work with them started from the question how can the bicycle use its structure to grow according to its own logic.' These bicycle sculptures are designed to be placed inside or outside, from the small scale, using two bicycles, to the monumental, comprising 3,144.

The present work is the first in which Ai has combined the two ideas, creating a chandelier from bicycles. The white crystals are suspended from the rims of the bicycles' wheels and cascade down in illuminated circles to create this dramatic, site-specific sculptural installation.

45 (detail overleaf)

Bicycle Chandelier, 2015

Bicycles and crystals, 500 x 430 cm

Courtesy of Ai Weiwei Studio

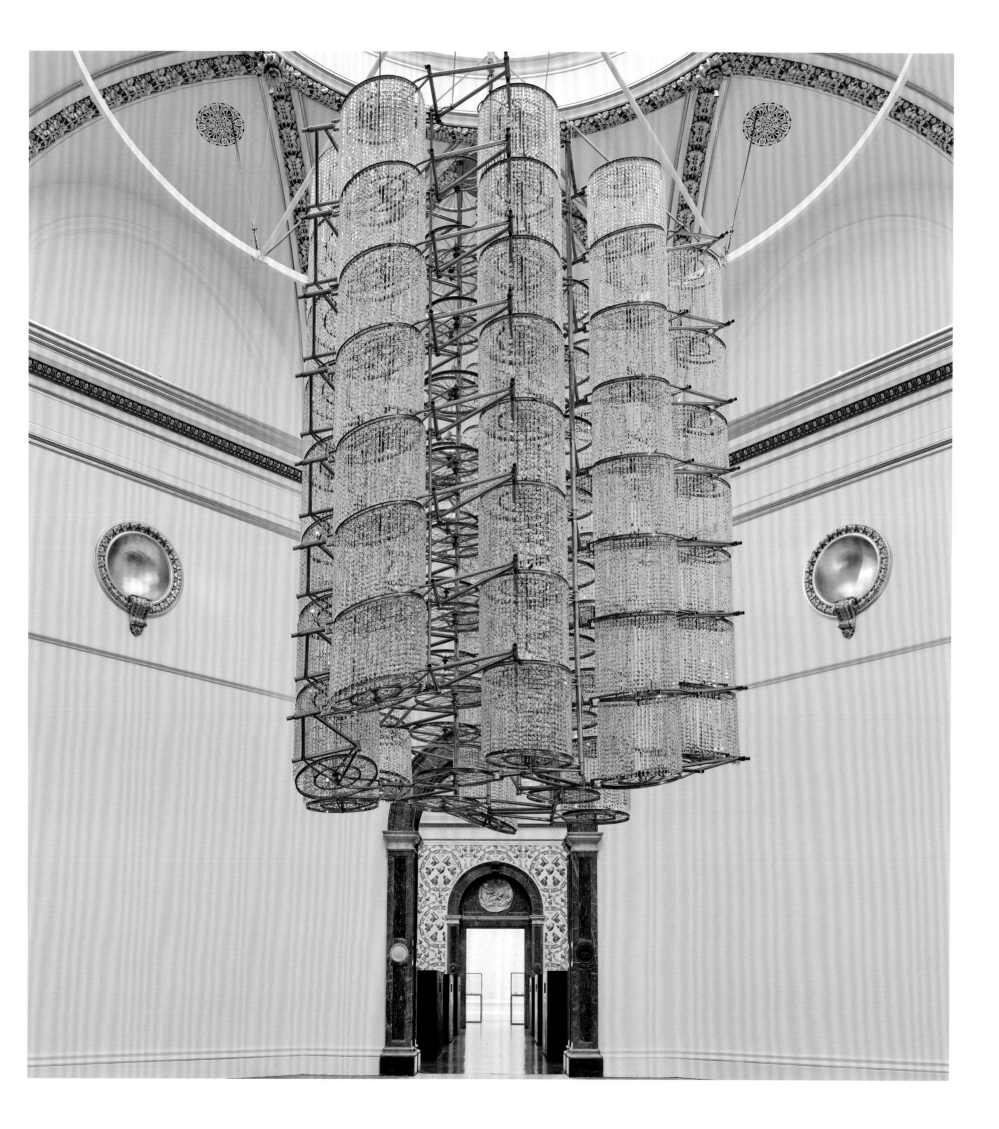

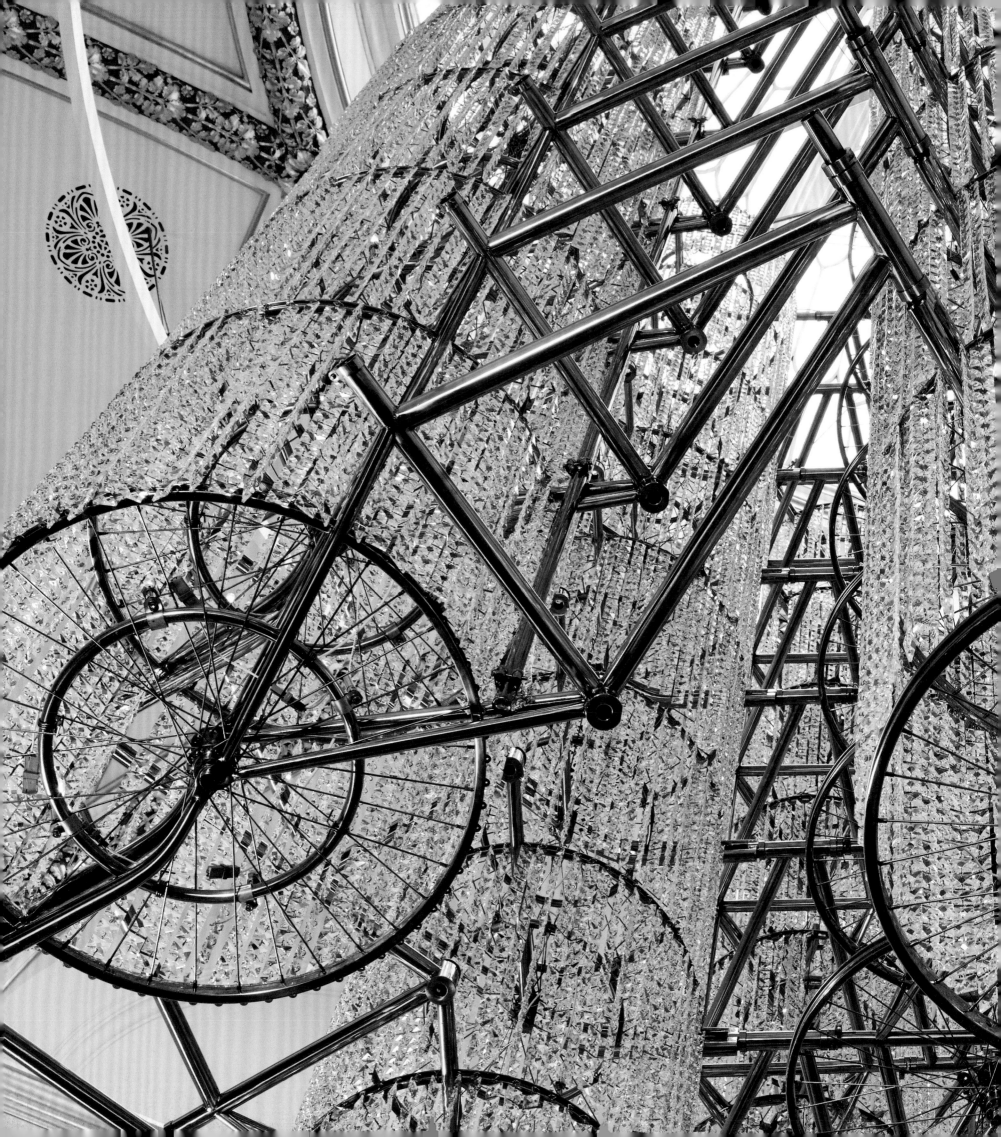

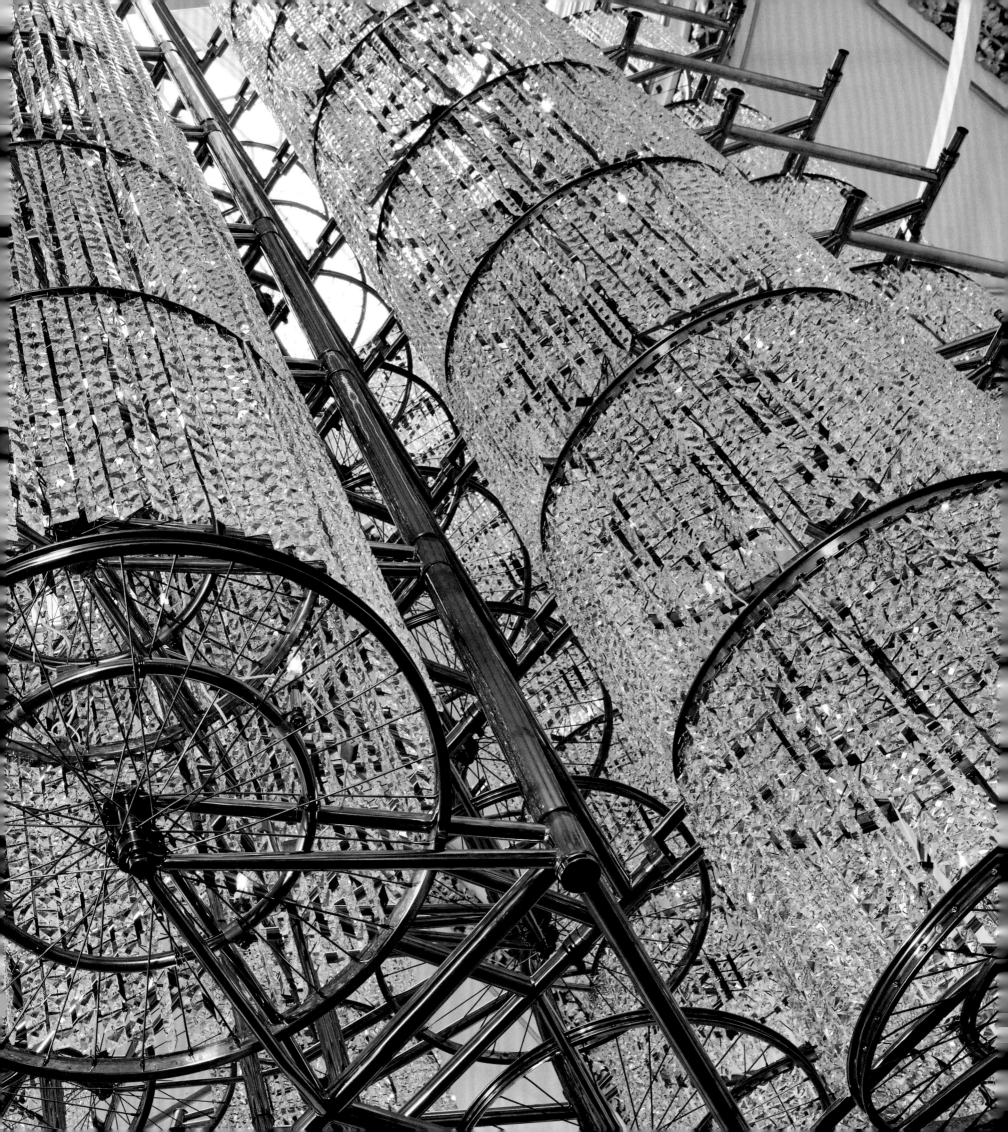

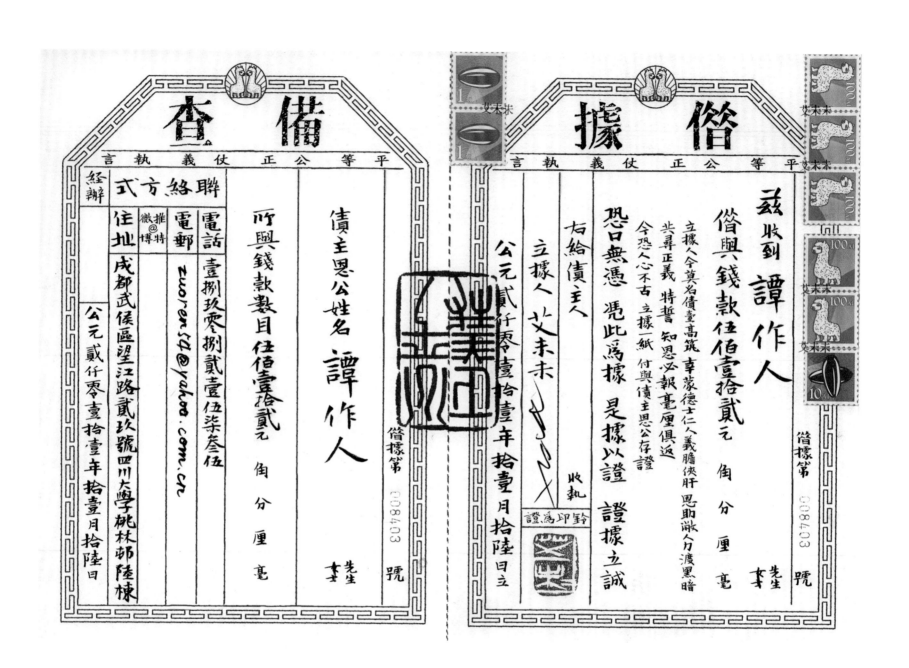

46

I.O.U. Wallpaper, 2011–13

Wallpaper, dimensions variable

Courtesy of Ai Weiwei Studio

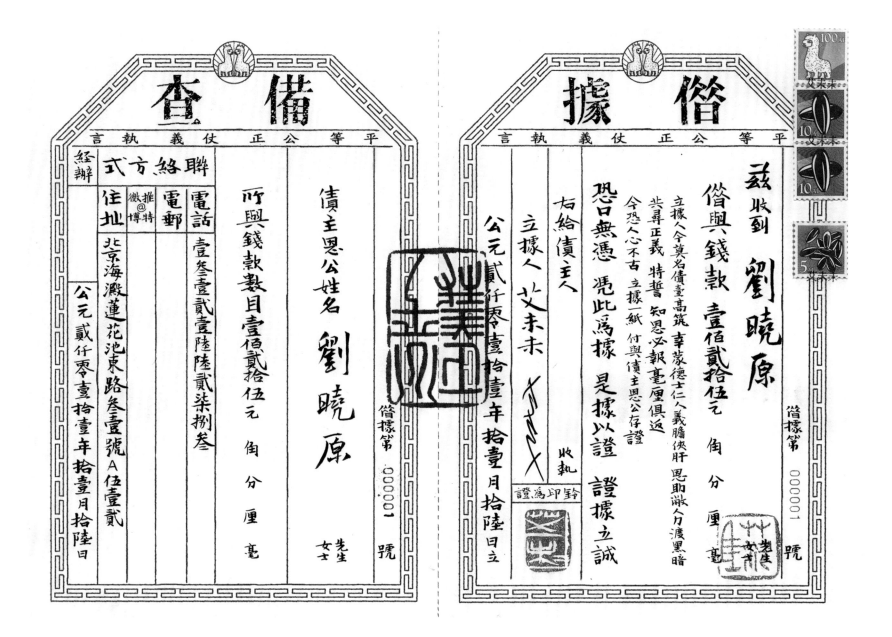

右幅（借據）

借據

平等　公正　仗義　執言

茲收到
借與錢款　劉曉原
壹佰貳拾伍元　佣　分　厘　毫

立據人今莫名債臺高築　幸蒙德士仁人義膽俠肝　思助澈人力渡黑暗
共尋正義　特誓　知恩必報毫厘俱返
今恐人心不古　立據一紙　付與債主恩公存證
恐日無憑　憑此爲據　是據以證　證據立誠
右給債主人
立據人　艾未未　收執
證爲即鈐
公元貳仟零壹拾壹年拾壹月拾陸日立

借據第　000001　號

左幅（備查）

備查

平等　公正　仗義　執言

債主恩公姓名　劉曉原
所興錢款數目壹佰貳拾伍元　佣　分　厘　毫
先生　女士

聯絡方式
電話　壹叁壹貳壹陸貳柒捌叁
電郵
微博@推特
住址　北京海澱蓮花池東路叁號A伍壹貳
經辦
公元貳仟零壹拾壹年拾壹月拾陸日

備查第　000001　號

225

ENDNOTES

BORN RADICAL (pages 30–45)
John Tancock

1   At the insistence of local officials Ai's name and works were removed from the exhibition 'Fifteen Years Chinese Contemporary Art Award' at the Power Station of Art, Shanghai, in 2014.

2   The 'Four Modernisations' refer to reforms in agriculture, industry, national defence, and science and technology.

3   For a full account of the club 'Wuming' ('No Name'), see Andrews and Kuiyi 2011.

4   For an account of the Stars exhibitions, see Rui 2007.

5   Lu Xun (1881–1936) was a great admirer of Käthe Kollwitz, both for the humanism of her work and for her use of the woodcut technique, which was extremely influential on early twentieth-century Chinese art.

6   Ai and Obrist 2011, p. 81.

7   Ai 2010.

8   Smith, Obrist and Fibicher 2010, p. 20.

9   Cai Guo-Qiang won the Golden Lion Award at the 1999 Venice Biennale.

10 See Wu Hung, *Rong Rong's East Village, 1993–1998*, New York, 2003.

11 Holzwarth 2014, p. 78.

12 Sarah Suzuki, 'Interview with Ai Weiwei', in Christophe Cherix, *Print/Out: Twenty Years in Print*, exh. cat., Museum of Modern Art, New York, 2012, p. 50.

13 Panjiayuan market, located near the Temple of Heaven in Beijing, still exists, although authentic objects are exceedingly scarce.

14 Interview with Stephanie Tung and John Tancock, 19 January 2015.

15 Liu Weiwei now has his own production workshop in Jingdezhen. Since 2006 he has worked closely with Ai Weiwei in the production of a considerable body of works in porcelain.

16 Interview with Stephanie Tung and John Tancock, 16 January 2015.

17 This series of works in porcelain was exhibited in 'A Point of Contact: Korean, Chinese, Japanese Contemporary Art', Daegu Art and Culture Hall, South Korea, in 1997.

18 Smith, Obrist and Fibicher 2010, p. 82.

19 See Wu 2014, pp. 342–45, and Andrews and Kuiyi 2012, p. 269.

20 Zhang Hui and Ai Weiwei, 'Interview with Ai Weiwei', from *White Cover Book*, Beijing, 1995, as translated in Glenside 2010, p. 23.

21 Published in Shanghai 2000, p. 9.

22 Yin Xiuzhen's installation *The Ruined Capital* (1996) at the Capital Normal University Art Museum, Beijing, consisted of furniture, cement and tiles from demolished buildings.

23 See 'Fragments', posted 29 April 2006 and reprinted in Ai and Ambrozy 2011, pp. 40–45.

24 Ai et al. 2009, pp. 97–98.

25 Wu 2014, p. 364, points out that these artists were informally known as the 'four great heavenly kings' (*si da tian wang*) of contemporary Chinese painting around the mid-2000s. He suggests that Liu Xiaodong and Zeng Fanzhi could also be added to the group.

26 In 2008 he curated 'Yang Zhichao Works 1999–2008' at the Eastlink Gallery, Shanghai.

27 See Wu 2014, pp. 362–63. The initial members of the China Contemporary Art Academy were Cai Guo-Qiang, Fang Lijun, Feng Mengbo, Lin Tianmiao, Liu Xiaodong, Luo Zhongli, Song Dong, Sui Jianguo, Qiu Zhijie, Wang Guangyi, Wang Gongxin, Wang Jianwei, Wu Ershan, Xu Bing, Xu Jiang, Ye Yongqing, Yue Minjun, Zeng Fanzhi, Zhan Wang, Zhang Xiaogang, and Zhou Chunya.

28 Ai and Ambrozy 2011, p. 123.

29 Brussels 2009.

30 In the Chinese edition of *The Art Book*, published by Phaidon Press in London and New York, 2012, Ai Weiwei's place was taken by Agostino di Duccio.

31 'Ai Weiwei' opened at Galleria Continua and Tang Contemporary on June 6; 'AB Blood Type' opened at Magician Space on 8 June; 'Tiger, Tiger, Tiger' opened at Chambers Fine Art on 13 June; 'Ai Weiwei' took place at Zhao Zhao's studio in Caochangdi on 19 June.

32 Brussels 2009, p. 147.

ARCHITECTURE CAN ALSO BE SILENT (pages 46–65)
Daniel Rosbottom

1 'Ai Weiwei', exhibition at the Albion Gallery, London, October – November 2008.

2 Interview with Jonathan Watts in the *Guardian*, 9 August 2007.

3 Ai Weiwei's blog post 'With Regard to Architecture', 22 January 2006, translated by Philip Tinari, quoted in Ai and Pins 2014.

4 Ai Weiwei's blog post 'Ordinary Architecture', 22 June 2006, translated by Philip Tinari, quoted in Ai and Pins 2014.

5 'With Regard to Architecture', *op. cit.*

6 Leslie Jacques, 'The Trouble with Mega Projects', *The New Yorker*, 11 April 2015.

7 Ai Weiwei's blog post 'Here and Now', 10 May 2006, translated by Lee Ambrozy, quoted in Ai and Pins 2014.

8 'With Regard to Architecture', *op. cit.*

10 'Here and Now', *op. cit.*

11 'Ordinary Architecture', *op. cit.*

12 'Here and Now', *op. cit.*

13 Chin-Chin Yap, 'A Handful of Dust', in Ai and Pins 2014, p. 37.

14 'With Regard to Architecture', *op. cit.*

15 'With Regard to Architecture', *op. cit.*

16 Michel Foucault, 'Space, Knowledge and Power', in Foucault and Rabinow 1984, p. 245.

17 David Howarth, 'Building Beyond Boundaries' (review of Ai Weiwei Exhibition at Kunsthaus Bregenz, Austria), *Architects' Journal*, vol. 234, no. 3, 4 August 2011, pp. 41–43.

18 Ai and Obrist 2011, p. 53.

19 Ai and Obrist 2011, p. 53.

20 For a fuller study of the relationships between Wittgenstein's house and Ai Weiwei's studio-house, see Anthony Pins, 'The Nudged Vernacular', in Ai and Pins 2014, pp. 132–151.

21 Ludwig Wittgenstein, *Tractatus Logico-Philosophicus*, 6.421, London, 2001, p. 86.

22 Ai Weiwei's blog post 'N Town', 19 March 2006, quoted in Ai and Ambrozy 2011, p. 28.

23 Ai and Obrist 2011, p. 15.

24 'N Town', *op. cit.*

25 Ai and Obrist 2011, p. 97.

26 Ai and Obrist 2011, p. 64.

27 'Conversation between Ai Weiwei and Eduard Kögel July 2007', in Kögel 2007, p. 6.

28 Kenneth Frampton, 'Rappel à L'ordre: The Case for the Tectonic', *Architectural Design*, vol. 60, no. 3–4, 1990, pp. 19–25.

29 'Conversation between Ai Weiwei and Eduard Kögel July 2007', in Kögel 2007, p. 8.

30 'The Nudged Vernacular', *op. cit.* p. 147.

31 'Urban Rural Conundrums – Off-center in Caochangdi, Beijing', Mary-Ann Ray and Robert Mangurian, *Journal of the International Institute*, University of Michigan, Fall 2003.

32 John Tancock, 'Prelude: Ai Weiwei in New York', in Ai, Tancock et al. 2011, pp. 17–23.

33 'Ai Weiwei: Fragments, Voids, Sections and Rings', interview by Adrian Blackwell, 21 June 2006, Archinect.com.

34 'Ai Weiwei: Fragments, Voids, Sections and Rings', interview by Adrian Blackwell, 21 June 2006, Archinect.com.

35 'Ai Weiwei: Interview with Curator Tessa Praun 2010', in *Ai Weiwei*, exh. cat., Magasin 3, Stockholm, February – June 2012.

36 Charles Merewether, 'Duration Within Time' (Excerpt), Ai and Pins 2014, p. 337.

37 'Introduction', *Sticks and Stones*, exh. cat., Alison and Peter Smithson, 1976, quoted in *The Charged Void: Architecture*, New York, 2001, p. 393.

38 Jacques Herzog, 'Conversation with Ai Weiwei Concept and Fake', *Parkett* 81, 2008, pp. 122–145.

39 Jacques Herzog, 'Conversation with Ai Weiwei Concept and Fake', *Parkett* 81, 2008, pp. 122–145.

40 Ai Weiwei, from the video *Wenchuan Rebar* 2012.

41 Reto Geiser, 'In the Realm of Architecture', Ai and Pins 2014, p. 133.

BIBLIOGRAPHY

Ai 2004
Ai Weiwei, *Ai Weiwei: Beijing 10/2003*, Beijing, 2004

Ai 2008
Ai Weiwei, *Becoming: Images of Beijing's Air Terminal 3*, Beijing and London, 2008

Ai et al. 2009
Ai Weiwei, Yung Ho Chang, Uli Sigg and Peter Pakesch, *Art and Cultural Policy in China*, Vienna, 2009

Ai and Ambrozy 2011
Ai Weiwei and Lee Ambrozy, *Ai Weiwei's Blog: Writings, Interviews, and Digital Rants 2006–2009*, Cambridge MA, 2011

Ai and Obrist 2011
Ai Weiwei, Hans Ulrich Obrist, *Ai Weiwei Speaks: With Hans Ulrich Obrist*, London 2011

Ai and Pins 2014
Ai Weiwei, Anthony Pins, *Ai Weiwei: Spatial Matters: Art, Architecture and Activism*, Cambridge MA and London, 2014

Ai and Weiqun 2006
Ai Weiwei and Chen Weiqun (eds), *Fragments*, Beijing, 2006

Ai, Tancock et al. 2011
Ai Weiwei, Uta Grosenick, John Tancock, Stephanie Tung, *Ai Weiwei New York 1983–1993*, Berlin, 2011

Alcatraz 2014
David Spalding (ed.), *@Large: Ai Weiwei on Alcatraz*, exh. cat., Alcatraz, published in San Francisco, 2014

Andrews and Kuiyi 2011
Julia F. Andrews and Kuiyi Shen, *Blooming in the Shadows: Unofficial Chinese Art, 1974–1985*, New York, 2011

Andrews and Kuiyi 2012
Julia F. Andrews and Kuiyi Shen, *The Art of Modern China*, Berkeley, 2012

Barcelona 2014
Llucià Homs and Rosa Pera, *Ai Weiwei: On the Table*, exh. cat., Palau de la Virreina, Barcelona, 2014

Beijing 2010
Ai Weiwei: New York Photographs, 1983–1993, exh. cat., Three Shadows Photography Art Centre, Beijing, 2010

Beijing 2014
John Tancock, *Ai Weiwei*, exh. cat., Chambers Fine Art, Beijing, 2014

Berlin 2014
Gereon Sievernich (ed.), *Ai Weiwei: Evidence*, exh. cat., Martin-Gropius-Bau, Berlin, published in Munich, 2014

Bortolotti et al. 2014
Maurizio Bortolotti, Gianmatteo Caputo, Greg Hilty, Hans Ulrich Obrist and Philip Tinari, *Ai Weiwei: Disposition*, London, 2014

Bovier and Schnetz 2012
Lionel Bovier and Salome Schnetz (eds), *Ai Weiwei: Fairytale, a Reader*, Zurich, 2012

Brussels 2009
Luc Tuymans, Ai Weiwei, Fan Di'an, *The State of Things, Brussels/Beijing*, exh. cat., BOZAR Center for Fine Arts, Brussels, and Beijing, 2009

Buergel, Kramer and Maas 2010
Roger M. Buergel, Dirk Kramer and Klaus Maas, *Ai Weiwei: Barely Something*, Duisburg, 2010

Chalabi and Van Cauteren 2015
Tamara Chalabi and Philippe Van Cauteren, *Traces of Survival: Drawing of Refugees in Iraq Selected by Ai Weiwei*, Antwerp, 2015

Costa 2010
Xavier Costa (ed.), *Ai Weiwei: With Milk___find something everybody can use*, Barcelona, 2010

Delson 2011
Susan Delson, *Ai Weiwei: Circle of Animals*, Munich, London and New York, 2011

Foster and Obrist 2009
Elena Ochoa Foster and Hans Ulrich Obrist (eds), *Ai Weiwei: Ways Beyond Art*, London and Madrid, 2009

Foucault and Rabinow 1984
Michel Foucault and Paul Rabinow, *The Foucault Reader*, New York, 1984

Gaensheimer 2013
Susanne Gaensheimer (ed.), *Ai Weiwei, Romuald Karmakar, Santu Mofokeng, Dayanita Singh: German Pavilion 2013: 55th International Art Exhibition: La Biennale di Venezia*, Berlin 2013

Glenside 2010
Ai Weiwei: Dropping the Urn: Ceramic Works, 5000 BCE – 2010 CE, exh. cat., Arcadia University Art Gallery, Glenside PA, 2010

Groningen 2008
Karen Smith, Sue-an van der Zijpp and Mark Wilson, *Ai Weiwei*, exh. cat., Groninger Museum, Groningen, 2008

Hilty and Tinari 2011
Greg Hilty and Philip Tinari, *Ai Weiwei*, London, 2011

Holzwarth 2014
Hans Werner Holzwarth (ed.), *Ai Weiwei*, Cologne, 2014

Klein 2010
Caroline Klein, *Ai Weiwei: Architecture*, Cologne, 2010

Kögel 2007
Eduard Kögel (ed.), *Ai Weiwei, Fake Design in the Village*, Aedes, 2007

Lauvergne 2004
Carole Lauvergne, *Ai Weiwei*, Ghent, 2004

Lilley 2014
Clare Lilley, *Ai Weiwei in the Chapel*, Wakefield, 2014

London 2010
Juliet Bingham, *Ai Weiwei: Sunflower Seeds*, exh. cat., Tate Modern, London, 2010

Lucerne 2007
Philip Tinari, Peter Pakesch, Urs Meile and Charles Merewether, *Ai Weiwei Works, 2004–2007*, exh. cat., Galerie Urs Meile, Lucerne; published in Zurich, 2007

Martin 2013
Barnaby Martin, *Hanging Man: The Arrest of Ai Weiwei*, London, 2013

Merewether 2003
Charles Merewether, *Ai Weiwei, Works: Beijing 1993–2003*, Beijing, 2003

Merewether 2008
Charles Merewether, *Ai Weiwei: Under Construction*, Sydney, 2008

Merewether and Price 2008
Charles Merewether and Matt Price, *Ai Weiwei, Herzog & de Meuron: Beijing, Venice, London*, London, 2008

Munich 2009
Ai Weiwei and Mark Siemons, *Ai Weiwei: So Sorry*, exh. cat., Haus der Kunst, Munich; published in Munich and New York, 2009

O'Brien, Larner and Feeley 2012
Sophie O'Brien, Melissa Larner and Claire Feeley (eds), *Herzog & de Meuron + Ai Weiwei: Serpentine Gallery Pavilion 2012*, Düsseldorf, 2012

Rui 2007
Huang Rui, *The Stars Times 1977–1984*, Beijing, 2007

Sassen, Pera and Furio 2014
Saskia Sassen, Rosa Pera and Vicenc Furio, *Ai Weiwei: Mirror and Hammer*, Barcelona, 2014

Smith 2008
Karen Smith, *Ai Weiwei: Illumination*, New York, 2008

Smith, Obrist and Fibicher 2010
Karen Smith, Hans Ulrich Obrist and Bernard Fibicher, *Ai Weiwei*, London and New York, 2010

Sorace 2014
Christian Sorace, 'China's Last Communist: Ai Weiwei', *Critical Inquiry*, vol. 40, no. 2, (Winter 2014), pp. 396–419

Spencer-Churchill et al. 2015
Edward Spencer-Churchill, Julian Schnabel, Emma Crichton-Miller, Michael Frahm and Ben Murphy, *Ai Weiwei at Blenheim Palace*, Woodstock, 2015

Stahel and Janser 2011
Urs Stahel and Daniela Janser (eds), *Ai Weiwei: Interlacing*, Goettingen, 2011

Wu 2014
Wu Hung, *Contemporary Chinese Art: A History*, New York, 2014

Shanghai 2000
Ai Weiwei and Feng Boyi (eds), *Buhezuo fangshi (Fuck Off)*, exh. cat., Eastlink Gallery, Shanghai, 2000

Warsh 2012
Larry Warsh (ed.), *Ai Weiwei: Weiweisms*, Princeton, 2012

Washington DC 2012
Mami Kataoka, Charles Merewether and Kerry Brougher, *Ai Weiwei: According to What?*, Hirshhorn Museum and Sculpture Garden, Washington DC; published in Munich, 2012

EXHIBITION HISTORY

SOLO EXHIBITIONS

2015
'Ruptures', Faurschou Foundation, Copenhagen, Denmark
'Ai Weiwei', Galleria Continua, Beijing, China
'Ai Weiwei', Tang Contemporary Art Center, Beijing, China
'AB Blood Type', Magician Space, Beijing, China
'Tiger, Tiger, Tiger', Chambers Fine Art, Beijing, China
'Beijing 2003', Being 3 Gallery, Beijing, China

2014
'@Large: Ai Weiwei on Alcatraz', Alcatraz Island, San Francisco, CA, USA
'Ai Weiwei in the Chapel', Yorkshire Sculpture Park, Wakefield, West Yorkshire, UK
'Ai Weiwei', Lisson Gallery, London, UK
'According to What?', Brooklyn Museum, Brooklyn, NY, USA
'Evidence', Martin-Gropius-Bau, Berlin, Germany
'Sunflower Seeds', Pinakothek der Moderne, Munich, Germany
'Baby Formula', Ayala Museum, Makati City, Metro Manila, Philippines
'Ai Weiwei', Christine König Galerie, Vienna, Austria

2013
'According to What?', Perez Art Museum Miami, Miami, FL, USA
'Ordos', Galleria Continua, Les Moulins, France
'Ai Weiwei: Screening Room', Bauer Hotel, Venice, Italy
'Baby Formula', Galerie Michael Janssen, Singapore
'According to What?', Art Gallery of Ontario, Toronto, Canada
'Ai Weiwei. Resistance and Tradition', Centro Andaluz de Arte Contemporaneo (CAAC), Seville, Spain
'Interlacing', Museu da Imagem e do Som, São Paulo, Brazil
'55th International Art Exhibition, Venice Biennale', German Pavilion, Venice, Italy
'Disposition', Zuecca Project Space, Complesse delle Zitelle, Giudecca, Chiesa di Sant'Antonin, Venice, Italy
'According to What?', Indianapolis Museum of Art, Indianapolis, IN, USA

2012
'Forge', Mary Boone Gallery, New York City, NY, USA
'New York Photographs 1983–1993', Ernst Museum (in collaboration with Alexander Ochs Galleries, Berlin | Beijing), Budapest, Hungary
'Ai Weiwei *Rebar-Lucerne*', Galerie Urs Meile, Lucerne, Switzerland
'Ai Weiwei', Galleria Continua San Gimignano, San Gimignano, Italy
'Ai Weiwei: According to What?', Hirshhorn Museum and Sculpture Garden, Washington DC, USA
'Perspectives: Ai Weiwei', The Arthur M. Sackler Gallery, Smithsonian Institution, Washington DC, USA
'Circle of Animals/Zodiac Heads: Gold', Museum of Contemporary Art San Diego, USA
'A Living Sculpture', Pippy Houldsworth Gallery, London, UK
'Ai Weiwei: New York Photographs 1983–1993', Moscow House of Photography, Moscow, Russia
'Circle of Animals/Zodiac Heads', Hirshhorn Museum, Washington DC, USA
'Circle of Animals/Zodiac Heads: Gold', Musée d'art contemporain de Montréal, Montréal, Canada
'Circle of Animals/Zodiac Heads', The Woodrow Wilson School at Princeton University, Princeton, NJ, USA
'Ai Weiwei', Lisson Gallery, Milan, Italy
'Ai Weiwei: Five Houses', Architecture Center Houston, Houston, TX, USA
'Interlacing', Kistefos-Museet, Jevnaker, Norway
'Ai Weiwei', De Pont Museum of Contemporary Art, Tilburg, the Netherlands
'Interlacing', Jeu de Paume, Paris, France
'Ai Weiwei', Magasin 3 Stockholm Konsthall, Stockholm, Sweden
'Circle of Animals/Zodiac Heads', Hermann Park, Houston, TX, USA
'Sunflower Seeds', Mary Boone Gallery, New York City, NY, USA

2011   'Louisiana Contemporary: Ai Weiwei', Louisiana Museum of Modern Art, Humlebaek, Denmark

'Ai Weiwei: New York Photographs 1983–1993', Martin-Gropius-Bau, Berlin, Germany

'Ai Weiwei: Absent', Taipei Fine Arts Museum, Taipei, Taiwan

'Dropping the Urn, Ceramics 5000 BCE – 2010 CE', Victoria and Albert Museum, London, UK

'Art | Architecture', Kunsthaus Bregenz, Bregenz, Austria

'Ai Weiwei: New York Photographs 1983–1993', Asia Society, New York, NY, USA

'Interlacing', Kunsthaus Graz, Graz, Austria

'Interlacing', Fotomuseum Winterthur, Winterthur, Switzerland

'Circle of Animals', Los Angeles County Museum of Art, Los Angeles, CA, USA

'Ai Weiwei: Works in the collection', DKM Museum, Duisburg, Germany

'Circle of Animals', Somerset House, London, UK

'Circle of Animals', Pulitzer Fountain, New York, NY, USA

'Ai Weiwei', Lisson Gallery, London, UK

'Sunflower Seeds', Kunsthalle Marcel Duchamp, Cully, Switzerland

'Ai Weiwei', Neugerriemschneider, Berlin, Germany

'Ai Weiwei – Teehaus', Museen Dahlem, Berlin, Germany

2010   'Ai Weiwei', Faurschou Gallery, Copenhagen, Denmark

'Cube Light', Misa Shin Gallery, Tokyo, Japan

'A Few Works from Ai Weiwei', Alexander Ochs Galleries, Berlin, Germany

'The Unilever Series: Ai Weiwei', Turbine Hall, Tate Modern, London, UK

'Hurt Feelings', Christine König Galerie, Vienna, Austria

'Ai Weiwei', Galerie Urs Meile, Lucerne, Switzerland

'Dropping the Urn, Ceramic Works 5000 BCE – 2010 CE', Museum of Contemporary Craft, Portland, USA (Travelling Exhibition)

'Ai Weiwei', Haines Gallery, San Francisco, USA

'Barely Something', Stiftung DKM, Duisburg, Germany

'Dropping the Urn, Ceramic Works 5000 BCE – 2010 CE', Arcadia University Gallery, Glenside, USA (Travelling Exhibition)

'Mermaid Exchange', Langelinie, Copenhagen, Denmark

2009   'Ai Weiwei', Friedman Benda, New York City, NY, USA

'With Milk ___ find something everybody can use', Mies van der Rohe Pavilion, Barcelona, Spain

'World Map', Faurschou Gallery, Beijing, China

'So Sorry', Haus der Kunst, Munich, Germany

'According to What?', Mori Art Museum, Tokyo, Japan

'Ways Beyond Art', Ivory Press Space, Madrid, Spain

'Four Movements', Phillips de Pury, London, UK

'Ai Weiwei: New York Photographs 1983–1993', Three Shadows Photography Art Centre, Beijing, China

2008   'Ai Weiwei', Albion Gallery, London, UK

'Ai Weiwei', Hyundai Gallery, Seoul, Korea

'Under Construction', Sherman Contemporary Art Foundation, Campbelltown Arts Centre, Sydney, Australia

'Illumination', Mary Boone Gallery, New York, NY, USA

'Go China! Ai Weiwei', Groninger Museum, Groningen, The Netherlands

'*Through* and Video Work *Fairytale*', Sherman Contemporary Art Foundation, Sydney, Australia

2007   'Fragments', Art Unlimited, Art 38 Basel, Basel, Switzerland
Galerie Urs Meile, Lucerne, Switzerland

'Ai Weiwei', Galerie Urs Meile, Beijing–Lucerne, Lucerne, Switzerland

'Traveling Landscapes', AedesLand, Berlin, Germany

2006   'Fragments', Galerie Urs Meile, Beijing–Lucerne, Beijing, China

2004   'Ai Weiwei', Kunsthalle Bern, Bern, Switzerland

'Ai Weiwei in Ghent, Belgium', Caermersklooster – Provinciaal Centrum voor Kunst en Cultuur, Ghent, Belgium

'Ai Weiwei', Robert Miller Gallery, New York, NY, USA

2003   'Ai Weiwei', Galerie Urs Meile, Beijing–Lucerne, Lucerne, Switzerland

1988   'Old Shoes – Safe Sex', Art Waves Gallery, New York, NY, USA

1982   'Ai Weiwei', Asian Foundation, San Francisco, CA, USA

SELECTED GROUP EXHIBITIONS

2015 'The 56th International Art Exhibition – All the World's Futures', Venice Biennale, Venice, Italy

'Go East', Art Gallery of New South Wales, Sydney, Australia

2014 'Taiping Tianguo: A History of Possible Encounters', e-flux, New York, USA

'State of Emergency', Davidson College, Belk Visual Arts Center, Davidson, USA

'Beyond and Between', Leeum Samsung Museum of Art, Seoul, South Korea

'Beyond Stuff', Mizuma Gallery, Singapore

'The 14th International Architecture Exhibition – Fundamentals', Venice Architecture Biennale, Venice, Italy

'Unscrolled: Reframing Tradition in Chinese Contemporary Art', Vancouver, Canada

2013 'The 55th International Art Exhibition – The Encyclopedic Palace', Venice Biennale, Venice, Italy

'Framed', Duddell's, Hong Kong

'Ground Zero', Lokanat Gallery, Yangon, Myanmar

'Island', Dairy Art Centre, London, UK

'Scotiabank Nuit Blanche 2013', Nathan Phillips Square, Toronto, Canada

'Emscherkunst 2013', Emscher River, Essen/Ruhr Valley, Germany

'Fuck Off 2', Groninger Museum, Groningen, The Netherlands

'A Journal of the Plague Year. Fear, Ghosts, Rebels. SARS, Leslie and the Hong Kong Story', Sheung Wan Civic Centre Exhibition Hall, Hong Kong

'Of Bridges and Borders', Parque Cultural of Valparaiso, Valparaiso, Chile

2012 Busan Biennale, Busan, South Korea

'Newtopia: The State of Human Rights', Kazerne Dossin Museum and Documentation Centre of the Holocaust and of Human Rights, Mechelen, Belgium

'Postmodernism: Style and Subversion 1970–1990', The Swiss National Museum, Zürich, Switzerland

'Art Basel', Basel, Switzerland

'Art and the City', Zürich, Switzerland

'Art+Press', Martin-Gropius-Bau, Berlin, Germany

'Lifelike', Walker Art Center, Minneapolis, MN, USA

2011 'Liu Wei & Ai Weiwei', Faurschou Gallery, Beijing, China

Gwangju Design Biennale, Gwangju, South Korea

'DaringDesign – Chinese and Dutch Designers with Guts', Netherlands Architecture Institute, Rotterdam, the Netherlands

'Art Parcours in St Alban-Tal', St Alban, Switzerland

'Shanshui', The Museum of Art Lucerne, Lucerne, Switzerland

'Six Rooms', Friedman Benda Gallery, New York, NY, USA

2010 '29th São Paulo Biennial', São Paulo Biennial, São Paulo, Brazil

'The 12th International Architecture Exhibition – People Meet in Architecture', Venice Architecture Biennale, Venice, Italy

'Acconci Studio + Ai Weiwei: A Collaborative Project', Para Site Art Space, Hong Kong

2009 'Fairytale', Herzliya Museum of Contemporary Art, Herzliya, Israel

'Mahjong: Contemporary Chinese Art from the Sigg Collection', The Peabody Essex Museum, Salem, MA, USA (Travelling Exhibition)

2008 'Liverpool Biennial International 08: Made Up', Tate Liverpool, Liverpool, UK

'The 11th International Architecture Exhibition – Out There: Architecture Beyond Buildings', Venice Architecture Biennale, Venice, Italy

2007 'The Sixth Shenzhen Contemporary Sculpture Exhibition – A Vista of Perspectives', OCAT Contemporary Art Terminal, Shenzhen, China

'Origin Point: Stars Group Retrospective Exhibition', Today Art Museum, Beijing, China

Documenta 12, Kassel, Germany

'Forged Realities', Universal Studios, Beijing, China

2006 'The 5th Asia-Pacific Triennial of Contemporary Art', Queensland Art Gallery, Queensland, Australia

'Zones of Contact', 15th Biennial of Sydney, Sydney, Australia

'Territorial. Ai Weiwei und Serge Spitzer', Museum für Moderne Kunst, Frankfurt am Main, Germany

'Herzog & de Meuron. No. 250. Eine Ausstellung', Haus der Kunst, Munich, Germany

'Fill in the Blanks', China Art Archives & Warehouse, Beijing, China

'Busan Biennial 2006', Busan Museum of Modern Art, Busan, Korea

2005   'The 2nd Guangzhou Triennial', Guangdong Museum of Art,
        Guangzhou, China

        'Herzog & de Meuron. No. 250. An Exhibition', Tate Modern,
        London, UK

        'Beauty and Waste in the Architecture of Herzog & de Meuron',
        Netherlands Architecture Institute, Rotterdam,
        The Netherlands

2004   'The 9th International Architecture Exhibition – Metamorph',
        Venice Architecture Biennale, Venice, Italy

        'On the Edge – Contemporary Chinese Photography & Video',
        Ethan Cohen Fine Arts, New York, USA

2002   'The 1st Guangzhou Triennial', Guangdong Museum of Art,
        Guangzhou, China

2001   'Take Part II', Galerie Urs Meile, Beijing–Lucerne, Lucerne,
        Switzerland

        'Tu Mu. Young Chinese Architecture', Aedes Galerie, Berlin,
        Germany

        'Take Part I', Galerie Urs Meile, Beijing–Lucerne, Lucerne,
        Switzerland

2000   'Fuck off', EastLink Gallery, Shanghai, China

1999   'Innovations Part I', China Art Archives & Warehouse, Beijing,
        China

        'd'Apertutto, La Biennale di Venezia, 48', International Art
        Exhibition, Venice, Italy

        'Modern China Art Foundation Collection', Caermersklooster –
        Provinciaal Centrum voor Kunst en Cultuur, Ghent, Belgium

1998   'Double Kitsch: Painters from China', Max Protetch, New York,
        NY, USA

1993   'Chinese Contemporary Art – The Stars 15 Years', Tokyo
        Gallery, Tokyo, Japan

1989   'The Stars: Ten Years', Hanart Gallery, Hong Kong

1987   'The Stars at Harvard: Chinese Dissident Art', Fairbank Center
        for East Asian Research, Harvard University, Cambridge, USA

1980   'The Second Stars Exhibition', National Art Museum of China,
        Beijing, China

1979   'The First Stars Exhibition', outside the National Art Museum
        of China, Beijing, China

LENDERS TO THE EXHIBITION

Ai Weiwei Studio

Collection of Lisa and Danny Goldberg

Lisson Gallery

M+ Sigg Collection, Hong Kong

Collection of Honus Tandijono

Tate, London

Collection of Larry Warsh

M. Neil Wong Hou-Lianq

And others who wish to remain anonymous

PHOTOGRAPHIC ACKNOWLEDGEMENTS

Artwork Acknowledgements

Artwork by Liam J. Andrews; © Daniel Rosbottom: fig. 22

Copyright Acknowledgements

All works of art are reproduced by kind permission of the owners. Every attempt has been made to trace copyright holders of works reproduced. Specific acknowledgements are as follows:

© Ai Weiwei: pp. 98–99, 139–42, 154, 168, 174, 188, 196, 210, 220; figs 3–9, 11–15, 17–21, 23–63, 65–6, 71–2, 74–9; cats 1–46

© Succession Marcel Duchamp/ADAGP, Paris and DACS, London 2015: figs 12, 35

Photographic Acknowledgements

All works of art are reproduced by kind permission of the owners. Every attempt has been made to trace the photographers of works reproduced. Specific acknowledgements are as follows:

Image courtesy of Ai Weiwei Studio: pp. 98–99, 122–23, 142, 160–61, 166–67, 170–71, 174, 186, 192, 196, 215 (top), 220; figs 3–7, 11–14, 16–21, 23–35, 37–60, 61, 62–3, 65, 72–4, 76, 78–9; cats 4, 7, 11, 12, 14–17, 20, 21, 27–30, 35–37, 39–42, 44 (pp. 216–17), 46

Courtesy of Filippo Armellin: fig. 71

Beijing, © Li Xiaobin: fig. 10

Beijing–Lucerne, Courtesy Galerie Urs Meile. Photo Oak Taylor-Smith: fig. 54

John Bodkin/DawkinsColour, London, © Royal Academy of Arts: pp. 7, 8, 10–11, 12–13, 14–15, 100, 106, 112, 128, 138–39, 154, 168, 176–77, 188–89, 210, 218, 222–23; cats 1–3, 5, 6, 8–10, 13, 18, 19, 22–26, 31, 32, 33 (p. 193), 34, 38, 43, 45

Copenhagen, courtesy Andreas Johnsen (photo Andreas Johnsen, design Neil Kellerhouse): fig. 70

Florence, Scala © 2015. Digital image, The Museum of Modern Art, New York: figs 12, 46

Gao Yuan: p. 2

Adrian Locke: fig. 2

London, courtesy Dazed; photograph by Gao Yuan: fig. 64

London, © Hampstead Theatre: fig. 69

London, courtesy New Statesman; photograph by Gao Yuan for Ai Weiwei Studio: fig. 67

London, Tate 2015: fig. 9

London, © View Pictures/UIG/Getty Images: fig. 66

Tim Marlow: fig. 1

Munich, Jens Weber: fig. 61 (detail on pp. 86–87 only)

Courtesy of Ben Murphy: fig. 77

New York, courtesy Alison Klayman/Never Sorry LLC; collection of Larry Warsh: fig. 68

Courtesy of Stockamp Tsai Collection: fig. 36

Courtesy of the Yorkshire Park. Photography: Jonty Wilde: fig. 75

INDEX

SUPPORTERS OF THE ROYAL ACADEMY

The President and the Trustees of the Royal Academy Trust are grateful to all its donors for their continued loyalty and generosity. They would like to extend their thanks to all those who have made a significant commitment, past and present, to the galleries, the exhibitions, the conservation of the Permanent Collection, the Library collections, the Royal Academy Schools, the Learning programme and other specific appeals.

Major Benefactors

HM The Queen
Her Majesty's Government
The 29th May 1961 Charitable Trust
The Aldama Foundation
The American Associates of the Royal Academy Trust
The Annenberg Foundation
Barclays Bank
BAT Industries plc
Sir David and Lady Bell
The late Tom Bendhem
The late Brenda M Benwell-Lejeune
John Frye Bourne
British Telecom
Conseulo and Anthony Brooke
The Brown Foundation
John and Susan Burns
Mr Raymond M Burton CBE
Jeanne and William Callanan
Sir Trevor Chinn CVO and Lady Chinn
The John S Cohen Foundation
The Roger De Haan Charitable Trust
Sir Harry and Lady Djangoly
The Dulverton Trust
Alfred Dunhill Limited
The John Ellerman Foundation
The Eranda Foundation
Esso UK plc
EY
Esmée Fairbairn Charitable Trust
The Fidelity UK Foundation
The Foyle Foundation
The Foundation for Sports and the Arts
Friends of the Royal Academy
Jacqueline and Michael Gee
The Getty Grant Programme
J Paul Getty Jnr Charitable Trust
Mr Thomas Gibson
Glaxo Holdings plc
Diane and Guilford Glazer
Mr and Mrs Jack Goldhill
Maurice and Laurence Goldman
The Horace W Goldsmith Foundation
HRH Princess Marie-Chantal of Greece
Sir Nicholas Grimshaw CBE PPRA
Mrs Robin Hambro
Mr and Mrs Jocelin Harris
The Philip and Pauline Harris Charitable Trust
The Charles Hayward Foundation
Heritage Lottery Fund
IBM United Kingdom Limited
The Idlewild Trust
Lord and Lady Jacobs
The JP Jacobs Charitable Trust
The Japan Foundation
Gabrielle Jungels-Winkler Foundation
Mr and Mrs Donald Kahn
The Lillian Jean Kaplan Foundation

The Kresge Foundation
The Samuel H Kress Foundation
The Kirby Laing Foundation
The Lankelly Foundation
The late Mr John S Latsis
The David Lean Foundation
The Leverhulme Trust
Lex Service plc
The Linbury Trust
Sir Sydney Lipworth QC and Lady Lipworth CBE
Ronald and Rita McAulay
McKinsey and Company Inc
John Madejski OBE DL
The Manifold Trust
Marks and Spencer
The Paul Mellon Estate
The Mercers' Company
The Monument Trust
The Henry Moore Foundation
The Moorgate Trust Fund
The late Mr Minoru Mori HON KBE and Mrs Mori
Museums and Galleries Improvement Fund
National Westminster Bank
Stavros S Niarchos
Simon and Midge Palley
The Peacock Charitable Trust
The Pennycress Trust
PF Charitable Trust
The Pidem Fund
The Pilgrim Trust
The Edith and Ferdinand Porjes Trust
The Porter Foundation
John Porter Charitable Trust
John A Roberts FRIBA
Sir Simon and Lady Robertson
The Ronson Foundation
Rothmans International plc
RTZ Corporation plc
Dame Jillian Sackler DBE
Jillian and Arthur M Sackler
Mr Wafic Rida Saïd
Mrs Jean Sainsbury
The Saison Foundation
The Sammermar Trust
The Basil Samuel Charitable Trust
Mrs Coral Samuel CBE
The Schroder Foundation
Sea Containers Ltd
Miss Dasha Shenkman
William and Maureen Shenkman
The Archie Sherman Charitable Trust
The late Pauline Sitwell
The Starr Foundation
Sir Hugh Sykes DL
Alfred Taubman
Sir Anthony and Lady Tennant
Ware and Edythe Travelstead
The Trusthouse Charitable Foundation
The Douglas Turner Trust
Sir Siegmund Warburg's Voluntary Settlement
The Weldon UK Charitable Trust
The Welton Foundation
The Weston Family
The Malcolm Hewitt Wiener Foundation
The Maurice Wohl Charitable Foundation
The Wolfson Foundation

*and others who wish
to remain anonymous*

Patrons

The Royal Academy is extremely grateful to all its Patrons, who generously support every aspect of its work.

Chair
Robert Suss

Platinum
Celia and Edward Atkin CBE
Mr and Mrs Christopher Bake
Mr and Mrs Patrick Doherty
Ms Ghizlan El Glaoui
Mr Stephen Gosztony
Mr Jim Grover
Mr Maurice Pinto
Mr and Mrs Jake Shafran
David and Sophie Shalit

Gold
Mr and Mrs Thomas Berger
Molly Lowell Borthwick
Sir Francis Brooke Bt
Christopher and Alex Courage
Mrs Robin Hambro
Ted Hirst
Mrs Elizabeth Hosking
Mr Michael Jacobson
Miss Joanna Kaye
The Licensing Company, London
Sir Sydney Lipworth QC and Lady Lipworth CBE
Sir Keith and Lady Mills
Lady Rayne Lacey
Jean and Geoffrey Redman-Brown
The Lady Renwick of Clifton
Richard Sharp
Jane Spack
David Stileman
Mr Robert John Yerbury

Silver
Ms Susanna Abu Zalaf
Lady Agnew
Mrs Anna Albertini
Miss H J C Anstruther
Ms Dina Aslanyan
Mrs Emma Avignon
Mrs Jane Barker
Catherine Baxendale
The Duke of Beaufort
Mrs J K M Bentley, Liveinart
Eleanor E Brass
Mrs Elie Brihi
Mrs Marcia Brocklebank
Jeremy Brown
Mrs Rosamond Brown
Mr and Mrs Zak Brown
Lord Browne of Madingley
Mr F. A. A. Carnwath CBE
Sir Roger and Lady Carr
Sir Charles and Lady Chadwyck-Healey
Mrs Ann Chapman-Daniel
Sir Trevor and Lady Chinn
Mr and Mrs George Coelho
Denise Cohen Charitable Trust
Sir Ronald and Lady Cohen
Ms Linda Cooper
Mr and Mrs Ken Costa
Mrs Caroline Cullinan
Julian Darley and Helga Sands
Gwendoline, Countess of Dartmouth
Mr Daniel Davies
Peter and Andrea De Haan
The de Laszlo Foundation
Dr Anne Dornhorst

Mr and Mrs Jim Downing
Ms Noreen Doyle
Mrs Janet Dwek
Mrs Sheila Earles
Lord and Lady Egremont
Susan Elliott
Bryan Ferry
Benita and Gerald Fogel
Mr Sam Fogg
Mrs Jocelyn Fox
Arnold Fulton
Mrs Jill Garcia
Mrs Mina Gerowin Herrmann
Lady Getty
Mr Mark Glatman
Lady Gosling
Professor Piers Gough CBE RA
Mr Gavin Graham
HRH Princess Marie-Chantal of Greece
Mrs Margaret Guitar
Mrs Jennifer Hall
Mr James Hambro
Sir John Hegarty and Miss Philippa Crane
Sir Michael and Lady Heller
Mrs Katrín Henkel
Lady Heseltine
Mrs Olivia Hoare
Anne Holmes-Drewry
Mr Philip Hudson
Mr and Mrs Jon Hunt
S Isern-Feliu
Mrs Caroline Jackson
Sir Martin and Lady Jacomb
Mrs Raymonde Jay
Alistair Johnston and Christina Nijman
Fiona Johnstone
Mrs Ghislaine Kane
Dr Elisabeth Kehoe
Princess Jeet Khemka
Mr D H Killick
Mr and Mrs James Kirkman
Mrs Aboudi Kosta
Mr and Mrs Herbert Kretzmer
Norman A Kurland and Deborah A David
Joan H Lavender
Mr Simon Lawless
Mrs Rachel Laxer
Mr George Lengvari and Mrs Inez Lengvari
Lady Lever of Manchester
Miss R Lomax-Simpson
Mrs Caroline Lord
The Hon Mrs Virginia Lovell
Mr and Mrs Henry Lumley
Gillian McIntosh
Andrew and Judith McKinna
Mr Nicholas Maclean
Sir John Mactaggart
Madeline and Donald Main
Scott and Laura Malkin
Mr Charles Martin
Mr and Mrs Richard C Martin
Zvi & Ofra Meitar Family Fund
Professor Anthony Mellows OBE TD and Mrs Anthony Mellows
Mr Daniel Mitchell
Mrs Susan Moehlmann
Ms Bona Montagu
Dr Ann Naylor
Mr Wade Newmark
Ann Norman-Butler
Mr Richard Orders
Mr Michael Palin
John Pattisson
Nicholas B Paumgarten

Mr and Mrs D J Peacock
Mr Philip Perry
David Pike
Mr and Mrs Anthony Pitt-Rivers
Mr Basil Postan
Mrs Becky Quintavalle
John and Anne Raisman
Mrs Bianca Roden
Rothschild Foundation
Miss Elaine Rowley
Mr and Mrs K M Rubie
The Lady Henrietta St George
Mr Adrian Sassoon
Mr and Mrs Kevin Senior
Christina Countess of Shaftesbury
Mr Robert N Shapiro
Major General and Mrs Jonathan Shaw
Mr Richard Simmons CBE
Alan and Marianna Simpson
Anne Elizabeth Tasca
Mr Tom Tempest-Radford
Lady Tennant
Anthony Thornton
Mr Anthony J Todd
Mrs Carolyn Townsend
Miss M L Ulfane
John and Carol Wates
Edna and Willard Weiss
The Duke and Duchess of Wellington
Anthony and Rachel Williams
Mrs Adriana Winters

Patron Donors
Stephen Barry Charitable Settlement
William Brake Charitable Trust
Jean Cass MBE and Eric Cass MBE
Peter and Elizabeth Goulds, L.A. Louver
Jacqueline and Marc Leland
Mr Eugene Ludwig
Mrs Josephine Lumley
The Michael H Sacher Charitable Trust
H M Sassoon Charitable Trust
Mrs Patricia Yunghanns

*and others who wish
to remain anonymous*

Benjamin West Group Patrons

Chair
Lady Judge CBE

Platinum
David Giampaolo
Charles and Kaaren Hale

Gold
Mr Steve Cardell
Lady Judge CBE
Mr Christian Levett
Ms Alessandra Morra

Silver
Lady J Lloyd Adamson
Mr Dimitry Afanasiev
Poppy Allonby
Mrs Spindrift Al Swaidi
Ms Ruth Anderson
Ms Sol Anitua
Mr Andy Ash
Marco and Francesca Assetto
Mrs Leslie Bacon
Mr and Mrs Benjelloun
Naomi and Ted Berk

Jean and John Botts
Ms Pauline Cacucciolo
Mrs Sophie Cahu
Brian and Melinda Carroll
Mrs Caroline Cartellieri Karlsen
Andrew and Stefanie Clarke
Mr and Mrs Paul Collins
Vanessa Colomar de Enserro
Ms Ruth Crabbe
Christophe de Taurines
Ms Karla Dorsch
Mr and Mrs Jeff Eldredge
Mr and Mrs Gunnar Engstrom
Nigel and Christine Evans
Mrs Stroma Finston
Cyril and Christine Freedman
Ronald and Helen Freeman
Ms Nicola Green
Mr and Mrs Jan Hagemeier
Mrs Dana Haimoff
Katie Jackson
Syrie Johnson
Suzanne and Michael Johnson
Miss Rebecca Kemsley
Lord and Lady Leitch
Mrs Stephanie Léouzon
Ms Ida Levine
Mr Guido Lombardo
Charles G Lubar
Cornelius Medvei
Mrs Victoria Mills
Neil Osborn and Holly Smith
Mr Tony O'Sullivan
Luciana and Alessandra Price
Lady Purves
Mr Aaron Rosenstein
Ms Elena Shchukina
Mr James B Sherwood
Mr Stuart Southall
Sir Hugh and Lady Sykes
Mr Ian Taylor
Miss Lori Tedesco
Mr and Mrs Julian Treger
Frederick and Kathryn Uhde
Mrs Neena Vaswani
Mr John Walden
Mr James Wasdell
Mr Craig D Weaver
Professor Peter Whiteman QC
Mr and Mrs John Winter
Ms Regina Wyles

*and others who wish
to remain anonymous*

Contemporary Circle Patrons

Chair
Susan Elliott

Platinum
Robert and Simone Suss

Gold
Joan and Robin Alvarez
Ms Ilaria Bulgari
Mr Jeremy Coller
Ms Miel de Botton
Matthew and Monika McLennan
Mr and Mrs Scott Mead
Simon and Sabi North
Mr and Mrs Simon Oliver
Yana and Stephen Peel
Mr Kevin Sneader and Ms Amy Muntner
Manuela and Iwan Wirth

Corporate Members of the Royal Academy

Launched in 1988, the Royal Academy's Corporate Membership Scheme has proved highly successful. Corporate membership offers benefits for staff, clients and community partners and access to the Academy's facilities and resources. The outstanding support we receive from companies via the scheme is vital to the continuing success of the Academy and we thank all members for their valuable support and continued enthusiasm.

Premier Level Members
American Express®
The Arts Club
Barclays Premier
Bird & Bird LLP
BNY Mellon
Catlin Group Limited
Cazenove Capital Management
Christie's
Deutsche Bank AG London
FTI Consulting
GlaxoSmithKline plc
HS1
Insight Investment Managment
JLL
JM Finn & Co.
JTI
KPMG LLP
Linklaters
Smith & Williamson
Sotheby's

Corporate Members
Bloomberg LP
The Boston Consulting Group UK LLP
Capital Group
Chestertons
Credit Agricole CIB
F & C Asset Management plc
GAM London Ltd
Generation Investment Management LLP
John Lewis Partnership
Lindsell Train
Marie Curie Cancer Care
Moelis & Company
Morgan Stanley
Native Land
Rathbones
Ridgeway Partners
The Royal Society of Chemistry
Trowers & Hamlins LLP
UBS Wealth Managment
Vitol SA
Weil, Gotshal & Manges

Associate Members
Bank of America Merrill Lynch
BNP Paribas
Bonhams 1793 Ltd
British American Tobacco
Clifford Chance
The Cultivist
EY
Heidrick & Struggles
Imperial College Healthcare Charity
International Inc.
Jones Day
Lazard
Lubbock Fine
Pentland Group plc
Timothy Sammons Fine Art Agents

Supporters of Past Exhibitions

The President and Council of the Royal Academy would like to thank the following supporters for their generous contributions towards major exhibitions in the last ten years:

2015
Jean-Etienne Liotard
2009–2016 Season supported by JTI
The Cockayne Foundation
Pictet
Mr and Mrs Bart T. Tiernan
The Jean-Etienne Liotard Supporters' Group

Joseph Cornell: Wanderlust
2009–2016 Season supported by JTI
The Terra Foundation for American Art
The Cornell Leadership Circle

Premiums, RA Schools Annual Dinner and Auction and RA Schools Show 2015
Newton Investment Management

247th Summer Exhibition
Insight Investment

Richard Diebenkorn
2009–2016 Season supported by JTI
The Terra Foundation for American Art

Rubens and His Legacy
BNY Mellon, Partner of the Royal Academy of Arts

2015 Architecture Programme
Lead supporter Turkishceramics

2014
Allen Jones RA
Lead Series Supporter JTI

Giovanni Battista Moroni
2009–2016 Season supported by JTI
UBI Banca

Anselm Kiefer
BNP Paribas
White Cube

Radical Geometry: Modern Art of South America from the Patricia Phelps de Cisneros Collection
2009–2016 Season supported by JTI
Christie's

Dennis Hopper: The Lost Album
Lead Series Supporter JTI
Nikon UK

Premiums, RA Schools Annual Dinner and Auction and RA Schools Show 2014
Newton Investment Management

246th Summer Exhibition
Insight Investment

Dream, Draw, Work: Architectural Drawings by Norman Shaw RA
Lowell Libson Ltd
Collections and Library Supporters Circle

Renaissance Impressions: Chiaroscuro Woodcuts from the Collections of Georg Baselitz and the Albertina, Vienna
JTI
Edwards Wildman

Sensing Spaces: Architecture Reimagined
Scott and Laura Malkin
AKT II
Arauco

2013
Bill Woodrow RA
Lead Series Supporter JTI
The Henry Moore Foundation

Daumier
2009–2016 Season supported by JTI

Australia
National Gallery of Australia
Qantas Airways
The Woolmark Company

Richard Rogers RA: Inside Out
Ferrovial Agroman
Heathrow Airport
Laing O'Rourke

Mexico: A Revolution in Art, 1910–1940
2009–2016 Season supported by JTI
Art Mentor Foundation Lucerne
Conaculta
James and Clare Kirkman
Mexican Agency for International Development Cooperation
Catherine and Franck Petitgas
Sectur
Visit Mexico
Mercedes Zobel

245th Summer Exhibition
Insight Investment

George Bellows
2009–2016 Season supported by JTI
Edwards Wildman

Premiums, RA Schools Annual Dinner and Auction and RA Schools Show 2013
Newton Investment Management

Manet: Portraying Life
BNY Mellon, Partner of the Royal Academy of Arts

2012
Mariko Mori
JTI

RA Now
JTI

Bronze
Christian Levett and Mougins Museum of Classical Art
Daniel Katz Gallery
Baron Lorne Thyssen-Bornemisza
John and Fausta Eskenazi
The Ruddock Foundation for the Arts
Tomasso Brothers Fine Art
Jon and Barbara Landau
Janine and J. Tomilson Hill
Embassy of the Kingdom of the Netherlands
Eskenazi Limited
Lisson Gallery
Alexis Gregory
Alan and Mary Hobart
Richard de Unger and Adeela Qureshi
Rossi & Rossi Ltd
Embassy of Israel

244th Summer Exhibition
Insight Investment

From Paris: A Taste for Impressionism – Paintings from the Clark
2009–2016 Season supported by JTI
Edwards Wildman
The Annenberg Foundation

Premiums, RA Schools Annual Dinner and Auction and RA Schools Show 2012
Newton Investment Management

Johan Zoffany RA: Society Observed
2009–2016 Season supported by JTI
Cox & Kings

Building the Revolution: Soviet Art and Architecture 1915–1935
2009–2016 Season supported by JTI
The Ove Arup Foundation
The Norman Foster Foundation
Richard and Ruth Rogers

David Hockney RA: A Bigger Picture
BNP Paribas
Welcome to Yorkshire: Tourism Partner
Visit Hull & East Yorkshire: Supporting Tourism Partner
NEC

2011
Degas and the Ballet: Picturing Movement
BNY Mellon, Partner of the Royal Academy of Arts
Region Holdings
Blavatnik Family Foundation

Eyewitness: Hungarian Photography in the Twentieth Century. Brassaï, Capa, Kertész, Moholy-Nagy, Munkácsi
2009–2016 Season supported by JTI
Hungarofest
OTP Bank

243rd Summer Exhibition
Insight Investment

Premiums, RA Schools Annual Dinner and Auction and RA Schools Show 2011
Newton Investment Management

Watteau: The Drawings
2009–2016 Season supported by JTI
Region Holdings

Modern British Sculpture
American Express Foundation
The Henry Moore Foundation
Hauser & Wirth
Art Mentor Foundation Lucerne
Sotheby's
Blain Southern
Welcome to Yorkshire: Tourism Partner

2010
GSK Contemporary – Aware: Art Fashion Identity
GlaxoSmithKline

Pioneering Painters: The Glasgow Boys 1880–1900
2009–2016 Season supported by JTI
Glasgow Museums

Treasures from Budapest: European Masterpieces from Leonardo to Schiele
OTP Bank
Villa Budapest

Daniel Katz Gallery, London
Cox & Kings: Travel Partner

Sargent and the Sea
2009–2016 Season supported by JTI

242nd Summer Exhibition
Insight Investment

Paul Sandby RA: Picturing Britain, A Bicentenary Exhibition
2009–2016 Season supported by JTI

The Real Van Gogh: The Artist and His Letters
BNY Mellon, Partner of the Royal Academy of Arts
Hiscox plc
Heath Lambert
Cox & Kings: Travel Partner

RA Outreach Programme
Deutsche Bank AG

2009
GSK Contemporary
GlaxoSmithKline

Wild Thing: Epstein, Gaudier-Brzeska, Gill
2009–2016 Season supported by JTI
BNP Paribas
The Henry Moore Foundation

Anish Kapoor
JTI
Richard Chang
Richard and Victoria Sharp
Louis Vuitton
The Henry Moore Foundation

J W Waterhouse: The Modern Pre-Raphaelite
2009–2016 Season supported by JTI
Champagne Perrier-Jouët
GasTerra
Gasunie

241st Summer Exhibition
Insight Investment

Kuniyoshi. From the Arthur R. Miller Collection
2009–2016 Season supported by JTI
Canon
Cox & Kings: Travel Partner

Premiums and RA Schools Show
Mizuho International plc

RA Outreach Programme
Deutsche Bank AG

2008
GSK Contemporary
GlaxoSmithKline

Byzantium 330–1453
J F Costopoulos Foundation
A G Leventis Foundation
Stavros Niarchos Foundation
Cox & Kings: Travel Partner

Miró, Calder, Giacometti, Braque: Aimé Maeght and His Artists
BNP Paribas

Vilhelm Hammershøi: The Poetry of Silence
OAK Foundation Denmark
Novo Nordisk

240th Summer Exhibition
Insight Investment

Premiums and RA Schools Show
Mizuho International plc

RA Outreach Programme
Deutsche Bank AG

From Russia: French and Russian Master Paintings 1870–1925 from Moscow and St Petersburg
E.ON
2008 Season supported by Sotheby's

2007
Paul Mellon's Legacy: A Passion for British Art
The Bank of New York Mellon
Georg Baselitz
Eurohypo AG

239th Summer Exhibition
Insight Investment

Impressionists by the Sea
Farrow & Ball

Premiums and RA Schools Show
Mizuho International plc

RA Outreach Programme
Deutsche Bank AG

The Unknown Monet
Bank of America

2006
238th Summer Exhibition
Insight Investment

Chola: Sacred Bronzes of Southern India
Cox & Kings: Travel Partner

Premiums and RA Schools Show
Mizuho International plc

RA Outreach Programme
Deutsche Bank AG

Rodin
Ernst & Young